300 BOOKS BY S. T. JOSHI

300 BOOKS BY S. T. JOSHI

A Comprehensive Bibliography

S. T. Joshi

Sarnath Press • Seattle

Contents

Introduction

This is scarcely the place for a full-scale history of my literary work, assuming anyone is even interested in such a thing. Suffice it to say that I began writing at a reasonably early age—although by no means as early as my chief subject of study, H. P. Lovecraft, who was writing stories and poems at the age of six or seven—and, after some early stumbles, found a niche where my writing could thrive.

The amusing thing, of course, is that English is not my native language. After my birth in Poona (now Punē), India, on 22 June 1958, I was brought to this country on 12 July 1963 by my parents, T. M. and P. T. Joshi. My mother was seeking to expand her career as a mathematician and secured a teaching position at the University of Illinois at Urbana. After staying with us (my mother, my two older sisters, and myself) for a short time, my father returned to India, where he resumed his work as an economist; he did not rejoin us until 1968. I began kindergarten in the fall of 1963, and one of my few memories of that time is sitting in a classroom with other children and listening to a teacher whom I could not understand. I was in no way alarmed or frightened, merely puzzled. Of course, I learned English quickly (and as quickly forgot my native language, Marahti). I still remember, at the age of seven or eight, poring through books of English grammar to resolve certain unanswered questions; and this academic approach to the language has perhaps never left me.

But, in fact, I was not actually much interested in reading, let alone writing, at this time. Instead, I quickly became Americanised to the point of becoming fascinated with both rock music (I was a devoted fan of The Beatles by 1964, although my mother also inculcated in me an abiding interest in classical music) and various American sports, notably football and baseball. When I was eleven, my sister Nalini expressed concern at my relative anti-intellectualism (although I always did well in school, since I found the lessons easy) and dragged me to a branch of the Muncie Public Library. (We had left Urbana in 1968, spending a year in Indianapolis before settling in Muncie, Indiana, in the fall of 1969.) I was not clear on what I should read—and, amusingly enough in light of my later atheism, became enraptured by C. S. Lewis's Chronicles of Narnia. Not having the slightest knowledge of Christianity, I was entirely unaware of the heavy Christian symbolism underlying these books, but read them merely as entertaining excursions into fantasy. But I also turned to darker material—namely, the anthologies for young adults (and later for adults) compiled by Rod Serling, Alfred Hitchcock, and others.

It was in 1972 that I decided to become a writer. Naturally, in light of my readings—which were heavily slanted toward both horror and detective fiction, although I also enjoyed "classic" mainstream fiction (I read the entirety of the Brontës on my own in high school, and was also fascinated by English history)—I started by trying to write fiction. My first story was a piece called "Murder" (printed here as an appendix), which was apparently written early during my freshman year of high school (Burris Laboratory School), in the fall of 1972. Although this piece was actually "published" in a school publication, *Literary Lapses,* that appeared in May 1973, I had two stories appear earlier: "The Picture" and "The Touch of Death," which appeared in a one-shot periodical named *Double Take,* dating to 1972. I no longer have this publication, but I am certain these stories were supernatural (as was "Murder").

I went on to write hundreds of stories over the next four years. I also produced an entire detective novel, *The Ordinary People* (about 175 double-spaced pages), along with about 120 pages of a second, *The Castle of Sebastian,* before abandoning it. In my youthful naïveté and arrogance, I actually submitted many of these stories to top-flight magazines like *Playboy* and *Ellery Queen's Mystery Magazine;* needless to say, all were turned down, and I amassed an impressive collection of rejection slips. The great majority of those stories have mercifully perished, but I unwisely embalmed some of them in the "literary magazine" that I founded and edited during my junior and senior years of high school, the *Forum.* (My English teacher should have told me that nearby Ball State University—of which Burris is in fact a branch—had its own literary magazine, *Ball State University Forum.* If I had known that, I would have chosen a different name.)

My *Forum* also included a certain number of my poems. I wrote more than a hundred poems—most of them quite short, and many of them in the free-verse manner of Stephen Crane. I even assembled an entire book of poems, *The Nothing Verses and Other Poems,* and submitted it (probably around 1975) to a poetry publisher, John F. Blair, who politely declined it. I also did some work for the school newspaper, the *Vanguard* (mostly book reviews), and worked on my high school yearbook during senior year as "Copy Editor," meaning I wrote every word of copy in the book, from brief articles to photo captions. The book was published in the spring of 1976, as I was graduating. I have not listed this work in the present compilation. I also ventured into actual journalism by writing a series of articles on school activities for one of the local papers, the *Muncie Evening Press.* The paper had asked a member of each of the four high schools to write an article of this sort every week, and I was chosen for the task, meaning I wrote one article every month or so.

I had tried my hand at literary criticism—if it can be called that—as early as 1973, when the first of two issues of another school publication, the *Cosmic Meld,* appeared. These issues were exclusively devoted to book reviews, and the second issue (January 1974) contains my first reviews of Lovecraft's work (*The Dunwich Horror and Others* and *Collected Poems,* respectively). I had lost my own copies of these periodicals, but years later a classmate I met at a convention gave me some copies. After a time, especially when I noted that my fiction was not selling (and, in all honesty, was quite mediocre and derivative of Lovecraft, Bradbury, and the other writers I was reading), I decided to try my hand at a more ambitious literary project: the treatise *Mystery and Horror Writers of the Twentieth Century.* I expound on the ups and downs of this project in an essay (written in 1975) that I print here as an appendix. The book, if anything, reflects my continued joint interest in horror fiction and detective fiction.

By no later than 1975, I was determined to focus on Lovecraft as a subject of critical study. It was in the summer of that year (between my junior and senior years of high school) that I conceived the idea for the anthology that later became *H. P. Lovecraft: Four Decades of Criticism* (1980). I began amassing material and also began getting in touch with other scholars of that period—beginning with R. Alain Everts (whose address I had found in a publication called *Spoor Directory*), who then put me in touch with Dirk W Mosig, then the leading authority on Lovecraft. Through Mosig I established contact with David E. Schultz, J. Vernon Shea, Peter Cannon, and many others.

Around this time I also wrote a short monograph, *H. P. Lovecraft: A Critical Analysis,* that was actually accepted by Shroud Publishers (Ken Krueger) of North Hollywood, California. Mercifully, Krueger never sent me a contract (or the payment of $250 that he promised) and subsequently fled south of the border to publish pornography in Mexico. This work was so awful that I would pay heavy blackmail to keep it out of print; I myself no longer have a copy. But it did allow me to pose as a "professional" critic and to allow me to get a foothold in Lovecraft scholarship.

Curiously enough, it was L. Sprague de Camp's *Lovecraft: A Biography* (which appeared in the spring of 1975) that inspired me to undertake Lovecraft research. I was then unaware of the manifold deficiencies of that work, but it clearly showed that Lovecraft was an interesting literary figure who deserved more study and analysis. It may have been through that biography that I learned that many of Lovecraft's papers and manuscripts were at the John Hay Library of Brown University; so, as I entered senior year of high school in the fall of 1975, I applied to Brown and luckily was accepted.

My six years at Brown (1976–82) were of course transformative; for not only did I receive an excellent education (gravitating away from English to the study of classics—Latin, Greek, ancient history, ancient philosophy), but I absorbed as much knowledge of Lovecraft as I could. Just before graduating from high school, I had received a somewhat casual offer from Kent State University Press to compile a new bibliography of Lovecraft for its Serif Series of Bibliographies and Checklists. Not knowing the first thing about bibliography, I assumed that I would merely act as a kind of secretary while receiving material from Mosig, Schultz, and other scholars. In the end, I did a good deal of the research myself—even spending ten days with Mosig in Georgia in the summer of 1977 cataloguing his collection, especially his rich holdings of foreign Lovecraftiana. I also made an expedition to New York earlier in 1977 to examine the holdings of the amateur journalism collection at the New York Public Library.

It was, of course, in the fall of 1976 that I met Marc A. Michaud, who had just started Necronomicon Press. We quickly formed a close personal and literary association, and my first work for Marc was a brief preface to his edition of *Writings in The Tryout* (1977). I went on to advise him on a number of his other projects; and we jointly compiled my first book, Lovecraft's *Uncollected Prose and Poetry* (1978), an assemblage of rare Lovecraftiana that I had stumbled upon as a result of my bibliographical work. Probably one of the most significant things we did was to establish *Lovecraft Studies* in 1979. This journal became the focus of a great deal of Lovecraft scholarship over the next two decades or so, although it carried on a genial rivalry with Robert M. Price's more lively and irreverent *Crypt of Cthulhu* (1981f.), to which I also contributed.

It was in the fall of 1978, after I had queried more than thirty different academic publishers, that Ohio University Press finally accepted *H. P. Lovecraft: Four Decades of Criticism,* although the book was not published until just after I had graduated with a B.A. in the summer of 1980. My bibliography was completed later that summer and published in 1981. (Neither Ohio University Press nor Kent State University Press knew how old I was when I signed contracts for these books.)

As I stayed on at Brown to receive an M.A. in 1982, I came close to completing another important project—the preparation of corrected texts of Lovecraft's fiction and other work. This project indeed required the full six years I spent at Brown, as I had to consult manuscripts, early printed sources, and other materials in order to arrive at a corrected text; I also, of course, had to learn the principles of textual scholarship, something that my training as a classicist markedly enhanced. No one had previously suspected the degree to which Lovecraft's work was, in the Arkham House editions, riddled with textual and typographical errors.

In the fall of 1982, at the World Fantasy Convention in New Haven, I met with James Turner, managing editor of Arkham House, and we began working out the laborious process of preparing the corrected editions. Much time was occupied in specifying exactly how I was to be credited; I insisted on receiving some kind of editorial credit, and Turner finally relented on the point. My three revised editions of the Lovecraft fiction appeared in 1984, 1985, and 1986; my revised edition of the revisions appeared in 1989. Turner had long been working (rather casually, it appears) on a volume of *Miscellaneous Writings*, but eventually turned the project over to me, and my edition appeared in 1995.

In the fall of 1982 I went to Princeton to enrol in a Ph.D. program in classical philosophy, but left after two years. Luckily I managed to secure a humble job in publishing, at Chelsea House Publishers in New York. I stayed there for eleven years, rising from associate editor to managing editor to senior managing editor. Much of my work at Chelsea House was involved in working on immense volumes of reprinted literary criticism, under the nominal editorship of Harold Bloom; in fact, I (along with my staff) did the major editing, with minimal input from Bloom. This work allowed me to gain a wide understanding of mainstream literature, which has proven immensely beneficial to my own literary work.

By this time I had become interested in exploring other weird writers beyond Lovecraft. I first received an opportunity to write about these writers from Darrell Schweitzer, who commissioned me to write long articles on Arthur Machen and Lord Dunsany for some critical anthologies he was assembling. These chapters became the nucleus for my book *The Weird Tale* (University of Texas Press, 1990), which I still regard as one of my better critical works. I almost immediately wrote a sequel, *The Modern Weird Tale*, covering selected weird writers of the last half-century. It was largely completed by 1992, but I had difficulty securing a publisher for it, and it did not appear until 2001 from McFarland, and then in a somewhat truncated form.

My interest in Lovecraft's predecessors led to the compilation of a bibliography (1993) and critical study (1995) of Dunsany, a few volumes of classic reprints for Dover, a three-volume edition of Arthur Machen's weird fiction (2001f.), and other volumes. Of course, my interest in Lovecraft remained paramount. The approach of his centennial inspired much work, including my philosophical treatise, *H. P. Lovecraft: The Decline of the West* (1990), and a major role in organising the H. P. Lovecraft Centennial Conference at Brown in the summer of 1990.

Lovecraft criticism seemed to experience a certain exhaustion after that conference, and little work was done in the years following. I continued editing the biannual journal *Lovecraft Studies* (founded in 1979) for Necronomicon Press; but pressure was building for someone to write a new biography of Lovecraft to replace de Camp's. I finally undertook the task, spending two full years (1993–95) writing a 500,000-word treatise. Again, I experienced difficulty securing a publisher, but Necronomicon Press came to my aid by publishing a somewhat abridged version as *H. P. Lovecraft: A Life* (1996). The book was widely reviewed (notably by Joyce Carol Oates in the *New York Review of Books*) and sold well, both in hardcover and in paperback. A few years thereafter, however, Marc experienced some personal difficulties, and his press became all but moribund.

Coincidentally, I struck up an acquaintance with Derrick Hussey, whom I persuaded (or perhaps badgered) into starting a new small press, initially devoted to Lovecraft, but whose scope has widened considerably. Hippocampus Press has become the focus of much of my work since its first publication, *The Annotated Supernatural Horror in Literature* (a book that I had, incredibly, compiled as early as 1981 for Greenwood Press), appeared in 2000.

In the fall of 1995, Chelsea House went temporarily bankrupt because of some bad investments, and the New York editorial office was shut down. This proved to be a blessing in disguise, for it compelled me to become a full-fledged freelance writer. I am certain that the majority of the more than 200 books I have published date to 1996 or later. By this time I had established a close working relationship with David E. Schultz, in spite of the fact that I lived in New York City and he lived in Milwaukee. We had initially worked hard to transcribe, and eventually publish, the totality of Lovecraft's letters—a project so huge that I had neglected to undertake it during my years at Brown, and one that will probably take at least another ten to fifteen years to complete. We also jointly became interested in Clark Ashton Smith (whose complete poetry we edited) and, through Smith, in George Sterling and then Ambrose Bierce. The appearance of Sterling's *Complete Poetry* in 2013 is a dream come true for both me and Schultz. Schultz and I (along with Lawrence I. Berkove) had earlier compiled an edition of Bierce's collected short fiction (2006).

Schultz and I prepared some editions of Lovecraft's letters for both Necronomicon Press and Night Shade Books, but this project quickly moved to Hippocampus Press. Necronomicon Press was also scheduled to publish my edition of Lovecraft's collected poetry, *The Ancient Track*, but the press's collapse shifted this project to Night Shade, where it appeared in 2001. For Hippocampus Press, I edited a five-volume edition of Lovecraft's *Collected Essays* (2004–06).

In the late 1990s my work began appearing in some wider venues. First, a book packager contacted me to assemble an *Annotated H. P. Lovecraft* for Dell (1997); it sold quite well. Soon thereafter, Penguin contacted me with the proposal to edit a volume of Lovecraft's stories for Penguin Classics; I was thrilled to undertake the task, and in the end edited three volumes for Penguin (1999–2004), along with editions of other weird writers (Blackwood, Dunsany, M. R. James, Machen). My literary interests also expanded beyond the weird altogether. My interest in George Sterling led me to H. L. Mencken, who I considered substantially understudied. I spent nine years transcribing the 12,000,000 words of Mencken's complete published work, and along the way began issuing editions of some of that body of work. I compiled bibliographies of Mencken (2009) and Gore Vidal (2007), with whom I was sporadically in touch before his death in 2012. I also compiled the anthology *Documents of American Prejudice* (Basic Books, 1999).

My interest in atheism was probably inspired initially by Lovecraft, but I subsequently read such philosophers as Nietzsche and Bertrand Russell, who solidified my views. I proposed an anthology of atheism to Prometheus Books, then and now the leading freethought publisher in America, and it appeared as *Atheism: A Reader* (2000); it is still in print. I subsequently wrote or compiled several other books for Prometheus, including a fiery and satirical treatise, *God's Defenders: What They Believe and Why They Are Wrong* (2003). I am now contemplating a full-scale history of atheism.

My treatise *The Rise and Fall of the Cthulhu Mythos* (2008) led me in an unexpected direction. I had written that book with the expectation that I would find the great majority of neo-Lovecraftian writing to be rubbish; but I was surprised to find that some authors (e.g., Caitlín R. Kiernan, Laird Barron, Donald Tyson, Brian Stableford, etc.) had actually produced creditable work. Over the course of years—in part through my compilation of *American Supernatural Tales* (2007) for Penguin—I had become acquainted with a number of these writers, and I now began assembling a volume of Cthulhu Mythos stories as a counterweight to anthologies by Derleth and others that I thought were inferior. I assembled the book—*Black Wings*—specifically with Arkham House in mind, since I was now on reasonably good terms with its proprietor, April Derleth, and wished to help it to revive its fortunes (it had not published a book since 2006—and, in fact, has still not done so). But after I completed the book in 2009, April sat on it for months without making a decision. Finally I had no choice but to withdraw it; I offered it to Pete Crowther of PS Publishing, who accepted it based only on the table of contents. The book came out in 2010 and was well received, and its three successors have also done well; paperback editions by Titan Books are in the process of appearing.

This arrangement with Titan Books was facilitated by Cherry Weiner, a literary agent who decided to take me on about this time. She also arranged for a lucrative deal for my compilation of a two-volume set, *The Madness of Cthulhu,* the first volume of which is expected to appear this fall. I hope to do more work with Titan in the future.

I continue to do all I can to promote many other weird writers, old and new. This work, which had begun in the 1980s and led to my editing of the Necronomicon Press journal *Studies in Weird Fiction* (1986f.), has also led to my working with various publishers (Midnight House, Chaosium, Tartarus Press, Arcane Wisdom) in reprinting texts by many classic authors. Lately, I have compiled many such books for Centipede Press, and they will be coming out over the next several years. Among them is a series of reasonably priced hardcover volumes, the Centipede Press Library of Weird Fiction, of which I am editor. I have had less success in editing lines of books of Cthulhu Mythos writing, as such series for Perilous Press and Arcane Wisdom languished after only a few titles were released.

My critical work on the field culminated with the two-volume *Unutterable Horror: A History of Supernatural Fiction* (2012), on which I worked for five years (2007–12). I was gratified that the book won the World Fantasy Award in 2013. Recently, Scarecrow Press has asked me to edit a series of critical studies of weird fiction, Studies in Supernatural Literature, and this series has made an auspicious start with its first several titles. I also hope to prepare more annotated reprints of classic weird fiction for Penguin Classics.

Perhaps the most unexpected development of my career is my resumption of fiction writing. Since abandoning such work in 1976, as I graduated from high school, I have dabbled in fiction only rarely. A few of my stories appeared in Brown's student magazine, *Issues.* I wrote a short detective novel, *Tragedy at Sarsfield Manor,* in 1979, but was unable to find a publisher for it. Then, in 2000, I wrote a slightly longer but still somewhat short (about 55,000 words) detective novel, *The Removal Company,* the core of whose plot was based on a short story by W. C. Morrow of that title. This too sat unpublished for years until Robert Reginald, of the revived Borgo Press (now an imprint of Wildside Press), said that he was willing to publish just about any book of mine on any subject. I proposed *The Removal Company,* and he brought it out in 2009 under a pseudonym that I had devised as far back as 1975, J. K. Maxwell (who had been the purported "editor" of my book of poems, *The Nothing Verses*). Imagine my dismay when I discovered later that another writer named J. K. Maxwell was the author of several books, at least one of which was a detective novel! I notified Reginald of the matter, and he quickly republished *The Removal Company* under my own name. I then wrote another short detective novel, *Conspiracy of Silence*, and Reginald proposed publishing it as one of a "double" (like the old Ace Doubles series), if I could write another work to balance it. I said I might be willing to rewrite my old *Tragedy at Sarsfield Manor*, but that it would not be even approximately as long (in fact, the rewrite came to only 27,000 words). Reginald said this was not a problem, and so he issued the two works as a "double" in 2010.

I never thought I would write a supernatural novel, since I figured that anything I would write in that vein would be a conscious or unconscious echo of something I had read. But I felt that the burgeoning subgenre of works with Lovecraft as a fictional character had not portrayed Lovecraft as accurately or as sympathetically as could be imagined, so I tried my hand at it in a 75,000-word novel, *The Assaults of Chaos*. Titan Books considered the book but ultimately declined it, so it came out from Hippocampus Press in 2013. As for shorter fiction, I had unwisely allowed Robert M. Price to publish a story I had written at the age of seventeen, "The Recurring Doom," in his anthology *Acolytes of Cthulhu* (2001). I did not think I would be writing anything more of the sort ever again, but recently Darrell Schweitzer talked me into writing an historical Cthulhu Mythos tale, "Incident at Ferney," set in the eighteenth century and featuring Voltaire as a character. I also resurrected an old (non-Lovecraftian) story, "'You'll Reach There in Time,'" for an anthology that Jason V Brock is about to publish. I also wrote a detective story, "Suicide in Brooklyn," that has Lovecraftian touches; it was published as a bonus booklet to accompany *The Assaults of Chaos*.

But by far the greatest proportion of my work for the past decade or so has been for Hippocampus Press, and I am immensely grateful to Derrick Hussey for not only publishing my own work but for allowing me to publish the new weird writings of a number of authors (W. H. Pugmire, Jonathan Thomas, Michael Aronovitz, etc.) whose work I think is of the highest quality. I have revived *Lovecraft Studies* in the form of the *Lovecraft Annual; Studies in Weird Fiction* was revived after a fashion as the *Weird Fiction Review* (Centipede Press, 2010f.), although this annual journal is devoted to fiction and poetry as well as articles; I edited the first ten issues of a journal, *Dead Reckonings*, that was meant to take the place of the well-received Necronomicon Press journal *Necrofile* (1991–99), devoted to reviews of contemporary publications in weird fiction; and I have published much of Lovecraft's work with Hippocampus—his essays, his poetry, and especially an ongoing series of his collected letters (coedited with David E. Schultz) that may extend to twenty-five volumes or more. I am the copyeditor for nearly all Hippocampus titles, and I hope that I have done a fair job at that onerous task.

The most significant project with Hippocampus was Lovecraft's *Collected Fiction: A Variorum Edition,* the first three volumes of which appeared in 2015 (the fourth volume appeared in 2017). This is a new edition of Lovecraft's fiction with textual variants in all relevant publications printed at the foot of the page. I had recorded the variants during my initial examination of the Lovecraft texts all the way back during my years at Brown (1976–82), and I felt that this information was worth presenting to devotees. I was commissioned by Joe Morey of Dark Renaissance Books to prepare a series of volumes of classic weird fiction, but his retirement due to health problems left the books without a home, until Hippocampus Press decided to issue them under the title "Classics of Gothic Horror."

In 2016 I established my own micro-press, Sarnath Press—the name I gave to books I issued through Amazon's CreateSpace and Kindle platforms. This imprint has allowed me to publish a great many books that I would not have wished to burden other publishers with; most notably, I have published more than twenty volumes of H. L. Mencken's collected essays and journalism, and I believe some of these books are being purchased by libraries. I also issued a volume of my collected fiction (excluding *The Assaults of Chaos*), entitled *The Recurring Doom* (2019). To commemorate my sixtieth birthday, I wrote my memoirs, *What Is Anything?* (2018). And to commemorate the publication of the revised edition of this volume, I assembled a book of my collected interviews, along with some otherwise unreprinted autobiographical essays.

My current work extends simultaneously in several directions: scholarship on Lovecraft (currently devoted largely to the editing of his letters, although I hope to write a treatise on the history of Lovecraft scholarship—and more generally a history of Lovecraft's emergence from obscurity to world renown); promoting the reading and study of classic weird fiction (by reprints, critical studies, and the like); promoting the work of selected contemporary weird writers; work on mainstream writers like Mencken and Vidal (I may pursue research on such diverse writers as Sinclair Lewis and Frank Norris if time ever permits); work on atheism (I was editor of a freethought journal, the *American Rationalist,* for six years). I of course continue to be active in the Lovecraft fan world: I have been the official editor of the Esoteric Order of Dagon, an amateur press association focused on Lovecraft and weird fiction, for more than twenty years, and continue to prepare occasional issues of a journal (first *Life Is a Hideous Thing,* and now *What Is Anything?*) to this day. Although time constraints (and profound lack of interest) do not permit me to engage in social media, I make every effort to respond to queries and requests for assistance when I receive e-mails, either directly or through my website (www.stjoshi.org).

I will confess that at times in recent years I find that my energy has been flagging, but I still feel as if I have many more years of productivity left in me. I certainly wish to complete some long-range-projects I have begun (such as the editing of the Lovecraft letters), and although it is unlikely that my subsequent career will take any unexpected turns, one never knows what the future holds. Meanwhile, I hope that this egotistical record of my publications—complete so far as I know it—will, if nothing else, stand as a monument to diligence. If I have any virtue, it is the ability to work hard and to complete projects I have begun. Any other virtues my work possesses I will have to leave to others to determine.

—S. T. JOSHI

A Note on This Compilation

This volume is not meant as a full-scale bibliography, although it is reasonably complete in certain particulars. I believe I have listed all my book publications, with their various printings and editions. The listing of my articles in books and periodicals is reasonably complete, although I may have overlooked some reprints of my work, some of which were never sent to me. The listing of my works in translation is quite incomplete, and I have neglected to list such things as a ten-volume Japanese edition of Lovecraft that appeared in the 1980s under my editorship, using my corrected texts. I have also failed to list most interviews of me, either in print or online, even though the great majority of these were actually written out by me rather than recorded verbally. I had initially kept track of my contributions to the Esoteric Order of Dagon and Necronomicon amateur press associations, but of late I have neglected to do so; but there is almost nothing in these periodicals that has not been published elsewhere. I have not listed any criticism of my work, either in the form of books, articles, or reviews, although there is a certain quantity of this material (some of which, again, I do not have in my possession). For this new edition, I have added an index of names, book titles, and periodicals.

Bibliography of S. T. Joshi

I. Books Written

1. *An Index to the Selected Letters of H. P. Lovecraft*
    a. West Warwick, RI: Necronomicon Press, 1980.
    b. West Warwick, RI: Necronomicon Press, 1991.

    Contents: Introduction; Explanatory Notes; The Index; Appendix I: A Brief Chronology of the Life of H. P. Lovecraft; Appendix II: List of Lovecraft's Correspondents; Appendix III: Index to Illustrations and Photographs; Appendix IV: Prose and Poetry Excerpts in the *Selected Letters*; Appendix V: Errata in the *Selected Letters*.

    Notes. An index that I compiled in six weeks one summer (1978, I think). I had offered it to Jim Turner of Arkham House, but he claimed he would be doing one of his own. By 1980 it became obvious that he wasn't, so Marc Michaud went ahead with the publication of mine.

2. *Lovecraft's Library: A Catalogue* (with Marc A. Michaud)
    a. West Warwick, RI: Necronomicon Press, 1980.
    b. New York: Hippocampus Press, 2002 (rev. and enlarged).
    c. New York: Hippocampus Press, 2012 (rev. ed.).
    d. New York: Hippocampus Press, 2017 (rev. ed.; with David E. Schultz).

    Contents. Introduction; Explanatory Notes; Lovecraft's Library [981 titles]; Weird &c. Items in Library of H. P. Lovecraft; Indices: A. Names; B. Titles; C. Works by Lovecraft; D. Publishers; E. Subjects.

    Notes. A volume that emerged from our discovery of the sketchy catalogue of HPL's library compiled by Mary Spink (now in the John Hay Library). Subsequent editions were considerably enlarged by the location of additional titles and by supplying of tables of contents of select items.

3. *H. P. Lovecraft and Lovecraft Criticism: An Annotated Bibliography*
    a. Kent, OH: Kent State University Press, 1981.
    b. Holicong, PA: Wildside Press, [2003].

    Contents: Introduction; Explanatory Notes; Abbreviations; I. Works by Lovecraft in English: A. Books by Lovecraft; B. Contributions to Periodicals: i. Fiction; ii. Nonfiction; iii. Poetry; iv. Revisions and Collaborations; v. Letters; C. Material Included in Books by Others; D. Works Edited by Lovecraft: i. Books; ii. Periodicals; E. Apocrypha and Other Miscellany: i. Apocrypha; ii. Lost Works; iii. Works Destroyed; iv. Items Included within Published Works by Lovecraft; v. Award-Winning Stories by Lovecraft; vi. Miscellany; II. Works by Lovecraft in Translation: A. Books by Lovecraft; B. Contributions to Periodicals: i. Fiction; ii. Nonfiction; iii. Poetry; iv. Revisions and Collaborations; v. Letters; C. Material Included in Books by Others; III. Works about Lovecraft: A. News Items and Encyclopedias; B. Bibliographies and Glossaries; C. Books and Pamphlets about Lovecraft; D. Criticism in Books or Periodicals; E. Academic Theses and Unpublished Papers: i. Academic Theses; ii. Unpublished Papers; F. Book Reviews: i. Books in English; ii. Books in Languages Other Than English; G. Special Periodicals and Unclassifiable Data: i. Periodicals Devoted Exclusively or Largely to Lovecraft; ii. Single Issues of Periodicals Devoted to Lovecraft; iii. Amateur Press Associations; iv. Unclassifiable Data; Supplement; IV. Indices: A. Works by Lovecraft; Works by Others; C. Names; D. Periodicals; E. Foreign Languages.

Notes. A book that I began in the summer of 1976, after the publisher (whom I had queried about *H. P. Lovecraft: Four Decades of Criticism* [II.2]) declined on that book but asked me to assemble a volume for its Serif Series of Bibliographies and Checklists. It took nearly four years to assemble. For the revised version, see item 33 below.

4.   *H. P. Lovecraft*
        a.1. Mercer Island, WA: Starmont House, 1982.
        a.2. Mercer Island, WA: Starmont House, 1984.
        a.3. Mercer Island, WA: Starmont House, 1987.
        Contents: Abbreviations; Acknowledgements; I. Chronology; II. Introduction: Life and Thought; III. The "Dunsanian" Tales; IV. The "New England" Tales; V. The Lovecraft Mythos; VI. Other Tales and Revisions; VII. Essays, Poetry, Letters; VIII. Conclusion; IX. Notes; X. Annotated Primary Bibliography; XI. Annotated Secondary Bibliography; Index.
        Notes. Starmont Reader's Guide 13. A small monograph that I wrote in about two weeks in 1981 after Dirk W. Mosig, to whom it had been assigned, abandoned Lovecraft scholarship. An extract was reprinted in *Twentieth-Century Literary Criticism,* Volume 22 (Detroit: Gale, 1987), 228-30. Another extract was reprinted in *Short Story Criticism,* Volume 3 (Detroit: Gale, 1989), 268-74. Yet another extract ("The 'Dunsanian' Tales") was reprinted in *Short Story Criticism,* Volume 52 (Detroit: Gale, 2002), 284-94.

5.   *H. P. Lovecraft and Lovecraft Criticism: An Annotated Bibliography: Supplement 1980–1984* (with L. D. Blackmore)

a.   West Warwick, RI: Necronomicon Press, 1985.

Contents: [Introduction], by Joshi and Blackmore; A Note on the Compilation [by Joshi and Blackmore]; I. Works by Lovecraft in English; II. Works by Lovecraft in Translation; III. Lovecraft Criticism; Errata.

Notes. A valuable addendum to the bibliography (item 3 above), much of it assembled by Blackmore.

6.   *Selected Papers on Lovecraft*

a.   West Warwick, RI: Necronomicon Press, 1989.

Contents: Introduction, by Steven J. Mariconda; Author's Note; Lovecraft's Alien Civilisations: A Political Interpretation; The Structure of Lovecraft's Longer Narratives; Lovecraft's Other Planets; Lovecraft's Revisions: How Much of Them Did He Write?; A Look at Lovecraft's Letters; Select Bibliography.

Notes. A book whose title is arrogantly modelled on Bertrand Russell's *Selected Papers* (1927). But it allowed me to print unabridged versions of essays that in some instances had appeared in truncated form in magazines.

7.   *The Weird Tale*

a.   Austin: University of Texas Press, 1990.

b.   Holicong, PA: Wildside Press, 2003.

Contents: Acknowledgments; Preface; Introduction; 1. Arthur Machen: The Mystery of the Universe; 2. Lord Dunsany: The Career of a *Fantaisiste*; 3. Algernon Blackwood: The Expansion of Consciousness; 4. M. R. James: The Limitations of the Ghost Story; 5. Ambrose Bierce: Horror as Satire; 6. H. P. Lovecraft: The Decline of the West; Epilogue: *Criticorum in Usum*; Notes; Critical Appendix; Bibliography; Index.

Notes. A volume that emerged out of Darrell Schweitzer's request for me to write long essays on Machen and Dunsany for some critical anthologies he was assembling. It is a book that I still think is one of the most satisfactory of my output. The chapter on Ambrose Bierce was reprinted in *Twentieth-Century Literary Criticism*, Volume 44 (Detroit: Gale, 1992), 43–51. The chapter on Algernon Blackwood was reprinted in *Short Story Criticism*, Volume 107 (Detroit: Gale, 2008). 183–201.

8.   *John Dickson Carr: A Critical Study*
       a.   Bowling Green, OH: Bowling Green State University Popular
              Press, 1990.
              Contents: Preface; Introduction; Part I: Henri Bencolin; Dr. Gide-
              on Fell; Sir Henry Merrivale; Other Detectives; The Historical Mys-
              teries; Short Stories and Radio Plays; Part II: Philosophy; The
              Theory and Practise of Detective Writing; Style and Characterisa-
              tion; Conclusion; Notes; Bibliography; Index.
              Notes. A book on my favourite detective writer—it took six months
              to prepare (five months spent reading Carr's 80 books, one month
              in writing).

9.   *H. P. Lovecraft: The Decline of the West*
       a.   Mercer Island, WA: Starmont House, 1990.
       b.   Berkeley Heights, NJ: Wildside Press, 2000.
              Contents: Preface; Introduction: On Methodology; Part I: The Phi-
              losophy: I. Lovecraft's Philosophical Development; II. Metaphysics;
              III. Ethics; IV. Aesthetics; V. Politics; Part II: The Fiction: I. Meta-
              physics; II. Ethics; III. Aesthetics; IV. Politics; Part III: The Decline
              of the West; Notes; Bibliography; Index.
              Notes. A book that T. E. Dikty of Starmont House suggested that I
              write for HPL's centennial. He wanted a book of about 75,000
              words, and I thought I had delivered a book of that length—but it
              turned out to be 125,000 words. It is an exhaustive study of HPL's
              philosophical thought and its incorporation into his fiction. I think
              a revised edition is in order.

10.   *An Index to the Fiction and Poetry of H. P. Lovecraft*
       a.   West Warwick, RI: Necronomicon Press, 1992.
              Contents: Explanatory Notes; Abbreviations; The Index.
              Notes. A useful reference work, I think. It has, however, been
              recompiled for Volume 4 of the *Collected Fiction* (Variorum Edition).

11.   *Lord Dunsany: A Bibliography* (with Darrell Schweitzer)
       a.   Lanham, MD: Scarecrow Press, 1993.
       b.   Lanham, MD: Scarecrow Press, [December] 2013 (rev. ed.; as
              Lord Dunsany: A Comprehensive Bibliography).
              Contents: Introduction; Explanatory Notes and Acknowledgments;
              I. Works by Dunsany in English; II. Works by Dunsany in Transla-
              tion; III. Dunsany Criticism; Indexes; About the Authors.
              Notes. A work that took years to research, as all bibliographies do.
              The revised edition contains much new work, both in regard to pub-

lications during Dunsany's lifetime and publications that appeared subsequent to the first edition.

12. *Lord Dunsany: Master of the Anglo-Irish Imagination*
     a. Westport, CT: Greenwood Press, 1995.
     b. Seattle: Sarnath Press, 2019 (revised; as *Creator of Gods and Men: Lord Dunsany and Fantasy Fiction*).

     Contents: Abbreviations; Preface; Introduction; 1. Pegāna and Its Analogues; 2. The Fantastic Drama; Interchapter: The Great War; 3. The Golden Age and Elfland; 4. The Nonhuman Perspective; 5. Jorkens; 6. The Comic Fantastic; 7. The Renunciation of Fantasy; Interchapter: Hitler's War; 8. Ireland; Conclusion; Bibliography; Index.

     Notes. Also a pretty satisfactory volume, I think—one in which I felt I had actually gotten into Dunsany's mind and understood the sources and purpose of his fiction and other writing.

13. *The Core of Ramsey Campbell: A Bibliography & Reader's Guide* (with Ramsey Campbell and Stefan Dziemianowicz)
     a. West Warwick, RI: Necronomicon Press, 1995.

     Contents: Preface, by Peter Straub; Explanatory Notes; A. Books Written; B. Books Edited; C. Fiction; D. Poetry; Index of Titles; Index of Names; Index of Periodicals.

     Notes. A work in which I took Campbell's ongoing bibliography of his own writings and put it into proper bibliographical format, with Stefan writing most of the plot summaries of the individual works. A revised edition is forthcoming, but it is unclear when—or whether—it will ever see print.

14. *H. P. Lovecraft: A Life*
     a.1. West Warwick, RI: Necronomicon Press, 1996.
     a.2. West Warwick, RI: Necronomicon Press, 1997.
     a.3. West Warwick, RI: Necronomicon Press, 2004. With new Afterword.

     Contents: Preface; 1. Unmixed English Gentry; 2. A Genuine Pagan (1890-1897); 3. Black Woods and Unfathomed Caves (1898-1902); 4. What of Unknown Africa? (1902-1908); 5. Barbarian and Alien (1908-1914); 6. A Renewed Will to Live (1914-1917 [I]); 7. Metrical Mechanic (1914-1917 [II]); 8. Dreamers and Visionaries (1917-1919 [I]); 9. Feverish and Incessant Scribbling (1917-1919 [II]); 10. Cynical Materialist (1919-1921 [I]); 11. Dunsanian Studies (1919-1921 [II]); 12. A Stranger in This Century (1919-1921 [III]); 13. The High Tide of My Life (1921-1922); 14. For My Own Amusement (1923-1924); 15. Ball and Chain (1924); 16. Moriturus

Te Saluto (1925–1926); 17. Paradise Regain'd (1926); 18. Cosmic Outsideness (1927–1928); 19. Fanlights and Georgian Steeples (1928–1930); 20. Non-Supernatural Cosmic Art (1930–1931); 21. Mental Greed (1931–1933); 22. In My Own Handwriting (1933–1935); 23. Caring about the Civilisation (1929–1937); 24. The End of One's Life (1935–1937); 25. Thou Art Not Gone (1937–1996); Notes; Bibliography; Index.

Notes. A book that took two full years to write—1993–95. I undertook it only after I determined that other candidates would not come through on a full-scale biography. The complete ms. came to more than 500,000 words; and after mainstream and academic publishers declined on it, Necronomicon Press issued it in somewhat abridged form—a mere 350,000 words. For the unabridged and revised edition, see items 34/35 below.

15. *A Subtler Magick: The Writings and Philosophy of H. P. Lovecraft*
  a. Mercer Island, WA: Starmont House, 1996.
  b. Berkeley Heights, NJ: Wildside Press, 1999.
      Contents: Introduction; An H. P. Lovecraft Chronology; 1. Life and Thought; 2. Early Fiction (1905–1921); 3. The "Dunsanian" Tales (1919–1921); 4. Regional Horror (1921–1926); 5. The Major Fiction: First Stage (1926–1930); 6. The Major Fiction: Second Stage (1931–1935); 7. Revisions and Collaborations; 8. Essays; 9. Poetry; 10. Letters; 11. Conclusion; Notes; Annotated Primary Bibliography; Annotated Secondary Bibliography; Index.

      Notes. A radical expansion of item 4 above, written contemporaneously with the biography.

16. *Sixty Years of Arkham House*
  a. Sauk City, WI: Arkham House, 1999.
  b. Seattle: Sarnath Press, [March] 2019 (as *Eighty Years of Arkham House*).
      Contents: Preface; Arkham House: 1939–1969, by August Derleth; Arkham House: 1970–1999, by S. T. Joshi; Bibliography: Arkham House; Mycroft & Moran; Stanton & Lee; Appendix: The "Lost" Arkhams; Reference Bibliography; Index of Names; Index of Titles.

      Notes. A volume commissioned by Peter Ruber, then managing editor of Arkham House, to commemorate the company's sixtieth anniversary. I included a complete bibliography of titles, the first and only time this was ever done for Arkham House books. The revised edition brings the listing down to 2010—the last date that any book bearing the Arkham House imprint appeared.

17.   *Ambrose Bierce: An Annotated Bibliography of Primary Sources* (with David
      E. Schultz)
      a.   Westport, CT: Greenwood Press, 1999.
           Contents: Preface; Introduction, by Joshi and Schultz; A. Separate
           Publications; B. Contributions to Books and Periodicals; C. Reprints;
           D. Manuscript Holdings; E. Unlocated Items; F. Appendix: Newly
           Discovered Items; Index: Titles; Index: Names; Index: Periodicals.
           Notes. Another bibliography that took years and much research
           travel to assemble.

18.   *The Modern Weird Tale*
      a.   Jefferson, NC: McFarland, [March] 2001.
      b.   Seattle: Sarnath Press, [June] 2019 (revised and expanded ed; as
           Weird Fiction in the Later 20th Century).
           Contents: Preface; Introduction; I. Shirley Jackson: Domestic Hor-
           ror; II. The Persistence of Supernaturalism: William Peter Blatty:
           The Catholic Weird Tale; Stephen King: The King's New Clothes;
           T. E. D. Klein: Urban Horror; Clive Barker: Sex, Death, and Fanta-
           sy; III. Ramsey Campbell: The Fiction of Paranoia; IV. The Alterna-
           tives to Supernaturalism: Killing Women with Robert Bloch,
           Thomas Harris, and Bret Easton Ellis; Thomas Tryon: Rural Horror;
           Peter Straub: From Ghost Story to Thriller; V. Pseudo-, Quasi-, and
           Anti-Weird Fiction: Robert Aickman: "So Little Is Definite"; Anne
           Rice: The Philosophy of Vampirism: Thomas Ligotti: The Escape
           from Life; Epilogue; Notes; Bibliography.
           Notes. A book that I actually finished around 1992, and meant as a
           sequel to *The Weird Tale*. It was scheduled to be published by Borgo
           Press, but the publisher went into abeyance around this time. I still
           have page proofs of the Borgo edition. I pigheadedly refused to
           abridge it when Southern Illinois University Press expressed interest
           but found the 150,000-word book too long to publish. Ironically
           enough, after McFarland finally did accept the book, it insisted on
           cuts very similar to those that Southern Illinois had requested! The
           German translation (see VIII.3) includes the book as it was originally
           intended—with chapters on Les Daniels, Dennis Etchison, and Da-
           vid J. Schow—as does the Sarnath Press reprint.

19.   *A Dreamer and a Visionary: H. P. Lovecraft in His Time*
      a.   Liverpool: Liverpool University Press, [March] 2001.
           Contents: Preface; 1. Unmixed English Gentry; 2. A Genuine Pagan
           (1890-97); 3. Black Woods and Unfathomed Caves (1898-1902);
           4. What of Unknown Africa? (1902-08); 5. Barbarian and Alien
           (1908-14); 6. A Renewed Will to Live (1914-1917 [I]); 7. Feverish

and Incessant Scribbling (1917–19); 8. Cynical Materialist (1919–21); 9. The High Tide of My Life (1921–22); 10. For My Own Amusement (1923–24); 11. Ball and Chain (1924); 12. Moriturus Te Saluto (1925–26); 13. Paradise Regain'd (1926); 14. Cosmic Outsideness (1927–28); 15. Fanlights and Georgian Steeples (1928–30); 16. Non-Supernatural Cosmic Art (1930–31); 17. Mental Greed (1931–33); 18. In My Own Handwriting (1933–35); 19. Caring about the Civilization (1929–37); 20. The End of One's Life (1935–37); Epilogue: Thou Art Not Gone; Notes; Index.

Notes. An abridgment of *H. P. Lovecraft: A Life,* whittled down to 150,000 words.

20. *Ramsey Campbell and Modern Horror Fiction*
    a. Liverpool: Liverpool University Press, [June] 2001.

       Contents: Abbreviations; Preface; My Roots Exhumed, by Ramsey Campbell; I. Biography and Overview; II. The Lovecraftian Fiction; III. The *Demons by Daylight* Period; IV. The Transformation of Supernaturalism; V. Dreams and Reality; VI. Horrors of the City; VII. Paranoia; VIII. The Child as Victim and Villain; IX. Miscellaneous Writings; Conclusion; Notes; Bibliography; Index.

       Notes. A volume written for Twayne's English Authors Series, but the publisher went defunct before the book could be published. It took me five years to find another publisher. An extract was published in *Guilty Pleasures and Other Dark Delights,* ed. Steve Dillon (n.p.: Things in the Well, 2019), 170–72 (as "On Ramsey Campbell's 'Scared Stiff'").

21. *An H. P. Lovecraft Encyclopedia* (with David E. Schultz)
    a. Westport, CT: Greenwood Press, [September] 2001.
    b. New York: Hippocampus Press, [April] 2004.

       Contents: Preface; Chronology; Abbreviations and Short Titles; The Encyclopedia; General Bibliography; Index.

       Notes. A useful reference work, I think. It was the ultimate product of a curious reference project I had conceived years before—the *Directory of Lovecraftians.*

22. *God's Defenders: What They Believe and Why They Are Wrong*
    a. Amherst, NY: Prometheus Books, [June] 2003.

       Contents: Introduction; 1. The Pragmatical Professor: William James; 2. The Bulldog and the Patrician: G. K. Chesterton and T. S. Eliot; 3. Surprised by Folly: C. S. Lewis; 4. God and the Yale Man: William F. Buckley, Jr.; 5. Religion and Politics: Stephen L. Carter; 6. Fire and Brimstone: Jerry Falwell; 7. Hand-Wringing from the Literati: Reynolds Price and Annie Dillard; 8. Beautiful Souls: Elisabeth Kübler-Ross; 9. Chatting with the Big Guy: Neale Donald Walsch; 10. Religion and Morals: Guenter Lewy; Conclusion; Index.

Notes. My first non-weird monograph, and one in which I like to think I initiated a new genre (unless some of my pungent reviews did so first)—"satirical criticism." It was, of course, very easy to lampoon these shoddy religious "thinkers."

23. *Primal Sources: Essays on H. P. Lovecraft*
  a. New York: Hippocampus Press, [December] 2003.

   Contents: Introduction; Lovecraft and the Munsey Magazines; Lovecraft and *Weird Tales*; A Look at Lovecraft's Letters; Lovecraft and the Films of His Day; Lovecraft's Library; Autobiography in Lovecraft; "Reality" and Knowledge; *In Defence of Dagon* and Lovecraft's Philosophy; The Rationale of Lovecraft's Pseudonyms; The Dream World and the Real World in Lovecraft; Lovecraft's Alien Civilisations: A Political Interpretation; Topical References in Lovecraft; Lovecraft, Regner Lodbrog, and Olaus Wormius; On "Polaris"; What Happens in "Arthur Jermyn"; "The Tree" and Ancient History; The Sources for "From Beyond"; Lovecraft and the *Regnum Congo*; Lovecraft and Dunsany's *Chronicles of Rodriguez*; On "The Descendant"; Some Sources for "The Mound" and *At the Mountains of Madness*; On "The Book"; Lovecraft's Fantastic Poetry.

   Notes. A follow-up to *Selected Papers on Lovecraft*.

24. *The Evolution of the Weird Tale*
  a. New York: Hippocampus Press, [September] 2004.

   Contents. Introduction; I. SOME AMERICANS OF THE GOLDEN AGE: W. C. Morrow: Horror in San Francisco; Robert W. Chambers: The Bohemian Weird Tale; F. Marion Crawford: Blood-and-Thunder Horror; Edward Lucas White: Dream and Reality; II. SOME ENGLISHMEN OF THE GOLDEN AGE: Sir Arthur Quiller-Couch: Ghosts and Scholars; Rudyard Kipling: The Horror of India; E. F. Benson: Spooks and More Spooks; L. P. Hartley: The Refined Ghost; III. H. P. LOVECRAFT AND HIS INFLUENCE: H. P. Lovecraft: The Fiction of Materialism; Frank Belknap Long: Things from the Sea; A Literary Tutelage: Robert Bloch and H. P. Lovecraft; Passing the Torch: H. P. Lovecraft and Fritz Leiber; IV. CONTEMPORARIES: Rod Serling: The Moral Supernatural; L. P. Davies: The Workings of the Mind; Les Daniels: The Horror of History; Dennis Etchison: Spanning the Genres; David J. Schow and Splatterpunk; Poppy Z. Brite: Sex, Horror, and Rock-&-Roll; Bibliography.

   Notes. Not really a follow-up to *The Weird Tale* and *The Modern*

Weird Tale, but a volume that collected my stray writings on various weird figures. Many of the pieces were introductions to editions of the authors in question.

25.   *The Angry Right: Why Conservatives Keep Getting It Wrong*
   a.   Amherst, NY: Prometheus Books, [August] 2006.
       Contents: Introduction; 1. Tin-pot Jeremiah: Russell Kirk; 2. Indiscretions of the Past: William F. Buckley, Jr.; 3. The Rise and Fall of Neoconservatism: Irving and William Kristol; 4. A Woman against Women: Phyllis Schlafly; 5. Laments of the Moralists: William J. Bennett and Gertrude Himmelfarb; 6. Fear from the Pulpit: David Limbaugh; 7. Loud and Wrong: Rush Limbaugh; 8. The Traitor Police: Ann Coulter, Michael Savage, and Sean Hannity; Conclusion; Index.
       Notes. Another attempt at "satirical criticism," again directed at easy targets.

26.   *Gore Vidal: A Comprehensive Bibliography*
   a.   Lanham, MD: Scarecrow Press, [June] 2007.
       Contents: Foreword, by Jay Parini; Introduction; Explanatory Notes; I. Works by Gore Vidal: A. Books and Pamphlets; B. Short Stories and Poems; C. Essays and Reviews; D. Plays; E. Screenplays; F. Published Letters; G. Manuscripts; H. Media Adaptations; I. Vidal in the Media; II. Gore Vidal in Translation: A. Books and Pamphlets; B. Contributions to Books and Periodicals; III. Works about Gore Vidal: A. Bibliographies; B. News Items and Encyclopedias; C. Interviews; D. Books about Vidal; E. Criticism in Books and Periodicals; F. Book Reviews; G. Media Reviews; H. Websites; I. Academic Papers; J. Miscellany; Index: A. Names; B. Titles by Vidal; C. Periodicals.
       Notes. A work that took about a year to assemble, most of the work done at the Cornell University library. I am still planning a monograph on Vidal.

27.   *Emperors of Dreams: Some Notes on Weird Poetry*
   a.   Sydney: P'rea Press, [December] 2008.
       Contents: Preface; Introduction; 1. George Sterling: Prophet of the Suns; 2. Clark Ashton Smith: Beauty Is for the Few; 3. H. P. Lovecraft: Alone in Space; 4. Samuel Loveman: Shelley in Brooklyn; 5. Donald Wandrei: Nightmare in Green; 6. Frank Belknap Long: The Gods Are Dead; 7. Some Contemporaries; Index.
       Notes. A book that the publisher, Charles Lovecraft, asked me to assemble. A pretty skimpy volume, given the largeness of the subject. The only new piece was the essay on Frank Belknap Long; the others are taken from previously published articles and introductions.

28. *The Rise and Fall of the Cthulhu Mythos*
     a.   Poplar Bluff, MO: Mythos Books, [December] 2008.
     b.   Poplar Bluff, MO: Mythos Books, [September 2009]. [with corrections and index]
     c.   New York: Hippocampus Press, [August] 2015 (as *The Rise, Fall, and Rise of the Cthulhu Mythos*).

     Contents: Preface; Introduction; I. Anticipations (1917–26); II. The Lovecraft Mythos: Phase I (1926–30); III. The Lovecraft Mythos: Phase II (1931–36); IV. Contemporaries (I); V. Contemporaries (II); VI. The Derleth Mythos; VII. Interregnum; VIII. The Scholarly Revolution; IX. Recrudescence; Epilogue; Notes; Bibliography; Index.

     Notes. A most entertaining book to write—one in which I found that Mythos writing (especially in recent years) wasn't quite so horrendous as I had imagined. It led directly to my assembly of the *Black Wings* anthologies and other such volumes. The Hippocampus edition has been extensively revised and updated.

29. *Classics and Contemporaries: Some Notes on Horror Fiction*
     a.   New York: Hippocampus Press, [June] 2009.

     Contents. Preface; I. SOME OVERVIEWS: Arkham House and Its Legacy; The Haunted House; Professionals and Amateurs; Some Thoughts on Weird Poetry; Bram and Bela and Mary and Boris; What the Hell Is Dark Suspense?; The Small Press; II. CLASSICS: Algernon Blackwood: The Starlight Man; Arthur Machen: A Minor Classic; William Hope Hodgson: Writer on the Borderland; E. F. Benson: Spooks and More Spooks; A. M. Burrage: The Ghost Man; Herbert S. Gorman: Where Is the Place Called Dagon?; Andrew Caldecott: The Well-Crafted Ghost; Rescuing Shirley Jackson; III. CONTEMPORARIES: Les Daniels: The Sardonic Vampire; Dennis Etchison and His Masters; Thomas Tryon: The Return of the Posthumous Collaboration; Stephen King and God; Peter Straub and the Blue Pencil; Ramsey Campbell: Alone with a Master; Clive Barker: Weird Fiction as Subversion; David J. Schow: Zombies, Tapeworms, and Kamikaze Butterflies; Donald R. Burleson: Enmeshed in the Bizarre; Norman Partridge: Here to Stay; Thomas Harris: Lecter as Albatross; Thomas Ligotti: The Long and the Short of It; Michael Cisco: Ligotti Redivivus?; Sherry Austin: The Southern Ghost Story; Shades of Edgar and Ambrose; IV. SCHOLARSHIP: The Charting of Horror Literature; Classics and Contemporaries; V. H. P. LOVECRAFT: Some Lovecraft Editions; The Cthulhu Mythos; Lovecraft as a Character in Fiction; Some Lovecraft Scholarship (Barton L. St Armand; Donald R. Burleson; Peter Cannon; Robert M. Price; Kenneth W. Faig, Jr; Edward W. O'Brien, Jr; Robert H. Waugh); Index; Acknowledgements.

Notes. A volume of my collected reviews that Derrick Hussey of Hippocampus charitably published. Its best feature is a cover portrait of me as an 18th-century gentleman by Allen Koszowski. An extract from "Ramsey Campbell: Alone with a Master" was reprinted in *Short Story Criticism,* Volume 19 (Detroit: Gale, 1995), 86–89.

30.   *H. L. Mencken: An Annotated Bibliography*
  a.   Lanham, MD: Scarecrow Press, [July] 2009.
       Contents: Introduction; Explanatory Notes; A. Books and Pamphlets; B. Works Edited or Translated: i. Books; ii. Magazines; iii. Newspapers; iv. Articles; C. Original Contributions to Books; D. Original Contributions to Magazines; E. Original Contributions to Newspapers; F. Interviews; Appendix A: "The Free Lance"; Appendix B: Unsigned Articles; Appendix C: H. L. Mencken as Randolph Bartlett; Appendix D: Author Index to Mencken's Book Reviews; Index: A. Names; B. Titles by Mencken; C. Periodicals.
       Notes. A product of my years of research on (and transcription of) Mencken's writings. This is only a primary bibliography; a secondary bibliography would be useful, but I am not much inclined to compile it. The introduction was reprinted in I.50 as "An Overview of Mencken's Life and Work."

31.   *Junk Fiction: America's Obsession with Bestsellers*
  a.   Rockville, MD: Borgo Press, [August] 2009.
       Contents: Introduction; 1. Queens of Romance: Danielle Steel, Barbara Taylor Bradford, and Nora Roberts; 2. An Aesthetic Pretender: John Grisham; 3. Mistresses of Mystery: Mary Higgins Clark, Sue Grafton, and Patricia Cornwell; 4. Pulse-Pounding Suspense: James Patterson and Nelson DeMille; 5. Cops, Robbers, and Spies: Robert Ludlum, Tom Clancy, and Clive Cussler; 6. Mavens of Horror: Stephen King and Dean Koontz; 7. Blood, Thunder, and Religion: Dan Brown and Irving Wallace; 8. Glamour, Fashion, and Sex: Jackie Collins, Judith Krantz, and Jacqueline Susann; Conclusion; Notes; Index.
       Notes. Another book of "satirical criticism" that I could find no publisher for among the academic press. It is flawed by being largely cynical plot summaries of the books I read, but I still think there is some value in it.

32.   *The Removal Company*
  a.   Rockville, MD: Borgo Press, [August] 2009 (as by "J. K. Maxwell").
  b.   Rockville, MD: Borgo Press, [2010] (as by "S. T. Joshi").
  c.   In I.53.

Contents: The Removal Company; Postscript (includes "The Removal Company," by W. C. Morrow).

Notes. My first detective novel—written, I think, as early as 2000. It is based very loosely on the story by W. C. Morrow, although set in a very different era (the early 1930s) and featuring my hard-boiled private investigator, Joe Scintilla.

33.   *H. P. Lovecraft: A Comprehensive Bibliography*
    a.   Tampa, FL: University of Tampa Press, [November] 2009.

       Contents: Introduction to the First Edition; Addendum (2008); I. WORKS BY LOVECRAFT IN ENGLISH: A. Books and Pamphlets; B. Contributions to Books and Periodicals: i. Fiction; ii. Essays; iii. Poetry; iv. Revisions and Collaborations; v. Letters; C. Works Edited by Lovecraft; D. Apocrypha and Miscellany: i. Apocrypha; ii. Works Lost or Destroyed; iii. Award-Winning Stories by H. P. Lovecraft; iv. Miscellany; II. WORKS BY LOVECRAFT IN TRANSLATION: A. Books and Pamphlets; B. Contributions to Books and Periodicals: i. Fiction; ii. Essays; iii. Poetry; iv. Revisions and Collaborations; v. Letters; III. WORKS ABOUT LOVECRAFT: A. News Items and Encyclopedias; B. Bibliographies and Indexes; C. Books and Pamphlets about Lovecraft; D. Criticism in Books and Periodicals: i. General Studies; ii. Biographies and Memoirs; iii. Studies of Individual Tales; iv. Essays, Poetry, Letters; v. Special Topics; vi. Lovecraft's Pseudomythology; vii. Influence and Reputation; viii. Lovecraft and Media; E. Academic Papers; F. Book Reviews: i. Books in English; ii. Books in Languages Other Than English; G. Special Periodicals and Miscellany: i. Periodicals Devoted Exclusively or Largely to Lovecraft; ii. Single Issues of Periodicals Devoted to Lovecraft; iii. Miscellany; IV. INDEXES: A. Names; B. Works by Lovecraft; C. Periodicals.

       Notes. A vast expansion and, in part, reorganisation of the original bibliography (item 3 above), to such a degree that I consider it a new work.

34/35.   *I Am Providence: The Life and Times of H. P. Lovecraft*
    a.   New York: Hippocampus Press, [September] 2010. 2 vols.
    b.   New York: Hippocampus Press, 2012 (paperback).

       Contents: Volume 1: Preface; 1. Unmixed English Gentry; 2. A Genuine Pagan (1890–1897); 3. Black Woods and Unfathomed Caves (1898–1902); 4. What of Unknown Africa? (1902–1908); 5. Barbarian and Alien (1908–1914); 6. A Renewed Will to Live (1914–1917 [I]); 7. Metrical Mechanic (1914–1917 [II]); 8. Dreamers and Visionaries (1917–1919 [I]); 9. Feverish and Incessant Scribbling (1917–

1919 [II]); 10. Cynical Materialist (1919–1921 [I]); 11. Dunsanian Studies (1919–1921 [II]); 12. A Stranger in This Century (1919–1921 [III]); 13. The High Tide of My Life (1921–1922); 14. For My Own Amusement (1923–1924); 15. Ball and Chain (1924); Notes; *Volume 2:* 16. The Assaults of Chaos (1925–1926); 17. Paradise Regain'd (1926); 18. Cosmic Outsideness (1927–1928); 19. Fanlights and Georgian Steeples (1928–1930); 20. Non-Supernatural Cosmic Art (1930–1931); 21. Mental Greed (1931–1933); 22. In My Own Handwriting (1933–1935); 23. Caring about the Civilisation (1929–1937); 24. Close to the Bread-Line (1935–1936); 25. The End of One's Life (1935–1937); 25. Thou Art Not Gone (1937–1010); Notes; Bibliography; Index.

Notes. The unabridged and updated version of *H. P. Lovecraft: A Life*—a full 550,000 words (with notes).

36.   *Conspiracy of Silence/Tragedy at Sarsfield Manor*
       a.   Rockville, MD: Borgo Press, [October] 2010.
       b.   In I.53.
             Contents: Conspiracy of Silence; Tragedy at Sarsfield Manor.

             Notes. My second (and third) detective stories, published as a "double." The first is a 55,000-word short novel; the second—a revision of a work that I originally wrote in 1979 (!)—comes to only 27,000 words.

37.   *Ten Years of Hippocampus Press: 2000–2010* (with Derrick Hussey and David E. Schultz)
       a.   New York: Hippocampus Pres, [December] 2010.
       b.   New York: Hippocampus Press, [August] 2015 (revised; as *Fifteen Years of Hippocampus Press*).
             Contents: Foreword, by Derrick Hussey; S. T. Joshi, "My Years with Hippocampus Press"; Publications of Hippocampus Press 2000–2010; Index of Authors, Editors, and Artists.

             Notes. A self-promotional item, to be sure, but useful for its chronological listing (with complete tables of contents) of all Hippocampus publications.

38.   *The Unbelievers: The Evolution of Modern Atheism*
       a.   Amherst, NY: Prometheus Books, [February] 2011.
             Contents: Introduction; 1. Thomas Henry Huxley: Gladiator-General for Science; 2. Leslie Stephen: A Logician Dissects Theology; 3. John Stuart Mill: Theism and Its Discontents; 4. Friedrich Nietzsche: Prophet of the Superman; 5. Mark Twain: God's Fool; 6. Clarence Darrow: Religion in the Dock; 7. H. L. Mencken: Cracker-

Barrel Philosopher; 8. H. P. Lovecraft: The Wonders of the Cosmos; 9. Bertrand Russell: The Sage of Cambridge; 10. Madalyn Murray O'Hair: Prayer out of the Schools; 11. Gore Vidal: Taking Aim at the Sky-God; 12. Richard Dawkins: Science vs. God; 13. Sam Harris: The Passionate Freethinker; 14. Christopher Hitchens: The Evils of Religion; Epilogue; Index.

Notes. A work that grew out of my work on *Icons of Unbelief* (II.74); the four chapters I wrote for that book are here, along with ten others.

39. *H. P. Lovecraft: Nightmare Countries*
  a. New York: Metro Books, [July] 2012.
  b. Seattle: Sarnath Press, [July] 2018 (as *H. P. Lovecraft: A Short Biography*).

    Contents: Introduction; 1. A Genuine Pagan (1890–1904); 2. Eccentric Recluse (1904–1914); 3. A Renewed Will to Live (1914–1924); 4. New York Exile (1924–1926); 5. The Creation of Cthulhu (1926–1931); 6. A Shadow over Life (1932–1937); 7. The Mythos Grows; Author Biography; Image Credits.

    Notes. A book commissioned by a book packager (Becker & Mayer) for exclusive distribution in Barnes & Noble bookstores. The text (less than 40,000 words) took no more than two weeks to write.

40/41. *Unutterable Horror: A History of Supernatural Fiction*
  a. Hornsea, UK: PS Publishing, [December] 2012.

    Contents: Volume 1 (From Gilgamesh to the End of the Nineteenth Century): Preface; I. Introduction; II. Anticipations; III. The Gothics; IV. Interregnum; V. Edgar Allan Poe; VI. Mid-Victorian Horrors; VII. The Deluge: British and European Branch; VIII. The Deluge: American Branch; Epilogue; Bibliographical Essay; Bibliography; *Volume 2 (The Twentieth and Twenty-first Centuries):* Preface; IX. The Titans; X. Other Early-Twentieth Century Masters; XI. Novelists, Satirists, and Poets; XII. H. P. Lovecraft and His Influence; XIII. American Pulpsmiths; XIV. Horrors at Midcentury; XV. Anticipations of the Boom; XVI. The Boom: The Blockbusters; XVII. The Boom: The Literati; XVIII. The Contemporary Era; Epilogue; Bibliographical Essay; Bibliography; Index.

    Notes. A book on which I worked for five years (2006–11). The first volume was ready as early as 2009, but I persuaded the publisher to hold off and release both books simultaneously. There are probably many omissions, but this is as comprehensive a study of weird fiction and its authors as I know of.

42.   *The Assaults of Chaos: A Novel about H. P. Lovecraft*
       a.   New York: Hippocampus Press, [July] 2013.
             Notes. A rather whimsical work in which the young Lovecraft (in
             1914, not quite twenty-four) heads off to England in the company of
             Ambrose Bierce and others and meets Arthur Machen, Lord Dun-
             sany, Algernon Blackwood, M. R. James, and William Hope Hodg-
             son in an adventure that turns supernatural. Nothing but a *jeu
             d'esprit.* The edition includes, as a bonus, a separate booklet, *Suicide
             in Brooklyn*—an 8000-word hard-boiled detective story with subtle
             Lovecraftian touches.

43.   *Lovecraft and a World in Transition: Collected Essays on H. P. Lovecraft*
       a. New York: Hippocampus Press, [August] 2014.
             Contents: Introduction; I. BIOGRAPHICAL STUDIES: Lovecraft and
             Weird Tales; Further Notes on Lovecraft and Music; Lovecraft's Li-
             brary; Lovecraft's Revisions: How Much of Them Did He Write?;
             Lovecraft and His Wife; Lovecraft and the Films of His Day; The
             Rationale of Lovecraft's Pseudonyms; Lovecraft and the Munsey
             Magazines; Lovecraft and Willis Conover; Barbarism and Civilisa-
             tion: Robert E. Howard and H. P. Lovecraft in Their Correspond-
             ence; II. PHILOSOPHICAL STUDIES: The Political and Economic
             Thought of H. P. Lovecraft; "Reality" and Knowledge: Some Notes
             on Lovecraft's Aesthetic; *In Defence of Dagon* and Lovecraft's Philos-
             ophy; Lovecraft's Alien Civilisations: A Political Interpretation;
             Lovecraft and a World in Transition; Lovecraft and the "Big Issue";
             H. P. Lovecraft: The Fiction of Materialism; Lovecraft on Religion;
             Time, Space, and Natural Law: Science and Pseudo-Science in Love-
             craft; III. THEMATIC AND TEXTUAL STUDIES: Autobiography in
             Lovecraft; Lovecraft's Other Planets; Textual Problems in Lovecraft;
             The Structure of Lovecraft's Longer Narratives; The Dream World
             and the Real World in Lovecraft; Topical References in Lovecraft;
             Humour and Satire in Lovecraft; A Guide to the Lovecraft Fiction
             Manuscripts at the John Hay Library; IV. STUDIES OF INDIVIDUAL
             WORKS: Who Wrote "The Mound?"; On "The Book"; On "Polaris";
             On "The Tree on the Hill"; Lovecraft and the *Regnum Congo;* The
             Sources for "From Beyond"; "On "The Descendant"; What Happens
             in "Arthur Jermyn"; "The Tree" and Ancient History; Lovecraft and
             Dunsany's *Chronicles of Rodriguez;* Some Sources for "The Mound"
             and *At the Mountains of Madness; The Case of Charles Dexter Ward;* Ex-
             cised Passages in "The Thing on the Doorstep"; V. ON LOVECRAFT'S
             ESSAYS, POETRY, AND LETTERS: "History of the *Necronomicon*"; "Su-
             pernatural Horror in Literature"; Two Spurious Lovecraft Poems; A

Look at Lovecraft's Letters; Lovecraft's Fantastic Poetry; Lovecraft, Regner Lodbrog, and Olaus Wormius; Lovecraft's Essays; VI. ON LOVECRAFT'S LEGACY AND INFLUENCE: The Development of Lovecraftian Studies, 1971–1982; R. H. Barlow and the Recognition of Lovecraft; The Lovecraft Centennial Conference: Concluding Address; A Literary Tutelage: Robert Bloch and H. P. Lovecraft; Passing the Torch: H. P. Lovecraft's Influence on Fritz Leiber; *Lovecraft at Last*; The Cthulhu Mythos; The Recognition of H. P. Lovecraft, 1937–2013; Sources; Index.

Notes. A volume of most (but not all) of my essays on Lovecraft, dating from as early as 1979 up to 2013.

44.   *200 Books by S. T. Joshi: A Comprehensive Bibliography*
   a.   New York: Hippocampus Press, [September] 2014.

   Contents: Introduction; I. Books Written; II. Books Edited; III. Editions of Works by H. P. Lovecraft; IV. Books Translated; V. Joshi as Series Editor: A. New Millennium Mythos; B. The Modern Mythos Library; C. Studies in Supernatural Literature; VI. Contributions to Books and Periodicals: A. Essays and Introductions; B. Reviews; C. Fiction; D. Poetry; E. Published Letters; F. Translations; VII. Journals Edited; VIII. Translations of Works by S. T. Joshi: A. Books; B. Contributions to Books and Periodicals; IX. Forthcoming Books; Appendix: Murder; The Writing of *Mystery and Horror Writers of the Twentieth Century*; Books Published by Year.

   Notes. The first version of the present compilation.

45.   *Driven to Madness with Fright: Further Notes on Horror Fiction*
   a.   n.p.: CreateSpace, [December] 2016.
   b.   Seattle: Sarnath Press, [September] 2018 (expanded ed.).

   Contents: I. THE CLASSICS: From Gothic to Weird; The Canon of American Weird Fiction; Weird Poetry, Then and Now; Poe as Revolutionary; The Life and Work of Ambrose Bierce; A Biography of the Mind; Shirley Jackson as a Classic; II. SOME CONTEMPORARIES: Terror in the Northwest; Campbell and Lovecraft; Rain, Rain, Everywhere; Fifty Years of Ramsey Campbell; Terror in a Sentence; The Sublime and the Ridiculous; Just Like the Movies; A Slow-Moving Tsunami; A Modern "Heart of Darkness"; Sculptures in Prose; The Mystery Man of Weird Fiction; Spanning the Genres with William F. Nolan; Of Revenants and Seedy Taverns; Road Dogs and Iron Dead; III. SOME ANTHOLOGIES: Driven to Madness with Fright; A Smorgasbord of Weird; Chambers, Lovecraft, and Pastiche; The Anthologies of Jason V Brock and William F. Nolan; IV. H. P. LOVECRAFT: HIS DISCIPLES AND HIS CRITICS: The Emergence of H. P.

Lovecraft; How Not to Edit Lovecraft; The Derleth Mythos; The Lovecraft Cult; The World of Lovecraft Fandom; The Return of Cosmic Horror; Old and New Cthulhu; Is the Well Running Dry?; A Distinctive Talent; Working Together; Darrell Schweitzer and the Mythos; "Life Is More Horrible Than Death"; Conflicted About Lovecraft; Sources.

Notes. A self-published collection of my book reviews (and some articles and introductions) subsequent to *Classics and Contemporaries* (I.29). The 2018 edition adds: A Promising Start; Terrors of the Natural World; Existential and Ontological Horror; Who Is Dr. Prozess?; and An Exponent of Quiet Horror to Section II; Carnacki Lives Again!; Horrors in Winnipeg; Pastiches of Pastiches; and A Mixed Bag to Section III; and How Not to Read Lovecraft; What Makes a Lovecraftian Story?; The Horror in the Card Catalog; and Lovecraft Alive to Section IV. "Campbell and Lovecraft" is augmented and transferred to Section IV.

46. *The Stupidity Watch: An Atheist Speaks Out on Religion and Politics*
   a. Seattle: Sarnath Press, [March] 2017.
   b. Seattle: Sarnath Press, 2018 (expanded ed.).

   Contents: Preface; Introduction: Living in a Religious Society; I. ESSAYS AND REVIEWS: A Confession of Unfaith; What Apostates Have to Say; Circling the Wagons; Yearning for Paradise Lost; The Caspar Miquetoast Humanist; A Christian "Intellectual" Speaks; Religious Freedom or Religious Coercion?; Satan, Monsters, and Bad People; Guns, Guns, and More Guns; The Pious Fight Back; Republicans: An Endangered Species; Christianity and Complexity; The Problem of Islamic Extremism; The Beatification of St. Kim; Atheism, Christianity, and Insanity; The Rise and Fall of Christianity; Christianity and Free Enterprise; The Bible and Gays; Atheism in Classical Antiquity; In-Your-Face Atheism; Why People Convert; A Fitting Burial; II. THE STUPIDITY WATCH; Index.

   Notes. A self-published collection of my writings for the *American Rationalist.* The expanded edition adds the following essays to the end of Section I: Trump and the Religious Right; Atheism and Women; Throwing In the Towel; The "Cake Artist" and His Bigotry; and The Party of Traitors.

47. *Varieties of the Weird Tale*
   a. New York: Hippocampus Press, [May] 2017.
   Contents: Introduction: Establishing the Canon of Weird Fiction; I. THE GOLDEN AGE: Some Notes on Ambrose Bierce (I. Bierce as Political Satirist; II. Bierce as Fabulist; III. What Happens in "The

Death of Halpin Frayser"); A Triumvirate of Fantastic Poets: Ambrose Bierce, George Sterling, and Clark Ashton Smith; Gertrude Atherton: Death and Women; Bram Stoker: *Dracula* and Others; Mary E. Wilkins Freeman: The Domestic Ghost; E. Nesbit: Lying Awake in the Dark; Edna W. Underwood: Dear Dead Women; Things in the Weeds: The Supernatural in Hodgson's Short Stories; II. THE ERA OF LOVECRAFT: M. R. James and the Classic Ghost Story; Some Notes on Lord Dunsany (I. The Pegāna Mythos; II. Jorkens; III. Christianity and Paganism in Two Dunsany Novels); Sax Rohmer: The Popular Weird Tale; Maurice Level and the Grand Guignol; Irvin S. Cobb and Gouverneur Morris: A Taste for the Weird; Bran Mak Morn and History; The Novels of Donald Wandrei; III. SOME CONTEMPORARIES: Science and Superstition: Fritz Leiber's Modernization of Gothic; Master and Pupil: August Derleth and Ramsey Campbell's First Book; Thomas Ligotti's *The Nightmare Factory*; Caitlín R. Kiernan and Sensuous Prose; Acknowledgments; Index.

Notes. Another collection of my miscellaneous essays on weird fiction, including the introductions to several editions of classic authors.

48.   *Lovecraft and Weird Fiction: Selected Blog Posts, 2009–2017*
  a.   Seattle: Sarnath Press, [December] 2017.
       Contents: Introduction; I. H. P. LOVECRAFT TODAY: Lovecraft's Worldwide Fame; Some Lovecraft Projects; Editing Lovecraft's Letters; The Variorum Lovecraft; Lovecraft in the Media; Some Lovecraft Discoveries; II. DEFENDING LOVECRAFT: On Roger Luckhurst; Daniel José Older and the World Fantasy Award; Laura Miller on Lovecraft; Charles Baxter on Lovecraft; Robert Dunbar on Lovecraft; Paula Guran on Lovecraft; III. On Weird Writers, Past and Present: *Unutterable Horror*; Work on Lord Dunsany; Work on Arthur Machen; Work on Clark Ashton Smith; Work on Ambrose Bierce and George Sterling; Work for Centipede Press; Work for Hippocampus Press; Work on Ramsey Campbell; Studies in Supernatural Literature; Some Worthy Contemporaries; On Scott Nicolay; IV. On S. T. Joshi: Who Is S. T. Joshi?; S. T. Joshi's Ascending Fame; *Black Wings* and Other Anthologies; The Fiction of S. T. Joshi; Joshi and Atheism; *Varieties of Crime Fiction*; Conventions and Other Destinations; NecronomiCon 2013, 2015, 2017; Joshi on Mencken; Some Other Projects; Joshi as Musician; On Book Reviewing; Brian Keene and the Joshi-Haters; Some Personal Matters; V. On General Subjects: Some Points of Grammar; The Horror of November 8; Real and Fake Liberalism; Books by S. T. Joshi; Index of Names.
       Notes. An amusing volume (I trust) reprinting many of my more controversial blogs (from my website, stjoshi.org) on various subjects,

as well as accounts of my progress on various of my volumes and other matters. Each section is arranged topically, with the date of each blog (or section of a blog) identified at the end of the extract.

49. *What Is Anything? Memoirs of a Life in Lovecraft*
     a. New York: Hippocampus Press, [June] 2018.
         Contents: Preface; 1. From India to Illinois (1958-68); 2. Indiana I (1968-72); 3. Indiana II (1972-76); 4. Brown (1976-80); 5. Brown and Princeton (1980-84); 6. Chelsea House I (1984-90); 7. Chelsea House II (1990-95); 8. New York (1995-2001); 9. Seattle I (2001-05); 10. Moravia (2005-08); 11. Seattle II (2008-12); 12. Seattle III (2013-18); Epilogue; Index.

         Notes. A book I have been threatening to write for years, and one that I managed to write mostly in the spring of 2017. The publisher issued it on my 60th birthday (June 22, 2018), unveiling it at a little gathering in New York, which I attended.

50. *H. L. Mencken as Artist and Critic: Essays on the Sage of Baltimore*
     a. Seattle: Sarnath Press, [July] 2018.
         Contents: An Overview of Mencken's Life and Work; H. L. Mencken, Free Lance; H. L. Mencken, Book Reviewer; H. L. Mencken and George Sterling; Mencken on Religion; Mencken as Creative Artist; Mencken and Terrorism; Mencken on Mencken; H. L. Mencken's America.

         Notes. A self-published collection of the introductions to my various editions of Mencken's writings. The opening essay is the introduction to my Mencken bibliography.

51. *21st-Century Horror: Weird Fiction at the Turn of the Millennium*
     a. Seattle: Sarnath Press, [November] 2018.
         Contents: Introduction; I. THE ELITE: Michael Aronovitz: Teller of Tales; Gemma Files: Sex, Myth, and Film; Adam Nevill: The Sense of Dread; Mark Samuels: Corporate Horror and Others; Simon Strantzas: The Cosmic and the Human; Jonathan Thomas: A Study in Contrasts; II. THE WORTHIES: Nicole Cushing: Suicide and Other Horrors; Richard Gavin: The Nature of Horror; Glen Hirshberg: The Sense of Place; John Langan: Tales from the Heart; Reggie Oliver: Ghosts and More Ghosts; Clint Smith: Decaying Cities, Decaying Lives; James Ulmer: Exponent of Quiet Horror; III. THE PRETENDERS: Laird Barron: Decline and Fall; Joe Hill: Like Father, Like Son; Brian Keene: Paperback Writer; Nick Mamatas: Failed Mimic; Paul Tremblay: Borrowing from His Predecessors; Jeff VanderMeer: An Aesthetic Catastrophe; Works Cited; Index.

Notes. A major book on which I worked for several years. But when I posted some of the more uncharitable chapters (i.e., those in the "Pretenders" section) online, I received such hostile reactions that several publishers were scared to publish the book. So I issued it myself.

52. *The Development of the Weird Tale*
 a. Seattle: Sarnath Press, [January] 2019.

 Contents: Mary Shelley: *Frankenstein* and Others; Théophile Gautier: The Eternal Feminine; A Forgotten Weird Fictionist: Henry Ferris; W. W. Jacobs: A Pessimistic Humourist; Barry Pain: The Occasional Weirdist; Algernon Blackwood and the Ghost Story; On "A Wine of Wizardry"; Samuel Loveman: Shelley in Brooklyn; Clark Ashton Smith: Poet of the Stars (A. Fiction; B. Prose-Poetry; C. *The Hashish-Eater*); The Poetry of Donald Wandrei; Thomas Burke: Look Back in Terror; D. H. Lawrence: Weird Fiction as Symbol; Surprised by Horror: The Fantasy Short Stories of C. S. Lewis; A Failed Experiment: Family and Humanity in Shirley Jackson's *The Sundial*; Some Novels by L. P. Davies (A. *Who Is Lewis Pinder?*; B. *Twilight Journey*; C. *The Shadow Before*); Atheism and Anticlericalism in the Films of Guillermo del Toro; Lovecraft and Some Lost Classics of the Supernatural: Walter de la Mare, *The Return* (1910); Algernon Blackwood, *Incredible Adventures* (1914); Arthur Ransome, *The Elixir of Life* (1915); Robert Hichens, *The Dweller on the Threshold* (1915); Leland Hall, *Sinister House* (1919); Eleanor M. Ingram, *The Thing from the Lake* (1921); Francis Brett Young, *Cold Harbour* (1924); Henri Béraud, *Lazarus* (1925); R. E. Spencer, *The Lady Who Came to Stay* (1931); Acknowledgments; Index.

 Notes. Another collection of my miscellaneous essays and introductions. The three pieces on L. P. Davies were written as introductions to reprints of the novels in question by an Irish publisher, but the reprints never occurred.

53. *The Recurring Doom: Tales of Mystery and Horror*
 a. Seattle: Sarnath Press, [February] 2019.

 Contents: Introduction; The Removal Company; Conspiracy of Silence; Tragedy at Sarsfield Manor; "You'll Reach There in Time"; The Recurring Doom; Personals; Suicide in Brooklyn; Incident at Ferney; Some Kind of Mistake; Acknowledgments.

 Notes. A book that fulfils a dream of mine since adolescence: a collection of my fiction (along with my two short detective novels and detective novella).

54.   *Something from Below*
       a.   Hornsea, UK: PS Publishing, [October] 2019.
            Notes. A weird novella. My most serious work of weird fiction to
            date. The book was also published in a 100-copy signed/limited edi-
            tion.

II. Books Edited

1.   *H. P. Lovecraft in "The Eyrie"* (with Marc A. Michaud)
       a.   West Warwick, RI: Necronomicon Press, 1979.
            Contents: Preface, by S. T. Joshi and Marc A. Michaud; Introduc-
            tion; A. Letters by H. P. Lovecraft: September 1923; October 1923;
            January 1924; March 1924; February 1926; January 1928; February
            1928; March 1928; January 1934; October 1936; B. Letters on Love-
            craft: H. Warner Munn (March 1925); H. P. Tead, Howard Ander-
            son (April 1925); H. S. Farnese (September 1925); August Derleth
            (March 1926); E. Hoffmann Price (April 1926); Ray Cummings, Au-
            gust Derleth (June 1926); J. Vernon Shea (October 1926); Henry S.
            Whitehead (May 1927); Jack Snow, Max F. Myers (December 1927);
            Edmond Hamilton (January 1928); R[obert] E. Howard (May 1928);
            Jack Snow (July 1928); J. W. Meek, Paul Hendrickson (August
            1928); A. V. Pershing, Jack T. Whitfield, Bernard Austin Dwyer
            (June 1929); E. L. Mengshoel (August 1929); Genevieve W. Fisher
            (September 1929); A. V. Pershing (November 1929); J. Wasso (Feb-
            ruary 1930); N. J. O'Neail (March 1930); Dale V. Simpson (April
            1930); Bernard Austin Dwyer (June 1930); H. P. Stiller (June 1930);
            Charles Rush, Jr. (November 1930); Harold Farnese (August 1931);
            J. Vernon Shea (September 1931); Anthony Amato, J. Vernon Shea,
            Robert Leonard Russell, Clark Ashton Smith (October 1931); How-
            ard J. Duerr (December 1931); G. W. Hockley (April 1932); E. L.
            Mengshoel (November 1932); John W. Bennett, Robert Bloch (Sep-
            tember 1933); Alexander Ostrow (October 1933); G. W. Hockley
            (January 1934); Bernard J. Kenton (May 1934); Henry Kuttner (Sep-
            tember 1934); Robert Nelson (March 1935); John Malone, Donald
            A. Wollheim, Lewis F. Torrance, B. M. Reynolds, Charles H. Burt
            (June 1935); Emil Petaja (August 1935); Henry Kuttner, Jacques
            Bergier (March 1936); B. M. Reynolds (October 1936); Henry Kutt-
            ner (February 1937); H. Warner Munn, Robert Bloch (April 1937);
            [Editor's note on Lovecraft's death], Lorne W. Power, Manly Wade
            Wellman, Robert Leonard Russell, Hazel Heald, Robert Bloch, Sea-
            bury Quinn (June 1937); Kenneth Sterling, Edmond Hamilton,
            Henry Kuttner, Earl Peirce, Jr., Bruce Bryan, Harold S. Farnese (July

1937); Hazel Heald, N. J. O'Neail, Paul S. Smith, Robert W. Lowndes, Samuel Gordon (August 1937); Francis Flagg, Jacques Bergier (September 1937); Elaine McIntire, Reginld A. Pryke, Donald A. Wollheim, Joseph Allen Ryan (October 1937); David Markham (November 1937); J. Vernon Shea (December 1937); Charles H. Burt (February 1938); Bernard Austin Dwyer (March 1938); E. Hoffmann Price, H. Sivia, J. Vernon Shea (April 1938); Jeffrey St. John Casserley (May 1938); Paul S. Smith (August 1938); Robert Black (October 1938); E. Hoffmann Price (December 1938); E. Hoffmann Price (May 1939); Thomas O. Mabbott (August 1939); Ray Douglas Bradbury (November 1939); Willis Conover, Jr. (December 1939); August Derleth and Donald Wandrei, Robert Rosen (May 1941); Harold Gauer (July 1941); August Derleth (January 1942); August Derleth (March 1944); Jack Snow (January 1946); Robert E. Briney, Steven Nickman, Leif Arjen, John Gatto, Irving Glassman (May 1952); "An Old Reader," J. N. Stewart, Jr. (July 1952); Joseph V. Wilcox (September 1952); James Wade (November 1952); Joseph V. Wilcox (January 1953); Notes; A Bibliography of H. P. Lovecraft in *Weird Tales*; Index to Contributors.

Notes. A book that had to be compiled the old-fashioned way: by transcribing *by hand*, in notebook after notebook, the various letters by and about HPL in *Weird Tales*. The copies of the magazine at the John Hay Library were too fragile for photocopying, so Michaud and I spent weeks copying out the letters in pen. The letters about Lovecraft were reprinted in *A Weird Writer in Our Midst* (item 82 below).

2.   *H. P. Lovecraft: Four Decades of Criticism*
a.   Athens: Ohio University Press, 1980.

    Contents: Preface; Kenneth W. Faig, Jr., and S. T. Joshi, "H. P. Lovecraft: His Life and Work"; S. T. Joshi, "Lovecraft Criticism: A Study"; S. T. Joshi, "A Chronology of Selected Works by H. P. Lovecraft"; T. O. Mabbott, "H. P. Lovecraft: An Appreciation"; Edmund Wilson, "Tales of the Marvellous and the Ridiculous"; Fritz Leiber, Jr., "A Literary Copernicus"; Peter Penzoldt, excerpts from *The Supernatural in Fiction*; George T. Wetzel, "The Cthulhu Mythos: A Study" (revised); Edward Lauterbach, "Some Notes on Cthulhuian Pseudobiblia"; Dirk W. Mosig, "H. P. Lovecraft: Myth-Maker"; J. Vernon Shea, "On the Literary Influences Which Shaped Lovecraft's Writings"; Fritz Leiber, Jr., "Through Hyperspace with Brown Jenkin: Lovecraft's Contribution to Speculative Fiction"; Peter Cannon, "The Influence of *Vathek* on H. P. Lovecraft's *The Dream-Quest of Unknown Kadath*"; Robert Bloch, "Poe and Lovecraft"; Peter Cannon, "H. P. Lovecraft in Hawthornian Perspective"; Barton L. St. Armand, "Facts in the Case of H. P. Lovecraft"; Dirk W. Mosig,

"'The White Ship': A Psychological Odyssey"; Richard L. Tierney, "Lovecraft and the Cosmic Quality in Fiction"; Paul Buhle, "Dystopia as Utopia: Howard Phillips Lovecraft and the Unknown Content of American Horror Literature"; Winfield Townley Scott, "A Parenthesis on Lovecraft as Poet"; R. Boerem, "A Lovecraftian Nightmare"; R. Boerem, "The Continuity of the *Fungi from Yuggoth*"; Clark Ashton Smith, "To Howard Phillips Lovecraft" [poem]; Appendix I: The Collected Works of H. P. Lovecraft (Arkham House edition); Appendix II: Supplementary Readings.

Notes. My first "real" book, begun in the summer of 1975 under the bland title *A Collection of H. P. Lovecraft Criticism.* I queried 33 academic publishers; a few (e.g., Cornell University Press) saw portions of the ms. but declined. Finally Ohio accepted it in the fall of 1978, but it did not come out until the summer of 1980, just as I was graduating (B.A.) from Brown.

3.   Sonia H. Davis, *The Private Life of H. P. Lovecraft*
        a.   West Warwick, RI: Necronomicon Press, 1985.
        b.   West Warwick, RI: Necronomicon Press, 1992.
             Contents: A Note on the Text; Introduction; The Private Life of H. P. Lovecraft, by Sonia H. Davis.
             Notes. An unabridged publication of Sonia's memoir of HPL.

4.   Donald Wandrei, *Collected Poems*
        a.   West Warwick, RI: Necronomicon Press, 1988.
             Contents: Foreword; *Ecstasy and Other Poems:* The Voice of Beauty; The Song of Autumn; Ecstasy; Let Us Love To-night; Vain Warning; On Some Drawings; Sanctity and Sin; To Myrrhiline; The Song of Oblivion; In Mandrikor; The Woodland Pool; Death and the Poet: A Fragment; Satiation; In Memoriam: George Sterling; Bacchanalia; Awakening; Red; Hermaphroditus; Aphrodite; Amphitrite; Philomela; A Drinking Song; At the Bacchic Revel; The Challenger; The Greatest Regret; Futility; From the Shadowlands of Memory; The Poet's Language; Nightmare; Valerian; *Dark Odyssey:* Largo; Aubade; Fata Morgana; Borealis; In Memoriam: No Name; Dark Odyssey; Look Homeward, Angel; Under the Glass; You Will Come Back; Aftr Bacchus, Eros; To Lucasta on Her Birthday; Villanelle à la Mode; For the Perishing Aphrodite; Morning Song; The Whispering Knoll; The Five Lords; Lost Atlantis; The Night Wind; The Plague Ship; The Voyagers' Return to Tyre; Chaos Resolved; Epithalamium; Epilude; *Poems for Midnight:* Phantom; The Corpse Speaks; The Woman at the Window; Shadowy Night; The Worm-King; Incubus; The Prehistoric Huntsman; Water Sprite; Witches' Sabbath; Forest

Shapes; The Dream That Dies; The Sleeper; The Moon-Glen Altar; The Morning of a Nymph; Death and the Traveler: A Fragment; King of the Shadowland; Ishmael; Sonnets of the Midnight Hours; Somewhere Past Ispahan; Uncollected Poems: Paphos; Poems from *Broken Mirrors* (Fling Wide the Roses, Drink!, The Dead Mistress, My Lady Hath Two Lovely Lips, Aftermath, Credo); Sonnets of the Midnight Hours (Dream-Horror, The Grip of Evil Dreams, The Creatures, The Red Specter, Doom); Chant to the Dead; Moon Magic (The Glow, The Song, The Overtone, The Dream); Dead Fruit of the Fugitive Years (The Dream Changes, Surrender, Through All My Days, The Second Beauty, Twice Excellent Perfection, This Larger Room, The Woman Answers, The Deadly Calm, Corroding Acids, With Cat-like Tread); Lyrics of Doubt (A Testament of Desertion, To the God of My Fathers); Marmora; The Cypress-Bog; A Queen in Other Skies; Epitaph to a Lady; Portrait of a Lady During a Half Hour Wait While She Finished Dressing; The Little Gods Wait; Solitary; Lines; I Am Man; Golden Poppy.

Notes. A volume that emerged out of my relations with Wandrei, who had died in 1987. An augmented edition was issued as *Sanctity and Sin* (item 71 below).

5.   Clark Ashton Smith, *Nostalgia of the Unknown: The Complete Prose Poetry* (with Marc & Susan Michaud and Steve Behrends)
  a.   West Warwick, RI: Necronomicon Press, 1988.
  b.   West Warwick, RI: Necronomicon Press, 1993.

Contents: Introduction, by the editors; From *Ebony and Crystal:* The Traveller; The Flower-Devil; Images (Tears, The Secret Rose, The Wind and the Garden, Offerings, A Coronal); The Black Lake; Vignettes (Beyond the Mountains, The Broken Lute, Nostalgia of the Unknown, Grey Sorrow, The Hair of Circe, The Eyes of Circe); A Dream of Lethe; The Caravan; The Princess Almeena; Ennui; The Statue of Silence; Remoteness; The Memnons of the Night; The Garden and the Tomb; In Cocaigne; The Litany of the Seven Kisses; From a Letter; From the Crypts of Memory [text taken from original manuscripts]; From the Crypts of Memory [text taken from *Ebony and Crystal*]; A Phantasy; The Demon, the Angel, and Beauty; The Shadows; December 1929: The Mirror in the Hall of Ebony; To the Daemon; The Abomination of Desolation; The Touch-Stone; The Lotus and the Moon; The Osprey and the Shark; The Forbidden Forest; The Mithridate; The Muse of Hyperborea; Chinoiserie; Additional Prose Poems: The City of Destruction [fragment]; The Image of Bronze and the Image of Iron [fragment]; The Crystals; The Lake of Enchanted Silence; The Mortuary; The Corpse and the

Skeleton; The Sun and the Sepulchre; The Frozen Waterfall; Preference; The Passing of Aphrodite; The Days; Offering; Narcissus; The Peril That Lurks among Ruins [text taken from original manuscript] (31); The Peril That Lurks among Ruins [text taken from a later manuscript]; [Untitled].

Notes. A volume in which I had almost no involvement aside from writing a portion of the introduction; but I am listed as editor, so the title is included here.

6.   Robert E. Howard, *Selected Letters 1923–1930* (with Glenn Lord and Rusty Burke)
   a.   West Warwick, RI: Necronomicon Press, 1989.
        Contents: Introduction, by Glenn Lord; The Letters.
        Notes. Another volume in which I was not much involved, aside from doing some light annotation of the letters.

7.   Robert E. Howard, *Selected Letters 1931–1936* (with Glenn Lord, Rusty Burke, and Steve Behrends)
   a.   West Warwick, RI: Necronomicon Press, 1991.
        Contents: Introduction, by Robert M. Price; The Letters.
        Notes. Same as above.

8.   *The H. P. Lovecraft Centennial Conference: Proceedings*
   a.   West Warwick, RI: Necronomicon Press, 1991.
        Contents: Introduction; PANEL I: LOVECRAFT AND NEW ENGLAND: Jason C. Eckhardt, "Introduction"; Henry L. P. Beckwith, "Lovecraft's Xenophobia and Providence Between the Wars"; Donald R. Burleson, "Providence and Lovecraft's Fiction"; Barton L. St. Armand, "Roots of Horror in New England"; Will Murray, "Lovecraft's Arkham Country"; "Discussion"; PANEL II: LOVECRAFT'S LIFE AND TIMES: Marc A. Michaud, "Introduction"; [Will Murray], "An Interview with Harry Brobst"; Kenneth W. Faig, Jr., "Lovecraft's Parents"; M. Eileen McNamara, M.D., "Lovecraft's Medical History"; David E. Schultz, "Personal Elements in Lovecraft's Writings"; Frank Belknap Long, "Lovecraft the Man"; PANEL III: LOVECRAFT'S STYLE AND IMAGERY: Steven J. Mariconda, "Introduction: Style and Imagery in Lovecraft"; Norman R. Gayford, "Lovecraft's Narrators"; Robert H. Waugh, "Lovecraft's Documentary Style"; John McInnis, "'The Colour out of Space' as the History of H. P. Lovecraft's Immediate Family"; R. Boerem, "Other Elements in 'The Colour out of Space'"; "Discussion"; PANEL IV: THE CRAFT OF THE HORROR FICTION WRITER: Les Daniels, "Lovecraft and Modern Horror"; Fred Chappell, "Remarks on *Dagon*"; Stefan Dziemianowicz, "Lovecraft and the

Modern Horror Writer"; Robert M. Price, "Robert E. Howard and Other *Weird Tales* Writers"; Frank Belknap Long, "Lovecraft in His Times"; "Discussion"; Panel V: LOVECRAFT'S PLACE IN WORLD LITERATURE: Paul Buhle, "Introduction"; Maurice Lévy, "Lovecraft and Surrealism"; Kalju Kirde, "Lovecraft in Germany"; Giuseppe Lippi, "Italy Today: Lovecraft as the Grand Master of the Macabre"; Gilles Menegaldo, "Lovecraft's Reception in France Since 1890"; Barton L. St. Armand, "Lovecraft and Borges"; PANEL VI: A REASSESSMENT OF LOVECRAFT'S LEGACY: Paul Buhle, "The Sense of Time in H. P. Lovecraft"; Will Murray, "Lovecraft as Pulp Writer"; Robert M. Price, "The Mythology of the Old Ones"; Donald R. Burleson, "Lovecraft: Dreams and Reality"; Peter Cannon, "The Current State of Lovecraft Studies"; "Discussion"; S. T. Joshi, "Concluding Address."

Notes. A volume that was compiled by my transcription of audio tapes of the various panel discussions at the Centennial Conference.

9.　　*An Epicure in the Terrible: A Centennial Anthology of Essays in Honor of H. P. Lovecraft* (with David E. Schultz)
　　a.　Rutherford, NJ: Fairleigh Dickinson University Press, 1991.
　　b.　New York: Hippocampus Press, [September] 2011.

　　Contents: Preface, by David E. Schultz; Introduction; Kenneth W. Faig, Jr., "The Parents of Howard Phillips Lovecraft"; Jason C. Eckhardt, "The Cosmic Yankee"; Will Murray, "Lovecraft and the Pulp Magazine Tradition"; Donald R. Burleson, "On Lovecraft's Themes: Touching the Glass"; Peter Cannon, "Letters, Diaries, and Manuscripts: The Handwritten Word in Lovecraft"; Stefan Dziemianowicz, "Outsiders and Aliens: The Uses of Isolation in Lovecraft's Fiction"; Steven J. Mariconda, "Lovecraft's Cosmic Imagery"; David E. Schultz, "From Microcosm to Macrocosm: The Growth of Lovecraft's Cosmic Vision"; Robert H. Waugh, "Landscapes, Selves, and Others in Lovecraft"; Robert M. Price, "Lovecraft's 'Artificial Mythology'"; R. Boerem, "Lovecraft and the Tradition of the Gentleman Narrator"; Norman R. Gayford, "The Artist as Antaeus: Lovecraft and Modernism"; Barton Levi St. Armand, "Synchronistic Worlds: Lovecraft and Borges"; "Contributors"; "Bibliography"; "Index."

Notes. A volume in which Schultz and I commissioned some of the leading Lovecraft scholars to write substantial original essays. A splendid volume, I think, still of value and relevance.

10.　　R. H. Barlow, *On Lovecraft and Life*
　　a.　West Warwick, RI: Necronomicon Press, October 1992.

　　Contents: Introduction; A Note on the Text; [Memories of Lovecraft (1934)]; Autobiography.

Notes. A little booklet featuring the full notes that Barlow took on Lovecraft's visit to Florida in 1934 (printed in truncated form in *The Dark Brotherhood and Other Pieces* [1966]) along with an unpublished autobiography, all found on a microfilm of Barlow material.

11.   *The Count of Thirty: A Tribute to Ramsey Campbell*
   a.   West Warwick, RI: Necronomicon Press, 1993.
         Contents: Introduction; Stefan Dziemianowicz, "An Interview with Ramsey Campbell"; S. T. Joshi, "Campbell: Before and After Lovecraft"; Simon MacCulloch, "Glimpses of Absolute Power: Ramsey Campbell's Concept of Evil"; Joel Lane, "Negatives in Print: The Early Novels of Ramsey Campbell"; Joel Lane, "Beyond the Light: The Recent Novels of Ramsey Campbell"; Bibliography.
         Notes. A slim volume of critical essays on Campbell, an author who needs considerably more discussion. The article "Campbell: Before and After Lovecraft" was reprinted in *Short Story Criticism*, Volume 19 (Detroit: Gale, 1995). 89–92.

12.   *H. P. Lovecraft in the Argosy: Collected Correspondence from the Munsey Magazines*
   a.   West Warwick, RI: Necronomicon Press, 1994.
         Contents: Introduction; I. *The Argosy:* November 1911: H. P. L[ovecraft], letter; July 1913: F. V. Bennett, "Grouch on Jackson"; September 1913: Hugh Forrest, "Rises to Protest"; H. P. Lovecraft, "Objects to Jackson"; November 1913: F. V. Bennett, "Bennett Back Again"; E. F. W. C., "Opposed to Jackson"; John Russell, "Verses for Jackson"; T. P. Crean, "Syracuse on Deck"; December 1913: E. E. Blankenship, "Virginia vs. Providence"; G. E. Bonner, "Challenge to Lovecraft"; A. Missbaum, "Agrees with Lovecraft"; Elizabeth E. Loop, "Elmira vs. Providence"; H. F. B., "Agrees with Lovecraft"; F. W. Saunders, "Bomb for Lovecraft"; January 1914: H. P. Lovecraft, "Lovecraft Comes Back: Ad Criticos"; A. F. B., "Defender of Jackson"; February 1914: H. P. Lovecraft, "Ad Criticos: Liber Secundus"; R. K. Kinsman, "Texas Comes In"; F. V. Bennett, "Old Friend Bennett"; W. J. Archibald, "Read Argosy Years"; D. W. Isenhour, "Agrees with Lovecraft"; T. P. Crean, "Replies to Lovecraft"; J. W. Landis, "Likes Readers' Opinions"; H. C. Doyle, "Prefers Long Stories"; March 1914: "Georgia Girl," "Georgia Girl Replies"; Clifford D. Ennis, "Wants Jackson Stories"; H. P. Lovecraft, "Correction for Lovecraft"; W. J. Thompson, "Canada for Jackson"; H. M. Fisher, "Congratulates Fred Jackson"; Roy M. Grover, "Praises Lovecraft's Poetry"; April 1914: Ira B. Forrest, "Wants New 'Goat'"; Chas. Yevens, "Criticises the Kickers"; F. V.

Bennett, "Bennett Gives News"; Mrs. H. E. Shepherd, "Enjoys Readers Opinions"; E. P. Rahs, "Objects to Criticism"; John Russell, "Reply to Lovecraft"; F. W. Saunders, "Ruat Caelum"; May 1914: J. C. Cummings, "Back to the Flagship"; John Russell, "Some More Verse"; A. L. Rossiter, "Sees Steady Improvement"; Richard Forster, "Wyoming to the Front"; H. R. G., "Liked 'Mesquite Ranch'"; Jack E. Brown, "Opinions of Cow-Puncher"; K. Morris, "New Argosy Perfect"; Mrs. W. S. Ritter, "Wants More Letters"; June 1914: John Russell, "Love versus Lovecraft"; E. E. Jennings, "Sympathy for the Editor"; H. Hargrove, "Regular Jackson Fan"; C. M. Turner, "Lovecraft in Irons"; Richard Daley, "Wants Bennett's Opinion"; Edwin M. Freeland, "Wants More Jackson"; July 1914: Ed. Ellisen, "'Some Funny Ones'"; E. M. W., "Sarcasm and the Log-Book"; Gus Hogan, "Can't They Be Satisfied?"; Grailquill, "A Polyglot Lobbyist"; August 1914: R. E. T., "Silence and Knockers"; R. McE., "Why Kick?"; S. L., "Taking No Chances"; G. E. Bonner, "Hurrah and a Tiger"; September 1914: Jack P. Roberts, "Read a Thousand Times"; October 1914: John Burr, letter; Merritt Dews, "Beats Them All"; J. H. Gambrel, "A Jackson Fan"; Mrs. A. V. Chevalier, "Just Grand"; Fred E. Kennedy, letter; J. D. Toppen, "Stop Kicking Him Round"; F. V. Bennett, letter; Abe Fry, "Flag Him!"; John Russell and H. P. Lovecraft, "The Critics' Farewell"; November 1914: Elmer V. Heise, "'Some Magazine'"; *December 1914*: H. Kendall, "Jackson Forever!"; Stanley H. Watson, letter; Ia. *Argosy* Letters Falsely Attributed to H. P. Lovecraft: November 15, 1919: Augustus T. Swift, "Argosy Serials Constantly Coming Out as Books"; May 22, 1920: Augustus T. Swift, "Not Out for Blood"; II. *The All-Story*: 8 February 1913: H. P. Lovecraft, "A Few Lines about 'Fishhead'"; 7 March 1914: H. P. Lovecraft, letter; 11 April 1914: S. P. N., "Gracious!"; 15 August 1914: H. P. Lovecraft, "For England and the All-Story"; Appendix: Poems by H. P. Lovecraft Not Published in the Munsey Magazines: "Ad Criticos: Liber Tertius" and "Liber Quartus"; "Frustra Praemunitus"; "De Scriptore Mulieroso"; "Sors Poetae"; "'The Poetical Punch' Pushed from His Pedestal"; "To Mr. Terhune, on His Historical Fiction."

Notes. Like *H. P. Lovecraft in "The Eyrie,"* a volume that transcribes letters (and poems) by and about HPL in the *Argosy* and related magazines.

13.	*Caverns Measureless to Man: 18 Memoirs of Lovecraft*
	a.	West Warwick, RI: Necronomicon Press, 1996.
		Contents: Introduction; [Rheinhart Kleiner], "The Kleicomolo"; George Julian Houtain, "Lovecraft"; F. Lee Baldwin, "H. P. Love-

craft: A Biographical Sketch"; Rheinhart Kleiner, "After a Decade and the Kalem Club"; E. Hoffmann Price, "The Sage of College Street"; Maurice W. Moe, "Howard Phillips Lovecraft: The Sage of Providence"; Hyman Bradofsky, "Amateur Affairs"; Rheinhart Kleiner, "Howard Phillips Lovecraft"; August Derleth, "A Master of the Macabre"; E. A. Edkins, "Idiosyncrasies of H.P.L."; Edward H. Cole, "Ave atque Vale!"; James F. Morton, "A Few Memories"; Muriel E. Eddy, "Howard Phillips Lovecraft"; Stuart M. Boland, "Interlude with Lovecraft"; John Wilstach, "The Ten-Cent Ivory Tower"; Fritz Leiber, "My Correspondence with Lovecraft"; Samuel Loveman, "Lovecraft as a Conversationalist"; Kenneth Sterling, "Caverns Measureless to Man"; "Bibliography."

Notes. A volume that Michaud urged me to assemble as a way of beating Peter Cannon's *Lovecraft Remembered* (Arkham House, 1998) into print. A slim and inconsequential book.

14.   Bram Stoker, *Best Ghost Stories* (with Richard Dalby and Stefan Dziemianowicz)
   a.   Mineola, NY: Dover Publications, 1997.
      Contents: Introduction, by Richard Dalby; The Crystal Cup; The Chain of Destiny; The Castle of the King; The Dualitists; The Burial of the Rats; The Judge's House; The Secret of the Growing Gold; The Coming of Abel Behenna; The Squaw; A Dream of Red Sands; Crooken Sands; Dracula's Guest; A Star Trap; A Gipsy Prophecy.

      Notes. The first of four editions of "classic" weird fiction commissioned by Dover. I also prepared an edition of Machen's *Three Impostors,* but this volume was cancelled because Dent came out with a similar volume around this time.

15.   Henry Ferris, *A Night with Mephistopheles: Selected Works of Henry Ferris*
   a.   Horam, UK: Tartarus Press, 1997.
      Contents: Introduction; *Stories:* A Leaf from the Berlin Chronicles; A Night with Mephistopheles; A Night in a Haunted House; A Night in the Bell Inn; The Mysterious Compact; Tobias Guarnerius; *Essays:* German Ghosts and Ghost-Seers; Of the Nightmare; Fireside Horrors for Christmas; Bibliography.

      Notes. A volume that came to be when I discovered that Ferris was the true author of "A Night in the Bell Inn," which had been attributed to J. S. Le Fanu. It later transpired that some of the other items were translations by Ferris from German texts. The introduction was reprinted in I.52.

16.   Arthur Machen, *The Line of Terror and Other Essays*
       a.   Bristol, RI: Hobgoblin Press, 1997.
             Contents: Introduction; The "Inhumanity" of Art; The Paradox of
       Literature; Realism and Symbol; Science and Art; God's Beasts; True
       Comfort; Folklore and Legends of the North; The Literature of Oc-
       cultism; The Black Art; Has Spiritualism Come to Stay?; Review of
       The War of the Worlds; Science and the Ghost Story; Poe the En-
       chanter; The Line of Terror; The Other Side; Bibliography.
             Notes. A slim volume of Machen's writings on weird fiction and re-
       lated subjects. A good volume of Machen's essays still needs to be
       compiled.

17.   Lord Dunsany, *The Complete Pegāna*
       a.   Oakland, CA: Chaosium, February 1998.
             Contents: Introduction; *The Gods of Pegāna*; [*Time and the Gods:*]
       Preface; Time and the Gods; The Coming of the Sea; A Legend of
       the Dawn; The Vengeance of Men; When the Gods Slept; The King
       That Was Not; The Cave of Kai; The Sorrow of Search; The Men of
       Yarnith; For the Honour of the Gods; Night and Morning; Usury;
       Mlideen; The Secret of the Gods; The South Wind; In the Land of
       Time; The Relenting of Sarnidac; The Jest of the Gods; The Dreams
       of the Prophet; The Journey of the King; *Beyond the Fields We Know:*
       Idle Days on the Yann; A Shop in Go-by Street; The Avenger of
       Perdóndaris.
             Notes. First complete edition of all the stories that Dunsany set in
       the invented realm of Pegāna. The introduction was reprinted in I.47
       as "The Pegāna Mythos."

18.   Algernon Blackwood, *The Complete John Silence Stories*
       a.   Mineola, NY: Dover Publications, 1998.
             Contents: Introduction; A Psychical Invasion; Ancient Sorceries;
       The Nemesis of Fire; Secret Worship; Camp of the Dog; A Victim of
       Higher Space.
             Notes. The second of my four Dover editions.

19.   Ambrose Bierce, *A Sole Survivor: Bits of Autobiography* (with David E.
       Schultz)
       a.   Knoxville: University of Tennessee Press, 1998.
             Contents: Introduction; A Note on the Text; Chronology; The Civ-
       il War (1861–1865); The Aftermath of the War (1865–1867); Early
       Days in San Francisco (1868–1872); The English Jaunt (1872–1875);
       Return to San Francisco (1875–1879); The Black Hills (1880–1881);
       The *Wasp* Years (1881–1886); The *Examiner* Years (1887–1905); The

End (1905–1913); A Sole Survivor: An Epilogue; Appendix; Notes; Sources; Further Reading; Index.

Notes. A volume that emerged out of our Bierce research, and especially out of my admiration of Bierce's "Bits of Autobiography," which make up a substantial portion of the book.

20. *Documents of American Prejudice*
   a. New York: Basic Books, 1999.

   Contents: Foreword: Healing Branches on a Tainted Tree, by Derrick Bell; Introduction; A Note on This Edition; Part 1: Some Overviews: Thomas Jefferson, "Notes on the State of Virginia"; Alexis de Tocqueville, "Democracy in America"; Oliver Wendell Holmes, "The Pilgrims of Plymouth"; Ralph Waldo Emerson, "Race"; Houston Stewart Chamberlain, "Foundations of the Nineteenth Century"; Madison Grant, "The Passing of the Great Race"; Dinesh D'Souza, "The End of Racism"; David Duke, "America at the Crossroads"; Part 2: Science and Pseudo-Science: Samuel Stanhope Smith, "An Essay on the Causes of the Variety of Complexion and Figure in the Human Species"; Robert Chambers, "Vestiges of the Natural History of Creation"; Joseph Arthur, Comte de Gobineau, "The Inequality of Human Races"; Charles Darwin, "The Descent of Man"; Jean Finot, "Race Prejudice"; C. B. Davenport, "The Effects of Race Intermingling"; Arthur R. Jensen, "How Much Can We Boost IQ and Scholastic Achievement?"; Richard J. Herrnstein and Charles Murray, "The Bell Curve"; Part 3: Aryans, Anglo-Saxons, and Teutons: Robert Knox, "The Races of Men"; William F. Allen, "The Place of the Northwest in General History"; John W. Burgess, "The Ideal of the American Commonwealth"; John L. Brandt, "Anglo-Saxon Supremacy"; Part 4: Manifest Destiny and Imperialism: John O'Sullivan, "Annexation"; Theodore Roosevelt, "The Winning of the West"; H. H. Powers, "The War as a Suggestion of Manifest Destiny"; Whitelaw Reid, "Our New Duties: Their Later Aspects"; Part 5: Social Darwinism and Eugenics: Francis Galton, "Hereditary Genius"; David Starr Jordan, "The Blood of the Nation"; William Graham Sumner, "The Challenge of Facts"; Albert Edward Wiggam, "The New Decalogue of Science"; Wesley Critz George, "The Biology of the Race Problem"; William Shockley, "Is Quality of U.S. Population Declining?"; Part 6: Prejudice and Religion: Ezra Stiles Ely, "The Duty of Christian Freemen to Elect Christian Rulers"; Robert Baird, "The Progress and Prospects of Christianity in the United States of America"; Horace Bushnell, "Christian Nurture"; Josiah Strong, "Our Country"; Part 7: Native Americans: Increase Mather, "The History of King Philip's War"; Mary Rowlandson, "A Narrative of the Captivity and Restauration of Mrs. Mary Rowlandson"; Jedediah Morse, "A Report to the Secretary of War of the United States, on Indian Affairs"; Andrew Jackson, "Fifth Annual Message"; Samuel George Morton, "Crania Americana"; Lewis H. Morgan, "League of the Iroquois"; General G. A. Custer, "My Life on the Plains"; Helen Hunt Jackson, "A Century of Dishonor"; Part 8: African Americans: Benjamin Rush, "Observations . . ."; Thomas Jefferson, "Letter to Henri Gregoire"; William Gilmore Simms, "Slavery in America"; George Fitzhugh, "Sociology for the South"; Abraham Lincoln, "Fourth Lincoln-Douglas Debate"; J. H. Van Evrie, "White Supremacy and Negro Subordination"; Henry Woodfin Grady, "The South and Her Problems"; Senator John T. Morgan, "The Race Question in the United States"; Frederick L. Hoffman, "Race Traits and Tendencies of the American Negro"; Charles Carroll, "The Negro a Beast"; Thomas Nelson Page, "The Negro: The Southerner's Problem"; Thomas Dixon, Jr., "The Clansman"; R. W. Shufeldt, "The Negro: A Menace to American Civilization"; Senator J. Thomas Heflin, "Letter to Sam H. Reading"; Theodore G. Bilbo, "Take Your Choice: Separation or Mongrelization"; Earl Lively, Jr., "The Invasion of Mississippi"; Anonymous, "Public Record of George C. Wallace"; Sgt. Stacey C. Koon, L.A.P.D., "Presumed Guilty"; Alan M. Dershowitz, "Reasonable Doubts"; Part 9: Jews: Roger Williams, "A Testimony . . ."; Hannah Adams, "The History of the Jews"; Lydia Maria Child, "Letters from New York"; Telehacmus Thomas Timayenis, "The Original Mr. Jacobs"; Mark Twain, "Concerning the Jews"; Thomas E. Watson, "The Leo Frank Case"; Joseph Jefferson O'Neil, "'Peace' Object, Says Ford, in an Attempt to Justify His Anti-Semitic Attitude"; Burton J. Hendrick, "The Jews in America"; William Dudley Pelley, "How I Would Treat the Jews"; Charles E. Coughlin, "Why Leave Our Own?"; William H. Murray, "Adam and Cain"; Gerald L. K. Smith, "Jews in Government"; Bradley R. Smith, "The Holocaust Controversy: The Case for Open Debate"; Part 10: Asian Americans: Henry George, "The Chinese in California"; Ambrose Bierce, "Prattle"; Samuel Gompers and Herman Gutstadt, "Meat vs. Rice: American Manhood Against Asiatic Coolieism"; Jack London, "The Yellow Peril"; Earl Warren, "Testimony of the Honorable Earl Warren"; An Intelligence Officer, "The Japanese in America"; Deval L. Patrick, "The Rise in Hate Crime"; Part 11: Latinos: Lansford W. Hastings, "The Emigrants' Guide to Oregon and California"; Walt Whitman, "Editorials for the *Brooklyn Daily Eagle*"; Hubert Howe Bancroft, "California Pastoral"; Edmond Wood, "Can Cubans Govern Cuba?"; John Box, "Restriction of Mexican Immigration"; Raymond G. Carroll, "Alien Workers in America"; Jack Lait and Lee Mortimer, "New

York: Confidential!"; Juan Gonzalez, "Roll Down Your Window"; Part 12: The Debate over Immigration: E. L. Godkin, "Aristocratic Opinions of Democracy"; Chauncey Depew, "Political Mission of the United States"; Thomas Bailey Aldrich, "Unguarded Gates"; Francis A. Walker, "Restriction of Immigration"; John Fiske, "Letter to William Lloyd Garrison"; John R. Commons, "Races and Immigrants in America"; Henry James, "The American Scene"; Edward Alsworth Ross, "The Old World and the New"; Lothrop Stoddard, "The Rising Tide of Color Against White World-Supremacy"; Calvin Coolidge, "Whose Country Is This?"; Clinton Stoddard Burr, "America's Race Heritage"; Charles W. Gould, "America: A Family Matter"; Henry Fairfield Osborn, "Shall We Maintain Washington's Ideal of Americanism?"; Henry Pratt Fairchild, "The Melting-Pot Mistake"; Edward R. Lewis, "America, Nation or Confusion"; Captain Eddie Rickenbacker, "'America Must Return to Fundamentals'"; Politicus, "Keeping America American"; Chang-Lin Tien, "America's Scapegoats"; Notes; Bibliography; Acknowledgments; Index.

Notes. An immense compilation that took years to assemble. Although issued by a mainstream publisher, the book attracted almost no attention because the publisher failed to do any kind of marketing or promotion.

21.   *Great Weird Tales*
    a.   Mineola, NY: Dover Publications, 1999.

    Contents: Introduction; Ralph Adams Cram, "The Dead Valley"; Fiona Macleod, "The Sin-Eater"; William Hope Hodgson, "The Voice in the Night"; W. C. Morrow, "His Unconquerable Enemy"; Ambrose Bierce, "My Favorite Murder"; Arthur Machen, "The Inmost Light"; Algernon Blackwood, "The Man Whom the Trees Loved"; F. Marion Crawford, "The King's Messenger"; Lord Dunsany, "The Unhappy Body"; M. P. Shiel, "Xélucha"; Frank Belknap Long, "The Eye Above the Mantel"; R. H. Barlow, "A Dim-Remembered Story"; Fitz-James O'Brien, "The Diamond Lens"; H. P. Lovecraft, "Facts concerning the Late Arthur Jermyn and His Family"; Bibliography.

    Notes. A volume whose title got us into trouble because the magazine *Weird Tales* claimed (correctly) that the phrase was trademarked. So I believe Dover had to pay a fee of some kind, but the book remained in print.

22.   Ambrose Bierce, *The Collected Fables of Ambrose Bierce*
    a.   Columbus: Ohio State University Press, 2000.

    Contents: Introduction; A Note on This Edition; The Fables of Zambri, the Parsee (includes Appendix: Fables from *Fun*); Fantastic

Fables (includes Æsopus Emendatus, Old Saws with New Teeth, Fables in Rhyme); Unreprinted Fables from *Fantastic Fables* (1899) (includes Æsopus Emendatus); Fables from *The Devil's Dictionary*; Uncollected Fables; Commentary; A Chronology of Bierce's Fables; Index of Titles; Index of Characters.

Notes. A volume that emerged out of my observation that Bierce's *Fantastic Fables* represented only a tiny proportion of his total output of fables, which number nearly 850. The introduction was reprinted in I.47 as "Bierce as Fabulist."

23. Sir Arthur Quiller-Couch, *The Horror on the Stair and Other Weird Tales*
  a. Ashcroft, BC: Ash-Tree Press, 2000.

  Contents: Introduction; Psyche; "Doubles" and Quits; Old Aeson; A Dark Mirror; The Magic Shadow; The Haunted Dragoon; A Blue Pantomime; The Roll-Call of the Reef; My Grandfahter, Hendry Watty; Widdershins; The Legend of Sir Dinar; Oceanus; The Seventh Man; The Room of Mirrors; A Pair of Hands; The Lady of the Ship; The Mystery of Joseph Laquedem; The Laird's Luck; Phoebus on Halzaphron; The Haunted Yacht; John and the Ghosts; The Talking Ships; The Horror on the Stair; The Bend of the Road; Mutual Exchange, Limited; Not Here, O Apollo!; Bibliography.

  Notes. A competent selection of Quiller-Couch's weird work, although few stories stand out. The introduction was reprinted in I.24 as "Sir Arthur Quiller-Couch: Ghosts and Scholars."

24. *Civil War Memories*
  a. Nashville, TN: Rutledge Hill Press, 2000.
  b. New York: Gramercy Books, 2003.
  c. New York: Barnes & Noble, 2009.

  Contents: Introduction; Bret Harte, "Prologue: The Reveille"; Anonymous, "My Revenge"; Thomas Bailey Aldrich, "Quite So"; W. C. Morrow, "The Three Hundred"; Stephen Crane, "Three Miraculous Soldiers"; Ambrose Bierce, "Three and One Are One"; Rebecca Harding Davis, "John Lamar"; Louisa May Alcott, "My Contraband"; W. C. Morrow, "The Bloodhounds"; Albion W. Tourgée, "'Corporal Billie'"; George Cary Eggleston, "'Little Lamkin's Battery'"; Mark Twain, "Lucretia Smith's Soldier"; Henry James, "The Story of a Year"; Grace B. King, "Bayou L'Ombre"; Harold Frederic, "The Eve of the Fourth"; John William De Forest, "An Independent Ku-Klux"; Kate Chopin, "A Wizard from Gettysburg"; Thomas Nelson Page, "The Gray Jacket of 'No. 4'"; Sarah Orne Jewett, "A War Debt"; Edward Lucas White, "The Little Faded Flag"; Henry Timrod, "Epilogue: The Two Armies."

Notes. A book that I compiled in exactly two weeks, after coming upon previously unreprinted stories by W. C. Morrow and Edward Lucas White. And yet, this has proved to be one of my most "popular" and frequently reprinted books!

25.   W. C. Morrow, *The Monster Maker and Other Stories* (with Stefan Dziemianowicz)
       a.   Seattle: Midnight House, 2000.
             Contents: Introduction; The Monster Maker; The Haunted Automaton; The Resurrection of Little Wang Tai; The Wrong Door; The Permanent Stiletto; Over an Absinthe Bottle; The Red Strangler; A Glimpse of the Unusual; The Gloomy Shadow; A Night with Death; A Story Told by the Sea; His Unconquerable Enemy; Two Singular Men; The Removal Company; The Haunted Burglar; A Mystery of South Park; The Faithful Amulet; The Woman of the Inner Room; An Original Revenge; In a Dark Room; The Unfaithful Clock; Some Queer Experiences; Bibliography.

             Notes. A volume that contains selected tales from *The Ape, the Idiot and Other People* (1897) along with a number of uncollected tales. The introduction was reprinted in I.24 as "W. C. Morrow: Horror in San Francisco." A much more exhaustive selection of Morrow's writings is under way for Centipede Press's Masters of the Weird Tale series.

26.   Ambrose Bierce, *The Unabridged Devil's Dictionary* (with David E. Schultz)
       a.   Athens: University of Georgia Press, 2000.
             Contents: Acknowledgments; Introduction, by Schultz and Joshi; List of Abbreviations; The Unabridged Devil's Dictionary; Appendix; Notes; List of Appearances of Definitions; Bibliography; Index.

             Notes. A book on which about three-fourths (or maybe ninetenths) of the work was done by Schultz.

27.   Robert W. Chambers, *The Yellow Sign and Other Stories*
       a.   Oakland, CA: Chaosium, 2000.
             Contents: Introduction; The King in Yellow (selections); The Maker of Moons (selections); The Mystery of Choice (selections); In Search of the Unknown; The Tracer of Lost Persons (selections); The Tree of Heaven (selections); Police!!!

             Notes. A huge selection of Chambers's weird writings. An even larger volume (adding *The Slayer of Souls* [1920]) is in press from Centipede Press. The introduction was reprinted in *Short Story Criticism,*

Volume 92 (Detroit: Gale, 2006). 21–25, and in I.24 as "Robert W. Chambers: The Bohemian Weird Tale."

28. *Atheism: A Reader*
  a. Amherst, NY: Prometheus Books, [October] 2000.

Contents: Introduction; PART 1: SOME OVERVIEWS: Thomas Henry Huxley, "Agnosticism"; Leslie Stephen, "An Agnostic's Apology"; Emma Goldman, "The Philosophy of Atheism"; Carl Van Doren, "Why I Am an Unbeliever"; PART 2: THE EXISTENCE OF GOD: Percy Bysshe Shelley, "A Refutation of Deism"; Robert G. Ingersoll, "What Is Religion?"; Bertrand Russell, "Is There a God?"; A. J. Ayer, "The Claims of Theology"; PART 3: THE IMMORTALITY MYTH: Lucretius, "On the Nature of Things"; John Stuart Mill, "Immortality"; Antony Flew, "Can We Survive Our Own Deaths?"; PART 4: THE NATURE OF RELIGIOUS BELIEF: David Hume, "The Natural History of Religion"; George Eliot, "Evangelical Teaching"; Charles Bradlaugh, "Humanity's Gain from Unbelief"; Anatole France, "Miracle"; PART 5: RELIGION AND SCIENCE: Charles Darwin, "Autobiography"; Friedrich Nietzsche, "The Antichrist"; H. L. Mencken, "The Scopes Trial"; Carl Sagan, "The Demon-Haunted World"; PART 6: RELIGION AND ETHICS: Paul-Henri Thiry, baron d'Holbach, "The System of Nature"; Thomas Paine, "The Age of Reason"; H. P. Lovecraft, "A Letter on Religion"; Walter Kaufmann, "The Faith of a Heretic"; PART 7: RELIGION AND THE STATE: Benedict de Spinoza, "Theologico-Political Treatise"; W. E. H. Lecky, "The Spirit of Rationalism in Europe"; Robert G. Ingersoll, "God in the Constitution"; Clarence Darrow, "The Lord's Day Alliance"; Gore Vidal, "Monotheism and Its Discontents"; PART 8: RELIGION AND SOCIETY: Elizabeth Cady Stanton, "The Christian Church and Woman"; J. M. Robertson, "The Priest and the Child"; Chapman Cohen, "Religion and Sex"; Further Reading.

Notes. My first book with Prometheus Books. I was unsure whether the publisher would be interested, because it had already issued two volumes of reprinted atheist writings assembled by Gordon Stein; but my book proved to be sufficiently distinct for them to take it. It is still in print and has sold well.

29. Ambrose Bierce, *The Fall of the Republic and Other Political Satires* (with David E. Schultz)
  a. Knoxville: University of Tennessee Press, [October] 2000.

Contents: Introduction; Fiction: Ashes of the Beacon; The Land Beyond the Blow; Letters from a Hdkhoite; The Aborigines of Oakland; A Scientific Dream; Across the Continent; John Smith, Liberator; "The Bubble Reputation"; For the Ahkoond; The Fall of the Republic; The Wizard of Bumbassa; Modern Penology; The Great Strike of 1895; Annals of the Future Historian; Essays: Government vs. Anarchy; Judges, Lawyers, and Juries; Capital Punishment; Tariffs, Trusts, and Labor; Insurance; Advances in Weaponry; Travel by Air; Dogs and Horses; Temperance; Reflections on the Future; Appendix: A Screed of the Future Historian; Notes; Sources.

Notes. Another book that emerged out of my admiration for a group of Bierce's writings—his political fantasies (some of them in Volume 1 of his *Collected Works*)—that had not attracted much attention. The introduction was reprinted in I.47 as "Bierce as Political Satirist."

30.   Rudyard Kipling, *The Mark of the Beast and Other Horror Tales*
   a.   Mineola, NY: Dover Publications, [December] 2000.

   Contents: Introduction; The Dream of Duncan Parenness; "The City of Dreadful Night"; The Phantom 'Rickshaw; The Strange Ride of Morrowbie Jukes; In the House of Suddhoo; Haunted Subalterns; By Word of Mouth; My Own True Ghost Story; The Wandering Jew; The Mark of the Bast; At the End of the Passage; "The Finest Story in the World"; The Recrudescence of Imray; The Lost Legion; "They"; The House Surgeon; "Swept and Garnished"; Glossary of Indian Terms; Bibliography.

   Notes. The fourth of my original Dover volumes, although I assembled another anthology later (see item 33). The introduction was reprinted in I.24 as "Rudyard Kipling: The Horror of India."

31.   *From Baltimore to Bohemia: The Letters of H. L. Mencken and George Sterling*
   a.   Rutherford, NJ: Fairleigh Dickinson University Press, 2001.

   Contents: Introduction; A Note on This Edition; Abbreviations; The Letters; Appendix: Mencken on Sterling's Death; Notes; Bibliography; Index.

   Notes. A volume in which I hoped that the Mencken association would elevate Sterling in the eyes of critics; but the end result was that I became thoroughly interested in Mencken and went on to do much work on him. The introduction was reprinted in I.50 as "H. L. Mencken and George Sterling."

32.   Arthur Machen, *The Three Impostors and Other Stories*
   a.   Oakland, CA: Chaosium, April 2001.

   Contents: Introduction; The Great God Pan; The Inmost Light; The Shining Pyramid; *The Three Impostors; or, The Transmutations.*

   Notes. The first of three volumes that reprinted nearly the totality of Machen's weird work.

33. Robert Hichens, *The Return of the Soul and Other Stories*
  a. Seattle, WA: Midnight House, [December] 2001.
      Contents: Introduction; The Return of the Soul; A Tribute of Souls; The Face of the Monk; Sea Change; The Cry of the Child; How Love Came to Professor Guildea; The Lady and the Beggar; The Figure in the Mirage.
      Notes. The first of a planned three-volume set of Hichens's weird writings, but the publisher went defunct before the other two volumes could appear. (They were not assembled.) I may do a large omnibus of Hichens's work for Centipede Press.

34. Clark Ashton Smith, *The Black Diamonds*
  a. New York: Hippocampus Press, [March] 2002.
      Contents: Introduction; The Black Diamonds.
      Notes. A work that dates (as far as my involvement with it goes) to 1979, when Marc Michaud and I began cataloguing Smith's papers for the John Hay Library. I found this manuscript, did a partial transcript, then—decades later—completed the transcript.

35. *Great Tales of Terror*
  a. Mineola, NY: Dover Publications, [March] 2002.
      Contents: Introduction; Sir Arthur Quiller-Couch, "The Haunted Dragoon"; William Sharp, "The Graven Image"; Robert Hichens, "The Return of the Soul"; Lafcadio Hearn, "Of a Promise Broken"; Walter de la Mare, "The Promise"; William Waldorf Astor, "The Ghosts of Austerlitz"; Violet Hunt, "The Coach"; James Hopper, "The Night School"; Théophile Gautier, "The Mummy's Foot"; Ambrose Bierce, "The Discomfited Demon"; W. F. Harvey, "The Tortoise"; J. Sheridan Le Fanu, "Borrhomeo the Astrologer"; Barry Pain, "The Diary of a God"; E. Nesbit, "The Three Drugs"; H. L. Mencken, "The Window of Horrors"; Thomas Burke, "The Man Who Lost His Head"; Erckmann-Chatrian, "The Queen of the Bees"; Gertrude Atherton, "The Caves of Death"; Arthur Machen, "The Soldiers' Rest"; Lord Dunsany, "Romance"; Algernon Blackwood, "The Man Who Found Out"; J. D. Beresford, "A Negligible Experiment"; R. H. Barlow, "The Root-Gatherers"; Notes on the Authors.
      Notes. My fifth Dover book (or sixth, if one counts the reprint of de la Mare's *The Return,* for which I wrote the introduction [see Section VI below]).

36. H. L. Mencken, *H. L. Mencken on American Literature*
  a. Athens: Ohio University Press, [May] 2002.

Contents: Introduction; A Note on This Edition; 1. The Travails of a Book Reviewer; 2. Establishing the Canon; 3. Some Worthy Second-Raters; 4. Trade Goods; 5. Some Thoughts on Literary Criticism; Notes; Glossary of Names; Index.

Notes. A pretty interesting compilation of Mencken's reviews, taken mostly from the *Smart Set* (1908–23) and *American Mercury* (1924–33). The introduction was reprinted as "H. L. Mencken, Book Reviewer" (although this piece also includes the unpublished introduction to another compilation, *H. L. Mencken on British Literature,* for which I have found no publisher).

37.   Algernon Blackwood, *Ancient Sorceries and Other Weird Stories*
       a.   New York: Penguin, [August] 2002.
             Contents: Introduction; Suggestions for Further Reading; A Note on the Text; Smith: An Episode in a Lodging House; The Willows; The Insanity of Jones; Ancient Sorceries; The Man Who Found Out; The Wendigo; The Glamour of the Snow; The Man Whom the Trees Loved; Sand.
             Notes. My first Penguin edition of the four "Modern Masters" as identified by Lovecraft.

38.   H. L. Mencken, *H. L. Mencken on Religion*
       a.   Amherst, NY: Prometheus Books, [September] 2002.
             Contents: Introduction; I. The Beliefs of an Iconoclast; II. Some Overviews; III. Protestants and Catholics; IV. Fundamentalists and Evangelicals; V. Spiritualism, Theosophy, and Christian Science; VI. The Scopes Trial; VII. Religion and Science; VIII. Religion and Politics; IX. Religion and Society; Epilogue: Memorial Service; Notes; Glossary of Names; Index.
             Notes. The second of my Mencken compilations, including the first complete reprinting of all his articles on the Scopes trial of 1925. The introduction was reprinted in I.50 as "Mencken on Religion."

39.   Ramsey Campbell, *Ramsey Campbell, Probably*
       a.   Harrogate, UK: PS Publishing, [October] 2002.
       b.   Hornsea, UK: PS Publishing/Drugstore Indian Press, 2015 (expanded ed.).
             Contents: Douglas E. Winter, "Ramsey Campbell, Absolutely"; I. On Horror Fiction: Fiedler on the Roof; The Crime of Horror; Dig Us No Grave; A Horror Writer's Lexicon; Horror Fiction and the Mainstream; Unconvincing Horror; To the Next Generation; II. On Horror and Fantasy Film: Beyond the Pale; Horror Films and Society; The Quality of Terror; Alone in the Pacific . . .; Pulsating Posteri-

ors . . .; Floundering on the Bottom; III. On Horror in Society: Turn Off; The Nearest to a Ghost; The Strange Case of Sean Manchester; IV. On Some Writers: Tim Powers; Terry Lamsley; *American Psycho*; S. Hudson; Shaun Hutson; Pete Atkins; Bob Shaw; John Brunner; K. W. Jeter; Alan David Price; Richard Christian Matheson; Poppy Z. Brite; Lovecraft: An Introduction; Robert E. Howard; Solomon Kane; R. R. Ryan; Robert Aickman; Stephen King; Clive Barker; Peter Straub; Dennis Etchison; James Herbert; Thomas Ligotti; Donald R. Burleson; V. On Ramsey Campbell: Near Madness; Chasing the Unknown; A Small Dose of Reality; Why I Write Horror Fiction; On Reading My Stories; Nightmares; Taking Drugs; Fame!; A School Visit; Writing and Depression; Editing Horror Anthologies; A Transient Engagement; Foreword: *Demons by Daylight*; Introduction: *The Height of the Scream*; Afterword: *The Doll Who Ate His Mother*; Afterword: *The Parasite*; Afterword: *The Nameless*; Introduction: *Dark Companions*; Afterword: *Night of the Claw*; Afterword: *Incarnate*; Afterword: *Obsession*; Afterword: *The Hungry Moon*; Afterword: *Scared Stiff*; Introduction: *Dark Feasts*; Afterword: *The Influence*; Afterword: *Alone with the Horrors*; Introduction: *Far Away & Never*; All the Ghosts That Made Me; Afterword.

Notes. An extensive but by no means comprehensive gathering of Campbell's nonfiction (essays, reviews, columns, etc.). It may be the only one of my books in which I have written absolutely nothing. A second volume, containing Campbell's more recent essays and reviews, is in the works.

40.   Clark Ashton Smith, *The Last Oblivion: Best Fantastic Poems* (with David E. Schultz)
a.   New York: Hippocampus Press, [November] 2002.
      Contents. Introduction; A Note on the Text; Acknowledgments; *The Hashish-Eater; or, The Apocalypse of Evil*; I. THE STAR-TREADER: The Star-Treader; Ode to the Abyss; Nirvana; The Song of a Comet; Lament of the Stars; In Saturn; Triple Aspect; The Abyss Triumphant; The Motes; Desire of Vastness; Shadows; A Dream of the Abyss; After Armageddon; The Ancient Quest; A Dream of Oblivion; Ode to Light; Ode to Matter; II. MEDUSA AND OTHER HORRORS: Nero; Medusa; Averted Malefice; The Medusa of the Skies; Saturn; In Lemuria; Satan Unrepentant; The Ghoul and the Seraph; The Medusa of Despair; A Vision of Lucifer; The Witch in the Graveyard; The Flight of Azrael; The Mummy; Minatory; To the Chimera; The Whisper of the Worm; The Envoys; Nyctalops; Jungle Twilight; Necromancy; The Witch with Eyes of Amber; Cambion;

The Saturnienne; Chance; Revenant; Song of the Necromancer; *Pour chercher du nouveau*; Witch-Dance; Not Theirs the Cypress-Arch; III. THE ELDRITCH DARK: A Song from Hell; The Titans in Tartarus; The Twilight Woods; Lethe; Atlantis; The Eldritch Dark; White Death; A Dead City; The Cloud-Islands; The City of the Titans; The City of Destruction; Beyond the Great Wall; Solution; *Rosa Mystica*; Symbols; The City in the Desert; The Melancholy Pool; Twilight on the Snow; The Land of Evil Stars; Memnon at Midnight; The Kingdom of Shadows; Moon-Dawn; Outlanders; Warning; The Nightmare Tarn; The Prophet Speaks; The Outer Land; In Thessaly; *Le Miroir des blanches fleurs*; The Moonlight Desert; Ougabalys; Desert Dweller; Amithaine; The Dark Chateau; Averoigne; Zothique; IV. SAID THE DREAMER: The Castle of Dreams; The Dream-God's Realm; Imagination; The Last Night; Shadow of Nightmare; A Song of Dreams; The Dream-Bridge; Said the Dreamer; Dolor of Dreams; *Luna Aeternalis*; Echo of Memnon; Nightmare; The Last Goddess; Love Malevolent; The Wingless Archangels; Enchanted Mirrors; Selenique; Maya; *Fantaisie d'Antan*; In Slumber; V. THE REFUGE OF BEAUTY: The Power of Eld; Strangeness; The Nereid; Exotique; Transcendence; The Tears of Lilith; Cleopatra; The Refuge of Beauty; Sandalwood; The Last Oblivion; Alienage; Adventure; Interrogation; Canticle; To Antares; Connaissance; Exorcism; Lamia; Farewell to Eros; Some Blind Eidolon; Bacchante; Resurrection; The Sorcerer to His Love; The Hill of Dionysus; Midnight Beach; Omniety; VI. TO THE DARKNESS: Ode on Imagination; Retrospect and Forecast; To the Darkness; A Dream of Beauty; The Pursuer; In the Desert; The Nameless Wraith; To the Daemon of Sublimity; Desolation; Inferno; Dissonance; Remembered Light; The Incubus of Time; *Laus Mortis*; The Hope of the Infinite; Antepast; Forgotten Sorrow; Lunar Mystery; The Funeral Urn; Mors; September; Ennui; VII. THE SORCERER DEPARTS: To Omar Khayyam; To Nora May French; On Rereading Baudelaire; To George Sterling: A Valediction; To Howard Phillips Lovecraft; H. P. L.; Soliloquy in a Ebon Tower; Cycles; Glossary; Bibliography; Index of Titles; Index of First Lines.

Notes. A selection of Smith's best weird verse, arranged in rough thematic categories.

41.   R. H. Barlow, *Eyes of the God: The Weird Fiction and Poetry of R. H. Barlow* (with Douglas A. Anderson and David E. Schultz)

a.   New York: Hippocampus Press, [November] 2002.

    Contents. Introduction, by Joshi and Anderson; FICTION: The Slaying of the Monster (with H. P. Lovecraft); Eyes of the God;

Annals of the Jinns: I. The Black Tower; II. The Shadow from Above; III. The Flagon of Beauty; IV. The Sacred Bird; V. The Tomb of the God; VI. The Flower God; VII. The Little Box; VIII. The Fall of the Three Cities; IX. The Mirror; X. The Theft of the Hsothian Manuscripts; XI. An Episode in the Jungle; The Hoard of the Wizard-Beast (with H. P. Lovecraft); The Battle That Ended the Century (with H. P. Lovecraft); The Fidelity of Ghu; The Inhospitable Tavern; The Misfortunes of Butter-Churning; "Till A' the Seas" (with H. P. Lovecraft); The Temple; The Adventures of Garoth; The Experiment; Collapsing Cosmoses (with H. P. Lovecraft); The Bright Valley; The Priest and the Heretic; The Summons; A Dream; A Memory; Pursuit of the Moth; The Root-Gatherers; A Dim-Remembered Story; The Night Ocean (with H. P. Lovecraft); Origin Undetermined; The Swearing of an Oath; The Questioner; The Artizan's Reward; Return by Sunset. POETRY: I. Poems 1936–1939; [Untitled]; Sonnet V; Sonnet VI; Sonnet VII; Song; [Untitled]; Sonnet; [Untitled]; [Untitled]; R. E. H.; St. John's Churchyard; Dirge for the Artist; Alcestis; N. Y.; [Untitled]; [Untitled]; Altamira; Cycle from a Dead Year; H. P. L.; I. March 1937; II. March 1938; [Untitled]; [Untitled]; H. P. L.; H. P. L.; March; [Untitled]; The Unresisting; Shub-Ad; Who Will Not Know; To Bacchus; [Untitled]; [Untitled]; Winter Mood; Burlesque; Frustration; To a Companion; Dawn Delayed; To a Wayfarer; [Untitled]; Fragments; To Alta, On Her Original American Sonnet; Sonnet; [Untitled]; [Untitled]; Fragments; [Untitled]; [Untitled]; [Untitled]; Quetzalcoatl; Quetzalcoatl; Out of the Dark; Prophecy; A Gull From a Cliff; [Untitled]; [Untitled]; [Untitled]; To Sleep; [Untitled]; Isolde; II. POEMS FOR A COMPETITION (1942): Date Uncertain; Nostalgia; For D.; Lines to Diana; The Gods in the Patio; The School Where Nobody Learns What; For Leon Trotzky and Huitzilopochtli; Sacre du Printemps; In Black and White; Explanation to M.; III. [STATEMENT ABOUT POETRY]; IV. VIEW FROM A HILL (1947): I. For D.; 1. From This Tree; 2. Air for Variations; 3. New Directions; 4. To a Friend on Sailing; 5. To One Rescued; II. Fresco of Priests and Beans; On a Feather Poncho; The Chichimecs; Stela of a Mayan Penitent; Tepuzteca, Tepehua; The Conquered; III. For Rosalie; blotted a beetle; Table Set for Sea-Slime; IV. Five Years; First Year: Sebastian; Second Year: Dream While Paris Was Threatened; Third Year: About a Mythical Factory-Area; Fourth Year: Letter to My Brother; Fifth Year: Viktoria; V. For E. and For W.; "¿Que Quieres? ¿Mis Costillas?" (For E.); Chili Sin Carne (For W.); VI: View from a Hill; To the Builders of a Dam; View from a Hill; Recantation; On the Lights of San Francisco; A Escoger; In

Order to Clarify; We Kept on Reading "Tuesday"; VII: For Barbara Mayer; On Leaving Some Friends at an Early Hour; V. A STONE FOR SISIPHUS (1949): Sonnet to Siva; Anniversary; Invocation; Evening; The Coming Fructification by Night of Our Cyrus; Of the Names of the Zapotec Kings; Framed Portent; Orientation to the West; VI. MISCELLANEOUS POEMS: Mourning Song; Admittance; The City; A Tapestry; Warning to Snake Killers; [Untitled]; Mythological Episode; Rainy-Day Pastime; The Heart; Mozart's G. Minor; [Miscellaneous Lines]; Letter for Last Christmas; [Untitled]; Colors; [Untitled]; [Untitled]; [Untitled]; [Untitled]; Poema de Salida; Intimations of Mortality; Bibliography; Index of Poetry Titles; Index of First Lines.

Notes. A complete publication of all the known fiction and poetry by Barlow; the fiction was edited by David E. Schultz and myself, the poetry by Anderson.

41A. Lord Dunsany, *The Last Book of Jorkens*
    a. San Francisco: Night Shade Books, 2002 [March 2003].

Contents: Foreword, by J. W. Doyle; A Fatal Mistake; A Prophet without Honour; A Big Bang; Jorkens' Regret; The Two Scientists; The Lost Charm; Bringing Things Up to Date; A Snake Story; The Deal; In the Mojave; A Modern Conqueror; The Little Light; Across the Colour Bar; A Bit of Counter-Espionage; A Wonderful Day; Not Guilty; The Explanation; A Deal with a Witch; Jorkens' Dilemma; A Plaything of Our Betters; The Visitor; On Wings of Song.

Notes. A limited paperback edition designed as a kind of foretaste of the *Collected Jorkens*. This was a book that Dunsany compiled late in life but never managed to get published.

42. Ambrose Bierce, *A Much Misunderstood Man: Selected Letters of Ambrose Bierce* (with David E. Schultz)
    a. Columbus: Ohio State University Press, [May] 2003 (hardcover).
    b. Columbus: Ohio State University Press, [April] 2016 (paperback).

Contents: List of Abbreviations; Introduction; A Note on This Edition; Selected Letters; Bibliography; Index.

Notes. An annotated edition of about one-quarter of Bierce's total correspondence. Schultz and I are still searching for a publisher for the complete correspondence (about 500,000 words).

43. George Sterling, *The Thirst of Satan: Poems of Fantasy and Terror*
    a. New York: Hippocampus Press, [October] 2003.

Contents. Introduction; I. The Testimony of the Suns: The Testimony of the Suns; Mystery; Three Sonnets on Oblivion; Oblivion; The Dust Dethroned; The Night of Gods; Three Sonnets of the

Night Skies (I—Aldebaran at Dusk; II—The Chariots of Dawn; III—The Huntress of Stars); The Evanescent; The Thirst of Satan; The Setting of Antares; Outward; The Face of the Skies; Ephemera; Disillusion; The Meteor; The Last Man. II. The Gardens of the Sea: The Nile; The Fog Siren; The Sea-Fog; Darkness; "Sad Sea-Horizons"; Sonnets by the Night Sea; The Gardens of the Sea; At the Grand Cañon; The Last of Sunset; Caucasus; The Caravan; III. The Muse of the Incommunicable: Memory of the Dead; The Altar-Flame; Ultima Thule; The Directory; In Extremis; Romance; A Mood; The Moth of Time; The Muse of the Incommunicable; "Omnia Exeunt in Mysterium": To One Self-Slain; Three Sonnets on Sleep; Illusion; Essential Night; To Life; To Science; Waste; Amber; The Dweller in Darkness; Here and Now; IV. The Black Vulture: The Black Vulture; The Sibyl of Dreams; The Last Monster; "That Walk in Darkness"; To the Mummy of the Lady Isis; Witch-Fire; Song; The Young Witch; Eidolon; The Sphinx; V. The Naiad's Song: The Haunting; The Naiad's Song; White Magic; The Golden Past; The Revenge; To a Girl Dancing; Flame; The Stranger; VI. A Wine of Wizardry: The Summer of the Gods; Nightmare; A Wine of Wizardry; The Apothecary's; Under the Rainbow; The Shadow of Nirvana; The Wiser Prophet; The Oldest Book; Farm of Fools; VII. The Passing of Bierce: To Edgar Allan Poe; To Ambrose Bierce; The Ashes in the Sea; The Coming Singer; The Passing of Bierce; Shelley at Spezia. VIII. The Rack: The Lords of Pain; A Dream of Fear; The Rack; Conspiracy; The Hidden Pool; The Death of Circe; To a Monk's Skull; To Pain; Epilogue: My Swan Song; George Sterling: An Appreciation, by Clark Ashton Smith; Commentary; Index of Titles; Index of First Lines.

Notes. A foretaste of Sterling's collected poetry. I understand, however, that this book has not sold well.

44. Lord Dunsany, *The Pleasures of a Futuroscope*
a. New York: Hippocampus Press, [October] 2003.
   Contents: Introduction; The Pleasures of a Futuroscope.
   Notes. Dunsany's last novel, previously unpublished. The manuscript was provided to me by Joe Doyle, the archivist at Dunsany Castle.
b. New York: Hippocampus Press, [July] 2005.

45. Arthur Machen, *The White People and Other Stories*
a. Oakland, CA: Chaosium, [October] 2003.
   Contents: Introduction; The Red Hand; Ornaments in Jade; The White People; A Fragment of Life; The Angels of Mons; The Great Return; Out of the Earth; The Coming of the Terror; The Happy Children.

Notes. The second volume in my Chaosium edition of Machen's weird fiction.

46.   H. L. Mencken, *Mencken's America*
       a.   Athens: Ohio University Press, [January] 2004.
             Contents: Introduction; A Note on This Edition; Prologue: On Living in the United States; 1. The American: A Treatise; 2. The American Landscape; 3. American Politics, Morality, and Religion; 4. American Art, Literature, and Culture; Epilogue: Testament; Notes; Glossary of Names; Sources; Index.
             Notes. An interesting volume of Mencken's writings on American culture, politics, and society. The introduction was reprinted in I.50 as "Mencken's America."

47.   Lord Dunsany, *In the Land of Time and Other Fantasy Tales*
       a.   New York: Penguin, [January] 2004.
             Contents: Introduction; Suggestions for Further Reading; A Note on the Text; *The Gods of Pegāna;* Time and the Gods; A Legend of the Dawn; In the Land of Time; The Relenting of Sarnidac; The Fall of Babbulkund; The Sword of Welleran; The Kith of the Elf-Folk; The Ghosts; The Fortress Unvanquishable, Save for Sacnoth; Blagdaross; Idle Days on the Yann; A Shop in Go-by Street; The Avenger of Perdóndaris; The Bride of the Man-Horse; Where the Tides Ebb and Flow; The Raft-Builders; The Prayer of the Flowers; The Workman; Charon; Carcassonne; Roses; The City; The Wonderful Window; The Coronation of Mr. Thomas Shap; The City on Mallington Moor; The Bureau d'Echange de Maux; The Exiles' Club; Thirteen at Table; The Last Dream of Bwona Khubla; The Tale of the Abu Laheeb; Our Distant Cousins; The Walk to Lingham; The Development of the Rillswood Estate; A Life's Work; The Policeman's Prophecy; The Two Bottles of Relish; The Cut; Poseidon; Helping the Fairies; The Romance of His Life; The Pirate of the Round Pond; Explanatory Notes.
             Notes. A book that I lobbied the Penguin editors for years to let me compile. It has apparently sold surprisingly well. Ursula K. Le Guin had a nice review of it in the *Los Angeles Times Book Review.*

48.   *Fritz Leiber and H. P. Lovecraft: Writers of the Dark* (with Ben J. S. Szumskyj)
       a.   Holicong, PA: Wildside Press, 2003 [January 2004].
             Contents: Introduction, by Ben J. S. Szumskyj; H. P. Lovecraft: Letters to Fritz and Jonquil Leiber; Stories and Poems by Fritz Leiber: Adept's Gambit; The Demons of the Upper Air; The Sunken Land;

Diary in the Snow; The Dreams of Albert Moreland; The Dead Man; A Bit of the Dark World; To Arkham and the Stars; The Terror from the Depths; Essays by Fritz Leiber: The Works of H. P. Lovecraft: Suggestions for a Critical Appraisal; Some Random Thoughts about Lovecraft's Writings; Leiber on Onderdonk; A Literary Copernicus; My Correspondence with Lovecraft; Lovecraft: A Symposium; The "Whisperer" Re-examined; Through Hyperspace with Brown Jenkin; The Cthulhu Mythos: Wondrous and Terrible; Lovecraft in My Life; Afterword, by S. T. Joshi.

Notes. A book that Szumskyj urged me to collaborate on. It contains the first complete publication of Lovecraft's surviving letters to Leiber.

49. Lord Dunsany, *The Collected Jorkens: Volume 1*
  a. San Francisco: Night Shade Books, [February] 2004.

     Contents: Brief Foreword to the Complete Edition of Jorkens, by Edward Plunkett, [20th] Lord Dunsany; Dunsany, Lord of Fantasy, by Arthur C. Clarke; Introduction, by S. T. Joshi; Bibliographical Notes; *The Travel Tales of Mr. Joseph Jorkens:* Preface; The Tale of the Abu Laheeb; The King of Sarahb; How Jembu Played for Cambridge; The Charm against Thirst; Our Distant Cousins; A Large Diamond; A Queer Island; The Electric King; A Drink at a Running Stream; A Daughter of Rameses; The Showman; Mrs. Jorkens; The Witch of the Willows; *Jorkens Remembers Africa:* Preface; The Lost Romance; The Curse of the Witch; The Pearly Beach; The Walk to Lingham; The Escape from the Valley; One August in the Red Sea; The Bare Truth; What Jorkens Has to Put Up With; Ozymandias; At the End of the Universe; The Black Mamba; In the Garden of Memories; The Slugly Beast; Earth's Secret; The Persian Spell; Stranger Than Fiction; The Golden Gods; The Correct Kit; How Ryan Got out of Russia; The Club Secretary; A Mystery of the East.

     Notes. Part of my ongoing attempt to bring Dunsany's work back into print. The introduction was reprinted in I.47 as part of "Jorkens."

50. Lord Dunsany, *The Collected Jorkens: Volume 2*
  a. San Francisco: Night Shade Books, [August] 2004.

     Contents: Brief Foreword to the Complete Edition of Jorkens, by Edward Plunkett, [20th] Lord Dunsany; Whiskey, Popcorn and Gold, by T. E. D. Klein; Introduction, by S. T. Joshi; Bibliographical Notes; *Jorkens Has a Large Whiskey:* Preface; Jorkens' Revenge; Jorkens Retires from Business; Jorkens Handles a Big Property; The Invention of Dr. Caber; The Grecian Singer; The Jorkens Family Emeralds; A Fishing Story; Jorkens in High Finance; The Sign; The Angelic Shepherd; The Neapolitan Ice; The Development of the

Rillswood Estate; The Fancy Man; The Lion and the Unicorn; A Doubtful Story; Jorkens Looks Forward; Jorkens among the Ghosts; Elephant Shooting; African Magic; Jorkens Consults a Prophet; A Matter of Business; The Invention of the Age; The Sultan, the Monkey and the Banana; Pundleton's Audience; The Fight in the Drawing-Room; The Ivory Poacher; *The Fourth Book of Jorkens:* Making Fine Weather; Mgamu; The Haunting of Halahanstown; The Pale-Green Image; Jorkens Leaves Prison; The Warning; The Sacred City of Krakovlitz; Jorkens Practices Medicine and Magic; Jarton's Disease; On the Other Side of the Sun; The Rebuff; Jorkens' Ride; The Secret of the Sphinx; The Khamseen; The Expulsion; The Welcome; By Command of Pharaoh; A Cricket Problem; A Life's Work; The Ingratiating Smile; The Last Bull; The Strange Drug of Dr. Caber; A Deal with the Devil; Strategy at the Billiards Club; Jorkens in Witch Wood; Lost; The English Magnifico; The Cleverness of Dr. Caber; Fairy Gold; A Royal Dinner; A Fight with Knives; Out West; In a Dim Room.

Notes. A combined reprint of *Jorkens Has a Large Whiskey* (1940) and *The Fourth Book of Jorkens* (1947). The introduction was reprinted in I.47 as part of "Jorkens."

51.   Samuel Loveman, *Out of the Immortal Night: Selected Works of Samuel Loveman* (with David E. Schultz)

a.   New York: Hippocampus Press, 2004.

   Contents. Introduction; I. Poetry: *Poems* (1911): In Pierrot's Garden; Ode to Ceres; Fra Angelico; Song; To P. G.; Lines; A Twenty-second Birthday; *The Hermaphrodite and Other Poems* (1936): The Hermaphrodite; River Pattern; Will o' the Wisp; Steener Haakonson Dances; Dream Song; Heckscher Building; Euphorion; Agathon; Arcesilaus; Lineage; For a Book of Poems; Ascension; Thomas Holley Chivers; The Ramapos; Oscar Wilde; John Clare in a Madhouse; The Minstrel; The Chopin-Player; A Dedication; Vice; Transience; Dolore; Bacchanale; To Simone's; Ad Fratrem; Isolation; Remonstrance; Proteus; A Voyage; Legend; The Return; Memoralia; Forest of Rhododendron; Understanding; Ecce Homo; Ariel; Visitor; Inarticulate; Madison Square; Contrast; Invocation; Song; Harbour; Admonition; Foes; Limbo; Interlude; Gates Mills; Wasteland; Amy Levy; Forest Hill; Andenkung; Dream of Spring; Finis; A Georgia Garden; Palingenesis; Belated Love; Nostalgia; Becalmed; Mutation; Dirge; To Dionysus; To Apollo; Quatrains (Poppies; Forgotten Poets; Space; Music; Simeon Solomon; Aftermath); A Chinese Pavilion; Ben De Casseres in Camden; Terminus; Uncollected Poems: A Poet; A Sonnet: Lethe; The Birth of Fear; Pierced; A Lily; Lost

Youth; Avalon; Hope; The Old Cobbler; Shadow-Land; The Song Unsung; Ship of Dreams; The Birth of Poesy; On Lost Friendship; Peccavi; The Plaint of Bygone Loves; Eventide (I. Sunset; II. Twilight; III. Night); David Gray; An Epitaph; Quatrains; To Alfred Noyes, Oversea; Michael Scott's Wooing; Thomas Dermody; Resurgam; Shadow-Love; Euthanasia; A Burden; A Song of Chamisso's; A Departure; W. E.; On the Passing of Youth; A Triumph in Eternity; Talent; [Untitled]; Adventure; In Sepulcretis; Saturday Evening; A Letter to G—— K——; Ernest Nelson; Heldenleben; Winter; To Satan; Christmas—1923; Genesis; Night Piece (Forest Hill); Monolith; Oscar Redivivus; Unfulfilled; To Mr. Theobald; To George Kirk on His 27th Birthday; Music; Vigil; To a Child; The Dead King; Kin; Episode; Rescue; Transit; An Admonition to the Ladies; Debs in Prison; For the Chelsea Book Shop [I]; For the Chelsea Book Shop [II]; Nepenthe; Quatrain; Reliquiae; Spring at El Retiro; Versailles; [Untitled]; The Goal; John Clare in 1864; II. Drama: Oedipus at Colonus; Belshazzar; Nero; Narcisse; Arcady; A Scene for *King Lear*; A Scene for *Macbeth*; The Sphinx: A Conversation; III. Translations: Twenty-four Translations from Heine; Catullus; Translations from Baudelaire: La Musique; Parfum Exotique; Horreur Sympathique; De Profundis Clamavi; La Beauté; Causerie; Chant d'Automne; Le Couvercle; Le Chat; La Fontaine de Sang; Sonnet d'Automne; Ciel Brouillé; Les Chats; Translations from Verlaine: Sagesse; Bruxelles; Romances sans Paroles; Il Bacio; La Bonne Chanson; Vert; Sappho; Sonnet: After Leconte de Lisle; God's Work; IV. Fiction: Antenor; The Faun; The Dog; An Impression; The One Who Found Pity; Christmas-Eve with Sherlock Holmes; V. Essays: Mr. Sterling and Minor Poets; A Keats Discovery; Modern Poetry (An Exorcism); A Note [to *Twenty-one Letters of Ambrose Bierce*]; A Convention Address; The Book of Life; Foreword to *Poppies and Mandragora*; Preface to *The Man from Genoa*; Hubert Crackanthorpe: A Realist of the Nineties; Marcel Proust; Literature and Dry-rot; A Letter on Hart Crane; Howard Phillips Lovecraft; Lovecraft as Conversationalist; Bibliography; Index of Poetry Titles; Index of First Lines.

Notes. A product of years of work by several hands, combing through amateur periodicals in search of material by Loveman. Probably more poetry and other work exists, but this book contains a substantial proportion of it. The introduction was reprinted in I.52.

52. Lord Dunsany, *The Collected Jorkens: Volume 3*
   a.   San Francisco: Night Shade Books, [April] 2005.

      Contents: Brief Foreword to the Complete Edition of Jorkens, by Edward Plunkett, [20th] Lord Dunsany; Foreword, by Michael Dirda; Introduction, by S. T. Joshi; Bibliographical Notes; *Jorkens Borrows Another Whiskey:* Preface; The Two-Way War; A Nice Lot of Diamonds; Letting Bygones Be Bygones; The Lost Invention; On Other Paths; The Partner; Poulet a la Richelieu; A Walk in the Night; One Summer's Evening; A Friend of the Family; An Eccentricity of Genius; Influenza; The Unrecorded Test Match; Idle Tears; Among the Neutrals; An Idyll of the Sahara; The Devil among the Willows; A Spanish Castle; The New Moon; The Gods of Clay; A Rash Remark; The Story of Jorkens' Watch; The Track through the Wood; Snow Water; The Greatest Invention; The Verdict; A Conversation in Bond Street; The Reward; Which Way?; A Desperado in Surrey; Misadventure; A Long Memory; An Absentminded Professor; Greek Meets Greek; *The Last Book of Jorkens:* A Fatal Mistake; A Prophet without Honour; A Big Bang; Jorkens' Regret; The Two Scientists; The Lost Charm; Bringing Things Up to Date; A Snake Story; The Deal; In the Mojave; A Modern Conqueror; The Little Light; Across the Colour Bar; A Bit of Counter-Espionage; A Wonderful Day; Not Guilty; The Explanation; A Deal with a Witch; Jorkens' Dilemma; A Plaything of Our Betters; The Visitor; On Wings of Song; Uncollected Tales: The Two Jenets; A Meeting of Spirits; The Ultimate Goal.

Notes. A combined reprint of *Jorkens Borrows Another Whiskey* (1954) and *The Last Book of Jorkens* (see item 41A), along with some miscellaneous material. The introduction was reprinted in I.47 as part of "Jorkens."

53.   Arthur Machen, *The Terror and Other Stories*
       a.   Oakland, CA: Chaosium, April 2005.
             Contents: Introduction; *The Terror;* The Lost Club; Munitions of War; The Islington Mystery; Johnny Double; The Cosy Room; Opening the Door; The Children of the Pool; The Bright Boy; Out of the Picture; Change; The Dover Road; Ritual; Appendix: The Literature of Occultism.

             Notes. The third and final volume of my Chaosium edition of Machen's weird fiction. The edition does not contain the complete contents of the late collections *The Cosy Room* (1936) and *The Children of the Pool* (1936), since some of the tales in those volumes are pretty poor.

54.   M. P. Shiel, *The House of Sounds and Others*
       a.   New York: Hippocampus Press, [July] 2005.
             Contents: Introduction; Xélucha; The Pale Ape; The Case of Euphemia Raphash; Huguenin's Wife; The House of Sounds; The Great King; The Bride; *The Purple Cloud;* Appendix: Vaila.

Notes. A volume that reprints those works by Shiel that most inspired Lovecraft.

55.   Clarence Darrow, *Closing Arguments: Clarence Darrow on Religion, Law, and Society*
 a.   Athens: Ohio University Press, [July] 2005.
        Contents: Introduction; A Note on This Edition; 1. On Philosophy and Religion: Is Life Worth Living?; Is the Human Race Getting Anywhere?; "The War on Modern Science"; Can the Individual Control His Conduct?; The Lord's Day Alliance; Why I Have Found Life Worth Living; Is There a Purpose in the Universe?; Does Man Live Again?; 2. On Law and Crime: The Right Treatment of Violence; Crime: Its Cause and Treatment; The Ordeal of Prohibition; Crime and the Alarmists; What to Do about Crime; Capital Punishment; 3. On Politics and Society: Woman Suffrage; Patriotism; Salesmanship; The Eugenics Cult; 4. On Clarence Darrow: *Farmington* [extracts]; George Bissett; At Seventy-two; Notes; Bibliographical Essay; Index.
        Notes. A volume that collects many interesting writings by Darrow, although much of his work remains uncollected.

56.   M. R. James, *Count Magnus and Other Ghost Stories*
 a.   New York: Penguin, [September] 2005.
        Contents: Introduction; Suggestions for Further Reading; A Note on the Text; Canon Alberic's Scrap-book; Lost Hearts; The Mezzotint; The Ash-Tree; Number 13; Count Magnus; "Oh, Whistle, and I'll Come to You, My Lad"; The Treasure of Abbot Thomas; A School Story; The Rose Garden; The Tractate Middoth; Casting the Runes; The Stalls of Barchester Cathedral; Martin's Close; Mr. Humphreys and His Inheritance; Appendix; Explanatory Notes.
        Notes. A volume designed to compete with the Oxford University Press edition of James's *Casting the Runs* (1987). The introduction was reprinted in part in I.47 as "M. R. James and the Classic Ghost Story."

57/58/59. *Supernatural Literature of the World: An Encyclopedia* (with Stefan Dziemianowicz)
 a.   Westport, CT: Greenwood Press, [September] 2005. 3 vols.
        Contents: Foreword, by Ramsey Campbell; Preface; Alphabetical List of Entries; Guide to Related Topics; Abbreviations of Frequently Cited Reference Works; The Encyclopedia; General Bibliography; Index of Fictional Characters; Index of Motifs; General Index; Notes on Contributors.

Notes. A reference work that took years to assemble and the work of many contributors. Overall, it is probably the most comprehensive work of its kind in the field.

60.   *The Shadow of the Unattained: The Letters of George Sterling and Clark Ashton Smith* (with David E. Schultz)
  a.   New York: Hippocampus Press, [December] 2005.

      Contents: Introduction; The Shadow of the Unattained; Appendix: To George Sterling, by Clark Ashton Smith; To George Sterling, by Clark Ashton Smith; To George Sterling, by Clark Ashton Smith; To the Editor of *Town Talk*, by Ambrose Bierce; The Coming Singer, by George Sterling; Preface to *Odes and Sonnets*, by George Sterling; Preface to *Ebony and Crystal*, by George Sterling; Recent Books of Fact and Fiction, by George Sterling; Poetry of the Pacific Coast—California, by George Sterling; To George Sterling: A Valediction, by Clark Ashton Smith; George Sterling: An Appreciation, by Clark Ashton Smith; George Sterling: Poet and Friend, by Clark Ashton Smith; To George Sterling, by Clark Ashton Smith; Glossary of Names; List of Extant Enclosures; Bibliography; Index.

      Notes. First complete publication of the joint correspondence between Smith and Sterling. The joint correspondence of Bierce and Sterling could be assembled, but Schultz and I have found no takers for such a volume.

61.   *In Her Place: A Documentary History of Prejudice against Women*
  a.   Amherst, NY: Prometheus Books, [March] 2006.

      Contents: Acknowledgments; Introduction; Part 1: Some Overviews: John Todd, "Woman's Rights"; Hugh L. McMenamin, "Evils of Woman's Revolt against the Old Standards"; George Frazier, "The Entrenchment of the American Witch"; Part 2: Woman's "Place": Elizabeth Sandford, "Woman, in Her Social and Domestic Character"; Margaret Bisland, "The Curse of Eve"; Lyman Abbott, "The Home Builder"; Charles W. Eliot, "The Normal American Woman"; Part 3: Scientists on Women: Alexander Walker, "Woman: Physiologically Considered"; Otto Weininger, "Sex and Character"; Steven Goldberg, "The Inevitability of Patriarchy"; Part 4: Women and Intellect: George J. Romanes, "Mental Differences between Men and Women"; Molly Elliot Seawell, "On the Absence of the Creative Faculty in Women"; James H. Leuba, "The Weaker Sex: A Scientific Ramble"; Part 5: Women and Education: Edward H. Clarke, M.D., "Sex in Education; or, A Fair Chance for the Girls"; A. Lapthorn Smith, "Higher Education of Women and Race Suicide"; John M. McBryde, Jr., "Womanly Education for Women";

Part 6: Women and Work: Anonymous, "Women's Mistakes about Work"; Emily Greene Balch, "The Education and Efficiency of Women"; Dr. Donald A. Laird and Eleanor C. Laird, "The Psychology of Supervising the Working Woman"; Patricia Coffin, "Memo to the American Woman"; Part 7: Women and Sex: John Martin, "Feminism: Its Fallacies and Follies"; Sigmund Freud, "Female Sexuality"; Kate Constance, "How to Get and Keep a Husband"; Part 8: Women and Marriage: Sir William Blackstone, "Commentaries on the Laws of England"; William A. Alcott, "The Young Wife"; William Johnston, "These Women"; George Gilder, "Men and Marriage"; Part 9: Women and Religion: Jonathan F. Stearns, "Female Influence, and the True Christian Mode of Its Exercise"; Catharine E. Beecher, "Woman's Profession as Mother and Educator"; John Paul MacCorrie, "'The War of the Sexes'"; John Erskine, "The Influence of Women and Its Cure"; Joseph H. Fichter, S.J., "The Decline of Femininity"; Part 10: Women and Suffrage: Orestes Augustus Brownson, "The Woman Question"; Horace Bushnell, "Woman Suffrage: The Reform against Nature"; Rossiter Johnson, "The Blank-Cartridge Ballot"; James Monroe Buckley, "The Wrong and Peril of Woman Suffrage"; Harold Owen, "Woman Adrift: The Menace of Suffragism"; Benjamin Vestal Hubbard, "Socialism, Feminism, and Suffragism: The Terrible Triplets"; William Parker, "The Fundamental Error of Woman Suffrage"; Part 11: Women Hating Women: Mrs. Amelia E. Barr, "Discontented Women"; Elizabeth Bisland, "The Abdication of Man"; Ida M. Tarbell, "The business of Being a Woman"; Part 12: Backlash—Men Fight Back: Harry Thurston Peck, "For Maids and Mothers: The Woman of To-day, and of To-morrow"; Harry Hibschman, "Equal Rights for Men"; Roy U. Schenk, "So Why Do Rapes Occur?"; Further Reading; Index.

Notes. A companion of sorts to *Documents of American Prejudice* (item 18 above); in fact, my original title was *Documents of American Misogyny.* It completes my trilogy of books (the third being *Atheism: A Reader* [item 26]) in which I tackle what I regard as three of the great scourges of humanity: religion, race prejudice, and sexism.

62. *Lovecraft's New York Circle: The Kalem Club, 1924–1927* (with Mara Kirk Hart)
   a. New York: Hippocampus Press, 2006.
   Contents: Preface, by Peter Cannon; Introduction, by Mara Kirk Hart; The Kalem Letters of George Kirk: Introduction, by Mara Kirk Hart; 1924; 1925; 1926; 1927; Writings by the Kalems: George Kirk: Book Collecting: The Prince of Hobbies; Rheinhart Kleiner: A Glee; At Providence in 1918; Epistle to Mr. and Mrs. Lovecraft; The Four

of Us (Rondeau); Brooklyn, My Brooklyn; Columbia Heights, Brooklyn; [Prisky]; On a Favorite Cat: Killed by an Automobile; To George W. Kirk, upon His 26th Birthday; To His Peculiar Friend, G. Kirk, Esq.; Your Street; Blue Pencil Anniversary Song; What My Ancestors Were Like; The Great Adventure; If I Had Lived a Hundred Years Ago; H. P. L.; Arthur Leeds: He Had to Pay the Nine-Tailed Cat; Frank Belknap Long: A Man from Genoa; Come, Let Us Make; The Man Who Died Twice; H. P. Lovecraft: Plaster-All; To Endymion; Providence; Waste Paper; Primavera; To an Infant; To George Kirk, Esq.; To George Willard Kirk, Gent., of Chelsea Village in New York, upon His Birthday, Novr. 25, 1925; Two Christmas Poems to G. W. K.; A Year Off; In Memoriam Oscar Incoul Verelst of Manhattan 1920–1926; Samuel Loveman: A Letter to G—— K——; To George Kirk on His 27th Birthday; For the Chelsea Book Shop [1]; For the Chelsea Book Shop [2]; For a Cat; For a Book of Poems; Admonition; Limbo; To H. P. L.; Genesis; Spring at El Retiro; Arcesilaus; John Clare in 1864; Everett McNeil: From *Tonty of the Iron Hand*; James Ferdinand Morton: To G.W.K. on His 27th Birthday; From *The Curse of Race Prejudice*; Appendix: After a Decade and the Kalem Club, by Rheinhart Kleiner; Bards and Bibliophiles, by Rheinhart Kleiner; Sources and Works Consulted; Index.

Notes. A fascinating compilation, chiefly spearheaded by my collaborator, and based on the many letters that George Kirk wrote to his fiancée about the comings and goings of the Kalem Club. Several of the pieces by the Kalem members are uncollected or unpublished.

63/64/65. *The Short Fiction of Ambrose Bierce: A Comprehensive Edition* (with Lawrence I. Berkove and David E. Schultz)

    a.   Knoxville: University of Tennessee Press, [September] 2006. 3 vols.

         Contents: Volume 1: General Introduction, by the editors; Explanatory Notes; Part 1. 1868–1876: Introduction, by Berkove; Letters from a Hdkhoite; The Aborigines of Oakland; A Scientific Dream; Across the Continent; The Haunted Valley; Some Fiction: From *The Fiend's Delight*; Crazy Tales: From *Nuggets and Dust*; Dr. Deadwood, I Presume; The Magician's Little Joke; Nut-Cracking; Sundered Hearts; A Fowl Witch; A Tale of Spanish Vengeance; Juniper; Four Jacks and a Knave; Seafaring; No Charge for Attendance; Feodora; A Tale of the Bosphorus; The Grateful Bear; The Early History of Bath; John Smith, Liberator; Converting a Prodigal; The Civil Service in Florida; Mrs. Dennison's Head; Pernicketty's Fright; Following the Sea; Tony Rollo's Conclusion; "The Following Dorg"; Maumee's Mission; Snaking; Maud's Papa; Jim Beckwourth's Pond; How to Saw Bears; The New Bedder; Samuel Baxter, M.D.; Jeph

Benedick's Grandmother; The Sanctity of an Oath; A Remarkable Adventure; The Dempsters; Authenticating a Ghost; Jo Dornan and the Ram; Banking at Mexican Hill; To Fiji and Return; Concerning Balloons; Two Stories about Johnson; A Champion of the Sex; How I Came to Like Dogs; Mr. Jim Beckwourth's Adventure; Why I Am Not Editing "The Stinger"; Corrupting the Press; Mr. Barcle's Mill; Little Larry; My Muse; The Night-Doings at "Deadman's"; A Providential Intimation; Confessions of a Sad Dog; The Wreck of the *Orion*; The Late John Sweetbosh, Esq.; Largo al Gapperino; The Baptism of Dobsho; The Race at Left Bower; A Literary Riot; A Shipwreckollection; Perry Chumly's Eclipse; Mr. Masthead, Journalist; Mr. Swiddler's Flip-Flap; The Lion at Bay; The Little Story; The Failure of Hope & Wandel; Curried Cow; Stringing a Bear; The Miraculous Guest; A Representative Inquest; Storm and Sunshine; An Upper Class Misdemeanant; A Holiday Experience; The Captain of the *Camel*; The Man Overboard; Part 2. 1878–1886: Introduction; The Famous Gilson Bequest; A Psychological Shipwreck; Sam Baxter's Eel; "A Bad Woman"; That Dog; "By Her Own Hand"; Infernia; Boarding a Bear; The Following Bear; A Holy Terror; George Thurston; A Mirage in Arizona; A Cargo of Cat; Jupiter Doke, Brigadier-General; The History of Windbag the Sailor; An Imperfect Conflagration; My Credentials; A Revolt of the Gods; "The Bubble Reputation"; A Story at the Club; An Inhabitant of Carcosa; Selected Textual Variants.

Volume 2: Part 3. 1887–1893: Introduction, by Berkove; Killed at Resaca; The Man out of the Nose; A Bottomless Grave; One of the Missing; For the Ahkoond; Hades in Trouble; The Fall of the Republic; The Kingdom of Tortirra; Bodies of the Dead [I]; Bodies of the Dead [II]; Sons of the Fair Star; Hither from Hades; A Son of the Gods; Behind the Veil; My Favorite Murder; A Tough Tussle; Whither?; One of Twins; The Tamtonians; The City of the Gone Away; Chickamauga; One Officer, One Man; A Horseman in the Sky; The Coup de Grâce; Two Haunted Houses; The Suitable Surroundings; The Affair at Coulter's Notch; The Golampians; A Watcher by the Dead; The Major's Tale; The Story of a Conscience; The Man and the Snake; An Occurrence at Owl Creek Bridge; The Realm of the Unreal; His Waterloo; The Middle Toe of the Right Foot; Burbank's Crime; Oil of Dog; The Widower Turmore; Haïta the Shepherd; Parker Adderson, Philosopher; A Lady from Redhorse; The Boarded Window; The Secret of Macarger's Gulch; The Mocking-Bird; The Thing at Nolan; A Baby Tramp; The Death of Halpin Frayser; An Adventure at Brownville; The Wizard of Bumbassa; The Applicant; One

Kind of Officer; John Bartine's Watch; The Hypnotist; A Jug of Sirup;
The Damned Thing; Selected Textual Variants.

Volume 3: Part 4. 1895–1904: Introduction, by Berkove; The
Great Strike of 1895; The Eyes of the Panther; An Affair of Out-
posts; Marooned on Ug; The War with Wug; Moxon's Master; The
Alternative Proposal; Trustland: A Tale of a Traveler; The Maid of
Podunk; The Extinction of the Smugwumps; Industrial Discontent
in Ancient America; At Old Man Eckert's; A Diagnosis of Death; A
Letter from a Btrugumian; The Future Historian and His Fatigue; A
Chronicle of the Time to Be; The Dog in Ganegwag; Part 5. 1905–
1910: Introduction; The Jury in Ancient America; A Vine on a
House; The Man with Two Lives; A Wireless Message; An Arrest;
The Conflagration in Ghargaroo; One Summer Night; John Mor-
tonson's Funeral; Staley Fleming's Hallucination; Insurance in Ancient America; A Baffled Ambuscade; Two Military Executions; The
Moonlit Road; An Execution in Batrugia; The Other Lodgers; Beyond the Wall; A Resumed Identity; Three and Three Are One; Rise
and Fall of the Aëroplane; The Stranger; The Dispersal; An Ancient
Hunter; Ashes of the Beacon; The Land Beyond the Blow; A Leaf
Blown In from Days to Be; Appendix A. Variant Texts (1. The *Jean-
nette* and the *Corwin*; 2. Bodies of the Dead; 3. Present at a Hanging;
4. A Fruitless Assignment; 5. The Isle of Pines; 6. A Cold Greeting;
7. The Difficulty of Crossing a Field; 8. An Unfinished Race; 9.
Charles Ashmore's Trail; 10. The Spook House; 11. A Doppelgang-
er); Appendix B. Bierce on His Fiction (1. Preface to *Tales of Soldiers
and Civilians*; 2. Preface to *In the Midst of Life*; 3. Preface to *Bubbles
Like Us* [*Can Such Things Be?*]; 4. Preface to *Can Such Things Be?*; 5.
Prefatory note to "The Ways of Ghosts"; 6. [On *Tales of Soldiers and
Civilians*]; 7. [On "The Damned Thing"]); Appendix C. Supplementary Texts (Texts by Bierce: [Before the Mirror]; The Evolution of a
Story; A Ghost in the Unmaking; The Clothing of Ghosts; A Screed
of the Future Historian; [Annals of the Future Historian]; An Untit-
led Tale; Alasper; Texts by Others: The Fortune of War; A Strange
Adventure, by W. C. Morrow); Selected Textual Variants; Bibliog-
raphy; Bierce's Civil War Stories Arranged Chronologically; Index to
Bierce's Fiction; General Index.

Notes. A book long in the making, and printing Bierce's total fictional work for the first time, as opposed to such volumes as Ernest
Jerome Hopkins's *The Complete Short Stories of Ambrose Bierce* (1970),
which leaves out at least 80 stories (out of 200 or so). I established
the text (based on research conducted by Schultz and myself), while
Berkove wrote most of the introductory matter.

66.   M. R. James, *The Haunted Dolls' House and Other Ghost Stories*
       a.   New York: Penguin, [October] 2006.

       Contents: Introduction; Suggestions for Further Reading; A Note on the Text; The Residence at Whitminster; The Diary of Mr. Poynter; An Episode of Cathedral History; The Story of a Disappearance and an Appearance; Two Doctors; The Haunted Dolls' House; The Uncommon Prayer-book; A Neighbour's Landmark; A View from a Hill; A Warning to the Curious; An Evening's Entertainment; There Was a Man Dwelt by a Churchyard; Rats; After Dark in the Playing Fields; Wailing Well; The Experiment; The Malice of Inanimate Objects; A Vignette; The Fenstanton Witch; Twelve Medieval Ghost-Stories (tr. Leslie Boba Joshi); Appendix; Explanatory Notes.

       Notes. The second of my M. R. James editions (see item 54 above), gathering his complete ghost stories. The introduction was reprinted in part in I.47 as "M. R. James and the Classic Ghost Story."

67/68. *Icons of Horror and the Supernatural*
       a.   Westport, CT: Greenwood Press, [January] 2007.

       Contents: Volume 1: List of Photos; Preface; Donald R. Burleson, "The Alien"; Matt Cardin, "The Angel and the Demon"; Brian Stableford, "The Cosmic Horror"; S. T. Joshi, "The Cthulhu Mythos"; Alan Warren, "The Curse"; Darrell Schweitzer, "The Devil"; Tony Fonseca, "The Doppelgänger"; Melissa Mia Hall, "The Ghost"; Scott Connors, "The Ghoul"; Steven J. Mariconda, "The Haunted House"; Brian Stableford, "The Immortal"; Richard Bleiler, "The Monster"; Paula Guran, "The Mummy"; *Volume 2:* Tony Fonseca, "The Psychic"; Mike Ashley, "The Sea Creature"; Hank Wagner, "The Serial Killer"; Melissa Mia Hall, "The Siren"; John Langan, "The Small-Town Horror"; K. A. Laity, "The Sorcerer"; Rob Latham, "The Urban Horror"; Margaret L. Carter, "The Vampire"; Stefan Dziemianowicz, "The Werewolf"; Bernadette Lynn Bosky, "The Witch"; June Pulliam, "The Zombie"; General Bibliography; Notes on Contributors; Index.

       Notes. An interesting volume in which contributors were asked to write 15,000-word essays on the topics in question. My essay of course led to the writing of *The Rise and Fall of the Cthulhu Mythos* (I.28).

69.   Clark Ashton Smith, *Complete Poetry and Translations*, Volume 3 (with David E. Schultz)
       a.   New York: Hippocampus Press, [May] 2007.
       b.   New York: Hippocampus Press, 2012 (paperback).

       Contents: Introduction; *Les Fleurs du mal,* by Charles Baudelaire: Preface/Préface; Spleen et Idéal: I. Bénédiction; II. The Albatross/

L'Albatros; III. Elevation/Elévation; IV. Corres-pondences/Correspon-
dances; V. [Untitled]; VI. The Beacons/Les Phares; VII. The Sick
Muse/La Muse malade; VIII. The Venal Muse/La Muse vénale; IX.
The Evil Monk/Le Mauvais Moine; X. L'Ennemi; XI. Le Guignon/Le
Guignon; XII. Anterior Life/La Vie antérieure; XIII. Travelling
Gypsies/Bohémiens en voyage; XIV. L'Homme et la mer; XV. Don
Juan aux enfers; XVI. To Theodore de Banville/A Théodore de
Banville; XVII. Chastisement of Pride/Châtiment de l'orgueil; XVIII.
Beauty/La Beauté; XIX. The Ideal/L'Idéal; XX. The Giantess/La
Géante; XXI. Le Masque; XXII. Hymn to Beauty/Hymne à la beauté;
XXIII. Exotic Perfume/Parfum exotique; XXIV. The Chevelure/La
Chevelure; XXV. [Untitled]; XXVI. [Untitled]; XXVII. *Sed non sati-
ata*; XXVIII. [Untitled]; XXIX. Le Serpent qui danse; XXX. Une
Charogne; XXXI. *De profundis clamavi*; XXXII. The Vampire/Le
Vampire; XXXIII. [Untitled]; XXXIV. The Remorse of the Dead/
Remords posthume; XXXV. The Cat/Le Chat; XXXVI. The Duel/
Duellum]; XXXVII. The Balcony/Le Balcon; XXXVIII. The
Possessed/Le Possédé; XXXIX. Un Fantôme; XL. [Untitled]; XLI.
Semper eadem; XLII. Tout entière; XLIII. [Untitled]; XLIV. Le
Flambeau vivant; XLV. Réversibilité; XLVI. Confession; XLVII. The
Spiritual   Dawn/L'Aube   spirituelle;   XLVIII.   Evening   Har-
mony/L'Harmonie du soir; XLIX. Le Flacon/Le Flacon; L. The
Poison/Le Poison; LI. Doubtful Skies/Ciel brouillé; LII. Le Chat;
LIII. Le Beau Navire; LIV. L'Invitation au voyage; LV. The Irrepar-
able/L'Irréparable; LVI. Causerie; LVII. Song of Autumn/Chant
d'automne; LVIII. A une Madone; LIX. Chanson d'après-midi; LX.
Sisina; LXI. Vers pour le portrait d'Honoré Daumier; LXII. *Franciscæ
meæ laudes*; LXIII. To a Creole Lady/A une Dame créole; LXIV.
Mœsta et errabunda; LXV. The Phantom/Le Revenant; LXVI. Sonnet
d'automne; LXVII. Tristesses de la lune; LXVIII. The Cats/Les
Chats; LXIX. The Owls/Les Hiboux; LXX. La Pipe; LXXI. Music/La
Musique; LXXII. Sépulture; LXXIII. Une Gravure fantastique;
LXXIV. Le Mort joyeux; LXXV. The Barrel of Hate/Le Tonneau de
la haine; LXXVI. La Cloche fêlée; LXXVII. Spleen; LXXVIII. Spleen;
LXXIX. Spleen; LXXX. Spleen; LXXXI. Obsession; LXXXII. Le Goût
du néant; LXXXIII. Alchemy of Sorrow/Alchimie de la douleur;
LXXXIV. Sympathetic Horror/Horreur sympathique; LXXXV. Le
Calumet de paix; LXXXVI. A Pagan's Prayer/La Prière d'un païen;
LXXXVII. The Cover/Le Couvercle; LXXXVIII. L'Imprévu; LXXXIX.
Examination at Midnight/L'Examen de minuit; XC. Madrigal of
Sorrow/Madrigal triste; XCI. The Adviser/L'Avertisseur; XCII. To a
Malabaress/A une Malabaraise; XCIII. The Voice/La Voix; XCIV.

Hymn/Hymne; XCV. The Rebel/Le Rebelle; XCVI. The Eyes of Bertha/Les Yeux de Berthe; XCVII. The Fountain/Le Jet d'eau; XCVIII. La Rançon; XCIX. Very Far from Here/Bien loin d'ici; C. Le Coucher du Soleil romantique; CI. On "Tasso in Prison" by Eugène Delacroix/Sur *Le Tasse en Prison* d'Eugène Delacroix; CII. The Gulf/Le Gouffre; CIII. The Lament of Icarus/Les Plaintes d'un Icare; CIV. Contemplation/Receuillement; CV. *L'Héautontimorouménos*; CVI. The Irremediable/L'Irrémédiable; CVII. The Clock/L'Horloge; Tableaux Parisiens: CVIII. Paysage; CIX. The Sun/Le Soleil; CX. Lola de Valence; CXI. La Lune offensée; CXII. A une Mendiante rousse; CXIII. Le Cygne; CXIV. Les Sept Vieillards; CXV. Les Petites Vieilles; CXVI. The Blind/Les Aveugles; CXVII. To a Passer-by/A une Passante; CXVIII. The Toiling Skeleton/Le Squelette laboureur; CXIX. Evening Twilight/Le Crépuscule du soir; CXX. The Game/Le Jeu; CXXI. The Dance of Death/Danse macabre; CXXII. The Love of Falsehood/L'Amour du mensonge; CXXIII. [Untitled]; CXXIV. [Untitled]; CXXV. Mists and Rains/Brumes et pluies; CXXVI. Parisian Dream/Rêve parisien; CXXVII. Le Crépuscule du matin; LE VIN: CXXVIII. L'Ame du vin; CXXIX. The Wine of the Rag-Pickers/Le Vin de chiffonniers; CXXX. The Wine of the Assassin/Le Vin de l'assassin; CXXXI. The Wine of the Solitary/Le Vin du solitaire; CXXXII. The Wine of Lovers/Le Vin des amants; Les Fleurs du Mal: CXXXIII. Epigraph for a Condemned Book/Epigraphe pour un livre condamné; CXXXIV. Destruction/La Destruction; CXXXV. Une Martyre; CXXXVI. Femmes damnées; CXXXVII. The Two Kind Sisters/Les Deux Bonnes Sœurs; CXXXVIII. The Fountain of Blood/La Fontaine de sang; CXXXIX. Allégorie; CXL. Beatrice/La Béatrice; CXLI. Un voyage à Cythère; CXLII. Love and the Cranium/L'Amour et le crâne; RÉVOLTE: CXLIII. The Denial of St. Peter/Le Reniement de Saint Pierre; CXLIV. Abel et Caïn; CXLV. Litany to Satan/Les Litanies de Satan; LA MORT: CXLVI. The Death of Lovers/La Mort des amants; CXLVII. La Mort des pauvres; CXLVIII. La Mort des artistes; CXLIX. La Fin de la journée; CL. La Rêve d'un curieux; CLI. The Voyage/; [Jetsam]: I. Les Bijoux; II. Lethe/Le Léthé; III. To Her Who Is Too Gay/A celle qui est trop gaie; IV. Lesbos; V. Femmes damnées: Delphine et Hippolyte; VI. The Metamorphoses of the Vampire/Les Métamorphoses du vampire; Translations from the French: Marie Dauguet: [Untitled]/[Epilogue]; Théophile Gautier: The Flower-Pot/Le Pot de fleurs; The Impassible/ L'Impassible; Pastel; Gérard de Nerval: Artemis/Artémis; Golden Verses/Vers dorés; José-Maria de Heredia: Antony and Cleopatra/ Antoine et Cléopâtre; The Coral Reef/Le Récif de corail; La Dogaresse; Nemea/Némée;

Oblivion/L'Oubli; On a Broken Statue/Sur un Marbre brisé; The Samurai/Le Samouraï; A Setting Sun/Soleil couchant; The Stained Window/ Vitrail; Victor Hugo: Twilight/Crépuscule; What One Hears on the Mountain/Ce qu'on entend sur la montagne; The Wheel of Omphale/Le Rouet d'Omphale; Tristan Klingsor: Plaisir d'Amour; Alphonse Louis Marie de Lamartine: The Lake/Le Lac; Charles Marie René Leconte de Lisle: The Black Panther/La Panthère noire; Ecclesiastes/L'Ecclésiaste; The Exhibitionists/Les Montreurs; The Howlers/Les Hurleurs; The Sleep of the Condor/Le Sommeil du condor; Solvet seclum; Charles van Lerberghe: Song/Chanson; Pierre Lièvre: Elysian Landscape/Paysage Elyséen [text not found]; The End of Supper/[title unknown; text not found]; Stuart Merrill: A Woman at Prayer/Celle qui prie; Alfred de Musset: Remember Thee/Rappelle-toi; Song/Chanson; Sully-Prudhomme: Siesta/Sieste; Albert Samain: I Dream/[Untitled]; [Myrtil and Palemone]/[Myrtil et Palémone]; Fernand Severin: Sonnet/Bois sacré; Paul Verlaine: IX (Ariettes Oubliées); Il Bacio; La Bonne Chanson; Crimen Amoris; En Sourdine; The Faun/Le Faune; Green; Moonlight/Claire de lune; Song from *Les Uns et les autres*; Spleen [Spleen]; To a Woman/A une femme; TRANSLATIONS FROM THE SPANISH: Gustavo Adolfo Bécquer: Invocation/Rimas LII; The Sower/Rimas LX; Where?/Rimas XXXVIII; The World Rolls On/Rimas I (Libro de los gorriones); José A. Calcaño: The Cypress/El ciprés; José Santos Chocaño: The Sleep of the Cayman/El sueño del caimán; Rubén Darío: The Song of Songs/El Cantar de los Cantares; Juana de Ibarbourou: Rustic Life/Vida aldeana; Jorge Isaacs: Luminary/ Luminar; Juan Lozano y Lozano: Rhythm/Ritmo; Amado Nervo: Night/ Noche; Appendix: XXVII. *Sed non Satiata*; LV. L'Irréparable; CXLI. Un Voyage à Cythère; The Peace-Pipe, by Henry Wadsworth Longfellow; Notes; Index of Titles; Index of First Lines.

Notes. Another book long in the making, and one on which I had somewhat more involvement than my collaborator, although my own knowledge of French was by this time rusty and my knowledge of Spanish rudimentary at best.

70.   *Warnings to the Curious: A Sheaf of Criticism on M. R. James* (with Rosemary Pardoe)

    a.   New York: Hippocampus Press, [August] 2007.

        Contents: Introduction; I. SOME NOTES ON BIOGRAPHY: Stephen Gaselee, "Montague Rhodes James 1862–1936"; Shane Leslie, "Montague Rhodes James"; Norman Scarfe, "The Strangeness Present: M. R. James's Suffolk"; Michael Cox, "M. R. James and Livermere"; II. GENERAL STUDIES: H. P. Lovecraft, "Supernatural

Horror in Literature"; Mary Butts, "The Art of Montague James"; L. J. Lloyd, "The Ghost Stories of Montague Rhodes James"; Simon MacCulloch, "The Toad in the Study: M. R. James, H. P. Lovecraft, and Forbidden Knowledge"; III. SOME SPECIAL TOPICS: Michael A. Mason, "On Not Letting Them Lie: Moral Significance in the Ghost Stories of M. R. James"; Ron Weighell, "Dark Devotions: M. R. James and the Magical Tradition"; David G. Rowlands, "M. R. James's Women"; Jacqueline Simpson, "'The Rules of Folklore' in the Ghost Stories of M. R. James"; Brian Cowlishaw, "'A Warning to the Curious': Victorian Science and the Awful Unconscious in M. R. James's Ghost Stories"; Steve Duffy, "'They've Got Him! In the Trees!' M. R. James and Sylvan Dread"; Mike Pincombe, "Homosexual Panic and the English Ghost Story: M. R. James and Others"; John Alfred Taylor, "'If I'm Not Careful': Innocents and Not-So-Innocents in the Stories of M. R. James"; Steven J. Mariconda, "'As Time Goes On I See a Shadow Coming': M. R. James's Grammar of Terror"; Scott Connors, "'What Is This That I Have Done?' The Scapegoat Figure in the Stories of M. R. James"; IV. STUDIES OF INDIVIDUAL TALES: Helen Grant, "The Nature of the Beast: The Demonology of 'Canon Alberic's Scrap-book'"; C. E. Ward, "A Haunting Presence"; Rosemary Pardoe, "'A Wonderful Book': George MacDonald and 'The Ash-Tree'"; Rosemary Pardoe, "Who Was Count Magnus? Notes towards an Identification"; Nicholas Connell, "A Haunting Vision: M. R. James and the Ashridge Stained Glass"; Martin Hughes, "A Maze of Secrets in a Story by M. R. James"; Jim Rockhill, "Thin Ghosts: Notes toward a Jamesian Rhetoric"; Roger Craik, "Nightmares of Punch and Judy in Ruskin and M. R. James"; Lance Arney, "An Elucidation (?) of the Plot of M. R. James's 'Two Doctors'"; Jacqueline Simpson, "Landmarks and Shrieking Ghosts"; Rosemary Pardoe, "Addendum"; Bibliography; Acknowledgments; Index.

Notes. A volume that constituted, as it were, my peace offering to the James community, since I realised I had been unduly harsh on him in my chapter in *The Weird Tale.*

71.   *The Agnostic Reader*
   a.   Amherst, NY: Prometheus Books, [September] 2007.
       Contents: Introduction; I. SOME OVERVIEWS: Thomas Henry Huxley, "Agnosticism and Christianity"; Edgar Fawcett, "Agnosticism"; Clarence Darrow, "Why I Am an Agnostic"; Bertrand Russell, "What Is an Agnostic?"; II. THE CRITICAL STUDY OF RELIGION: David Friedrich Strauss, "The Life of Jesus Critically Examined"; Edward Burnett Tylor, "Primitive Culture"; Robert G. Ingersoll,

"About the Holy Bible"; Edward Westermarck, "Christianity and Morals"; III. AGNOSTICISM AND SCIENCE: John William Draper, "History of the Conflict Between Religion and Science"; Moncure Daniel Conway, "The Pre-Darwinite and Post-Darwinite World"; Albert Einstein, "Science and Religion"; Isaac Asimov, "In the Beginning . . ."; IV. THE DEFICIENCIES OF RELIGION: Arthur Schopenhauer, "The Christian System"; W. K. Clifford, "The Ethics of Religion"; Charles T. Gorham, "Christianity and Civilization"; V. Christianity in Decline: W. E. H. Lecky, "Rationalism in Europe"; Leslie Stephen, "Are We Christians?"; Harry Elmer Barnes, "The Twilight of Christianity"; Walter Lippmann, "God in the Modern World"; VI. THE AGNOSTIC WAY OF LIFE: G. W. Foote, "Secularism the True Philosophy of Life"; H. L. Mencken, "On Happiness"; Corliss Lamont, "The Ethics of Humanism"; Further Reading.

Notes. A volume that my publisher asked me to compile. Not as interesting as *Atheism: A Reader,* I think, but still containing some compelling material.

72.   *American Supernatural Tales*
 a.   New York: Penguin, [October] 2007.
 b.   New York: Penguin, [September] 2013 (as part of Penguin Horror, ed. Guillermo del Toro).

Contents: Introduction; Suggestions for Further Reading; Washington Irving, "The Adventure of the German Student"; Nathaniel Hawthorne, "Edward Randolph's Portrait"; Edgar Allan Poe, "The Fall of the House of Usher"; Fitz-James O'Brien, "What Was It?"; Ambrose Bierce, "The Death of Halpin Frayser"; Robert W. Chambers, "The Yellow Sign"; Henry James, "The Real Right Thing"; H. P. Lovecraft, "The Call of Cthulhu"; Clark Ashton Smith, "The Vaults of Yoh-Vombis"; Robert E. Howard, "Old Garfield's Heart"; Robert Bloch, "Black Bargain"; August Derleth, "The Lonesome Place"; Fritz Leiber, "The Girl with the Hungry Eyes"; Ray Bradbury, "The Fog Horn"; Shirley Jackson, "A Visit": Richard Matheson, "Long Distance Call"; Charles Beaumont, "The Vanishing American"; T. E. D. Klein, "The Events at Poroth Farm"; Stephen King, "Night Surf"; Dennis Etchison, "The Late Shift"; Thomas Ligotti, "Vastarien"; Karl Edward Wagner, "Endless Night"; Norman Partridge, "The Hollow Man"; David J. Schow, "Last Call for the Sons of Shock"; Joyce Carol Oates, "Demon"; Caitlin R. Kiernan, "In the Water Works"; Sources; Acknowledgments.

Notes. A volume that Penguin asked me to compile, for a hefty fee. I was forced to leave out stories by Edith Wharton, Mary E. Wilkins Freeman, and some others for space reasons. I assembled a table of contents for a *British Supernatural Tales*, but it has not yet been taken up; it may be in the future.

73.   Donald Wandrei, *Sanctity and Sin: The Collected Poems and Prose Poems of Donald Wandrei*
   a.   New York: Hippocampus Press, [June] 2008.
        Contents: Introduction; *Ecstasy and Other Poems:* The Voice of Beauty; Song of Autumn; Ecstasy; Let Us Love To-night; Vain Warning; On Some Drawings; Sanctity and Sin; To Myrrhiline; Song of Oblivion; In Mandrikor; The Woodland Pool; Death and the Poet: A Fragment; Satiation; In Memoriam: George Sterling; Bacchanalia; Awakening; Red; Hermaphroditus; Aphrodite; Amphitrite; Philomela; A Drinking Song; At the Bacchic Revel; The Challenger; The Greatest Regret; Futility; From the Shadowlands of Memory; The Poet's Language; Nightmare; Valerian; *Dark Odyssey:* Largo; Aubade; Fata Morgana; Borealis; In Memoriam: No Name; Dark Odyssey; Look Homeward, Angel; Under the Grass; You Will Come Back; After Bacchus, Eros; To Lucasta on Her Birthday; Villanelle à la Mode; For the Perishing Aphrodite; Morning Song; The Whispering Knoll; The Five Lords (Black; Green; Red; Purple; Chorus; White); Lost Atlantis; The Night Wind; The Voyagers' Return to Tyre; The Plague Ship; Chaos Resolved; Epithalamium; Epilude; POEMS FOR MIDNIGHT: Phantom; The Corpse Speaks; The Woman at the Window; Shadowy Night; The Worm-King; Water Sprite; Incubus; The Prehistoric Huntsman; Witches' Sabbath; Forest Shapes; The Dream That Dies; The Sleeper; The Moon-Glen Altar; The Morning of a Nymph; Death and the Traveler: A Fragment; King of the Shadowland; Ishmael; *Sonnets of the Midnight Hours* (After Sleep; Purple; The Old Companions; The Head; In the Attic; The Cocoon; The Metal God; The Little Creature; The Pool; The Prey; The Torturers; The Statues; The Hungry Flowers; The Eye; The Rack; Escape; Capture; In the Pit; The Unknown Color; Monstrous Form; Nightmare in Green; What Followed Me?; Fantastic Sculpture; The Tree; The Bell; The Ultimate Vision); Somewhere Past Ispahan; Uncollected Poems: The Poet's Lament; There Was a Smell of Dandelions; The Classicist; Pedagogues; Street Scene . . .; Chant to the Dead; The School of Seduction; Poems from *Broken Mirrors* (Fling Wide the Roses; Drink!; The Dead Mistress; My Lady Hath Two Lovely Lips; Aftermath; Credo; In Mandrikor); *Sonnets of the Midnight Hours* (Dream-Horror; The Grip of Evil Dreams; The Creatures; The Red Specter; Doom); *Moon Magic* (The Glow; The Song; The Overtone; The Dream); *Dead Fruit of the Fugitive Years* (The Dream Changes; Surrender; Though All My Days; The Second Beauty; Twice Excellent

Perfection; This Larger Room; The Woman Answers; The Deadly Calm; Corroding Acids; With Cat-like Tread); *Lyrics of Doubt* (A Testament of Desertion; To the God of My Fathers. Marmora; The Cypress-Bog; The Monster Gods; A Queen in Other Skies; Epitaph to a Lady; Portrait of a Lady During a Half Hour Wait While She Finished Dressing; The Little Gods Wait); [Poems from *Invisible Sun*]; [Limerick]; Elegy; September Hill; I Am Man; Golden Poppy; Solitary; Lines; Poems in Prose: The One Who Died; The Messengers; The Pursuers; Paphos; The Woman at the Window; Ebony and Silver; The Death of the Flowers; The Purple Land; The Lost Moon; Dreaming Away My Life; The Black Flame; The Shrieking House; The Kingdom of Dreams; Unforgotten Night; Santon Merlin; A Legend of Yesterday; From "The Tower of Sound"; An Epitaph on Jupiter; Commentary; Index of Titles; Index of First Lines.

Notes. An exhaustive revision of *Collected Poems* (item 4 above), with the addition of Wandrei's prose poems and much other matter, some of it supplied by D. H. Olson.

74/75. Clark Ashton Smith, *The Complete Poetry and Translations*, Volumes 1 and 2 (with David E. Schultz)
   a.   New York: Hippocampus Press, [July] 2008.
   b.   New York: Hippocampus Press, 2012 (paperback).
        Contents: Volume 1 (*The Abyss Triumphant*): Introduction; The Voice of Silence (1910–1911): Cloudland; The Fountain of Youth; The Road of Pain; Reincarnation; Lethe; A White Rose; Death; Companionship; Illusion; The Call of the Wind; The Expanding Ideal; Imagination; The Sunrise; Night; To a Yellow Pine; A Sierran Sunrise; The Sierras; The Wind and the Moon; Moonlight; The Altars of Sunset; To George Sterling; The Voice of Silence; Weavings; The West Wind; Before Sunrise; At Nadir; The Besieging Billows; The Butterfly; The Meaning; To the Nightshade; The Garden of Dreams; Ode to Matter; Ode to Poetry; The Pageant of Music; Autumn Dew; The Eclipse; The Falling Leaves; The Freedom of the Hills; The Hosts of Heaven; Ode on the Future of Song; The Suns and the Void; To George Sterling; Moods of the Sea; Sonnets of the Seasons; Spring; Summer; The Wizardry of Winter; The Storm; To the Morning Star; The Flower of the Night; A Sunset; War; Wings of Perfume; The Island of a Dream; Autumn's Pall; The Music of the Gods; The Night of Despair; Somnus; At Midnight; The Fanes of Dawn; The Summer Hills; To George Sterling; The Wind-Threnody; The Voice in the Pines; Black Enchantment; The Burden of the Suns; The Castle of Dreams; A Dream of Oblivion; A Dream of Darkness; The Revelation; The Dream-God's Realm; Ephemera;

The Eternal Gleam; Evening; The Harbour of the Past; In Extremis; Lost Beauty; Nature's Orchestra; The Past; The Present; The Future; Time the Wonder; The Palace of Jewels; The Past; The Potion of Dreams; The Power of Eld; Romance; The Song of the Worlds; Sonnet on Music; Sonnet on Oblivion; Sonnet to the Sphinx; Sphinx and Medusa; The Sphinx of the Infinite; The Tartarus of the Suns; The Temple of Night; The Throne of Winter; Time; To a Cloud; To a Mariposa Lily; To a Snowdrop; To Ambition; To the Crescent Moon; To the Morning Star; To Thomas Paine; To Thomas Paine; Twilight; The Twilight Woods; The Vampire Night; The Waning Moon; The Abyss Triumphant (1911–1912): Antony to Cleopatra; Poetry; The Last Night; The Eternal Snows; The Moonlight Desert; Nocturne; Ode to Music; The Dream-Weaver; Ode to the Abyss; Medusa; The Messengers; Chant to Sirius; The Horizon; A Dream of Beauty; A Live-Oak Leaf; Wind-Ripples; A Song from Hell; The Palace of Jewels; The Star-Treader; To George Sterling; The Dream-Bridge; The Nemesis of Suns; Retrospect and Forecast; The Song of a Comet; Said the Dreamer; Saturn; The Shadow of the Unattained; The Pursuer; Echo of Memnon; Nero; The Mad Wind; Finis; Ode to Light; In the Desert; The Return of Hyperion; To the Daemon Sublimity; Atlantis; Averted Malefice; The Balance; The Cherry-Snows; Copan; A Dead City; The Eldritch Dark; Epitaph for the Earth; Fairy Lanterns; The Fugitives; Lament of the Stars; Lethe; The Masque of Forsaken Gods; The Maze of Sleep; The Medusa of the Skies; The Night Forest; Nirvana; Ode on Imagination; Pine Needles; The Price; The Retribution; Shadow of Nightmare; The Snow-Blossoms; A Song of Dreams; The Song of the Stars; Song to Oblivion; The Soul of the Sea; The Summer Moon; To the Darkness; To the Sun; The Unremembered; White Death; The Winds; The Morning Pool; The Abyss Triumphant; The Last Goddess; Satan Unrepentant; The Titans in Tartarus; The Cloud-Islands; Remembered Light; The Sorrow of the Winds; Luna Aeternalis; [In the Ultimate Valleys]; The Nereid; A Phantasy at Twilight (1913–1917): The Ghoul; The Land of Evil Stars; The Clouds; The Doom of America; Nightmare; The City of the Titans; Desire of Vastness; The Medusa of Despair; The Refuge of Beauty; The Years Restored; The Witch in the Graveyard; The Sea-Gods; The Ministers of Law; Decadence; Somnus; To Beauty; The City of Destruction; The Orchid of Beauty; A Phantasy of Twilight; Beauty Implacable; The Nameless Wraith; The Ancient Quest; Aspect of Iron; Beyond the Door; The Harlot of the World; Psalm to the Desert; Inheritance; Memnon at Midnight; The City in the Desert; The Blindness of Orion; The Mirrors of Beauty; The Flight of Azrael; Duality; Love Malevolent; Exotique; Alien Memory; Fire of Snow; In the Wind; Lunar Mystery; Moon-Dawn; The Mummy; Morning on an Eastern Sea; Reclamation; Afterglow; Nocturne; The Crucifixion of Eros; Suggestion; Arabesque; Belated Love; November Twilight; Desolation; Coldness; The Kingdom of Shadows; Give Me Your Lips; Strangeness; Impression; The Exile; Ave atque Vale; The Tears of Lilith; Alexandrines; Autumnal; The Whisper of the Worm (1918–1920): A Vision of Lucifer; Sepulture; Palms; Mors; Dissonance; Eidolon; Haunting; Image; In November; Memorial; A Precept; Requiescat in Pace; In Saturn; Winter Moonlight; Inferno; The Whisper of the Worm; The Chimera; Autumn Orchards; Disillusionment; Ode to Peace; Antepast; Ashes of Sunset; At Sunrise; Crepuscule; The Melancholy Pool; Mirage; Mirrors; The Motes; Recompense; Satiety; Triple Aspect; Twilight on the Snow; Fantasie; Song of Sappho's Arabian Daughter; Forgetfulness; Transcendence; To the Beloved; Laus Mortis; The Traveller; Ombos; The Absence of the Muse; Quest; Symbols; Heliogabalus; The Hope of the Infinite; Flamingoes; Rosa Mystica; For a Wine-Jar; To Omar Khayyam; Beyond the Great Wall; Ennui; In Lemuria; Solution; The Ghoul and the Seraph; Tempus; The Dials; Silhouette; To Whom It May Concern; Speculation; Ode to Aphrodite; The Oracle; A Memory; To a Northern Venus; In Alexandria; The Incubus of Time; Amor Aeternalis; *The Hashish-Eater* (1920); The Infinite Quest (1920–1922): The Dream; Requiescat; To Nora May French; Psalm; A Psalm to the Best Beloved; Cleopatra; Nightfall; Ecstasy; Secret Love; The Hidden Paradise; The Infinite Quest; Exotic Memory; Satiety; Fawn-Lilies; Artemis; Plum-Flowers; Chance; Union; Song; Love Is Not Yours, Love Is Not Mine; Poplars; The Fugitives; The Song of Aviol; Song; The Love-Potion; The Song of Cartha; Chant of Autumn; A Fragment; Enchanted Mirrors (1923–1926): Selenique; Semblance; Change; Don Juan Sings; The Nymph; By the River; Fashion; The Witch with Eyes of Amber; On the Canyon-Side; We Shall Meet; The Secret; Contradiction; Alienage; Moments; Exchange; Metaphor; The Wingless Archangels; A Valediction; Cocaigne; Forgotten Sorrow; Septembral; Afterwards; The Barrier; The Funeral Urn; Dolor of Dreams; Brumal; Autumn Orchards; Remembrance; Departure; Diversity; The End of Autumn; On Re-reading Baudelaire; Lemurienne; You Are Not Beautiful; December; The Pagan; A Meeting; Adventure; Transmutation; The Last Oblivion; To the Chimera; Immortelle; In Autumn; Estrangement; A Catch; Consolation; The Temptation; Apologia; Incognita; Enigma; Query; Loss; Concupiscence; Maya; Dead Love; A Prayer; Enchanted Mirrors; Minatory; Interrogation; Madrigal; Sandalwood; October; The Envoys; Ode; Un Couchant; A Sunset; Un

Madrigal; A Madrigal; The Saturnienne; Apostrophe; Chansonette; Idylle païenne; Idylle païenne; Retrospect and Forecast; Sonnet lunaire; Sonnet lunaire; À Mi-Chemin; À Mi-Chemin; L'Abîme; Le Cauchemar; Chanson de rêve; Le Cheveu; Éloignement; Exotique; La Méduse des cieux; To George Sterling: A Valediction; After Armageddon; Juvenilia: [Untitled]; [Fragment 1]; [Fragment 2]; [Fragment 3]; [Fragment 4]; [Fragment 5]; [Fragment 6]; Benares; The Prayer Rug; The Rubaiyat of Seyyid; Sunrise; The Skull; The Orient; Time; To an Eastern City; Fortune; The Ocean; Allah; Arab Song; Arabian Love-Song; Bedouin Song; The City of the Djinn; The Desert; A Dream of Vathek; A Dream of Zanoni; Eblis Repentant; From the Persian; From the Persian; From the Persian; Haroun Al-Raschid; The Inscription; Jewel of the Orient; Jewel of the Orient; Kismet; Mohammed; The Muezzin; Ode from the Persian; Odes of Alnaschar; Omar's Philosophy; The Palace of the Jinn; The Prayer Rug; The Prince and the Peri; Quatrain; Quatrains; Quatrains; The Snare; Song; Quatrains on Jewels; The Diamond; The Pearl; The Turquoise; The Ruby; The Opal; Rubaiyat; Rubaiyat; Rubaiyat of Saiyed; The Seekers; Some Maxims from the Persian; Stamboul; Suleyman Jan ben Jan; The Temple; The World; Youth and Age; Zuleika; Asia; Aurungzeb's Mosque; The Burning Ghauts; The Burning-Ghauts at Benares; Dawn; Delhi; A Dream of India; The Ganges; Alchemy; The Book of Years; Courage; The Days of Time; The Departed City; A Dream; Fear; The Fear of Death; The Feast; Hate and Love; Hope; The Land o' Dreams; The Leveler; Love; The Lure of Gold; Mercy; The Moon; Perseverance; Poem [?]; Resignation; The River; The River of Life; Sea-Lure; The Sea-Shell; Silence; Solitude; Summer Idleness; To the Best Beloved; The World; [Fragment 7].

Volume 2 (The Wine of Summer): Spectral Life (1927–1929): Les Violons; Au Bord du Léthé; The Nevermore-to-Be; Fantaisie d'antan; Canticle; A Fable; De Consolation; De Consolation; Simile; Trope; Venus; One Evening; Tristan to Iseult; Souvenance; To Antares; Song; Amor Autumnalis; Warning; Temporality; Chansonette; Chansonette; Credo; The Autumn Lake; Le Lac d'automne; On a Chinese Vase; November; Chanson de Novembre; Chanson de Novembre; Exorcism; Winter Moonlight; Connaissance; Harmony; Moon-Sight; Sonnet; Similitudes; Calendar; February; Variations; Sufficiency; Lichens; Vaticinations; Nyctalops; The Hill-Top; L'Amour suprême; L'Amour suprême; Alexandrins; Absence; Une Vie spectrale; Spectral Life; Seins; Les Marées; Paysage païen; Le Souvenir; Rêvasserie; La Mare; Le Miroir des blanches fleurs; Le Miroir des blanches fleurs; The Dragon-Fly; September; Shadows; Evanescence; Fellowship; Ougabalys; Ineffability; The Nightmare

Tarn; Cumuli; Refuge; Some Older Bourn (1930–1938): Answer; Song at Evenfall; Jungle Twilight; Madrigal of Evanescence; Solicitation; An Old Theme; Psalm; The Pool; Revenant; A Dream of the Abyss; In Slumber; Necromancy; Outlanders; Dominion; In Thessaly; The Phoenix; The Outer Land; Day-Dream; Contra Mortem; The Cycle; Kin; Sanctuary; Simile; Le Refuge; Le Refuge; La Forteresse; The Fortress; Sonnet; Ennui; Adjuration; Song of the Necromancer; Rêves printaniers; Rêves printaniers; Amour bizarre; L'Ensorcellement; Le Fabliau d'un dieu; Orgueil; Sea-Memory; Farewell to Eros; Indian Summer; Mystery; Touch; To Howard Phillips Lovecraft; The Prophet Speaks; Desert Dweller; Requiescat; Wizard's Love; The Last and Utmost Land (1939–1947): From Arcady; Ode; Sestet; Bacchante; Resurrection; Witch-Dance; Song of the Bacchic Bards; Anteros; Lamia; Interim; Sonnet; To One Absent; Silent Hour; Grecian Yesterday; But Grant, O Venus; Bond; Madrigal of Memory; "That Last Infirmity"; The Thralls of Circe Climb Parnassus; Dialogue; The Mime of Sleep; The Old Water-Wheel; Fragment; Yerba Buena; Consummation; Humors of Love; Town Lights; The Sorcerer to His Love; To George Sterling; L'Espoir du néant; Amor Hesternalis; "All Is Dross That Is Not Helena"; Future Pastoral; Wine of Summer; In Another August; Nocturne: Grant Avenue; Classic Epigram; Twilight Song; Supplication; Erato; Anodyne of Autumn; The Hill of Dionysus; Before Dawn; Amor; Interval; Postlude; Strange Girl; De Profundis; Midnight Beach; Illumination; Omniety; Even in Slumber; Moly; Cambion; The Knoll; For an Antique Lyre; On Trying to Read *Four Quartets*; Greek Epigram; Lines on a Picture; Alternative; Hymn; The Sorcerer Departs; Surréalist Sonnet; Paean; Do You Forget, Enchantress?; The Horologe; Parnassus à la Mode; Sea Cycle; Dancer; Nevermore; Reverie in August; Tin Can on the Mountain-Top; Some Blind Eidolon; The Pursuer; To Bacchante; Calenture; Copyist; Love and Death; Quintrains; Essence; Epitaph for an Astronomer; The Heron; Bird of Long Ago; Late November Evening; Mithridates; Mummy of the Flower; Nightmare of the Lilliputian; Passing of an Elder God; Poets in Hades; Quiddity; Someone; Dying Prospector; Experiments in Haiku (1947): Strange Miniatures; Unicorn; Untold Arabian Fable; A Hunter Meets the Martichoras; The Limniad; The Sciapod; The Monacle; Feast of St. Anthony; Paphnutius; Philtre; Borderland; Lethe; Empusa Waylays a Traveller; Perseus and Medusa; Odysseus in Eternity; The Ghost of Theseus; Distillations; Fence and Wall; Growth of Lichen; Cats in Winter Sunlight; Abandoned Plum-Orchard; Harvest Evening; Willow-Cutting in Autumn; Declining Moon; Late Pear-Pruner; Nocturnal Pines; Phallus Impudica; Stormy

Afterglow; Geese in the Spring Night; Foggy Night; Reigning Empress; The Sparrow's Nest; The Last Apricot; Mushroom-Gatherers; Spring Nunnery; Nuns Walking in the Orchard; Improbable Dream; Crows in Spring; High Mountain Juniper; Storm's End; Pool at Lobos; Poet in a Barroom; Fallen Grape-Leaf; Gopher-Hole in Orchard; Basin in Boulder; Indian Acorn-Mortar; Old Limestone Kiln; Love in Dreams; Night of Miletus; Tryst at Lobos; Mountain Trail; Future Meeting; Classic Reminiscence; Goats and Manzanita-Boughs; Bed of Mint; Chainless Captive; California Winter; January Willow; Snowfall on Acacia; Flight of the Yellow-Hammer; Sunset over Farm-Land; Flora; Windows at Lamplighting Time; Old Hydraulic Diggings; Hearth on Old Cabin-Site; Builder of Deserted Hearth; Aftermath of Mining Days; River-Canyon; Childhood; School-Room Pastime; Boys Telling Bawdy Tales; Fight on the Play-Ground; Water-Fight; Boys Rob a Yellow-Hammer's Nest; Nest of the Screech-Owl; Grammar-School Vixen; Girl of Six; Mortal Essences; Snake, Owl, Cat or Hawk; Slaughter-House in Spring; Cattle Salute the Psychopomp; Slaughter-House Pasture; Field Behind the Abatoir; Plague from the Abatoir; La Mort des amants; Vultures Come to the Ambarvalia; For the Dance of Death; Berries of the Deadly Nightshade; Water-Hemlock; Felo-de-se of the Parasite; Pagans Old and New; Initiate of Dionysus; Bacchic Orgy; Abstainer; Picture by Piero di Cosimo; Bacchants and Bacchante; Garden of Priapus; Morning Star of the Mountains; Bygone Interlude; Prisoner in Vain; Epitaphs; Braggart; Slaughtered Cattle; The Earth; Miscellaneous Haiku; Illuminatus; Limestone Cavern; Maternal Prostitute; Ocean Twilight; Radio; Tule-Mists; If Winter Remain (1948–1950): Hellenic Sequel; No Stranger Dream; On the Mount of Stone; Only to One Returned; Sonnet for the Psychoanalysts; Avowal; Tolometh; If Winter Remain; Almost Anything; "That Motley Drama"; Pour Chercher du nouveau; Dans l'univers lointain; In a Distant Universe; High Surf: Monterey Bay; Isaac Newton; La Muse moderne; The Mystical Number; Pantheistic Dream; Rêve panthéistique; Poèmes d'amour; Sandalwood and Onions; The Dark Chateau; Don Quixote on Market Street; The Isle of Saturn; "O Golden-Tongued Romance"; Averoigne; Zothique; Le poéte parle avec ses biographes; The Poet Talks with the Biographers; Beauty; La Hermosura; Las Poetas del optimismo; The Poets of Optimism; El Cantar de los seres libres; Song of the Free Beings; ¿Donde duermes, Eldorado?; Where Sleepest Thou, O Eldorado?; Los Dueños; Dominium in Excelsis; Parnaso; Parnassus; Las Alquerías perdidas; Lost Farmsteads; Cantar; Song; Eros in the Desert; Dice el soñador; Says the Dreamer; Memoria roja; Red Memory; Dos Mitos y una fábula; Two Myths

and a Fable; La Nereida; La Isla de Circe; The Isle of Circe; Lo Igno-
to; The Unknown; Leteo; [Lethe]; Añoranza; Melancholia; El
Vendaval; El Vendaval; Farmyard Fugue; Didus Ineptus; Amithaine;
Malediction; Shapes in the Sunset; Sinbad, It Was Not Well to Brag;
El Eros de ébano; Eros of Ebony; THE DEAD WILL CUCKOLD YOU
(1950); THE SORCERER DEPARTS (1951–1961): The Stylite; Two on a
Pillar; Not Theirs the Cypress-Arch; Alpine Climber; Hesperian Fall;
"Not Altogether Sleep"; Seeker; Soliloquy in a Ebon Tower; The
Twilight of the Gods; Qu'Importe?; ¿Qué sueñas, Musa?; What
Dreamest Thou, Muse?; Que songes-tu, Muse?; Ye Shall Return;
Lives of the Saints; Secret Worship; The Song of Songs; STYES
WITH SPIRES; In Time of Absence; Nada; Seer of the Cycles; I
Shall Not Greatly Grieve; Geometries; Alchemy; Sacraments; Delay;
Verity; La Isla del náufrago; Isle of the Shipwrecked; Thebaid; Sa-
turnian Cinema; Dedication: To Carol; The Centaur; Lawn-Mower;
Tired Gardener; High Surf; H. P. L.; Cycles; FRAGMENTS AND
UNTITLED POEMS: Al borde del Leteo; Ballad of a Lost Soul; The
Brook; Demogorgon; Despondency; The Flight of the Seraphim; For
Iris; Haunting; The Milky Way; Night; The Night Wind; No-Man's-
Land; Ode on Matter; The Regained Past; The Saturnienne; Sonnets
of the Desert; The Temptation; To a Comet; To Iris; To Iris; To the
Sun; The Vampire Night; [miscellaneous fragments]; Broceliande;
[miscellaneous fragments]; Twilight Pilgrimage; [miscellaneous frag-
ments]; Limericks; Ripe Mulberries; From "Ode to Antares"; From
"The Song of Xeethra"; From "Song of the Galley Slaves"; From
"Song of King Hoaraph's Bowmen"; From "Ludar's Litany to
Thasaidon"; From "Ludar's Litany to Thasaidon"; Appendix: Prospective Tables of Contents: The Jasmine Girdle; The Jasmine Gir-
dle and Other Poems; Incantations; The Abalone Song;
Translations: The Desire of Loving [a translation of "Le Désir
d'Aimer" by Hélène Picard; [Sandalwood]; Voices; Notes; Index of
Titles; Index of First Lines.

Notes. Two volumes for which I unfairly received top billing (for
the lame reason that Vol. 3 of the edition—item 67 above—had
already appeared, in which I was listed as top editor), since Schultz
had been working on this edition for years, maybe decades, and I got
in only at a very late stage of compilation. The paperback edition
prints several additional poems.

76.   Gertrude Atherton, *The Caves of Death and Other Stories*
   a.   Tampa, FL: University of Tampa Press, [August] 2008.
         Contents: Statement; Introduction; The Caves of Death; Death
         and the Woman; A Tragedy; When the Devil Was Well; Miss Mark-

ham's Wedding Night; The Striding Place; The Greatest Good of the Greatest Number; The Dead and the Countess; The Bell in the Fog; Notes; Afterword; Suggestions for Further Reading; About the Editor; About the Series Editors; About the Book.

Notes. A smallish book of Atherton's weird tales, including some unreprinted items. The introduction was reprinted in I.47 as "Gertrude Atherton: Death and Women."

77.   *Icons of Unbelief: Atheists, Agnostics, and Secularists*
      a.   Westport, CT: Greenwood Press, [November] 2008.

            Contents: Series Foreword; Preface; Jenin Younes, "Ayaan Hirsi Ali"; Donald Tribe, "Charles Bradlaugh"; Donald R. Burleson, "Richard Dawkins"; Richard Gillilan, "Daniel C. Dennett"; John Shook, "John Dewey"; Mauro Murzi, "Albert Einstein"; Max Deutscher, "The Existentialists"; Edd Doerr, "The Founding Fathers"; Kirk Bingaman, "Sigmund Freud"; Jenin Younes, "Sam Harris"; Sherrie Lyons, "Thomas Henry Huxley"; Tom Flynn, "Robert G. Ingersoll"; Bill Cooke, "Paul Kurtz"; Robert M. Price, "H. P. Lovecraft"; S. T. Joshi, "H. L. Mencken"; S. T. Joshi, "John Stuart Mill"; Béla Szabados and Andrew Lugg, "Kai Nielsen"; Weaver Santaniello, "Friedrich Nietzsche"; Frank R. Zindler, "Madalyn Murray O'Hair"; Wilda Anderson, "The *Philosophes*"; Keith M. Parsons, "Bertrand Russell"; John Shook, "Carl Sagan"; S. T. Joshi, "Leslie Stephen"; Richard Bleiler, "Mark Twain"; S. T. Joshi, "Gore Vidal"; Jean-Claude Pecker, "Voltaire"; General Bibliography; About the Contributors; Index.

            Notes. A volume analogous to *Icons of Horror and the Supernatural* (items 65/66 above), although the essays were not quite as lengthy. I reprinted my four pieces in *The Unbelievers* (I.37).

78.   Mark Twain, *What Is Man? and Other Irreverent Essays*
      a.   Amherst, NY: Prometheus Books, [January] 2009.

            Contents: Introduction; What Is Man?; Reflections on the Sabbath; About Smells; The Indignity Put upon the Remains of George Holland by the Rev. Mr. Sabine; The Revised Catechism; The Second Advent; The Character of Man; Letter from the Recording Angel; Three Statements from the 1880s; Bible Teaching and Religious Practice; Man's Place in the Animal World; Thoughts of God; "Was the World Made for Man?"; As Concerns Interpreting the Deity; God; Christian Citizenship; The Ten Commandments; Reflections on Religion; Little Bessie; Things a Scotsman Wants to Know.

Notes. A volume commissioned by the publisher, and containing some of Twain's more outrageous remarks on and lampoons of religion.

79.   H. L. Mencken, *Collected Poems*
   a.   New York: Hippocampus Press, [September] 2009.
         Contents: Introduction; To R. K.; The Four-Foot Filipino: A Ballad of the Trenches; The Tin-Clads; Joe and Bobs; Auroral; One Man Band; A Frivolous Rondeau; A Few Lines; The Roorback and the Canard; Chrysanthemum; Canzonette; [Untitled]; An Ante-Christmas Rondeau; The Dawn of Love; [Untitled]; Fidelis ad Urnum; [Untitled]; A Ballad of Impecuniosity; A War Song; A Madrigal; A Song for Autumn; Nocturne; An Ode to a "Stein"; The Filipino Maiden; A Rondeau of Two Hours; When the Pipe Goes Out; Thanksgiving Day; Adlai; A Dirge; A Bacteriologal Romance; To O. P. K.; And Now Comes Congress; The Man That Guards the Grub; A Ballad of Looking; Well Buried; The Orf'cer Boy; A Paradox; Madrigal; The Song of the Slapstick; An Old, Old Story; Love and the Rose; The Coming of Winter; Outside, Old Year!; To Isaackhanmofakhammeddovlet; The Boy and the Man; The Donation Party; To Kruger; A Rondeau of Statesmanship; In Eating Soup; Serenade; Im Hinterland; The Snow; A Ballad of Fierce Fighters; The Pantoum of Congress; To Mrs. Nation; In Vaudeville; A Slug of Pessimism; An Ode to Nelson A.; To G. W.; A Sonnet to a Wienerwurst; The Ballade of the Rank and File; To Wu Ting Fang, Envoy Extraordinary and Minister Plenipotentiary; On Phyllis at the Play; Theatrical Alphabet; April; Dawn; A Villanelle; The Transport Gen'ral Ferguson; Faith; The Spanish Main; The Rondeau of Riches; A Ballade of Protest; Preliminary Rebuke; The Song of the Olden Time; The Ballad of Ships in Harbor; The Violet; September; Arabesque; The Rhymes of Mistress Dorothy; Roundel; Within the City Gates; Il Penseroso; Finis; War; On Passing the Island of San Salvador; Starting for the Play; Good-By, Divine Sarah!; The Old Trails; The Ballade of Cockaigne; Song; Invocation; The Voices; APPENDIX: A Kruger, by Edmond Rostand; Notes; Index of Titles; Index of First Lines.
         Notes. Something of an indulgence. This slim volume contains a great many uncollected poems by Mencken (mostly from very early newspaper columns of 1900–05). It seemed unlikely that any mainstream publisher would issue it, but Derrick Hussey kindly let me issue it under his imprint. The introduction was reprinted in I.50 as part of "Mencken as Creative Artist."

80.   Arthur Machen, *The Great God Pan and Other Weird Stories*
      a.   Modesto, CA: Arcane Wisdom, 2009 [January 2010].
           Contents: Introduction; The Great God Pan; The Three Impostors;
           The Shining Pyramid; The White People; A Fragment of Life; The
           Bowmen; Appendix 1: Introduction to *The Three Impostors* (1923);
           Appendix 2: Introduction to *The Angels of Mons* (1915); Notes; Bibli-
           ography.
           Notes. Yet another edition of Machen, this time annotated; it un-
           wittingly served as the prelude for my Penguin edition.

81.   H. L. Mencken, *Mencken on Mencken: New Autobiographical Writings*
      a.   Baton Rouge: Louisiana State University Press, [January] 2010.
           Contents: Introduction; A Note on This Edition; Prologue: Henry
           Louis Mencken (1905); Memories of a Long Life; Author and Jour-
           nalist; Thinker; World Traveler; Epilogue: Henry Louis Mencken
           (1936); Notes; Glossary of Names; Bibliography of Original Appear-
           ances; Index.
           Notes. A volume based on a number of late memoirs that Menck-
           en wrote but failed to include in his three standard autobiographical
           volumes.

82.   *Black Wings: New Tales of Lovecraftian Horror*
      a.   Hornsea, UK: PS Publishing, [March] 2010.
      b.   New York & London: Titan Books, 2012 (as *Black Wings of
           Cthulhu*).
           Contents: Introduction; Caitlín R. Kiernan, "Pickman's Other
           Model (1929)"; Donald R. Burleson, "Desert Dreams"; Joseph S.
           Pulver, Sr., "Engravings"; Michael Shea, "Copping Squid"; Sam Gaf-
           ford, "Passing Spirits"; Laird Barron, "The Broadsword"; William
           Browning Spencer, "Usurped"; David J. Schow, "Denker's Book";
           W. H. Pugmire, "Inhabitants of Wraithwood"; Mollie L. Burleson,
           "The Dome"; Nicholas Royle, "Rotterdam"; Jonathan Thomas,
           "Tempting Providence"; Darrell Schweitzer, "Howling in the Dark";
           Brian Stableford, "The Truth about Pickman"; Philip Haldeman,
           "Tunnels"; Michael Cisco, "Violence, Child of Trust"; Norman Par-
           tridge, "Lesser Demons"; Ramsey Campbell, "The Correspondence
           of Cameron Thaddeus Nash"; Adam Niswander, "An Eldritch Mat-
           ter"; Michael Marshall Smith, "Substitutions"; Jason Van Hollander,
           "Susie"; Notes on Contributors.
           Notes. My first original anthology of horror tales—an outgrowth of
           my work on *The Rise and Fall of the Cthulhu Mythos*, and originally de-
           signed for publication with Arkham House. But after April Derleth
           sat on the ms. for months without making a decision, I took it to PS

Publishing. Pete Crowther, the publisher, accepted the book without reading it—based solely on the table of contents.

83.   Montague Glass, *Potash and Perlmutter: Stories of the American Jewish Experience*
      a.   San Bernardino, CA: Borgo Press, [March] 2010.
           Contents: Introduction; The Early Bird; Firing Miss Cohen; Taking It Easy; The Perfect 36; An Up-to-Date Feller; The Walking Delegate; The Fly in the Ointment; "R. S. V. P."; Deeds—Not Words; Sympathy; The Trail of the Silk; Dead Men's Shoes; The Raincoat King; Brothers All; Lucky Numbers; Revolutionizing the Revolution Business; The Approaching Royal Visit; Keeping Expenses Down; APPENDIX: The Truth about Potash and Perlmutter; "Some of My Best Friends Are—"; Bibliography; About the Author.
           Notes. A book that came about through my interest in H. L. Mencken, who was very cordial to the work of Glass in his book review columns. He proved to be a very intriguing writer—something of a predecessor to Leo Rosten as an example of American Jewish humour.

84.   Edna W. Underwood, *Dear Dead Women: The Weird Stories of Edna W. Underwood*
      a.   Leyburn, UK: Tartarus Press, [May] 2010.
           Contents: Introduction; The Painter of Dead Women; The Mirror of La Granja; Liszt's Concerto Pathétique; Sister Seraphine; The Sacred Relics of Saint Euthymius; The Opal Isles; The House of Gauze; The King; An Orchid of Azia; Bibliography.
           Notes. A collection founded on Underwood's rare collection *A Book of Dear Dead Women* (1911), with the addition of a later novella. The introduction was reprinted in I.47 as "Edna W. Underwood: Dear Dead Women."

85.   *Encyclopedia of the Vampire*
      a.   Santa Barbara, CA: Greenwood Press, [November] 2010.
           Contents: Preface; Alphabetical List of Entries; Guide to Related Topics; The Encyclopedia; General Bibliography; About the Editor and Contributors; Index.
           Notes. A volume commissioned by the publisher, but one in which I took little interest. It probably shows.

86.   *A Weird Writer in Our Midst: Early Criticism of H. P. Lovecraft*
      a.   New York: Hippocampus Press, [December] 2010.

Contents: Introduction; I. RECOLLECTIONS OF LOVECRAFT: Howard P. Lovecraft [1890–1937], by Walter J. Coates; Amateur Affairs, by Hyman Bradofsky; [Letter to the Editor], by Robert Bloch; Interlude with Lovecraft, by Stuart M. Boland; Howard Phillips Lovecraft, by Muriel E. Eddy; I Met Lovecraft, by Paul Livingston Keil; The Man Who Came at Midnight, by Ruth M. Eddy; II. CRITICISM IN LOVECRAFT'S LIFETIME: A Note on Howard P. Lovecraft's Verse, by Rheinhart Kleiner; Howard P. Lovecraft's Fiction, by W. Paul Cook; The Vivisector, by Zoilus [Alfred Galpin]; Preface to *The Shunned House*, by Frank Belknap Long, Jr.; A Weird Writer Is in Our Midst, by Vrest Orton; The Sideshow, by B. K. Hart; What Makes a Story Click?, by J. Randle Luten; III. COMMENTS FROM READERS (extracts from the letter columns of *Weird Tales* and *Astounding Stories*); IV. CRITICISM FROM THE FAN WORLD: H. P. Lovecraft, Outsider, by August Derleth; A Master of the Macabre, by August Derleth; Disbelievers Ever, by R. W. Sherman; The Last of H. P. Lovecraft, by J. B. Michel; What of H. P. Lovecraft? or, A Commentary upon J. B. Michel, by Autolycus; H. P. Lovecraft: Strange Weaver, by J. Chapman Miske; Lovecraft and Benefit Street, by Dorothy Walter; [Letters to the Editor], by Thomas Ollive Mabbott; A Plea for Lovecraft, by W. Paul Cook; Let's All Jump on H.P.L., by P. Schuyler Miller; Howard Phillips Lovecraft, by Michael Harrison; The Lovecraft Cult, by Arthur F. Hillman; Lovecraft Is 86, by Francis T. Laney; Rusty Chains, by John Brunner; Some Notes on HPL, by Sam Moskowitz, Fritz Leiber, Edward Wood, and John Brunner; V. NOTICES FROM THE LITERARY COMMUNITY: Mystery and Adventure, by Will Cuppy; Horror Story Author Published by Fellow Writers, by Anonymous; [Review of *The Outsider and Others*], by T. O. Mabbott; Such Pulp as Dreams Are Made On, by Robert Allerton Parker; Macabre, Lyrical and Weird, by Peter De Vries; Mystery and Adventure, by Will Cuppy; Nightmare in Cthulu, by William Poster; Books Alive, by Vincent Starrett; Bookman's Holiday, by Charles Collins; Mystery and Adventure, by Will Cuppy; Poesque Doodles, by Marjorie Farber; Books Alive, by Vincent Starrett; The Phoenix Nest, by William Rose Benét; [Review of *Supernatural Horror in Literature*], by Fred Lewis Pattee; Pilgrims through Space and Time, by J. O. Bailey; Imagination Runs Wild, by Richard B. Gehman; Books Alive, by Vincent Starrett; A Bookman's Notebook, by Joseph Henry Jackson; Sabbat-Night Reading, by E. O. D. Keown; Of Good and Evil, by [Anthony Powell]; The Genius Who Lived Backwards, by Vincent H. Gaddis; Appendix: Some Vignettes; Notes; Index.

Notes. A volume I had long planned. I took occasion to reprint the letters about Lovecraft in *Weird Tales* (from *H. P. Lovecraft in "The Eyrie"* [item 1 above]), adding the letters in *Astounding Stories* (1936) and sundry other material, including early reviews of the Arkham House books.

87. W. H. Pugmire, *The Tangled Muse*
  a. Lakewood, CO: Centipede Press, [December] 2010. [withdrawn]
  b. Lakewood, CO: Centipede Press, [February] 2011.

  Contents: Introduction; Totem Pole; Beyond the Realm of Dream; Born in Strange Shadow; The Darkest Star; Dust to Dust; Heritage of Hunger; An Imp of Aether; Child of Dark Mania; The Hands That Reek and Smoke; Host of Haunted Air; The Woven Offspring; The Zanies of Sorrow; The Phantom of Beguilement; A Vestige of Mirth; An Eidolon of Nothing; The Fungal Stain; Hour of Their Appetite; The Sign That Sets the Darkness Free; Jigsaw Boy; Balm of Nepenthe; The Saprophytic Fungi; *Stupor Mundi*; His Splintered Kiss; Your Metamorphic Moan; The Boy with the Bloodstained Mouth; Bloom of Sacrifice; Time of Twilight; He Who Made Me Dream; Garden of Shattered Faces; Some Buried Memory; Inhabitants of Wraithwood; The Tangled Muse; In Memoriam: Oscar Wilde; Afterword, by W. H. Pugmire.

  Notes. A fine selection of the best stories by one of our leading neo-Lovecraftians. The first printing had to be scrapped because of some disagreement with the artist.

88. Ambrose Bierce, *The Devil's Dictionary, Tales, & Memoirs*
  a. New York: Library of America, [August] 2011.

  Contents: In the Midst of Life (Tales of Soldiers and Civilians); Can Such Things Be?; The Devil's Dictionary; Bits of Autobiography; Selected Stories; Chronology; Note on the Texts; Notes.

  Notes. A volume whose compilation I had discussed for years with the editors of the Library of America. It seems to have been well received.

89. Maurice Level, *Tales of the Grand Guignol*
  a.1. Lakewood, CO: Centipede Press, [September] 2011.
  a.2. Lakewood, CO: Centipede Press, n.d.
  b. Mineola, NY: Dover, [March] 2016 (abridged; as *Thirty Hours with a Corpse and Other Tales of the Grand Guignol*).

  Contents: Introduction; *The Grip of Fear*; *Tales of Mystery and Horror:* The Debt Collector; The Kennel; Who?; Illusion; In the Light of the Red Lamp; A Mistake; Extenuating Circumstances; The Confession; The Test; Poussette; The Father; "For Nothing"; In the Wheat; The

Beggar; Under Chloroform; The Man Who Lay Asleep; Fascination; The Bastard; That Scoundrel Miron; The Taint; The Kiss; A Maniac; The 10:50 Express; Blue Eyes; The Empty House; The Last Kiss; Under Ether; The Spirit of Alsace; At the Movies; The Little Soldier; The Great Scene; After the War; The Appalling Gift; Night and Silence; The Cripple; The Look; The Horror on the Night Express; Thirty Hours with a Corpse; She Thought of Everything; *Those Who Return.*

Notes. A volume containing virtually the entirety of Level's fiction (short stories and two novels) that had been translated into English. The very small (100 copies) first printing was quickly exhausted, so the publisher eventually issued a second print of about 300 copies. The Dover edition prints only the short stories, omitting the two novels. The introduction was reprinted in I.47 as "Maurice Level and the Grand Guignol."

90.   Barry Pain, *The Undying Thing and Others*
    a.   New York: Hippocampus Press, [September] 2011.

       Contents: Introduction; "Bill"; The Glass of Supreme Moments; Exchange; The Diary of a God; This Is All; The Moon-Slave; The Green Light; The Magnet; The Case of Vincent Pyrwhit; The Bottom of the Gulf; The End of a Show; The Undying Thing; The Gray Cat; The Four-Fingered Hand; The Tower; The Unfinished Game; The Unseen Power; The Widower; Smeath; Linda; Celia and the Ghost; The Tree of Death; Not on the Passenger-List; The Reaction; The Missing Years; *The Shadow of the Unseen* (with James Blyth); Bibliography.

       Notes. A volume spanning the totality of Pain's copious but very uneven weird work. His short novel *An Exchange of Souls* had been reprinted earlier by Hippocampus. The introduction was reprinted in I.52.

91.   Arthur Machen, *The White People and Other Weird Stories*
    a.   New York: Penguin, [October] 2011.

       Contents: Foreword: The Ecstasy of St. Arthur, by Guillermo del Toro; Introduction; Suggestions for Further Reading; A Note on the Texts; The Inmost Light; Novel of the Black Seal; Novel of the White Powder; The Red Hand; The White People; A Fragment of Life; The Bowmen; The Soldiers' Rest; The Great Return; Out of the Earth; The Terror; Explanatory Notes.

       Notes. Another volume long in the making, and one that the Penguin Classics editors were only inclined to publish if del Toro delivered a foreword. He did, so the book came out. It completes my

Penguin editions of the "big four" weird writers (Machen, Dunsany, Blackwood, James) as identified by Lovecraft.

92.   Donald Wandrei, *Dead Titans, Waken!; Invisible Sun*
      a.   Lakewood, CO: Centipede Press, [October] 2011.
      b.   Nampa, ID: Fedogan & Bremer, [August] 2017.
            Contents: A Note on the Texts; Dead Titans, Waken!; Invisible Sun; Notes; Afterword.
            Notes. A book compiled as early as 1999 for Fedogan & Bremer, but their temporary collapse prevented publication for more than a decade. *Invisible Sun* is a previously unpublished mainstream novel with some weird touches. The afterword was reprinted in I.47 as "The Novels of Donald Wandrei."

93.   *Dissecting Cthulhu: Essays on the Cthulhu Mythos*
      a.   Lakeland, FL: Miskatonic River Press, [December] 2011.
            Contents: Introduction; I. SOME OVERVIEWS: Richard L. Tierney, "The Derleth Mythos"; Dirk W. Mosig, "H. P. Lovecraft: Myth-Maker"; David E. Schultz, "Who Needs the 'Cthulhu Mythos'?"; Simon MacCulloch, "Lovecraft Waits Dreaming"; S. T. Joshi, "The Cthulhu Mythos: Lovecraft vs. Derleth"; Steven J. Mariconda, "Toward a Reader-Response Approach to the Lovecraft Mythos"; II. THE BOOKS: Robert M. Price, "Genres in the Lovecraftian Library"; Robert M. Price, "Higher Criticism and the *Necronomicon*"; Dan Clore, "The Lurker at the Threshold of Interpretation"; III. THE GODS: Robert M. Price, "Demythologizing Cthulhu"; Robert M. Price, "The Last Vestige of the Derleth Mythos"; Will Murray, "Behind the Mask of Nyarlathotep"; Will Murray, "On the Natures of Nug and Yeb"; IV. THE LANDSCAPE: Robert D. Marten, "Arkham Country: In Rescue of the Lost Searchers"; Will Murray, "Where Was Foxfield?"; Edward W. O'Brien, "Lovecraft's Two Views of Arkham"; V. INFLUENCES: Marco Frenschowski, "Hali"; Jason C. Eckhardt, "Cthulhu's Scald: Lovecraft and the Nordic Tradition"; David E. Schultz, "The Origin of Lovecraft's 'Black Magic' Quote"; Robert M. Price, "Robert E. Howard and the Cthulhu Mythos"; Stefan Dziemianowicz, "Divers Hands"; Suggestions for Further Reading.
            Notes. A volume commissioned by the publisher, containing many of the better essays about the Mythos.

94.   *The Ghost of Fear and Others* (H. P. Lovecraft's Favorite Horror Stories, Volume 1)
      a.   Welches, OR: Arcane Wisdom, [March] 2012.
      b.   Portland, OR: Dark Regions Press, 2016.

Contents: Introduction; Lord Dunsany, "Idle Days on the Yann"; Nathaniel Hawthorne, "Fragments from the Journal of a Solitary Man"; E. F. Benson, "The Man Who Went Too Far"; Rudyard Kipling, "The Mark of the Beast"; Fiona Macleod, "The Sin-Eater"; M. P. Shiel, "The House of Sounds"; Seabury Quinn, "The Phantom Farmhouse"; Théophile Gautier, "One of Cleopatra's Nights"; E. Hoffmann Price, "The Stranger from Kurdistan"; Edgar Allan Poe, "The Facts in the Case of M. Valdemar"; Arthur Machen, "Novel of the White Powder"; F. Marion Crawford, "The Dead Smile"; H. G. Wells, "The Ghost of Fear"; Edward Lucas White, "Lukundoo"; Arthur J. Burks, "Bells of Oceana"; John Buchan, "The Wind in the Portico."

Notes. A volume that originated with the idea of an anthology (compiled by Marc A. Michaud and myself) called *H. P. Lovecraft's Favourite Horror Stories.* The ms. was fully assembled perhaps as early as 1985 or earlier, but we found no takers for it.

95.   H. L. Mencken, *The Collected Drama of H. L. Mencken: Plays and Criticism*
   a.   Lanham, MD: Scarecrow Press, [June] 2012.

     Contents: Introduction; Part I. The Plays: The Artist: A Drama without Words; In the Vestry Room; Seeing the World; Asepsis: A Deduction in Scherzo Form; Death: A Philosophical Discussion; The Wedding: A Stage Direction; Heliogabalus: A Buffoonery in Three Acts (with George Jean Nathan); Part II. Mencken on Drama: "By Way of Introduction" to *George Bernard Shaw: His Plays*; William Shakespeare; A Drama of Ideas; A Plea for Comedy; Et-Dukkehjemiana; The Revival of the Printed Play; The New Dramatic Literature; Brieux and Others; The Terrible Swede; Synge and Others; Gerhart Hauptmann; Thirty-five Printed Plays; The Ulster Polonius; Ibsen: Journeyman Dramatist; Notes; Index.

     Notes. A volume based on my fondness for Mencken's full-length play *Heliogabalus* (1920) and my discovery that he wrote a number of other plays that had rarely been reprinted. The volume was fleshed out by some of his writings on the drama, always incisive. The introduction was reprinted in I.50 as part of "Mencken as Creative Artist."

96.   *Black Wings II: New Tales of Lovecraftian Horror*
   a.   Hornsea, UK: PS Publishing, [July] 2012.
   b.   London: Titan Books, February 2014 (as *Black Wings of Cthulhu 2*).

     Contents: Introduction; John Shirley, "When Death Wakes Me to Myself"; Tom Fletcher, "View"; Caitlín R. Kiernan, "Houndwife"; Jonathan Thomas, "King of Cat Swamp"; Nick Mamatas, "Dead Media"; Richard Gavin, "The Abject"; Melanie Tem, "Dahlias"; John Langan, "Bloom"; Jason C. Eckhardt, "And the Sea Gave Up the Dead"; Don Webb, "Casting Call"; Darrell Schweitzer, "The Clockwork King, the Queen of Glass, and the Man with the Hundred Knives"; Nicholas Royle, "The Other Man"; Steve Rasnic Tem, "Waiting at the Crossroads Motel"; Brian Evenson, "The Wilcox Remainder"; Rick Dakan, "Correlated Discontents"; Donald Tyson, "The Skinless Face"; Jason V Brock, "The History of a Letter"; Chet Williamson, "Appointed."

Notes. My second anthology of original horror tales. The publisher has said that I can keep compiling such volumes indefinitely every 12–18 months. He may rue those words!

97. *The Dead Valley and Others* (H. P. Lovecraft's Favorite Horror Stories, Volume 2)
 a. Welches, OR: Arcane Wisdom, [November] 2012.
 b. Colusa, CA: Dark Renaissance Books, 2014.

Contents: Introduction; Fitz-James O'Brien, "The Diamond Lens"; Guy de Maupassant, "The Horla"; A. Merritt, "The Moon Pool"; M. R. James, "Count Magnus"; Ambrose Bierce, "The Damned Thing"; Ralph Adams Cram, "The Dead Valley"; John Metcalfe, "The Bad Lands"; Anthony M. Rud, "Ooze"; Irvin S. Cobb, "Fishhead"; Robert W. Chambers, "The Harbor-Master"; Algernon Blackwood, "Ancient Sorceries"; Henry S. Whitehead, "Cassius"; Hanns Heinz Ewers, "The Spider"; H. Russell Wakefield, "Blind Man's Buff."

98. H. L. Mencken, *Bluebeard's Goat and Other Stories*
 a. Chester Springs, PA: Dufour Editions, [December] 2012.

Contents: Introduction; The Cook's Victory; Like a Thief in the Night; A Double Rebellion; The Crime of McSwane; The Bend in the Tube; The Last Cavalry Charge; The Barbarous Bradley; Epithalamium; The Visionary; From the Memoirs of the Devil; A Statesman; The Memory of Edna; Bluebeard's Goat; The Charmed Circle; The Window of Horrors; Wall-Paper; The Victim; The Homeric Sex; The Man of God; The Hypocrite; Wives; Here's to the Dead!; Meditation; *Some Jeux d'Esprit:* The Scholar; The Prayer of a Little Frog; The Greatest Gift; The Incomparable Physician; The Rescuers; The Bleeding Heart; The Omission; She Did Not Believe Me; Bibliography.

Notes. A volume that completes my reprinting of Mencken's creative work—poetry, plays, and fiction. The introduction was reprinted in I.50 as part of "Mencken as Creative Artist."

99. Edward Lucas White, *The Stuff of Dreams: The Weird Stories of Edward Lucas White*
 a. Welches, OR: Arcane Wisdom, [March] 2013.

b. Mineola, NY: Dover Publications, [April] 2016.

Contents: Introduction; The House of the Nightmare; The Flambeau Bracket; Amina; The Message on the Slate; Lukundoo; The Pig-skin Belt; The Song of the Sirens; The Picture Puzzle; The Snout; Sorcery Island; Azrael; The Ghoula; Edward Lucas White on Dreams.

Notes. A volume that had been assembled many years before for a British publisher who issued a contract but did not publish the book. The introduction was first printed in I.24 as "Edward Lucas White: Dream and Reality."

100. William F. Nolan, *Nolan on Bradbury*

a. New York: Hippocampus Press, [March] 2013.

Contents: Preface, by William F. Nolan; Introduction, by Jason V Brock; Editor's Introduction; Ray Bradbury, "About Bill Nolan"; *Articles:* R. B.: A Biographical Sketch; Portrait of a Writer; The Bradbury Years; Bradbury: Prose Poet in the Age of Space; The Great White Whale; The Best of Ray Bradbury; Ray Bradbury; Leigh Brackett and Ray Bradbury; Ray Bradbury: Space Age Moralist; Bradbury in the Pulps; Introduction to *The Last Circus and The Electrocution*; Afterword to "The Fireman"; Introduction to *Ray Bradbury Review* (1988 edition); A Half-Century of Creativity; Behind the Illustrations: The Real Ray Bradbury; Fifty Years with Bradbury: A Birthday Tribute; Ray Bradbury: Space-Age Legend; Ray, Ray, and Ray; William F. Nolan Interviews Ray Bradbury; A Bradbury Top Ten, Plus Fifty: My Personal Evaluation of Ray's Finest Stories; *Stories:* The Immortal Ones; Mr. B. Goes to Hollywood; The Joy of Living; And Miles to Go Before I Sleep; To Serve the Ship; Dead Call; Fair Trade; The Dandelion Chronicles; *Tributes to Ray Bradbury:* William F. Nolan, "Goodbye, Old Pal"; Jason V Brock, "Kneeling at the Dandelion Shrine"; John C. Tibbetts, "Ray Bradbury's Good Companions"; S. T. Joshi, "A Master of Symbol and Metaphor"; Greg Bear, "Afterword: The Return of Ray B."; Select Bibliography.

Notes. A volume that grew out of my friendship with Nolan and his friends Jason V Brock and Greg Bear; not to mention my increasing interest in Ray Bradbury. The book came out around the time of Nolan's 85th birthday. I was pleased to see it win a Bram Stoker Award for best nonfiction volume of the year.

101. *Dreams of Fear: Poetry of Terror and the Supernatural* (with Steven J. Mariconda)

a. New York: Hippocampus Press, [April] 2013.

Contents: Introduction, by Joshi and Mariconda; I. The Ancient World: Homer, "From the *Odyssey*"; Euripides. "From *Medea*"; Catullus, "Attis (Poem 64)"; Horace, "Epode 5"; II. From the Middle Ages to the Eighteenth Century: Dante Alighieri, "*Inferno* (Cantos 3 and 18)"; Christopher Marlowe, "From *Dr. Faustus*"; William Shakespeare, "From *Hamlet*," "From *Macbeth*"; John Donne, "The Apparition"; John Milton, "From *Paradise Lost*"; John Gay, "A True Story of an Apparition"; David Mallet, "William and Margaret"; William Collins, "Ode to Fear"; III. The Gothics and Romantics: Johann Wolfgang von Goethe, "The Erl-King," "The Bride of Corinth," "The Dance of Death"; Mary Robinson, "The Haunted Beach"; William Blake, "Fair Elenor"; Robert Burns, "Tam o'Shanter"; Friedrich von Schiller, "A Funeral Fantasie"; Nathan Drake, "Ode to Superstition"; James Hogg, "The Witch of the Gray Thorn"; Sir Walter Scott, "William and Helen," "The Wild Huntsman"; Samuel Taylor Coleridge, "The Rime of the Ancient Mariner," "Kubla Khan"; Robert Southey, "To Horror"; Matthew Gregory Lewis, "Alonzo the Brave and Fair Imogine"; Thomas Moore, "The Lake of the Dismal Swamp"; George Gordon, Lord Byron, "Darkness"; Percy Bysshe Shelley, "Ghasta; or, The Avenging Demon!!!," "Sister Rosa: A Ballad"; John Clare, "The Nightmare"; John Keats, "La Belle Dame sans Merci: A Ballad"; Heinrich Heine, "The Lorelei"; Thomas Hood, "The Demon-Ship"; IV. The Later Nineteenth Century: Victor Hugo, "The Vanished City"; Thomas Lovell Beddoes, "The Ghosts' Moonshine," "The Boding Dreams," "Doomsday"; Henry Wadsworth Longfellow, "Haunted Houses," "The Haunted Chamber"; Edgar Allan Poe, "The City in the Sea," "The Haunted Palace," "The Conqueror Worm," "Dream-Land," "Ulalume"; Alfred, Lord Tennyson, "The Kraken"; Oliver Wendell Holmes, "The Broomstick Train; or, The Return of the Witches"; Robert Browning, "Childe Roland to the Dark Tower Came"; James Russell Lowell, "The Ghost-Seer"; Charles Baudelaire, "The Phantom," "The Irremediable"; William Allingham, "A Dream"; George MacDonald, "The Homeless Ghost"; George Meredith, "Phantasy"; Thomas Bailey Aldrich, "Eidolons," "The Lorelei," "Apparitions"; Algernon Charles Swinburne, "The Witch-Mother"; Thomas Hardy, "The Dead Man Walking"; Ambrose Bierce, "A Vision of Doom"; Julian Hawthorne, "Were-Wolf"; William Ernest Henley, "[Untitled]"; Guy de Maupassant, "Horror"; Edwin Markham, "Wail of the Wandering Dead," "The Wharf of Dreams"; Emile Verhaeren, "The Miller"; A. E. Housman, "Hell Gate"; Katharine Tynan, "The Witch"; Madison Cawein, "The Forest of Shadows," "The Wood Water," "The Night-Wind," "Hallowmas"; W. B. Yeats, "The Phantom Ship"; Dora Sigerson Shorter, "The Skeleton in the Cupboard," "The Fetch"; AE (George William Russell), "A Vision of Beauty"; V. The Twentieth Century: George Sterling, "A Dream of

Fear," "A Wine of Wizardry," "The Thirst of Satan"; Edwin Arlington Robinson, "The Dead Village," "The Dark House"; Christopher Brennan, "[Untitled]"; Paul Laurence Dunbar, "The Haunted Oak"; Walter de la Mare, "Fear," "The Listeners," "Drugged"; Robert W. Service, "The Cremation of Sam McGee"; Robert Frost, "Ghost House," "The Demiurge's Laugh"; William Hope Hodgson, "Storm"; Park Barnitz, "Mad Sonnet," "Mankind"; Edward Thomas, "Out in the Dark"; Herman George Scheffauer, "Phantasmagoria," "Lilith of Eld," "The Shadow o'er the City"; Lord Dunsany, "Songs from an Evil Wood," "The Watchers"; Wilfrid Wilson Gibson, "The Whisperers," "The Lodging House"; John Masefield, "The Haunted"; John G. Neihardt, "The Voice of Nemesis"; Siegfried Sassoon, "Haunted," "Goblin Revel"; Vincent Starrett, "Villon Strolls at Midnight"; Georg Heym, "The Demons of the Cities"; Rupert Brooke, "Dead Men's Love"; Samuel Loveman, "Ship of Dreams"; Conrad Aiken, "La Belle Morte"; H. P. Lovecraft, "Despair," "To a Dreamer," "The Wood," "From *Fungi from Yuggoth*"; Harold Vinal, "Apparition," "Ghostly Reaper"; Clark Ashton Smith, "Ode to the Abyss," "The Eldritch Dark," "The Medusa of Despair," "The Tears of Lilith," "A Vision of Lucifer"; Robert Graves, "The Haunted House"; Frank Belknap Long, "The Goblin Tower," "The Abominable Snow Men"; Robert E. Howard, "Dead Man's Hate," "Recompense"; Donald Wandrei, "Nightmare," "The Woman at the Window," "From *Sonnets of the Midnight Hours*"; Joseph Payne Brennan, "The Scythe of Dreams"; Stanley McNail, "The House on Maple Hill"; Donald Sidney-Fryer, "Midnight Visitant"; Richard L. Tierney, "The Evil House," "To the Hydrogen Bomb"; Bruce Boston, "The Nightmare Collector," "Ghost Blood"; Brett Rutherford, "Fête"; G. Sutton Breiding, "The Worm of Midnight," "Black Leather Vampire"; W. H. Pugmire, "The Outsider's Song"; Gary William Crawford, "The Formicary"; Keith Daniels, "Stonehenge"; Leigh Blackmore, "Terror Australis"; Ann K. Schwader, "The Coming of Chaos"; Acknowledgments.

Notes. Another volume long in the making, and one that seems to me on the whole an anthology superior to Derleth's *Dark of the Moon* (1947).

102. *Ambrose Bierce* (Masters of the Weird Tale)
    a.   Lakewood, CO: Centipede Press, [April] 2013.
        Contents: Introduction; Artist's Dedication; I. Tales of the Civil War: Killed at Resaca; George Thurston; One of the Missing; Jupiter Doke, Brigadier General; Chickamauga; A Son of the Gods; A Tough Tussle; A Horseman in the Sky; One Officer, One Man; An Affair of Outposts; The Affair at Coulter's Notch; The Coup de

Grâce; An Occurrence at Owl Creek Bridge; One Kind of Officer; A Baffled Ambuscade; The Major's Tale; The Story of a Conscience; Parker Adderson, Philosopher; The Mocking-Bird; A Man with Two Lives; Two Military Executions; A Resumed Identity; Three and One Are One; II. Tales of Supernatural and Psychological Horror: The Haunted Valley; The Night-Doings at "Deadman's"; The Famous Gilson Bequest; A Fruitless Assignment; An Inhabitant of Carcosa; Bodies of the Dead; Present at a Hanging; A Psychological Shipwreck; A Holy Terror; Charles Ashmore's Trail; The Difficulty of Crossing a Field; The Isle of Pines; A Cold Greeting; One of Twins; The Spook House; The Suitable Surroundings; The Man and the Snake; The Man out of the Nose; The Death of Halpin Frayser; An Adventure at Brownville; The Damned Thing; An Unfinished Race; A Watcher by the Dead; The Realm of the Unreal; The Middle Toe of the Right Foot; Haïta, the Shepherd; The Boarded Window; The Secret of Macarger's Gulch; The Thing at Nolan; A Baby Tramp; The Applicant; Moxon's Master; John Bartine's Watch; A Jug of Sirup; A Diagnosis of Death; A Wireless Message; The Moonlit Road; Perry Chumly's Eclipse; An Imperfect Conflagration; At Old Man Eckert's; A Vine on a House; The Eyes of the Panther; An Arrest; Staley Fleming's Hallucination; Beyond the Wall; The Other Lodgers; The Stranger; Authenticating a Ghost; A Story at the Club; The Hypnotist; A Bottomless Grave; My Favorite Murder; Oil of Dog; The Widower Turmore; One Summer Night; John Mortonson's Funeral; III. Tall Tales, Comic and Political Fantasies: The Aborigines of Oakland; A Scientific Dream; For the Ahkoond; Ashes ofthe Beacon; John Smith, Liberator; Story Sources; Credits.

Notes. An extensive selection of Bierce's weird work, although the publisher decided to omit the long political fantasy *The Land Beyond the Blow.*

103/104/105.   George Sterling, *Complete Poetry* (with David E. Schultz)
  a.   New York: Hippocampus Press, [May] 2013. 3 vols.

     Contents: Volume 1 (*Chords of Fire*): Preface, by Kevin Starr; Introduction; *The Testimony of the Suns and Other Poems:* Dedication; Memorial Day; Poesy; The City of Music; To One Loved; The Summer of the Gods; The Lords of Pain; The Fog Siren; To Miss Constance Crawley in "Everyman"; To Imagination; To a Lily; "With the Strength of Dreams"; The Testimony of the Suns; Music; A White Rose; The Soul's Exile; In the Beginning; Memory of the Dead; To My Wife; The Haunting; War; Nightmare; The Spirit of Beauty; To Katherine; Mystery; To My Sister; The Poets; The Reincarnation; On Reading the Poems of Father Tabb; The Parting; Words for Lange's

"Blumenlied"; The Altar-Flame; To One Asking Lighter Songs; The Sea-Fog; The Nile; Darkness; The Ideal; To Colonel John S. Engs; "Sad Sea-Horizons"; Evening; Ultima Thule; The Swoon; The City and the Silence; The Directory; The Triumph of Bohemia; *A Wine of Wizardry and Other Poems:* A Wine of Wizardry; The Islands of the Blest; The Lover Waits; To Edgar Allan Poe; In Extremis; Romance; The Forest Mother; A Violet; The Wild Iris; To an Elder Poet; The Homing of Drake; The Cloud; Three Sonnets on Oblivion (Oblivion; The Dust Dethroned; The Night of Gods); Helen Peterson; Tasso to Leonora; Of America; Beauty; The Soul Prismatic; Pride and Conscience; An April Morning; Madrigal; To Ina Coolbrith; A Mood; A Visitor; A Dream of Fear; Night in Heaven; Personal Sonnets (To My Wife as May Queen; To Ambrose Bierce; Nora May French; To Robert I. Aitken; To Charles Rollo Peters; The Man I Might Have Been); *The House of Orchids and Other Poems:* Duandon; Three Sonnets of the Night Skies (I. Aldebaran at Dusk; II. The Chariots of Dawn; III. The Huntress of Stars); The Evanescent; Memory; The Moth of Time; The Black Vulture; The House of Orchids; Sonnets on the Sea's Voice; Autumn; Stars of the Noon; The Apothecary's; The Swimmers; Beneath the Redwoods; Music at Dusk; The Tides of Change; Morning Twilight; An Altar of the West; The Faun; The Voices; A Character; The Guerdon of the Sun; The Gardens of the Sea; The Sibyl of Dreams; The Music of Sleep; Duty; The Echo and the Quest; Justice; The Fleet; Remorse; Moonlight in the Pines; At the Grave of Serra; White Magic; Three Sonnets by the Night Sea; After the Storm; The Harlot's Wakening; The Midges; Personal Poems (To Ambrose Bierce; To Hall B. Rand; To Vernon L. Kellogg; Charles Warren Stoddard; The Ashes in the Sea); The Forty-Third Chapter of Job; *Sonnets to Craig:* Repentance; Thy Picture; To Craig; The Unalterable; Foreboding; Question; From the Gloom; Lost Music; Resurrection; The Heart of Music; Verses to Craig; Parting; A Prayer; Lonely; Autumn; Absence; Worship; Homeward; The Kiss; By Lonely Waters; Passion's Hour; Intimation; Shadows of Thee; The Unattainable; The Font of Beauty; Hope's Paradise; The Soul-Giver; The Inexorable Hour; At the Lily's Heart; The Joys Unchanging; Love the Transmuter; Search Rewarded; Bliss Decreed; The Burden of the Past; Past Flesh and Soul; Sunset; Love's Companions; Love's Shadow; At Dusk; The Spirit of Dusk; Eros in Heaven; The Star of Separation; A Midnight; Transmutation; God's Lily; From Dawn to Dream; Fire of Dreams; Thy Child-Picture; Evanescence; Sorrow and Joy; Beauty Afar; From Arcady; Loneliest; Belovéd; Hesperia; The Eternal Visitant; Evening Music; Love and Joy; Doubt and Worship; Love's Sacrament; Divinity; Enchantment; Coronation; Revelation; Adoration; My Love; The Unavailing; Love's Primacy; To Thy Heart; From Two Skies; The Abiding Presence; Love Complete; By the Western Ocean; A Vision; Love Desolate; The Pain of Beauty; A Constancy of Sleep; Dream's Alchemy; Soul of the World; Dreamland; The Shadow of Immortality; Until Thou Comest; Reborn; The Silent Fane; The Lute-Player; The Heritage of the Skies; Love and Sorrow; In Vain; The Hidden Goddess; Love's Mercy; Song's Futility; At Sunset; The Immortal; Blossom or Bird; Longing; The New Goddess; To the Moon; Lost in Light; The Path to Paradise; Appendix; Worship's Acme; Before Dawn; Separation; [Untitled]; *Poems to Vera:* To Vera; Inclusion; The Song-Font; My Songs; To Vera; "I Loved Thee, Atthis, Long Ago!"; To Vera; To Vera; Intimation; At Noon; The Cup-Bearer; Iphigenia; The Face of the Star; Afterward; Confession; To Vera; Absence; Mystery; "Out of the Night"; Star of the Soul; Before Dawn; To Vera at Night; To Vera (Birthday Ode); To Vera (Blank Verse); *Beyond the Breakers and Other Poems:* Beyond the Breakers; The Master-Mariner; The Voice of the Dove; Night-Sentries; The Muse of the Incommunicable; The Coming Singer; At the Grand Cañon; Nightfall; Ode on the Centenary of the Birth of Robert Browning; Afterward; "Tidal, King of Nations"; The Last Monster; Christmas Under Arms; War; Ascension; The Thirst of Satan; Scrutiny; Ballad of Two Seas; Ballad of St. John of Nepomuk; The Rack; Willy Pitcher; "Beyond the Sunset"; Respite; Kindred; "That Walk in Darkness"; In the Market-Place; The Palette; The Hunting of Dian; A Winter Dawn; A Winter Sunset; Forenoon by the Pacific; A Legend of the Dove; Said the Wind.; The Mission Swallows; "Omnia Exeunt in Mysterium"; "On a Western Beach"; Then and Now; Menace; The Secret Room; Past the Panes; From the Mountain; Discord; Lineage; To One Self-Slain; Night on the Mountain; The Abandoned Farm; To H. G. Wells; Caeli Enarrant; "You Never Can Tell"; Dawn from a Western Mountain; The Setting; The Sleepers; The Sleep of Birds; Spring in Monterey; The Last Days; Natural History Items; Father Coyote; The Lagoon; Relativity; The Plaint of the Cotton-Tails; A Possibility; *Yosemite: An Ode; The Caged Eagle and Other Poems:* The Slaying of the Witch; To Twilight; Henri; Conspiracy; Indian Summer; Ballad of the Fatal Word; On the Sale of the Love-Letters of a Dead Poet; Mediatrix; A Dog Waits His Dead Mistress; Humility in Art; An Autumn Thrush; The Fall of the Year; October; In Autumn; The Caged Eagle; Time and Tears; To an Old Nurse; To the Mummy of the Lady Isis; The Ramparts and the Rose; On a Portrait of Lincoln; The Tryst; A Yellow Rose; Shakespeare; The Shadow of Nirvana; The Return; Moloch; Three Sonnets on Sleep; Man; On a

City Street; Illusion; Essential Night; The Gleaner; California; Poems on the Panama-Pacific International Exposition (Ode on the Opening; The Builders; The Evanescent City); Personal Poems (Frank Unger; To Xavier Martinez, Painter; The Light-Giver; To Margaret Anglin); On the Great War (The Song of the Valkyrs; The Dream of Wilhelm II; Earth's Anthem; To Germany; Betrayal; Belgium, August, 1914; England, August, 1914; To the War-Lords; The War-God; The Little Farm; The House of War; "As It Was in the Beginning"; To Belgium; The Two Prayers; Aftermath; The War-Machine; Bombardment; Germany; The Death-Chords; The Feast; War's Music; The Aeroplane; Before Dawn; The Turk; The New Kings; To France; The Night of Man; To the Allied Arms; The Battlefield at Night; Kingship; The Death of Rupert Brooke; The Helots; The Crown-Prince at Verdun; Before Dawn in America; Gun-Practice; To England; Civilization at Bay; The Day of Decision; Broadway, New York, 1916; The "Lusitania"; War: The Past; War: The Present; War: The Future); *Additional War Poems from* The Binding of the Beast and Other Poems: To Germany [VI]; The Binding of the Beast; To France at Verdun; In a Thousand Years; Germany in Belgium; Germany on the Seas; A Vision of Germania; To the Hun; *The Play of Everyman.*

Volume 2 (To a Girl Dancing): Rosamund; Lilith; Sails and Mirage and Other Poems: The Queen Forgets; Saul; Ocean Sunsets; Sanctuary; Spring in Carmel; The Setting of Antares; The Deserted Nest; Kingship; The First Food; The Wind; A Lost Garden; The Glass of Time; Reason; Sonnets by the Night-Sea; Sails; Mirage; The Skull of Shakespeare; Two Met; The Common Cult; The Lost Nymph; The Wine of Illusion; To Life; The Roman Wall; "His Own Country"; Lost Colors; The Passing of Bierce; Everest; Afternoon; A Compact?; Autumn in Carmel; Poe's Gravestone; The Secret Garden; Norman Boyer; Of One Asleep; To a Girl Dancing; The Far Feet; Hesperian; The Face of the Skies; The Morning Star; The Evening Star; To Charles Rollo Peters; To Ruth Chatterton; The Cool, Grey City of Love; The Princess on the Headland; To the Moon; The Hidden Pool; The Death of Circe; The Pathway; The Last Island; Infidels; Vox Humana; An Elegy; Sonnets on the Sea's Voice; The Dead Captain; Wind in Pines; *Truth; Truth: A Grove Play; Strange Waters;* Appendix: Light; By Carmel Mission; A Poet Has Risen, by Ambrose Bierce; A Poet and His Poem, by Ambrose Bierce; An Insurrection of the Peasantry, by Ambrose Bierce; Introduction to Lilith, by Theodore Dreiser; Notes; Index of Titles; Index of First Lines.

Volume 3 (The Stranger at the Gate): Dated Poems: Farewell; The Sea Waif; The Spaniards in Cuba; To ————; The Furies; In Farewell;

To Leopold of Belgium; Brotherhood; Feb. 21, '08; To Mrs. J. B. C;
Love's Shrine; The Cliff Dwellers; Inauguration Day, 1909; Ro-
mance! Romance!; The Pinions; To Artemis Hunting; Song in Fami-
ly Club Jinks for 1912; The Golden Past; The Abalone Song; The
Loosing; The Seasons; The Path of Portola; R. L. S; Hope; The Star
of Love; To Stella; "Seasonal to Date"; To Albert Bierce; To the
Goddess of Liberty; The Vision of Portola; Heat in the City; August
1st, 1914; The Blind; At Morning; Night Sounds; The Fish Hawk;
At the Last; On Fifth Avenue; The Lifted Wings; Stress of Beauty;
Ships of a Day; Under the Rainbow; Back to Back against the
Mainmast; Ballad of the Bells; The First Snow; The Beach by Winter
Twilight; Easter Dawn on Rubidoux; Lilies of Stone; Rendezvous;
To the Unknown Goddess; "57"; Transmutation; Art; Joan of Arc;
To Jack London; A Brother to Christ; Butterflies; Farmer Haynes'
Niece; California to the Artist; Before Dawn; Holy River of Sleep; A
Star; To Jack; To Robinson Jeffers; Democracy; The Passing of Buf-
falo Bill; To Sir Ernest Shackleton; The Revenge; The Friends of
Wilhelm; "You Coward!"; To General White and Visiting Officers;
The Path of Gold; The Immutable; You Are So Beautiful; The Sym-
boled Spirit; Song of the Swineherds; "The White Logic"; The Flag;
Moll; Songs from *The Twilight of the Kings* (1918); A Morning Hymn;
The Messenger; Ever of You; We're A-Going; The Dust Hopes; Ser-
vice; Nov. 11, 1918; The World-Rachel; Lucifer; To Joyce Kilmer;
Outward; Visual Beauty; Altars of War; The Modern Muse; Memo-
rial Day, 1919; [The Doughboy's Love Song]; From the Train; Morn-
ing in the Pines; To Raphael Weill; To Rachmaninoff; To Science;
My Brook; Three Voices; Art and Life; Witch-Fire; Autumnal Love;
To One Asleep; To Ned Greenway; To Louis Untermeyer; "Indulge
the Genial Hour!"; Incarnation; Good and Evil; The Three Gifts; To
Frank Mathieu; Distance; Rainbow's End; The "Bohemian Club";
Beyond the Music; Love and Time; Careless; The Wiser Prophet;
Lost Sunsets; Three Sonnets on Beauty; The Parting of the Ways;
The Day of Decision; Youth and Time; The Gulls; At Midnight;
Flame; Happiest; The Kiss of Consummation; To an Irate Father;
Problem; The Twilight of the Grape; Pumas; Ode to Shelley; Beauty
Renounced; To Edwin Markham on His Seventieth Birt; The Wild
Swan; Warning; The Killdee; The Night Migration; The Voice of the
Wheat; The Trapping of Rung; To a Water-Fowl; The Midway
Peace; Penitence; The Tracker; A Moth; To Serra of Carmel; The
Stranger at the Gate; Ephemera; Shelley at Spezia; Sorcery; Venus
Letalis; Song; A Critic; The Sailor Turns Street-Sweeper; The City by
the Sea; Long Island Pebbles; The Wings of Beauty; Waste; The Kiss;
To a Stenographer; Gulls at Night; By Another Sea; Mystery; Sup-

pose Nobody Cared; The Fog-Sea; The Housebreaker; Fog-Horns; The Black Hound Bays; The Dog; Return, Romance!; Chivalry; The Stranger; Eidolon; To Carl Sandburg; The Strange Bird; A Sceptic's Fate; After Sunset; A Lumberjack Yearns; The First-Born; The Flight; A Knee Is Bent; The Last of Sunset; Old Partings; The Pirate's Grave; Amber; The Daughters of Disillusion; The Young Witch; The Pony Express; Paradox; Transition; One Poem; Wet Beaches; Three Mysteries; Vigil; What Porridge Had John Keats?; Nepenthe; The Night-Watch; To a Reformer; A Face in the Crowd; High Noon; To Wordsworth; From the Valley; The Voice of the Deep; "The Ice-Age"; To Charles Warren Stoddard; Two Pictures by Dickman; The Little Hills; The Unconditioned; Dear to Me; Old Anchors; The Street; Three That Knew Helen; Solitude; Farm of Fools; A Deserted Farm; Once; Caucasus; The Sailing of Keats; Which Was, and Never Shall Be; The Aëroplane; To Bernice di Pasquali; "The Grizzly Giant"; Hostage; Life, Toil, and Love; Wayfarers; Disillusion; Ballad of the Seeker; Compensation; An Old Pine; To a Monk's Skull; Miocene; The Dreamer; Hope; An Old Road; The Fleet Comes; The Hawk's Nest; The Oldest Book; The Faithful; The Transfusion; The Steelyard; Familiar Beauty; Seismos; Sierran Dawn; Yerba Buena: July 9, 1846; To George Edwards; A Day of Truce; Ballad of the Grapes; Ballad of the Swabs; The Way to the West; The Grey Man; Infusion; The Unborn; The Meteor; Beauty and Truth; The Caravan; Echo; An Old Poem; The Pathfinders; To Friend W. Richardson; The Last Man; Late Tidings; Repartee; The Balance; North Wind; The Quarrel; Peace; Love and Custom; Lost Companion; Implication; On Certain Verses; Grasshopper; Safe; Insincerities; To California; Wings; The Restoration; The Seventh Veil; Coup de Grace; Counsel; Silence; An Old Indian Remembers; Adullam; My Swan Song; Abraham Lincoln; "And on Earth Peace, to Men of Good Will; At Villa Montalvo; The Ballad of the Ghost-Arrow; Contributor; The Dark Nation; The Dweller in Darkness; The Final Faith; Sacrament; Sorrow; The Sowers; To Pain; To Ray Coyle; *Undated Poems:* Above the Sea; Above the Stream; After Sunset; Amara; Annus Mirabilis; Answering; Arabian Lullaby; Archer and Arrow; The Ashes of Astarte; At the Club; At the Keyboard; At the Sea's Verge; Autumn; Autumn in California; Autumnal Hope; Before an Ocean; Beyond the Tides; Blue Ranges; Breakers; By the Sea of Time; The Carmel Millionaire; The Castaways; Change; The City and the Night; The Cocktail Song; Cold Altars; The Coming of Helen; Communion; Comparison; Completion; Comradeship; Conclusion; Confiteor; Contrition; Conviction; Coronal; A Couch of Love; A Cry of the Heart; The Cynic; "Dad" Tatlow Advises; Darling!; Dawn; A Day; Deep-Sea Limericks; The Desert; Devotion; Division; A Dream of Arcady; The Dusks of Destiny; Earth-Worms; Endearment; Enigma; Entreaty; Exiles; "A Fair Exchange"; Far and Near; Far Day; The Far Goddess; Far Peace; Farewell and Meeting; Fate's Flower; Flags o' Truce; For E. H. Sothern; Foreshadowed; Forest Music; Forever and Ever; From Dawn to Dusk; From Sun to Star; The Fugitives; Fulfillment; The Futile Song; The Glory of the Globe; The Goal; Goddess-Love; Good-Bye; Haunted; Heart-ache; Her Welcome; Here and Now; The Hidden Garden; The Horse in War; Hotaling's Fancy Farm; A Hymn for Americans; The Immortal Moment; In the Shadow; In the Valley; In the Valley; Inarticulate; Inclusion; Interpeace; Journey's End; June; The Last Mirage; The Last of Beauty; The Last of the Year; The Last Veil; Lilies of Lethe; A Listener; Lonely Beauty; The Lost Empire; Love Adoring; Love and Faith; Love and the Sea; Love at Sunset; Love at Twilight; Love Inexhaustible; Love Song; Love's Consummation; Love's Farewell; Love's Hunger; Love's Silence; The Lutes of Exile; Magdalene; Man and Woman; Martyrdom; Meeting; Melodie in E; Memory and Rain; The Merciful Man; The Messenger; The Mirror; The Moon of Memory; The Music of Memory; Myrrh; Night-Separation; The Night-Wind; Nimrod; November Carol; The Oceans; "The Old Black-a Bull"; "Old Cats o' Carmel"; On His Blindness; On the Late Payment of Rent—Followed by a Massacre in Piedmont; One Day; Origin; Pain and Joy; The Palace of the Moon; Parted; Parted; Passion's Prayer; Pavement; The Peace of the Hills; A Prayer; Protest; The Quest; The Rain; Recompense; Recompense; The Redwoods; Redwoods by Morning; The Redwoods Wait; Reflections on the Cat; Regret; Relatives; Remembered; Renouncement; "The Return of Faith"; Revealing Music; Revelation; Rosa Mystica; Rosa Mystica; Rose of the Winds; Roses of Sunset; Sarah the Whale; The Sea; Separation; Serenade; Silver Sword; The Sisters; Song; Song; Song; Song; Song; The Song of Henry Maxwell; Song of the Pirates; Song's Lesson; Sonnets of Realization; Sonnets of the True Beauty; The Sphinx; Spontaneity 37; Spontaneity 40; Spontaneity 42; Spontaneity 44; Spontaneity 92; Star and Storm; Starlight; Stars; Surety; The Swimmer; Tears; Testimony; That Which Abides; Thou and I; Through Love's Eyes; Thy Lineage; To a Dusk-Rose; To Anne Bremer; To Antonoë; To Astarte; To Love the God; To Mrs. Phoebe A. Hearst; To One Who Passed; To Stella; To the Bosom of Antonoë, Handmaiden of; To the True Heart; To Wilhelm II; To Ylla; To You; To You; Together; Too Late; Transfiguration; Twilight at Midway Point; Twilight Song; The Two Buzzards; The Unattainable; Until the Dawn; Valerie; A Visitant; A Voice; The Wayfarer; The

Wayside Garden; Western Twilight; What It's Like; What Shall Be; Willy Smith at the Ball Game; Wind and Rain; "With Brief Thanksgiving"; Wonderment; The Woof of the Stars; The Word-Shrine; Yearning; Young Love; [Untitled Poems]; [Untitled Fragments]; [Untitled Fragmentary Poetic Drama]; Appendix; Holy River of Sleep; We're A-Going; A Christmas Hymn; [Untitled], by François Coppée; Notes; Index of Titles; Index of First Lines.

Notes. The ultimate product of the research begun by Schultz and myself in 1995, assembling all known poems (and other writings) by Sterling. The volume required extensive correspondence with and travel to the many libraries (especially the Bancroft Library at the University of California) that owned Sterling poetry manuscripts.

106. *Critical Essays on Lord Dunsany*
a. Lanham, MD: Scarecrow Press, [August] 2013.

Contents: Acknowledgments; Introduction; I. BIOGRAPHIES AND MEMOIRS: Clayton Hamilton, "Lord Dunsany: Personal Impressions"; Oliver St. John Gogarty, "Lord Dunsany"; Hazel Littlefield, "Dunsany: King of Dreams: A Personal Portrait"; II. GENERAL STUDIES: W. B. Yeats, "Introduction to *Selections from the Writings of Lord Dunsany*"; Montrose J. Moses, "Lord Dunsany's Peculiar Genius"; H. P. Lovecraft, "Lord Dunsany and His Work"; Benjamin De Casseres, "Lord Dunsany"; Patrick Maume, "Dreams of Empire, Empire of Dreams: Lord Dunsany Plays the Game"; Max Duperray, "'The Laughter of the Gods': Contextualizing Lord Dunsany"; III. ON DUNSANY'S FICTION: Padraic Colum, "Introduction to *A Dreamer's Tales and Other Stories*"; Arthur C. Clarke, "Dunsany Lord of Fantasy"; John Wilson Foster, "A Dreamer's Tales: The Stories of Lord Dunsany"; Angelee Sailer Anderson, "Lord Dunsany: The Potency of Words and the Wonder of Things"; Megan Mitchell, "Jorkens"; IV. ON DUNSANY'S PLAYS: H. L. Mencken, "Mencken on Dunsany"; Rebecca West, *"If"*; Ludwig Lewisohn, "Dunsany"; Ben P. Indick, "Beyond the Fields: The Theatre of Lord Dunsany"; V. ON INDIVIDUAL WORKS: Edward Thomas, "A Tory Young Hopeful"; William Rose Benét, "Sleep's Painted Scene"; Faye Ringel, *"The King of Elfland's Daughter* and the Patterns of Romance"; Iris Fernández Muniz, "The Influence of *Don Quixote* on *Don Rodriguez*"; S. T. Joshi, "Christianity and Paganism in Two Dunsany Novels"; Darrell Schweitzer, "Dunsany's Retreat from the Fantastic"; VI. ON INFLUENCES: Susan Bassnett, "From Gods to Giants: Theatrical Parallels Between Edward Dunsany and Luigi Pirandello"; Beatriz Vegh, "'The Strength of Imaginative Idiom': From Lord Dunsany's to Faulkner's 'Carcassonne'"; S. T. Joshi, "Lovecraft's 'Dunsanian Studies'"; Skye Cervone, "Recovering the Effects of Lord Dunsany and J. R. R. Tolkien"; Index.

Notes. A comprehensive collection of essays on Dunsany, some reprinted (including an early review of *The Gods of Pegāna* by Edward Thomas), and some original. Part of my series, Studies in Supernatural Literature.

107. Edgar Allan Poe, *The Raven: Tales and Poems* (uncredited)
   a.   New York: Penguin, [September] 2013.

   Contents: "Haunted Castles, Dark Mirrors: On the Penguin Horror Series" by Guillermo del Toro; Introduction; A Note on the Texts; TALES: Metzengerstein; MS. Found in a Bottle; Shadow—A Parable; Silence—A Fable; Berenicë; Morella; Ligeia; The Fall of the House of Usher; William Wilson; The Conversation of Eiros and Charmion; The Man of the Crowd; A Descent into the Maelström; The Colloquy of Monos and Una; Eleonora; The Oval Portrait; The Masque of the Red Death; The Pit and the Pendulum; The Tell-Tale Heart; The Black Cat; The Premature Burial; Some Words with a Mummy; The Imp of the Perverse; The Facts in the Case of M. Valdemar; The Cask of Amontillado; Hop-Frog; POEMS: Dreams; Spirits of the Dead; A Dream; Sonnet—To Science; Fairy-Land; [Alone]; Fairy Land [II]; The Valley of Unrest; The City in the Sea; Sonnet—Silence; Lenore; Dream-Land; The Raven; Ulalume—A Ballad; The Bells; A Dream within a Dream; For Annie; Eldorado; Annabel Lee.

   Notes. The introduction was reprinted in *Driven to Madness with Fright* (I.45) as "Poe as Revolutionary."

108. Sax Rohmer, *Brood of the Witch-Queen*
   a.   Lakewood, CO: Centipede Press, [December] 2013.

   Contents: Introduction; The Death-Ring of Sneferu; Breath of Allah; The Whispering Mummy; Lord of the Jackals; Harun Pasha; In the Valley of the Sorceress; The Haunting of Low Fennel; The Valley of the Just; The Master of Hollow Grange; The Curse of a Thousand Kisses; The Man with the Shaven Skull; The White Hat; Tchériapin; The Hand of the Mandarin Quong; The Key of the Temple of Heaven; *Brood of the Witch-Queen.*

   Notes. A compilation of the best (or, perhaps, least bad) supernatural or quasi-supernatural stories by Rohmer, along with a novel that HPL enjoyed. The introduction was reprinted in I.47 as "Sax Rohmer: The Popular Weird Tale."

109. *The Original Atheists: First Thoughts on Nonbelief*
   a. Amherst, NY: Prometheus Books, 2014 [December 2013].

Contents: Introduction; I. THE FRENCH AND GERMAN ENLIGHT-
ENMENT: Jean Meslier, From *Testament* (1729); Julien Offray de La
Mettrie, From *Man a Machine* (1748); Étienne Bonnot de Condillac,
"On the Origin and Progress of Divination" (1749); Voltaire
(François-Marie Arouet), From *Philosophical Dictionary* (1764); Paul-
Henri Thiry, Baron d'Holbach, From *The System of Nature* (1770);
Denis Diderot, "Conversation with the Abbé Barthélemy" (1772-
73); Immanuel Kant, From *Critique of Pure Reason* (1781); II. THE
BRITISH ENLIGHTENMENT: John Locke, "Of Faith and Reason, and
Their Distinct Provinces" (1690); Anthony Collins, From *A Treatise
of Free-Thinking* (1713); David Hume, "Of Miracles" (1748); Jeremy
Bentham and George Grote, From *Analysis of the Influence of Natural
Religion on the Temporal Happiness of Mankind* (1822); III. THE AMERI-
CAN ENLIGHTENMENT: Thomas Jefferson, [Selections]; Ethan Allen,
From *Reason, the Only Oracle of Man* (1784); James Madison, "A Me-
morial and Remonstrance against Religious Assessments" (1784-85);
Thomas Paine, From *The Age of Reason* (1794); Bibliography; Index.

Notes. A compilation of writings on atheism and related topics
from the eighteenth-century philosophers (French, German, British,
American). I translated the Condillac selection and revised other
translations.

110. *Black Wings III: New Tales of Lovecraftian Horror*
      a. Hornsea, UK: PS Publishing, [February] 2014.
      b. New York & London: Titan Books, [March] 2015 (as *Black Wings
         of Cthulhu 3*).

      Contents: Introduction; Jonathan Thomas, "Houdini Fish"; Donald
      R. Burleson, "Dimply Dolly Doofy"; Richard Gavin, "The Hag Stone";
      Jessica Amanda Salmonson and W. H. Pugmire, "Underneath an
      Arkham Moon"; Darrell Schweitzer, "Spiderwebs in the Dark"; Caitlín
      R. Kiernan, "One Tree Hill (The World as Cataclysm)"; Jason V
      Brock, "The Man with the Horn"; Mollie L. Burleson, "Hotel del
      Lago"; Donald Tyson, "Waller"; Don Webb, "The Megalith Plague";
      Joseph S. Pulver, Sr., "Down Black Staircases"; Peter Cannon, "China
      Holiday"; Lois H. Gresh, "Necrotic Cove"; Mark Howard Jones, "The
      Turn of the Tide"; Sam Gafford, "Weltschmerz"; Simon Strantzas,
      "Thistle's Find"; Brian Stableford, "Further Beyond."

      Notes. Another original anthology with much good work.

111. Clark Ashton Smith, *The Dark Eidolon and Other Fantasies*
      a. New York: Penguin Classics, [February] 2014.

Contents: Introduction; Suggestions for Further Reading; A Note on the Texts; *Short Stories:* The Tale of Satampra Zeiros; The Last Incantation; The Devotee of Evil; The Uncharted Isle; The Face by the River; The City of the Singing Flame; The Holiness of Azédarac; The Vaults of Yoh-Vombis; Ubbo-Sathla; The Double Shadow; The Maze of the Enchanter; Genius Loci; The Dark Eidolon; The Weaver in the Vault; Xeethra; The Treader of the Dust; Mother of Toads; Phoenix; *Prose Poems:* The Image of Bronze and the Image of Iron; The Memnons of the Night; The Demon, the Angel, and Beauty; The Corpse and the Skeleton; A Dream of Lethe; From the Crypts of Memory; Ennui; The Litany of the Seven Kisses; In Cocaigne; The Flower-Devil; The Shadows; The Passing of Aphrodite; To the Daemon; The Abomination of Desolation; The Mirror in the Hall of Ebony; The Touch-Stone; The Muse of Hyperborea; *Poetry:* The Last Night; Ode to the Abyss; A Dream of Beauty; The Star-Treader; Retrospect and Forecast; Nero; To the Daemon Sublimity; Averted Malefice; The Eldritch Dark; Shadow of Nightmare; Satan Unrepentant; The Ghoul; Desire of Vastness; The Medusa of Despair; The Refuge of Beauty; The Harlot of the World; Memnon at Midnight; Love Malevolent; The Crucifixion of Eros; The Tears of Lilith; Requiescat in Pace; The Motes; *The Hashish-Eater;* A Psalm to the Best Beloved; The Witch with Eyes of Amber; We Shall Meet; On Re-reading Baudelaire; To George Sterling: A Valediction; Anterior Life; Hymn to Beauty; The Remorse of the Dead; Exorcism; Nyctalops; Outlanders; Song of the Necromancer; To Howard Phillips Lovecraft; Madrigal of Memory; The Old Water-Wheel; The Hill of Dionysus; If Winter Remain; Amithaine; Cycles; Explanatory Notes.

Notes. A volume that, once again, I lobbied Penguin for years to issue. It seems to have been well received.

112.   Michael Aronovitz, *The Voices in Our Heads*
a.   n.p.: Horrified Press, [February 2014].

Contents: Foreword, by Tamara Thorne; The Falcon; The Echo; The Green-Eyed Breath Vampire with the Cheap Striped Tuxedo and Monocle Tattoo; The Puddles; The Rain Barrel; Prequel; The Sculptor; The Grave Keeper; The Soldier; The Addict; The Shape; The Trickster; Acknowledgments.

Notes. I was unexpectedly listed as editor of this book, even though all I did was routine copyediting. The author is one of the more dynamic figures in contemporary weird fiction.

113.   *Searchers After Horror: New Tales of the Weird and Fantastic*
a. Nampa, ID: Fedogan & Bremer, [March] 2014.

Contents: Introduction; Melanie Tem, "Iced In"; John Shirley, "At Home with Azathoth"; Michael Aronovitz, "The Girl Between the Slats"; Richard Gavin, "The Patter of Tiny Feet"; Ramsey Campbell, "At Lorn Hall"; Caitlín R. Kiernan, "Blind Fish"; W. H. Pugmire, "An Element of Nightmare"; Gary Fry, "The Reeds"; Steve Rasnic Tem, "Crawldaddies"; Jonathan Thomas, "Three Dreams of Ys"; Lois H. Gresh, "Willie the Protector"; Hannes Bok, "Miranda's Tree"; Simon Strantzas, "The Beautiful Fog Ascending"; Nick Mamatas, "Exit Through the Gift Shop"; Darrell Schweitzer, "Going to Ground"; Ann K. Schwader, "Dark Equinox"; Brian Stableford, "Et in Arcadia Ego"; Jason V Brock, "The Shadow of Heaven"; Nancy Kilpatrick, "Flesh and Bones"; John D. Haefele, "The Sculptures in the House"; Donald Tyson, "Ice Fishing"; Notes on Contributors.

Notes. An original anthology focusing on the motif of the "weird place." One of my best recent efforts, I think (entirely due, of course, to the excellence of the authors' contributions).

114. *Carl Jacobi* (with John Pelan)
    a.   Lakewood, CO: Centipede Press, [April] 2014.

        Contents: John Pelan, "Chronicles in Crimson"; The Unpleasantness at Carver House; Revelations in Black; Satan's Roadhouse; Coffin Crag; Matthew South and Company; The Kite; The Tunnel; The Elcar Special; Flight of the Flame Fiend; The Cocomacaque; The Tomb from Beyond; Eternity When?; Smoke of the Snake; Carnaby's Fish; Rails of the Yellow Skull; Portrait in Moonlight; The Music Lover; The Chadwick Pit; Witches in the Cornfield; Spawn of Blackness; The Satanic Piano; The Aquarium; Bride of the Tree Men; Ghoul Game; The Spanish Camera; The Random Quantity; House of the Ravens; Death Rids the Plateau; Sagasta's Last; A Pair of Swords; The Lorenzo Watch; A Quire of Foolscap; Murder for Medusa; Phantom Brass; Incident at the Galloping Horse; The Bells Toll Blood; The La Prello Paper; Manuscript for the Damned; The Singleton Barrier; Mive; Offspring; The Corbie Door; The Digging at Pistol Key; The Coach on the Ring; The Return of Fabian Blair; Josephine Gage; The Phantom Pistol; The Hand of Every; The Phantom from 512; Head in His Hands; Chameleon Town; Hamadryad; The Devil Deals; The Black Garden; Death's Outpost; The Last Drive; The Cane; The Monument; Laughter in the Wind; The Face in the Wind; Woman of the Witch Flowers; Wings for a Monster; Dyak Reward; Mr Iper of Hamilton; The Royal Opera House; Dwayne Olson, "Carl Jacobi Remembered"; Story Sources; Artwork; Credits.

Notes. An immense volume containing nearly the totality of the stories from Jacobi's three Arkham House volumes, along with much other work (including many "weird menace" stories both old and new).

115.   Robert W. Chambers, *The King in Yellow* (uncredited)
     a.   New York: Fall River Press, [April] 2014.

       Contents: Introduction; The Repairer of Reputations; The Mask; In the Court of the Dragon; The Yellow Sign; The Demoiselle d'Ys; The Prophets' Paradise; The Street of the Four Winds; The Street of the First Shell; The Street of Our Lady of the Fields; Rue Barrée; Appendix: Critics on Robert W. Chambers; Endnotes; Suggested Reading.

       Notes. An annotated edition of *The King in Yellow* prepared in a week, to capitalise on the sudden popularity of Chambers as a result of his influence on the HBO television show *True Detective*.

116.   *Edgar Allan Poe* (Library of Weird Fiction)
     a.   Lakewood, CO: Centipede Press, [April] 2014.

       Contents: Introduction; Metzengerstein; MS. Found in a Bottle; The Assignation; Shadow—A Parable; Silence—A Fable; Berenice; Morella; The Unparalleled Adventure of One Hans Pfaall; King Pest; The Narrative of Arthur Gordon Pym; Ligeia; The Devil in the Belfry; The Man That Was Used Up; The Fall of the House of Usher; William Wilson; The Conversaion of Eiros and Charmion; The Man of the Crowd; The Murders in the Rue Morgue; A Descent into the Maelström; The Colloquy of Monos and Una; Never Bet the Devil Your Head; Eleonora; The Oval Portrait; The Masque of the Red Death; The Pit and the Pendulum; The Tell-Tale Heart; The Black Cat; The Oblong Box; The Premature Burial; Mesmeric Revelation; The Balloon Hoax; Some Words with a Mummy; The Imp of the Perverse; The Facts in the Case of M. Valdemar; The Sphinx; The Cask of Amontillado; Hop-Frog; Von Kempelen and His Discovery; The Light-House; Dreams; Spirits of the Dead; A Dream; The Lake—To ——; Sonnet—To Science; Fairy-Land; "Alone"; Fairy Land; The Sleeper; The Valley of Unrest; The City in the Sea; Sonnet—Silence; Lenore; Dream-Land; Eulalie; The Raven; Ulalume; The Bells; A Dream within a Dream; For Annie; Eldorado; Annabel Lee; Bibliography.

       Notes. The first volume of a series of comprehensive and relatively inexpensive compilations of the work of the great writers of weird fiction.

117.   *Algernon Blackwood* (Library of Weird Fiction)
     a.   Lakewood, CO: Centipede Press, [April] 2014.

Contents: Introduction; A Haunted Island; Smith: An Episode in a Lodging House; The Listener; The Willows; The Insanity of Jones; The Woman's Ghost Story; A Psychical Invasion; Ancient Sorceries; The Wendigo; The Sea Fit; The Glamour of the Snow; The Golden Fly; The Man Whom the Trees Loved; Sand; The Wings of Horus; The Regeneration of Lord Ernie; The Damned; A Descent into Egypt; Bibliography.

118. *William Hope Hodgson* (Library of Weird Fiction)
   a. Lakewood, CO: Centipede Press, [April] 2014.
       Contents: Introduction; The House on the Borderland; The Ghost Pirates; The Goddess of Death; A Tropical Horror; From the Tideless Sea; The Mystery of the Derelict; The Voice in the Night; Out of the Storm; The Gateway of the Monster; The House among the Laurels; The Whistling Room; The Horse of the Invisible; The Searcher of the End House; The Thing Invisible; The Derelict; The Thing in the Weeds; The Finding of the *Graiken*; The Haunted *Pampero*; Demons of the Sea; The Haunted *Jarvee*; The Hog; The Riven Night; The Room of Fear; Bibliography.

119. Fritz Leiber, *Adept's Gambit: The Original Version*
   a. Welches, OR: Arcane Wisdom, [June] 2014.
       Contents: Introduction; Adept's Gambit; H. P. Lovecraft, "On 'Adept's Gambit'" (letter to Fritz Leiber, 19 December 1936); Notes.
       Notes. A slim volume long in the works. John Pelan had discovered the original (or, at least, an earlier) version of "Adept's Gambit," one that had fleeting references to HPL's myth-cycle. Pelan appeared to have misplaced the text for some time, but then turned it over to me, and I prepared the edition, annotating the story and including HPL's long letter of comment on it.

120. *A Mountain Walked: Great Tales of the Cthulhu Mythos*
   a. Lakewood, CO: Centipede Press, [August] 2014.
   b. Portland, OR: Dark Regions Press, [October] 2015.
       Contents: Introduction; Mearle Prout, "The House of the Worm"; Robert Barbour Johnson, "Far Below"; C. Hall Thompson, "Spawn of the Green Abyss"; James Wade, "The Deep Ones"; Erland Mørk, [Art Portfolio]; Ramsey Campbell, "The Franklyn Paragraphs"; Walter C. DeBill, Jr., "Where Yidhra Walks"; Allen Koszowski, [Art Portfolio]; T. E. D. Klein, "Black Man with a Horn"; Thomas Ligotti, "The Last Feast of Harlequin"; Neil Gaiman, "Only the End of the World Again"; Lois H. Gresh, "Mandelbrot Moldrot"; Stanley C. Sargent, "Black Brat of Dunwich"; Stanley C. Sargent, [Art Port-

folio]; W. H. Pugmire, "The Phantom of Beguilement"; Joseph S. Pulver, Sr., ". . . Hungry . . . Rats"; Donald Tyson, "Virgin's Island"; Cody Goodfellow, "In the Shadow of Swords"; Jonathan Thomas, "Mobymart After Midnight"; Mark Samuels, "A Gentleman from Mexico"; Laird Barron, "Man with No Name"; Caitlín R. Kiernan, "John Four"; Rhys Hughes, "Sigma Octantis"; Gemma Files, "[Anasazi]"; Patrick McGrath, "The Wreck of the *Aurora*"; T. C. Boyle, "Thirteen Hundred Rats"; Michael Shea, "Beneath the Beardmore"; Denis Tiani, "Rupa Worms from Outer Space"; H. P. Lovecraft, "Pickman's Model" (illustrated by John Kenn Mortensen); H. P. Lovecraft, "The Lurking Fear" (illustrated by Thomas Ott); Drazen Kozjan, "Excerpts from a Notebook"; Julien Bazinet, [cartoons]; Notes on Contributors.

Notes. An immense compilation that grew out of a much smaller volume that I had compiled as early as 2008 for Mythos Books. Many of the stories in the latter part of the volume were solicited by the publisher, who also included other items (art portfolios, illustrated versions of two HPL stories, etc.). The Dark Regions Press paperback edition omits many of these items (including the stories by Laird Barron and T. C. Boyle) and adds Jason V Brock's "The Man with the Horn."

121. *The Madness of Cthulhu: Volume 1*
   a.   London & New York: Titan Books, [September] 2014.
        Contents: Jonathan Maberry, "Foreword"; Introduction; Arthur C. Clarke, "At the Mountains of Murkiness"; Harry Turtledove, "The Fillmore Shoggoth"; Lois H. Gresh, "Devil's Bathtub"; John Shirley, "The Witness in Darkness"; William Browning Spencer, "How the Gods Bargain"; Caitlín R. Kiernan, "A Mountain Walked"; Robert Silverberg, "Diana of the Hundred Breasts"; Michael Shea, "Under the Shelf"; Melanie Tem, "Cantata"; Heather Graham, "Cthulhu Rising"; Darrell Schweitzer, "The Warm"; Jonathan Maberry, "A Footnote in the Black Budget"; J. C. Koch, "Little Lady"; Joseph S. Pulver, Sr., "White Fire"; Jonathan Thomas, "A Quirk of the Mistral"; Donald Tyson, "The Dog Handler's Tale"; Notes on Contributors.

122. Ramsey Campbell and August Derleth, *Letters to Arkham: The Letters of Ramsey Campbell and August Derleth, 1961–1971.*
   a.   Hornsea, UK: PS Publishing, [November] 2014.
        Contents: Introduction; The Letters; Glossary of Names; Bibliography; Index.

        Notes. A complete publication of the joint correspondence of Campbell and Derleth. The Campbell side was supplied by Peter

Ruber of Arkham House; the Derleth side was supplied by Campbell himself. I annotated the text extensively, with an extensive bibliography of books and films mentioned in the letters. The book won the British Fantasy Award.

123. *William Hope Hodgson: Voices from the Borderland* (with Massimo Berruti and Sam Gafford).
 a. New York: Hippocampus Press, [November] 2014.
  Contents: Sam Gafford, "Introduction"; I. SOME STUDIES OF HODGSON'S LIFE AND EARLY RECEPTION: Sam Gafford, "Houdini v. Hodgson: The Blackburn Challenge"; A. Langley Searles, "William Hope Hodgson: In His Own Day"; "Pioneering Essays" (H. P. Lovecraft, "The Weird Work of William Hope Hodgson"; Clark Ashton Smith, "In Appreciation of William Hope Hodgson"; H. C. Koenig, "William Hope Hodgson: Master of the Weird and Fantastic"; August Derleth, "William Hope Hodgson"; Ellery Queen, "William Hope Hodgson and the Detective Story"; Fritz Leiber, "William Hope Hodgson: Writer of Supernatural Horror"); II. SOME SPECIAL TOPICS: Brian Stableford, "William Hope Hodgson"; Emily Alder, "The Dark Mythos of the Sea: William Hope Hodgson's Transformation of Maritime Legends"; S. T. Joshi, "Things in the Weeds: The Supernatural in Hodgson's Short Stories"; Mark Valentine, "Against the Abyss: *Carnacki the Ghost-Finder*"; Phillip A. Ellis, "William Hope Hodgson in the Underworld: Mythic Aspects of the Novels"; Sam Gafford, "Decay and Disease in the Fiction of William Hope Hodgson"; Sam Gafford, "Hodgson's Women"; III. STUDIES OF INDIVIDUAL TALES: Leigh Blackmore, "Things Invisible, Human and Ab-Human in Two of Hodgson's Carnacki Stories"; Sid Birchby, "Sexual Symbolism in W. H. Hodgson"; Mark Valentine, "The 'Wonder Unlimited'—The Tales of Captain Gault"; Henrik Harksen, "*The House on the Borderland:* On Humanity and Love"; IV. COMPARATIVE STUDIES: Andy Sawyer, "Time Machines Go Both Ways: Past and Future in H. G. Wells and W. H. Hodgson"; Brett Davidson, "The Long Apocalypse: The Experimental Eschatologies of H. G. Wells and William, Hope Hodgson"; John D. Haefele, "Shadow out of Hodgson"; Marcos Legaria, "Robert H. Barlow's 'A Memory' in William Hope Hodgson's *The Night Land*"; S. T. Joshi, Sam Gafford, and Mike Ashley, "William Hope Hodgson: A Bibliography"; Index.

124. *Fred Chappell* (Masters of the Weird Tale)
 a. Lakewood, CO: Centipede Press [November] 2014.

Contents: Introduction, by Fred Chappell; *Dagon*; Linnaeus Forgets; Ladies from Lapland; The Snow That Is Nothing in the Triangle; Barcarole; Weird Tales; The Somewhere Doors; The Adder; Ember; Duet; Miss Prue; Mankind Journeys Through Forests of Symbols; Silent; The Evening of the Second Day; H. P. Lovecraft; The Sea Text; Prologue; Rider; Halloween Moon Over Huddle Knob Graveyard; Source; Alma; After Revelation; The Lodger; Gift of Roses; Hooyoo Love; The White Cat; Remnants; Uncle Moon in Raintree Hills; Interview with Fred Chappell, by Darrell Schweitzer; Bibliography.

125.   *Black Wings IV: New Tales of Lovecraftian Horror*
    a.   Hornsea, UK: PS Publishing, [March] 2015.
    b.   London: Titan Books, March 2016 (as *Black Wings of Cthulhu 4*).
        Contents: Introduction; Fred Chappell, "Artifact"; W. H. Pugmire, "Half Lost in Shadow"; Richard Gavin, "The Rasping Absence"; Caitlín R. Kiernan, "Black Ships Seen South of Heaven"; Jason V Brock, "The Dark Sea Within"; Gary Fry, "Sealed by the Moon"; Cody Goodfellow, "Broken Sleep"; Darrell Schweitzer, "A Prism of Darkness"; Ann K. Schwader, "Night of the Piper"; Jonathan Thomas, "We Are Made of Stars"; Melanie Tem, "Trophy"; John Pelan and Stephen Mark Rainey, "Contact"; Lois H. Gresh, "Cult of the Dead"; Will Murray, "Dark Redeemer"; Simon Strantzas, "In the Event of Death"; Stephen Woodworth, "Revival"; Donald Tyson, "The Wall of Asshur-sin"; Charles Lovecraft, "Fear Lurks Atop Tempest Mount."

126.   *David Case* (Masters of the Weird Tale)
    a.   Lakewood, CO: Centipede Press, [July] 2015.
        Contents: Introduction, by Ramsey Campbell; Anachrona; The Cell; The Dead End; The Hunter; Fengriffen; Among the Wolves; Strange Roots; Neighbours; A Cross to Bear; Twins; The War Is Over; Brotherly Love; The Foreign Bride; The Ogre of the Cleft; Jimmy; The Terrestrial Enemy; Stranger Than You Know; David Case Interview, by Johnny Mains; Story Sources.

127.   *The Madness of Cthulhu: Volume 2*
    a.   London & New York: Titan Books, [September] 2015.
        Contents: Kim Newman, "Foreword"; Introduction; Kevin J. Anderson, "20,000 Years Under the Sea"; Brian Stableford, "Tsathoggua's Breath"; Alan Dean Foster, "The Door Beneath"; William F. Nolan, "Dead Man Walking"; Nancy Kilpatrick, "A Crazy Mistake"; Cody Goodfellow, "The Anatomy Lesson"; Jason C. Eckhardt, "The Hollow Sky"; Steve Rasnic Tem, "Deep Fracture";

Donald Tyson, "The Dream Stones"; Laird Barron, "The Blood in My Mouth"; Karen Haber, "On the Shores of Destruction"; Erik Bear and Greg Bear, "Object 00922UU"; Mark Howard Jones, "The Last Ones"; K. M. Tonso, "Last Rites"; Notes on Contributors.

128. Dennis Etchison, *It Only Comes Out at Night and Other Stories*
    a.   Lakewood, CO: Centipede Press, [October] 2015 (uncredited).
    b.   Vancouver, WA: Cycatrix Press, 2018.

      Contents: Introduction; Wet Season; Sitting in the Corner, Whimpering Quietly; Daughter of the Golden West; The Machine Demands a Sacrifice; It Only Comes Out at Night; Calling All Monsters; We Have Been Here Before; On the Pike; I Can Hear the Dark; The Nighthawk; The Dead Line; It Will Be Here Soon; You Can Go Now; On Call; The Late Shift; The Spot; The Chill; Somebody Like You; Deathtracks; The Dark Country; The Chair; Talking in the Dark; The Woman in Black; Deadspace; The Olympic Runner; Call 666; The Scar; The Blood Kiss; When They Gave Us Memory; Call Home; The Dog Park; A Wind from the South; The Last Reel; The Dead Cop; No One You Know; Inside the Cackle Factory; The Detailer; Got to Kill Them All; In a Silent Way; One of Us; Red Dog Down; Tell Me I'll See You Again; Author's Notes; Story Sources.

      Notes. A book that began as an omnibus of Etchison's complete short fiction (I transcribed about 60 of his stories from his story collections and elsewhere), but in the end Etchison used only 38 of the stories.

129. *The Cold Embrace: Weird Stories by Women*
    a.   Mineola, NY: Dover, [May] 2016.

      Contents: Introduction; Mary Shelley, "Transformation"; Elizabeth Gaskell, "Curious If True"; Mary Elizabeth Braddon, "The Cold Embrace"; Amelia B. Edwards, "The Engineer's Story"; Margaret Oliphant, "The Secret Chamber"; E. Nesbit, "From the Dead"; Vernon Lee, "Winthrop's Adventure"; Mrs. J. H. Riddell, "The Last of Squire Ennismore"; Sarah Orne Jewett, "In Dark New England Days"; Charlotte Perkins Gilman, "The Yellow Wall Paper"; Gertrude Atherton, "Death and the Woman"; Mary E. Wilkins Freeman, "The Hall Bedroom"; Edith Wharton, "The Eyes"; Edna W. Underwood, "The Painter of Dead Women"; Ellen Glasgow, "The Shadowy Third"; Marjorie Bowen, "Scoured Milk"; Mrs. H. D. Everett, "The Death Mask"; Virginia Woolf, "A Haunted House"; May Sinclair, "Where Their Fire Is Not Quenched"; Notes on the Authors.

Notes. An anthology of weird tales by female writers from Mary Shelley up to the 1920s. Dover had initially proposed to have me edit two further volumes, including material right up to the present day; but a change in management nixed the plans.

130. *Black Wings V: New Tales of Lovecraftian Horror*
a. Hornsea, UK: PS Publishing, [June] 2016.
b. New York & London: Titan Books, [December] 2017 (as *Black Wings of Cthulhu 5*).

    Contents: Introduction; Jonathan Thomas, "Plenty of Irem"; Nicole Cushing, "Diary of a Sane Man"; Robert H. Waugh, "The Woman in the Attic"; Caitlín R. Kiernan, "Far from Any Shore"; W. H. Pugmire, "In Blackness Etched, My Name"; Cody Goodfellow, "Snakeladder"; Jason C. Eckhardt, "The Walker in the Night"; Lynne Jamneck, "In Bloom"; John Reppion, "The Black Abbess"; Mollie L. Burleson, "The Quest"; David Hambling, "A Question of Blood"; Mark Howard Jones, "Red Walls"; Donald Tyson, "The Organ of Chaos"; Donald R. Burleson, "Seed of the Gods"; Sunni K Brock, "Fire Breeders"; Sam Gafford, "Casting Fractals"; Darrell Schweitzer, "The Red Witch of Chorazin"; Nancy Kilpatrick, "The Oldies"; Stephen Woodworth, "Voodoo"; Wade German, "Lore."

131. *And Death Shall Have No Dominion: A Tribute to Michael Shea* (with Linda Shea)
a. New York: Hippocampus Press, [September] 2016.

    Contents: Editor's Note, by Linda Shea; Salutation to the World as Beheld at Dawn from Atop Mount Eburon; Foreword: Michael Shea Remembered, by Dan Temianka; FICTION: Credit Card; The Growlimb; In Memory Drive Slow; King Gil Gomez and Monkey-Do; VERSE: The Greek Plowman; Two Nights; From *A Quest for Simbilis*; From *Nifft the Lean*; From *In Yana, the Touch of Undying*; From *The Mines of Behemoth*; From *The A'Rak*; From *Epistle to Lebanoi*; From *Mr. Cannyharme*; From "The Angel of Death"; From "Fat Face"; From "The Recruiter"; From "Beneath the Beardmore"; Life is pretty fucking complicated; TRIBUTES: Shine On, Dark Star, by Laird Barron; A Memory of Michael Shea, by Cody Goodfellow; How I Met Michael Shea, by Sam Hamm; "Grab the Morning, You'll Have the Day": An Elegy for Michael Shea, by Maya Khosla; Memories of Michael Shea, by Marc Laidlaw; Read More Michael Shea, by John O'Neill; Remembering Michael, by W. H. Pugmire; Abysses, Mountains, and Skies; or, How My Vision Was Enlarged, by Jessica Amanda Salmonson; My Memories of Michael, by Jerad

Walters; Michael Shea, by Jason V Brock; Images; Afterword, by Michael Shea; A Michael Shea Bibliography; Notes on Contributors.

Notes. A book that took rather a long time to assemble, intended as a tribute to Shea, who died in early 2014. An interesting mix of memoirs of Shea along with rare writings (including a substantial amount of verse and some scintillating unreprinted or unpublished stories).

132. *Gothic Lovecraft* (with Lynne Jamneck)
   a.   Vancouver, WA: Cycatrix Press, 2016 [January 2017].

   Contents: Introduction; Donald R. Burleson, "The Shadow over Lear"; Don Webb, "The Revelation at the Abbey"; Jonathan Thomas, "Old Goodman Brown"; Lois H. Gresh, "Square of the Inquisition"; John Shirley, "The Rime of the Cosmic Mariner"; Mollie L. Burleson, "A Yuletide Carol"; Donald Tyson, "Curse of the House of Usher"; Mark Howard Jones, "The Rolling of Old Thunder"; Nancy Kilpatrick, "Always a Castle?"; Caitlín R. Kiernan, "As Red as Red"; Robert S. Wilson, "Four Arches"; Gwyneth Jones, "The Old Schoolhouse"; Orrin Grey, "Dream House"; Lynda E. Rucker, "The Unknown Chambers"; Notes on Contributors.

   Notes. A worthy assemblage of original tales that fused Gothic elements with Lovecraftian themes. The idea was devised by my coeditor.

133. *Nightmare's Realm: New Tales of the Weird and Fantastic*
   a.   Portland, OR: Dark Regions Press, [April] 2017.

   Contents: Introduction; H. P. Lovecraft, "Prologue: To a Dreamer"; Ramsey Campbell, "The Dreamed"; Darrell Schweitzer, "A Predicament"; Jason V Brock, "Kafkaesque"; David Barker, "Beneath the Veil"; John Shirley, "Dreams Downstream"; Nancy Kilpatrick, "Death-Dreaming"; Richard Gavin, "Cast Lots"; Steve Rasnic Tem, "The Wake"; Caitlín R. Kiernan, "Dead Letter Office"; Donald Tyson, "The Art of Memory"; John Langan, "What You Do Not Bring Forth"; W. H. Pugmire, "The Barrier Between"; Gemma Files, "Sleep Hygiene"; Jonathan Thomas, "Purging Mom"; Simon Strantzas, "The Fifth Stone"; Stephen Woodworth, "In the City of Sharp Edges"; Reggie Oliver, "An Actor's Nightmare"; Edgar Allan Poe, "Epilogue: Dream-Land"; Notes on Contributors.

   Notes. A "theme" anthology that I had long wished to compile—and one that, to my delight, turned out splendidly, with some highly imaginative treatments of the general theme of dreams, nightmares, and so on.

134. Lord Dunsany, *The Ghost in the Corner and Other Stories* (with Martin Andersson)
    a. New York: Hippocampus Press, [May] 2017.
        Contents: Introduction; TALES AND SKETCHES, 1931–1957: The Use of Man; The Ghost in the Corner; Very Secret; Tales for the Dark Continent; Advance Regulations; A Modern Portrait; The Rations of Murdoch Finucan; A Day on the Bog; Little Tim Brannehan; The Burrahoola; Kind Pagan Lights; A Witch in the Balkans; A Talk in the Dark; Mid Snow and Ice; A Treasure of India; Two Young Officers; The Unforgivable Choice; The Old Detective's Tale; TALES FROM THE 1956 COLLECTION: Helping the Fairies; The Story of Tse Gah; The Dwarf Holóbolos and the Sword Hogbiter; Progress; One Night in Eldorado; The Traveller to Thundercliff; The Lucky Escape; How Mickey Paid His Debt; Lost Lyrics; The Dance at Weirdmoor Caste; As It Seems to the Blackbird; The Haunting of Whitebeams; The Romance of His Life; A Theory of Evolution; Stolen Power; The Cook of Santamaria; The Awakening; A Goat in Trousers; A Breeze at Rest; A Channel Rescue; In the Governor's Palace; Hard Horses; The Blundering Curate; A Tale of the Irish Countryside; The Price of the World; When Mrs. Fynn Was Young; At the Scene of the Crime; A Victim of Bad Luck; In a Hotel Lounge; The Chambermaid of the Splendide; The Motive; The Quiet Laugh; Bibliography.

        Notes. A volume of Dunsany's uncollected and unpublished works that had long been in the works; it was initially titled *A Walk in the Wastes of Time* and contained uncollected essays as well as stories, but has now been refashioned to contain only later stories, some of them discovered by Martin Andersson on visits to Dunsany Castle.

135. H. L. Mencken, *A Saturnalia of Bunk: Selections from* The Free Lance, *1911–1915*
    a. Athens: Ohio University Press, [August] 2017.
        Contents: Introduction; I. On Being a Free Lance; II. The Central Questions of Existence; III. The Follies of American Government and Society; IV. The Bozart; V. Men, Women, and the Vote; VI. The Bane of Religion; VII. The Vice Crusade 1: General Notes; VIII. The Vice Crusade 2: Prohibition and Other Panaceas; IX. The Vice Crusade 3: Prostitution; X. Sundry Forms of Quackery; XI. The Great War; Notes; Glossary of Names; Index.

        Notes. A book that took a long time to achieve print. I had transcribed Mencken's 1200 "Free Lance" columns from the *Baltimore Evening Sun* years before, and then spent quite a bit of time assembling extracts of them into thematic chapters. Almost none of the material had been previously reprinted, either by Mencken or by later compilers. The introduction was reprinted in I.50 as "H. L. Mencken, Free Lance."

136. *The Red Brain: Great Tales of the Cthulhu Mythos*
   a.   Portland, OR: Dark Regions Press, [November] 2017.
        Contents: Introduction; Edith Miniter, "Falco Ossifracus: By Mr. Goodguile"; Donald Wandrei, "The Red Brain"; Clark Ashton Smith, "The Beast of Averoigne"; C. Hall Thompson, "The Will of Claude Ashur"; Ramsey Campbell, "The Pattern"; Thomas Ligotti, "The Sect of the Idiot"; Brian McNaughton, "Meryphillia"; Caitlín R. Kiernan, "The Peddler's Tale; or, Isobel's Revenge"; Jonathan Thomas, "Integrity"; W. H. Pugmire, "Pickman's Lazarus"; Mark Samuels, "The Crimson Fog"; Ray Garton, "Misanthrope"; Acknowledgments.
        Notes. A volume that was meant to capitalise on the unexpected success of the paperback edition of *A Mountain Walked* (item 120 above). The last three stories are previously unpublished.

137. Michael Shea, *Demiurge: The Complete Cthulhu Mythos Tales*
   a.   Portland, OR: Dark Regions Press, [November] 2017.
        Contents: Introduction; Fat Face; Nemo Me Impune Lacessit; The Presentation; The Pool; The Recruiter; The Battery; Copping Squid; Dagoniad; Tsathoggua; Beneath the Beardmore; Momma Durtt; Under the Shelf; Demiurge; Acknowledgments.
        Notes. A volume that gathers the entirety of Shea's Lovecraftian fiction, including the complete contents of *Copping Squid* (item V.A.1 below). The title novella is previously unpublished; I had urged the author to turn it into a full-length novel, but he died before he could do so. A superb unpublished Lovecraftian novel, *Mr. Cannyharme* (an elaboration of, of all things, "The Hound"), remains unpublished, although I have prepared it for publication.

138. *Black Wings VI: New Tales of Lovecraftian Horror*
   a.   Hornsea, UK: PS Publishing, [November] 2017.
   b.   New York & London: Titan Books, [September] 2018 (as *Black Wings of Cthulhu 6*).
        Contents: Introduction; Ann K. Schwader, "Pothunters"; Darrell Schweitzer, "The Girl in the Attic"; Jonathan Thomas, "The Once and Future Waite"; Lynne Jamneck, "Oude Goden"; William F. Nolan, "Carnivorous"; Ashley Dioses, "On a Dreamland's Moon"; Aaron Bittner, "Teshtigo Creek"; Caitlín R. Kiernan, "Ex Libris"; Mark Howard Jones, "You Shadows That in Darkness Dwell"; Adam Boli-

var, "The Ballad of Asenath Waite"; Nancy Kilpatrick, "The Visitor"; Tom Lynch, "The Gaunt"; Donald Tyson, "Missing at the Morgue"; Don Webb, "The Shard"; David Hambling, "The Mystery of the Cursed Cottage"; K. A. Opperman, "To Court the Night"; W. H. Pugmire, "To Move Beneath Autumnal Oaks"; Steve Rasnic Tem, "Mister Ainsley"; Jason V Brock, "Satiety"; Stephen Woodworth, "Provenance Unknown"; D. L. Myers, "The Well."

Notes. The sixth volume of the series. I initiated an informal contest among four poets to see who could write the best poem for the volume; but in the end I decided to accept all the poems.

139.   *Arthur Machen* (Library of Weird Fiction)
    a.   Lakewood, CO: Centipede Press, [December] 2017.

Contents: Introduction; The Great God Pan; The Inmost Light; The Shining Pyramid; *The Three Impostors*; The Red Hand; *Ornaments in Jade* (The Rose Garden; The Turanians; The Idealist; Witchcraft; The Ceremony; Psychology; Torture; Midsummer; Nature; The Holy Things); The White People; A Fragment of Life; The Bowmen; The Soldiers' Rest; The Monstrance; The Dazzling Light; The Great Return; The Terror; Johnny Double; The Bright Boy; APPENDIX: Folklore and Legends of the North; Introduction to *The Angels of Mons*; Introduction to *The Three Impostors*; Bibliography.

Notes. A hefty volume of Machen for my Library of Weird Fiction series.

140.   D. H. Lawrence, *The Rocking-Horse Winner and Other Superatural Tales*
    a.   Lakewood, CO: Centipede Press, [March] 2018.

Contents: Introduction; Odour of Chrysanthemums; The Prussian Officer; "Tickets, Please!"; The Blind Man; The Border Line; The Woman Who Rode Away; The Last Laugh; Glad Ghosts; The Rocking-Horse Winner; The Lovely Lady; Mother and Daughter; Story Notes.

Notes. A volume that had been commissioned nearly two decades earlier by Ash-Tree Press, but its financial troubles prevented it from publishing the book. Some of the items are only marginally "weird," but all are compelling and powerful. The introduction was reprinted in I.52.

141.   E. Nesbit, *From the Dead: The Complete Weird Stories of E. Nesbit*
    a.   New York: Hippocampus Press, [May] 2018.

Contents: Introduction; John Charrington's Wedding; The Ebony Frame; The Mass for the Dead; Uncle Abraham's Romance; The Mystery of the Semi-Detached; From the Dead; Man-Size in Marble;

Hurst of Hurstcote; The Power of Darkness; The Shadow; The Head; The Three Drugs; In the Dark; The New Samson; Number 17; The Five Senses; The Violet Car; The Haunted House; The Pavilion; Appendix: From *My School-Days*; Bibliography.

Notes. The first of eight volumes that had been commissioned by Joe Morey of Dark Renaissance Books; but his retirement from publishing for health reasons compelled him to abandon the plan. The series was to be called Classic Weird Fiction; but when Derrick Hussey of Hippocampus Press decided to pick up the series, he felt that the phrase "weird fiction" had been overused and suggested Classics of Gothic Horror. And so it was. The introduction was reprinted in I.47.

142. Mary E. Wilkins Freeman, *Lost Ghosts: The Complete Weird Stories of Mary E. Wilkins Freeman*
   a.   New York: Hippocampus Press, [May] 2018.
   Contents: Introduction; A Symphony in Lavender; A Far-away Melody; A Gentle Ghost; The Twelfth Guest; The Little Maid at the Door; Silence; The White Witch; The School-Teacher's Story; The Prism; The Wind in the Rose-bush; The Vacant Lot; Luella Miller; The Shadows on the Wall; The Hall Bedroom; The Southwest Chamber; The Lost Ghost; The Witch's Daughter; The Jade Bracelet; Giles Corey, Yeoman; Bibliography.
   Notes. The second volume of my Classics of Gothic Horror series. I believe this is the first volume to contain the totality of Freeman's weird writing, including the play *Giles Corey, Yeoman* (about the Salem witch trials): it has, strictly speaking, nothing weird about it, but certain phases of it are grimly terrifying. The introduction was reprinted in I.47.

143. Thomas Burke, *Johnson Looked Back: The Collected Weird Stories of Thomas Burke*
   a.   New York: Hippocampus Press, [June] 2018.
   Contents: Introduction; The Bird; The Tablets of the House of Li; The Bloomsbury Wonder; The Hands of Mr. Ottermole; Desirable Villa; The Secret of Francesco Shedd; The Yellow Imps; Miracle in Suburbia; Yesterday Street; Funspot; Uncle Ezekiel's Long Sight; The Horrible God; Father and Son; Johnson Looked Back; Two Gentlemen; The Black Courtyard; The Gracious Ghosts; Jack Wapping; One Hundred Pounds; The Man Who Lost His Head; Murder under the Crooked Spire; The Lonely Inn; The Watcher; Events at Wayless-Wagtail; The Hollow Man; The Golden Gong; Bibliography.
   Notes. The third volume of the Classics of Gothic Horror series. Burke had long been a favourite of mine, ever since I read his story

collection *Night-Pieces* (reprinted here in its entirety, along with several other works) as a teenger in Muncie, Indiana. The introduction was reprinted in I.52.

144. W. W. Jacobs, *Twin Spirits: The Complete Weird Stories of W. W. Jacobs*
    a. New York: Hippocampus Press, [June] 2018.
        Contents: Introduction; A Strange Compact; The Lost Ship; In Mid-Atlantic; The Rival Beauties; The Brown Man's Servant; Over the Side; Jerry Bundler; Three at Table; The Well; Twin Spirits; Captain Rogers; In the Library; The Monkey's Paw; The Castaway; The Toll-House; The Vigil; The Three Sisters; Sam's Ghost; His Brother's Keeper; The Interruption; APPENDIX: The Ghost of Jerry Bundler (with Charles Rock); In the Library (with Herbert C. Sargent); The Monkey's Paw (by Louis N. Parker); Bibliography.
        Notes. The fourth volume in my Classics of Gothic Horror series. I was particularly pleased to include three play versions of some of Jacobs's short stories, two co-written by Jacobs and the third written by another writer. The introduction was reprinted in I.52.

145/146.   *Robert Aickman* (Masters of the Weird Tale)
    a. Lakewood, CO: Centipede Press, [July] 2018. 2 vols.
        Contents: Volume 1: Introduction; "An Afternoon with Aickman," by T. E. D. Klein; The Trains; The Insufficient Answer; The View; Your Tiny Hand Is Frozen; Ringing the Changes; The Waiting Room; The School Friend; Bind Your Hair; Choice of Weapons; Just a Song at Twilight; Larger Than Oneself; My Poor Friend; The Wine-Dark Sea; The Visiting Star; A Roman Question; The Inner Room; No Stronger Than a Flower; The Cicerones; The Houses of the Russians; Ravissante; Into the Wood; Never Visit Venice; The Unsettled Dust; The Swords; Meeting Mr. Millar; The Same Dog; *Volume 2:* Pages from a Young Girl's Journal; The Clock Watcher; The Real Road to the Church; Niemandswasser; The Hospice; Compulsory Games; Wood; Growing Boys; The Fetch; Laura; Le Miroir; Residents Only; Raising the Wind; Marriage; Hand in Glove; The Next Glade; No Time Is Passing; The Breakthrough; Letters to the Postman; The Stains; Mark Ingestre: The Customer's Tale; Rosamund's Bower; Bibliography; Credits.
        Notes. A mammoth edition of Aickman's canonical 48 "strange stories."

147. Mary Shelley, *Frankenstein and Others: The Complete Weird Fiction of Mary Shelley*
    a. New York: Hippocampus Press, [September] 2018.

Contents: Introduction; Frankenstein; or, The Modern Prometheus; Valerius: The Reanimated Roman; Roger Dodsworth: The Reanimated Englishman; Transformation; The Invisible Girl; The Mortal Immortal; Bibliography.

Notes. The fifth volume in the Classics of Gothic Horror series, timed for the 200th anniversary of the publication of *Frankenstein*. Introduction reprinted in I.52.

148.　H. L. Mencken, *Writings in the* Smart Set, *Volume 1: 1908–1911*
　　a.　Seattle: Sarnath Press, [October] 2018.

　　　Contents: Introduction; The Good, the Bad and the Best Sellers; Oyez! Oyez! All Ye Who Read Books; A Road Map of the New Books; The Literary Olio; The Literary Clinic; The Novels That Bloom in the Spring, Tra-La!; Some Novels—and a Good One; Books for the Hammock and Deck Chair; The Best Novels of the Year; Novels and Other Books—Chiefly Bad; The Books of the Dog Days; The Last of the Victorians; What about Nietzsche?; "A Doll's House"—with a Fourth Act; George Bernard Shaw as a Hero; Books to Read and Books to Avoid; The Literary Heavyweight Champion; A Glance at the Spring Fiction; In Praise of a Poet; The Greatest of American Writers; A Fictioneer of the Laboratory; A Hot Weather Novelist; The Mackaye Mystery; Meredith's Swan Song; A Guide to Intelligent Eating; Mainly about Novels; The Leading American Novelist; The Revival of the Printed Play; A Stack of Novels; The Meredith of Tomorrow; Novels—the Spring Crop; The Horse Power of Realism; Novels for Hot Afternoons; The New Dramatic Literature; A 1911 Model Dream Book; Brieux and Others; A Novel of the First Rank; An Overdose of Novels.

　　　Notes. The first volume in what will probably be an immense series: the Collected Essays and Journalism of H. L. Mencken. I have had electronic files of Mencken's complete writings on my computer system since at least 2010, and I figured it was time to do something with them.

149.　H. L. Mencken, *Writings in the* Smart Set, *Volume 2: 1912–1913*
　　a.　Seattle: Sarnath Press, [October] 2018.

　　　Contents: Horsetales; Conrad, Bennett, James et al.; Rounding Up the Novels; The Prophet of the Superman; An Antidote to "Yankee Doodle"; Pertinent and Impertinent; The Bards in Battle Royal; Pertinent and Impertinent; The Terrible Swede; A Dip into the Novels; Zola; Prose Fiction ad Infinitum; Synge and Others; Novels Bad, Half Bad and Very Bad; A Visit to a Short Story Factory; Again the Busy Fictioneers; The Burden of Humor; Gerhart Hauptmann; Pertinent and Impertinent; The Beeriad; The Burbling of the Bards; Pertinent and Impertinent; Good Old Baltimore; Weep for the White Slave!; Pertinent and Impertinent; The American; At Large in London; A Nietzschean, a Swedenborgian and Other Queer Fowl; Pertinent and Impertinent; The American: His Morals; Various Bad Novels; Pertinent and Impertinent; The American: His Language; A Counterblast to Buncombe; Pertinent and Impertinent; The American: His Ideas of Beauty; Getting Rid of the Actor; Pertinent and Impertinent; The American: His Freedom; "With Your Kind Permission—"; Pertinent and Impertinent; Post-Impressions of Cities; Marie Corelli's Sparring Partner; Pertinent and Impertinent; The Russians.

Notes. Volume 2 of the Collected Essays and Journalism of H. L. Mencken.

150.   H. L. Mencken, *Writings in the* Smart Set, *Volume 3: 1914–1915*
   a.   Seattle: Sarnath Press, [November] 2018.

Contents: Pertinent and Impertinent; A Pestilence of Novels; Pertinent and Impertinent; The American: His New Puritanism; Anything But Novels!; Pertinent and Impertinent; The Raw Material of Fiction; Pertinent and Impertinent; Roosevelt, Bulwer-Lytton and Anthony Comstock; Pertinent and Impertinent; The Harp, the Sackbut and the Psaltery; The Bridge Game and How I Beat It to a Finish; The Anatomy of the Novel; Pertinent and Impertinent; Galsworthy and Others; Adventures among the New Novels; Pertinent and Impertinent; Thirty-Five Printed Plays; The Science of Four-Flushing; A Review of Reviewers; Ah, che la morte!; The Rewards of Science; Thoughts on Mortality; The Old Trails; The Ballade of Cockaigne; The Barbarous Bradley; Song; The Blind Goddess; Veneration; Epithalamium; The City of Seven Sundays; Critics of More or Less Badness; Water-Wagon Enchantments; The Innumerable Caravan; An Ode to Munich; Mr. John Smith; Death: A Discussion; After All, What's the Use?; Mush for the Multitude; From the Memoirs of the Devil; A Litany for Music Lovers; Is Civilization, Then, a Failure?; The Interior Hierarchy; A Few Pages of Notes; A Gamey Old Gaul; The Flapper; Contributions to a Thesaurus of American Synonyms for "Whiskers"; From the Chart; An American Statesman; Litany for Magazine Editors; Lachrymose Love; Invocation; The Ballad of Ships in Harbor; A Prayer for Puritans; Beethoven; The Voices; The Wedding; The Bugaboo of the Sunday Schools; The Grandstand Flirts with the Bleachers; Neapolitan Nights; The Troubadours A-twitter; Post-Impressions of Poets; A Panorama of Women; Here Are Novels!; The Scholar; The Prometheus of the Western World; Four Notes; A Panorama of Men; The Sawdust Trail; A Snapshot of an Ideal Husband; The Prayer of a Little Frog; The Genealogy of Etiquette; The Exile Returns; A Footnote for Critics; The Literature of a Moral Republic; The Greatest Gift; The Incomparable Physician; After All, Why Not?; Children of Apollo; The Memory of Edna; A Literary Behemoth.

Notes. Volume 3 of the Collected Essays and Journalism of H. L. Mencken.

151. H. L. Mencken, *Writings in the* Smart Set, *Volume 4: 1916–1917*
   a. Seattle: Sarnath Press, [November] 2018.

   Contents: The Rescuers; Partly about Books; Saved!; A Massacre in a Mausoleum; The Great American Art; Halls; Notes from a Day-Book; The Publishers Begin Their Spring Drive; The Bleeding Heart; The Deathbed; Tra-la! Tra-la-la! Tra-la-la-la!; Contribution toward a List of Euphemisms for "Drunk"; A Soul's Adventures; The Puritan; Savonarolas A-sweat; A Footnote on the Duel of Sex; A Panorama of Babies; Degenerate Days; A Litany for Hangmen; The Ulster Polonius; Portrait of a Tragic Comedian; The Creed of a Novelist; The Omission; Professors at the Bat; Chanson d'Amour à la Carte; The Literary Shambles; Suffering among Books; The Rough-House on Parnassus; The Books of the Irish; The Infernal Feminine; Shocking Stuff; The Genius; The Plague of Books; Rosemary; Bluebeard's Goat; The Conclusions of a Man of Sixty; The Cult of Dunsany; The Charmed Circle; The Conclusions of a Man of Sixty; The Cynic; The Conqueror; Criticism of Criticism of Criticism; The Window of Horrors; Si Mutare Potest Aethiops Pellum Suam . . .; Rosemary (Part 2); Woman, Lovely Woman!; Wall-Paper; Whoopers and Twitterers; Addenda to Wilstach; Critics Wild and Tame.

   Notes. Volume 4 of the Collected Essays and Journalism of H. L. Mencken.

152. H. L. Mencken, *Writings in the* Smart Set, *Volume 5: 1918–1919*
   a. Seattle: Sarnath Press, [December] 2018.

   Contents: Seven Pages about Books; She Did Not Believe Me; The National Letters; Literæ Humaniores; Unmentionables: An Inquiry into the Advertising Pages; Business; The Stream of Fiction; Hark, Hark, the Lark!; The Public Prints; The Victim; The Carousel; A Sub-Potomac Phenomenon; The Homeric Sex; Rattling the Subconscious; The Man of God; Suite Élégiaque; The Hypocrite; Dithyrambs against Learning; The Late Mr. Wells; Wives; Nothing Much Is Here, Alas!; Here's to the Dead!; Sunrise on the Prairie; Mainly Fiction; Répétition Générale; Meditation; Notes of a Poetry-Hater;

Répétition Générale; Prof. Veblen and the Cow; Répétition Générale; The Infernal Mystery; Répétition Générale; The Coroner's Inquest; Répétition Générale; Novels, Chiefly Bad; Répétition Générale; Along the Potomac; Arnold Bennett; Répétition Générale; Mark Twain; Répétition Générale; Novels for Indian Summer; Répétition Générale; Exeunt Omnes.

Notes. Volume 5 of the Collected Essays and Journalism of H. L. Mencken.

153. H. L. Mencken, *Writings in the* Smart Set, *Volume 6: 1920–1921*
  a. Seattle: Sarnath Press, [December] 2018.

  Contents: Répétition Générale; The Flood of Fiction; Répétition Générale; From the Diary of a Reviewer; Répétition Générale; Roosevelt and Others; The So-Called Fair; Répétition Générale; On Journalism; Répétition Générale; More Notes from a Diary; Répétition Générale; Reflections on Poetry; Répétition Générale; Observations upon the National Letters; Répétition Générale; Books More or Less Amusing; Répétition Générale; Notes and Queries; Répétition Générale; Gropings in Literary Darkness; A Litany for Bibuli; Répétition Générale; A Panorama of Patriots; Notes in the Margin; Répétition Générale; Conversations; Chiefly Americans; A Panorama of Idiots; Répétition Générale; Conversations: On Women; Consolation; Things I Remember; Répétition Générale; Conversations; The Anatomy of Ochlocracy; Ad Imaginem Dei Creavit Illum . . .; Répétition Générale; The Cat and His Shadow; A Soul's Adventures; Répétition Générale; Melomania; Conversations; Notes on Poetry.

  Notes. Volume 6 of the Collected Essays and Journalism of H. L. Mencken.

154. *Ave atque Vale: Reminiscences of H. P. Lovecraft* (with David E. Schultz)
  a. West Warwick, RI: Necronomicon Press, [December] 2018.

  Contents: Introduction; I. SOME OVERVIEWS: Edward H Cole, "Ave atque Vale!"; James F. Morton, "A Few Memories"; W Paul Cook, *In Memoriam: Howard Phillips Lovecraft—Recollections, Appreciations, Estimates;* Samuel Loveman, "Howard Phillips Lovecraft"; Frank Belknap Long, "Some Random Memories of H.P.L."; Rheinhart Kleinerm "A Memoir of Lovecraft"; Wilfred B. Talman, "The Normal Lovecraft: A Memoir to Restore Balance to the Shade of a Man of Delightful Character"; Sonia H. Davis, *The Private Life of H. P. Lovecraft,* "Memories of Lovecraft"; Hyman Bradofsky, "Amateur Affairs"; II. CHILDHOOD AND EARLY ADULTHOOD (1890–1922): Harold W Munro, "Lovecraft, My Childhood Friend"; Clara Hess,

Letter to Winfield Townley Scott; Andrew Francis Lockhart, "Little Journeys to the Homes of Prominent Amateurs"; L. Sprague de Camp, "Young Man Lovecraft"; Arthur Goodenough, "From 'Further Recollections of Amateur Journalism'"; Horace L. Lawson, "Lovecraft Was My Mentor"; George Julian Houtain, "20 Webster Street"; Maurice W Moe, "Howard Phillips Lovecraft: The Sage of Providence"; Ira A. Cole, "A Tribute from the Past"; Rheinhart Kleiner, "Discourse on H. P. Lovecraft"; Alfred Galpin, "Memories of a Friendship"; Paul Livingston Keil, "I Met Lovecraft"; III. EARLY PROFESSIONAL CAREER (1923-1930): Muriel E. Eddy. "Howard Phillips Lovecraft"; Ruth M. Eddy, "The Man Who Came at Midnight"; George Kirk, "The Kalem Letters"; Rheinhart Kleiner, "Bards and Bibliophiles"; Samuel Loveman, "Lovecraft as a Conversationalist"; Vrest Orton, "Recollections of H. P. Lovecraft"; Zealia Bishop, "H. P. Lovecraft: A Pupil's View"; Donald Wandrei, "Lovecraft in Providence"; H. Warner Munn, "H.P.L.: A Reminiscence"; Frank Belknap Long, "One Day in the Life of H. P. Lovecraft"; IV. LATER YEARS (1931-1937): Will Murray, "An Interview with Harry K. Brobst"; E. Hoffmann Price, "The Sage of College Street," "Howard Phillips Lovecraft," "H. P. Lovecraft the Man"; Ernest A. Edkins, "Idiosyncrasies of H.P.L."; Helen V. Sully, "Some Memories of H.P.L."; Dorothy C. Walter, "Three Hours with H. P. Lovecraft"; Robert H. Barlow, "[Memories of HPL (1934)]," "The Wind That Is in the Grass: A Memoir of H. P. Lovecraft in Florida"; Robert Bloch, Letter to *Fantasy Commentator*; Duane W. Rimel, "H. P. Lovecraft as I Knew Him"; Kenneth Sterling, "Caverns Measureless to Man"; Stuart M Boland, "Interlude with Lovecraft"; William L. Crawford, "Lovecraft's First Book"; Fritz Leiber, "My Correspondence with Lovecraft"; Marian F. Bonner, "Miscellaneous Impressions of H.P.L."; Mary V. Dana, "A Glimpse of H.P.L."; John B. Michel, "The Last of H. P. Lovecraft"; V. BRIEF TRIBUTES: Walter J. Coates, "Howard P. Lovecraft [1890-1937]"; Arthur Harris, "From 'More Regrettable Passings'"; Charles W. Smith, "Howard Phillips Lovecraft"; Ernest A. Edkins, "O Artemidorus, Farewell!"; Donald J. Moe, "From Maurice Moe's Son"; George W Macauley, "A Walk in the Field"; Hazel Heald, Letter to *Weird Tales*; Robert Bloch, Letter to *Weird Tales*; Clark Ashton Smith, "In Memoriam: H. P. Lovecraft," Letter to *Weird Tales*, Letter to *Science-Fiction Critic*; Donald A. Wollheim, "Howard Phillips Lovecraft"; Robert W. Lowndes, "A Tribute to Lovecraft"; Henry George Weiss (Francis Flagg), "The Genius of Lovecraft"; VI. Poetic Tributes: August Derleth, "Elegy in Spring"; Samuel Loveman, "To H. P. L."; Clark Ashton Smith, "To Howard Phillips Lovecraft"; Biographical Notes; Bibliography; Index.

Notes. A volume that is not meant to supersede but to complement Peter Cannon's superlative *Lovecraft Remembered* (Arkham House, 1998). In particular, we wished to include the original version of Sonia Davis's memoir (*The Private Life of H. P. Lovecraft* [II.3]), since Peter had chosen to include an edited version. We also wished to encourage Marc Michaud, who was in the process of reviving Necronomicon Press after a long hiatus.

155.   H. L. Mencken, *Writings in the* Smart Set, *Volume 7: 1921–1922*
    a.   Seattle: Sarnath Press, [January] 2019.
        Contents: Dianthus Caryophyllus; Répétition Générale; Conversations; The Land of the Free; A Panorama of Holy Clerks; Répétition Générale; Conversations; Books about Books; Répétition Générale; Conversations: On Marriage; Literary Notes; Répétition Générale; The South Begins to Mutter; Répétition Générale; From the Diary of a Reviewer; Répétition Générale; Notes on Books; Répétition Générale; Iron Infallibility; More Notes on Books; Répétition Générale; Variations on a Familiar Theme; Répétition Générale; Book Article No. 158; From the Diary of a Diner-Out; Répétition Générale; Frank Harris and Others; Répétition Générale; Taking Stock; Répétition Générale; The Niagara of Novels; Répétition Générale; Reflections on Prose Fiction; Répétition Générale; Demagogery as Art and Science.
        Notes. Volume 7 of the Collected Essays and Journalism of H. L. Mencken.

156.   H. L. Mencken, *Writings in the* Smart Set, *Volume 8: 1922–1923*
    a.   Seattle: Sarnath Press, [January] 2019.
        Contents: Répétition Générale; Saving the World; Répétition Générale; The Intellectual Squirrel-Cage; Répétition Générale; The Coroner's Inquest; Répétition Générale; Portrait of an American Citizen; Répétition Générale; Chiefly Pathological; Répétition Générale; The Monthly Feuilleton; Répétition Générale; Confidences; Répétition Générale; Specimens of Current Fiction; Répétition Générale; Conversations; Adventures among Books; Répétition Générale; Americanism: Exterior View; Répétition Générale; John Strom, Thrice Doctor; Nordic Blond Art; Répétition Générale; Notices of Books; Répétition Générale; Some New Books; Répétition Générale; Biography and Other Fiction; Répétition Générale; New York; Répétition Générale; Holy Writ; Répétition Générale; Notices of Books; Répétition Générale; Fifteen Years.
        Notes. Volume 8 of the Collected Essays and Journalism of H. L. Mencken.

157. H. L. Mencken, *Miscellaneous Magazine Contributions, 1899–1909*
  a. Seattle: Sarnath Press, [February] 2019.
       Contents: To Rudyard Kipling; The Four-Foot Filipino; The Tin-Clads; Joe and Bobs; Auroral; The Cook's Victory; The Woman and the Girl; A Footnote on Journalism; The Transport Gen'ral Ferguson; Like a Thief in the Night; The Flight of the Victor; The Point of the Story; A Double Rebellion; A Ballade of Protest; Hurra Lal, Peacemaker; The Crime of McSwane; Firing and a Watering; The Passing of a Profit; Charles J. Bonaparte: A Useful Citizen; Arthur Pue Gorman; James, Cardinal Gibbons; On the Edge of Samar; The Heathen Rage; The Fear of the Savage; The Bend in the Tube; Marketing Wild Animals; "The Star Spangled Banner"; On Passing the Island of San Salvador; The King and Tommy Crips; The Last Cavalry Charge; Popular Medical Fallacies; Cancer, the Unconquered Plague; If Your Baby Had Pneumonia; If My Baby Had Scarlet Fever; What You Ought to Know about Your Baby; What You Ought to Know About Your Baby; What You Ought to Know about Your Baby; What You Ought to Know about Your Baby; What You Ought to Know about Your Baby; What You Ought to Know about Your Baby; What You Ought to Know about Your Baby; The Slaughter of the Innocents; What You Ought to Know about Your Baby; The Fine Art of Conjugal Bliss; The Slap-Stick Burlesque; E Pluribus Unum; The Baldhead Man; Dr. William Osler; In Defense of Profanity; Cardinal Gibbons; The Gastronomic Value of the Knife; The Psychology of Kissing; The Artist—A Drama without Words.
       Notes. Volume 9 of the Collected Essays and Journalism of H. L. Mencken.

158. H. L. Mencken, *Miscellaneous Magazine Contributions, 1910–1923*
  a. Seattle: Sarnath Press, [February] 2019.
       Contents: How to Put On a Collar; The Legal Liabilities of the Best Man; Et-Dukkehjemiana; Dreiser's Novel; Thoughts on Present Discontents; Newspaper Morals; The Literary Show; The Literary Show; The Literary Show; The Literary Show; The Literary Show; The Literary Show; The Literary Show; The Literary Show; The Literary Show; The Mailed Fist and Its Prophet; The Literary Show; America Produces a Novelist; Ludendorff; The Dreiser Bugaboo; Ibsen: Journeyman Dramatist; The Literary Capital of the United States; A Mysterious Matter; At Last! A Man with Good Eyes!; The National Literature; Meditation in E Minor; Huneker II. on Huneker I.; Star-Spangled Men; A Pathological Movie; The Book of Reuben; Chapters of Medical History; Liquor and Literature; The Novels of W. L. George; The American Novel; That "Nervous Breakdown"; Sinister

Inquiry from the South; A Short View of Gamalielese; The American Language; James Huneker; Havelock Ellis; Morning Song in C Major; The Motive of the Critic; An Iconoclast at Washington; On Living in the United States; Release from Puritans, Pedagogues and Anglo-Saxons; The Follies of Washington; Frank Harris' New Portraits; [Review]; American Puritanism at Bay; Pio Baroja; The New Freedom; Crome Yellow: A Review; Spiritual Autopsies; Dream and Awakening; Maryland: Apex of Normalcy; Mr. Mencken Replies; The Harvard Affair [symposium]; "What I Am Going to Read This Summer"[symposium]; Three Years of Prohibition in America; The Prohibition Swindle in America; Mr. Mencken, War and the Editor; Hoch Iowisch; Help for German Authors; From an Editor and a Gentleman; Paltry Professors and History; Dr. Saleeby on Prohibition; Mr. Harding's Second Term; The Style of Lincoln; Gentlemen with Complexes; An Eminent American; The Ten Dullest Authors: A Symposium; The Dead Letter of Prohibition; Calvinism: New Style; Is the South a Desert; The American Tradition; H. L. Mencken; What I Think of Santa Claus [symposium]; When We Americans Dine.

Notes. Volume 10 of the Collected Essays and Journalism of H. L. Mencken.

159. Théophile Gautier, *The Mummy's Foot and Other Fantastic Tales*
    a. New York: Hippocampus Press, 2018 [actually February 2019].
        Contents: Introduction; Omphale: A Rococo Story; Clarimonde; One of Cleopatra's Nights; The Mummy's Foot; Arria Marcella: A Souvenir of Pompeii; Avatar; Jettatura; Spirite: A Fantastic Tale.
        Notes. The sixth volume in the Classics of Gothic Horror series. Introduction reprinted in I.52.

160. H. L. Mencken, *Essays and Introductions, 1899–1922*
    a. Seattle: Sarnath Press, [March] 2019.
        Contents: Old Court Houses of Maryland; Loudon Park Cemetery: 1835–1902; A Word at the Start; History of the Firm; [Advertising text]; Henry Louis Mencken; Summer in Jamaica; Introduction to *A Doll's House*; Introduction to *Little Eyolf*; Introduction to *The Gist of Nietzsche*; Preface to *Blanchette and The Escape*; [Statement]; Strange, Far-Off Places; [Preface]; Preface to *A House of Pomegranates*; Introduction to *Ventures in Common Sense*; [Letter]; Bibliography; Introduction to *Youth and Egolatry*; Introduction to *We Moderns*; Willa Cather; Introduction to *The Line of Love*; Preface to *Tales of Mean Streets*; Introduction to *The Nietzsche-Wagner Correspondence*; Introduction to *Democracy and the Will to Power*; Politics; Der Kritiker Poe;

George Bernard Shaw: His Plays; The Antichrist by Friedrich Nietzsche (tr. Mencken).

Notes. Volume 11 of the Collected Essays and Journalism of H. L. Mencken. His introductions and other contributions to books do not fill a full volume, so I reprinted his first treatise, *George Bernard Shaw: His Plays* (1905) and his translation of Nietzsche's *Antichrist* (1920).

161. H. L. Mencken, *Newspaper Work, 1899–1901*
   a.   Seattle: Sarnath Press, [March] 2019.

   Contents: Gossip about Sports; Democrats at Work; Rev. J. Addison Smith; With the Gold Hunters; Now for Manila; Made One Society; Hayes a Workingman; Sousa Warmly Greeted; Want Lower Taxes; Discussing the Issues; Oratorio's "Elijah"; Cuddy and His Wagon; Germany's Attitude; Raleigh's Chief Bugler; May Day Yesterday; John Wesley's Life; Levvy's Big Project; Labor Is the King; Successful Recital; Body Identified; Peabody Students; In Mercy's Name; Entertaining a Prophet; Rain Brings Relief; Mr. M'Intire's Trip; Through with Books; The Stage Reporter Quite an Equal of the Yellow Journalist; Daring Dashes for Freedom; A Matter of Ethnology; At the Edge of the Spanish Main; Its Day Is Going; Where Orchards Are Called Weeds; Seen on the Streets of Kingston; A Recent Crucifixion in Jamaica; Rhyme and Reason; Rhyme and Reason; Rhyme and Reason; Knocks and Jollies; Knocks and Jollies; Knocks and Jollies; Terse and Terrible Texts; Knocks and Jollies; Terse and Terrible Texts; Knocks and Jollies; Terse and Terrible Texts; Hailed the Truce; Dove of Peace Takes Flight; Knocks and Jollies; The Boy and the Man; Terse and Terrible Texts; To Kruger; Knocks and Jollies; Terse and Terrible Texts; Solons Still in Warpaint; Surplus Less Than Expected; Solons Plan a Coup d'Etat; Knocks and Jollies; Solons Victorious after a Hard Fight; After the Din of the Battle; Would Revise City Charter; Courts Will Take a Stand; Subways Can Be Improved; City's Troubles in the Courts; No Peace at the City Hall; Terse and Terrible Texts; Commissioners Ignore Civil Service Rules; His Honor's Discovery; School Children's Lives Are in Danger; "Get Together," Says Gephart; "Investigating" a Life Saver!; Senator and Solicitor; Health Demands Sewers and Schools; Only a Trifle Spent to Keep Streets Clean; Interest on City's Debt Is Decreased; Knocks and Jollies; Plays and Players; Stands Firm for Olin Bryan; Debt Is Decreased by Two Million; Appeal Tax Court Has Many Recommendations; Western Md. Sale Not Easy; Banks Refuse to Raise Rate; Mayor Hayes' Plan Faulty; M'Cuen Advises City Ownership; Plays and Players; Levy Muddle at

Annapolis; Mayor Hayes Was Non Est; Fendall Wants Sewers and Wood Pavements; Legal Wits Argue Law; Battles of the Lawyers Ended; Knocks and Jollies; Waiting for the Verdict; Solons Wearied of Their Work; Engineer Phelps' Hot Reply to His Critics; Lauterbach Offers $5,500,000 for W. M. R. R.; Knocks and Jollies; Terse and Terrible Texts; Nominations of the Mayor; Municipality May Secure Dollar Gas; Good Microbes Will Conquer Bad Microbes; Knocks and Jollies; Solons Have Faith in the Female Refuge; Telephone Wires Must Be Buried Immediately; Carswell Wins Lighting Case; Mayor Wins His Case; Tax Rate Will Be Low; Mayor Hayes Congratulated; Dove of Peace Is Back Again; Mayor Urges Prompt Tax Levy; Mayor's Message a Bitter Pill for Council; Solons Bow to Defeat; Mayor Has Confidence in His Sewerage Plans; Collection of Taxes Will Begin March 15; Sinking Fund Increase Greater Than Ever; Old Water Board Severely Criticised; Hayes Sewerage Plan Described in Detail; Charter Changes Suggested by Mayor; Collection of Taxes Begins with a Rush; The Theatrical Alphabet; Anti-Secret Session Ordinance Rejected; Immense Fire Losses during Present Year; Fire Board Discusses High Insurance Rates; Candidates for Council; The Hayes Volunteer Cabinet; Mayor Signs His School Bill; Contests in Many Wards; Afraid the People Are Hunting Snakes; Delay for Sewerage; Mayor's Plans Met Defeat; Councilmanic Fight Is Waxing Warm; Terse and Terrible Texts; Beginning of the End in Sight for Solons; How the City Fathers Served Constituents; Terse and Terrible Texts.

Notes. Volume 12 of the Collected Essays and Journalism of H. L. Mencken.

162.   *Robert Aickman* (Library of Weird Fiction)
    a.   Lakewood, CO: Centipede Press, [April] 2019.
        Contents: Introduction; Your Tiny Hand Is Frozen; The Trains; The Waiting Room; Ringing the Changes; Larger Than Oneself; The Wine-Dark Sea; The Visiting Star; Ravissante; The Swords; Meeting Mr Millar; Pages from a Young Girl's Journal; The Hospice; Growing Boys; The Fetch; Marriage; No Stronger Than a Flower; Letters to the Postman; The Stains; Bibliography.

        Notes. A truncated edition of the Masters of the Weird Tale volume (item 145/146 above), containing 18 of what I regard as Aickman's best stories.

163.   H. L. Mencken, *Newspaper Work, 1901–1904*
    a.   New York: Sarnath Press, [May] 2019.
        Contents: Office Holders to Fight for Hayes; Impenetrable Gloom

in the Mayor's Office; The Collapse of the Hayes Machine; Terse and Terrible Texts; City Council Nearing End of Its Official Life; Council Adjourns to Attend the Ball Game; Only One Leper Is in the City; Baseball Adopted as the Solons' Sport; Terse and Terrible Texts; Terse and Terrible Texts; Tracks Cleared for Herald Relief Train; They Thank the Herald from Their Hearts; Herald's Work Highly Praised; Good Things in the Car Greeted with Cries of Joy; Thousands of Hungry and Destitute Were Relieved; Florida City Is Still in Need of Assistance from the Outside World; Baltimore and the Rest of the World; Gaudy Display in the Council Chamber; Train Glimpses of the South; Baltimore and the Rest of the World; Baltimore and the Rest of the World; Untold Tales I; Untold Tales II; Untold Tales III; Untold Tales IV; Untold Tales V; Untold Tales VI; Untold Tales VII; Untold Tales VIII; Untold Tales IX; Untold Tales X; Untold Tales X; Untold Tales XI; Untold Tales XII; Untold Tales XIII; Untold Tales XIV; Untold Tales XV; Untold Tales XVI; Untold Tales XVII; Untold Tales XVIII; Untold Tales XIX; Untold Tales XX; Untold Tales XXI; Untold Tales XXII; Untold Tales XXIII; Untold Tales XXIV; Untold Tales XXV; Untold Tales XXVI; Untold Tales XXVII; Untold Tales XXVIII; Untold Tales XXIX; Untold Tales XXX; Untold Tales XXXI; Baltimore and the Rest of the World; Baltimore and the Rest of the World; Baltimore and the Rest of the World; The Shame of "Shorty" Ferguson; Impressions of One of the Prince's Staff; Wireless Interview with Prince Henry; With the Cranks at the Mayor's Office; Gen. Kitchener, War Machine; The Island War: A Tale of a Monarchy; A Pilgrimage to Old Mt. Vernon; Senator Fairbanks Will Accept the Second Place on the Ticket; Maryland in Van of National Convention; Convention Crowds Resemble a Durbar; Virginia Delegation Had a Lively Fight; Senator Depew Causes First Enthusiasm; Harry S. Cummings Much in Demand; Listless Delegates and Many Empty Seats Marked Opening of Republican Convention; "Uncle Joe" Cannon Worked the Convention of Republicans to a High Pitch of Enthusiasm; Theodore Roosevelt Named for President; Charles W. Fairbanks for Vice-President; Enthusiasm Lacking in Democratic Hosts; Maryland Delegates Penned in Hotel; Painful Indifference Prevails at St. Louis; Maryland Delegates Visit World's Fair; Enthusiastic Cheers for Mr. Cleveland Mark Opening of Big Democratic Convention, But the Opposition to Parker Is Waning; William J. Bryan, Once Powerful, Goes Down to Defeat Before the Forces That Will Nominate Chief Judge Parker; Hinges of St. Louis Lid Broken; Marylanders Prepare to Return Home; Parker's Name Placed Before Democratic Convention Accompanied by Demonstration of Greatest Enthusiasm; Herbert Remains True Gorman Man; Marylanders Start for Home Today; Hon. Henry G. Davis for Vice-President; Wornout Democratic Delegates Depart from Scenes of the Strenuous Struggle Which Ended in Declaration for Gold; Weary Marylanders Are Returning Home; "The Serenade"; Vaudeville at the Maryland; "The Maid and the Mummy"; A Chat with Miss Kline; "The Second Fiddle"; Some New Books; Notes in the Margin; "Red Feather" Redivivus; Notes in the Margin; "The Yankee Consul"; Notes in the Margin; "Why Smith Left Home"; Notes in the Margin.

Notes. Volume 13 of the Collected Essays and Journalism of H. L. Mencken.

164. H. L. Mencken, *Newspaper Work, 1904–1906*
a.   Seattle: Sarnath Press, [June] 2019.

Contents: Vaudeville at the Maryland; Notes in the Margin; "The Virginian"; Miss Walsh in "Resurrection"; Notes in the Margin; Creatore and His Band; Notes in the Margin; Mrs. Campbell at the Academy; Notes in the Margin; Vaudeville at the Maryland; Notes in the Margin; Miss Adelaide Keim as Hamlet; Notes in the Margin; Notes in the Margin; Better Times in Baltimore; Notes in the Margin; "Is He Man or Devil?"; Notes in the Margin; Baltimore's Recovery from Fire; Notes in the Margin; Notes in the Margin; Notes in the Margin; "Much Ado About Nothing"; Plays and Players; Red Wagon Stories; Poetry and the Public; Plays and Players; The Passing of "The Hill"; "On Going to Church"; The Theatrical Season; War; A Book of Dramatists; Planning the Paper; "The Girl of the Golden West"; By the Way; Down the Line; Mrs. Fiske and Her Company; Some Plays of the Day; A Drama with a Sunday-School Moral; Mere Opinion; "La Belle Marseillaise"; The Tardy Recognition of the Hon. Louis Michel; The National Theater Foolishness; Mere Opinion; Mere Opinion; Plays Mme. Bernhardt Will Present in Baltimore: I.; Mere Opinion; Plays Mme. Bernhardt Will Present in Baltimore: II.; Mere Opinion; Plays Mme. Bernhardt Will Present in Baltimore: III.; Mere Opinion; Certain Dramas of Importance; Mere Opinion; Mere Opinion; Mere Opinion; Mere Opinion; Mere Opinion; Nectar of the Eastern Sho'; Hustled His Way to Congress; UNSIGNED EDITORIALS: The Land of the Dollar; Wilhelm and His Germans; An Age of Wars; An American "Scoop"; On Newspaper English; The Good Old Summertime; Where Science Fails; The Price of Dominion; Newspapers and Progress; The New Bugaboo; The Sextet from "Lucia"; A Gain for Baltimore; A Bald-Headed Romeo; "Therefore, Be It Resolved"; Race Suicide Absurdities; More Chicago Science; On Pride of Ancestry; Oyama; An Unmanly Outrage; The Russian Masses; Oligarchy and Its Limits; The Crop of New Words; On Christian Endeavor; Long Live Romance!; Martyrs of the Dog Days; Roosevelt and Lawson; Grand Opera in English; Wilhelm vs. Bismarck; Virtue on the Scales; The Carnival of Graft; Bristow and Loomis; A Case of Good Riddance; The Penalty of Failure; What's in a Name?; Justice to the Dead; A Literary Note; Goodbye the Railsplitters; A Needed Reform; Exit the Stock Company; Introducing a New Poet; The Panama Quitters; Archbishop Chapelle; English as a Slobber; M. Witte's Ablutions; The Battleship Kansas; On Primeval Grafting; The Decay of the Actor; A Blow to Unionism; The Hon. Mr. Fitzsimmons; Standard Oil Savants; Enter a Richmond Bard; How Grafting Helps Us; The Art of Grafting; A Lay Sermon; The Literary Life; Politeness as an Asset; The Craze for Eminence; After the Republic—What?; Mr. Roosevelt's Luck; Trouble in the Levant; Gen. Lord Kitchener; History Repeats Itself; Is the Novel Doomed?; On High Ambitions; The Crop of New Songs; A Tariff War; An Eminent Baltimorean; To Curb the Legislatures; A Misguided Vice-Prophet; The Crop of Sensations; Actors Out of Work; Freedom in Montenegro; On Wedding Music; O Tempora! O Mores!; Dead Beats in the Army; Why Wear a Mustache?; Let Joy Be Unconfined; A Jewish African State; A Free Press in Montenegro; The Failure of Socialism; At It Again; Catholic Church Music; Mr. Chas. J. Bonaparte; Hustlers and Fossils; On Selecting Candidates; Happiness and the Sexes; Japan and the Future; Exit the Republicans; On International Law; Our Odorous Legislatures; Rivals; Austria versus Hungary; The Roosevelt Doctrine; The Future of Austria; Exit the American Boss; A New German Empire?; Cause and Effect in Russia; New Matrimonial Rules; The Fair Typewriter; Why This Portentous Silence?; Good Old Baltimore!; The Pratt Library's Needs; Pennypacker the Virtuous; The Unbeautiful Cobblestone; A Grievous Wrong Righted; The Baldheaded Man; Mark Twain; The Roosevelt Doctrine; The End Is in Sight; T. Hayes, Aet. 62; Piano Playing as an Art; Sam Pennypacker, C. P.; Pooh! Pooh!; Cardinal Gibbons on Agitators; On Wasted Talent; More Pay for Those Who Guard Us; No Need for Help; A Lucky Calamity; Let Us Be Good!; Baltimore Needs No State Aid; Let There Be Light; Lambs for the Pyre; Our Fair Visitors; In the Hot Weather; Alfred Beit; The Major and the Ladies; Over the Border; Mr. Frohman's Plays.

Notes. Volume 14 of the Collected Essays and Journalism of H. L. Mencken.

165.	H. L. Mencken, *Writings in the* Baltimore Sun, *1906–1909*
	a.	Seattle: Sarnath Press, [June] 2019.

Contents: The Truth Seeker; A Chorus Girl Famine Makes Managers Tremble; "Mizpah" at Academy; Theatres Last Night; Theatres Last Night; Frank Daniels Returns; Theatres Last Night; Theatres Last Night;' Theatres Last Night; Theatres Last Night; Theatres Last Night; Problems in Yiddish Plays; Shaw Comedy at Ford's; Theatres Last Night; Lulu Glaser without a Song; Mr. Robertson at Ford's; Theatres Last Night; "Hypocrites" Is Here; De Angelis at Academy; Marie Cahill at Ford's; "A Doll's House" at Albaugh's; Carlotta Nilsson at Academy; Theatres Last Night; Farnum as d'Artagnan; New Play at Albaugh's; "Chorus Lady" at Ford's; Miss Marlowe's Gloria; Waltz Dream Is Here; Miss Robson at Ford's; "Toddles" at Ford's; Ibsen Play at Academy; "'09" Has Its Premiere; Nazimova at Academy; Zangwill's Play Here; Belasco Play Here; "The Test" at Ford's; Kennedy's Play at Academy; "The Thief" at Academy; Marlowe at Academy; Premier at Academy; "The Devil" at Academy; A Book of Criticism; Miss Scheff In New Play; The Auditorium Opens; "Only Law" at Auditorium; "Israel" at Academy; Dodson at Ford's; "Bright Eyes" at Ford's; UNSIGNED EDITORIALS: The "Gallus" Problem; Sunbeams; The Theatrical Season; Exit the Servant Girl; The Hon. Hoke Smith vs. The Hon. Clark Howell; Grossvater Wilhelm; Literary False Alarms; A Too Valiant Knight; A Governor Who Looks as Well as Performs the Part; The Honeymoon Wanes; Exit the Populists; A Needed Reform; Kaiser Wilhelm; What Is a Whangdoodle?; A Scientific Footnote; Chewing Gum; Why Married Women Weep at Weddings; Problems That Press Us; Sauerkraut Weather; The Woes of Critics; The Blessed Pretenders; A Plea for Whiskers; Thoughts on Scrapple; Lights in the Parlor; On Hog and Hominy; A Sheep in Wolf's Clothing; Mr. Graves' Warning; The True Christmas Spirit; "Why Men Are Afraid to Get Married"; A Wise and Upright Jurist; Influenza and Kissing; The Major and the Sealions; The Sweetair Lyceum; On Planked Shad; A Pernicious Ordinance; The Peach-Crop Liar; The Awful Cost; The Whiskers Problem; Baseball; The Passing of a Civilization; The Martyrs of June; Thoughts on the Sublime and Beautiful; A Mount for Mr. Taft; Japan as a Bugaboo; The Sweet Girl Graduate; Mayor Mahool's Proposed Tax on Bachelors; Sir Conan Doyle's Treason; The Ideal Man; The Uselessness of Money; More Birth-Rate Alarms; The Science of Psychology; On Matchmakers; On Tenors; The Climate of Baltimore; A Culinary Favorite; A Vile Pretender; An Elegy on Graves; A Rhapsody on Rabbit; Professor James' Startling Discovery; A Preposterous Pretense; Matrimony and Crime; A Footnote on Mothers-in-Law; On Whiskers; The Strains of "Lohengrin"; Some Needed Legislation; An Apology; Senseless Superstitions; The Valiant McCuen; The

Waltz; The Cultivation of Sauerkraut; The Suicide Tables; A Psychological Footnote; The Surgeon on the Bridge; Science and Statistics; The Leap-Year Peril; Literature and the Mountain Dew; In the Face of Peril; The Slaughter of the Innocents; The Clank of the Chain; Money; The German; The Trade of the Editor; The Stupendous Casey; An Unnecessary Law; A Vindication; A Fair Critic Answered; The Turn of the Tide; A Fallacy Exploded; St. Lohengrin's Day; On the Soul Kiss; A Triumph of Jurisprudence; An Illinois Martyr; The June Bride and the Law of Compensation; A Happy Man; On Cruelty to Tenors; Advice to Prospective Mothers-in-Law; The Mint Crop; A Welcome to Honeymooners; The Father-in-Law; What Is Worse Than a Tenor?; Is Chicago Still upon the Map?; On Journalism; New Wedding March Needed; The Colonel at the Bat; The Colonel on the Job; Nuptial Statistics; The King and Swell Dressing; Taxes and Celibacy; Why Does a Man Marry?; A Curious Legal Problem; Meditations upon a Depressing Theme; A Hospitable Madness with Method in It; How Much Should a Woman Eat?; Thoughts on Eating; Sauerkraut Redivivus; The Best Man; The Hon. John Temple Graves; A Perennial Nuisance; The Case of Mr. Brooker; Poor John; The Value of a Man; Sauerkraut as an Antiseptic; The Leap-Year Record; Mr. Hayes' Sinister Humor; Buffalo Bill's Successor; In Praise of Kissing; A Hero in Need; The Menace of the Fly; The German Singers; English Songs; The Promise to Obey; The Old Songs Forever; Mrs. Jane Germon; John D.'s Theological Tests; A Curious Coincidence; The Chesapeake Oyster; Thoughts on Good Eating; The Horse; Let Us Have Opera; Pity the Poor President; Baltimore's Great White Way; The Maryland Tomato; Where Pie Is Not Pie; Indian Summer Joys; Are Married Women Slaves?; An Inhuman Innovation; A Mother in Israel; The Heart of Baltimore; Enough Is Sufficient; Welcome to Our Fair Republic; Farewell to Cook and Peary; Gaynor vs. the Field; Missionaries to the Rich; At Pimlico; Mrs. and Mr. Mary Roe; A Hero of the Shenandoah; The Limburgundian Theory of Immunity; Facts about Scrapple; The Human Conflagration; Cleanliness as a Nuisance; The Fiddlers Are Tuning Up; The Charm of Jail Life; Mr. Taft Fails to Score; The Theatrical Season; A Connoisseur of Carnage; Mayor Johnson Safe; Cranberry Pie: A Defense; The Chewing Gum Famine; Diseases Multiply; An Essay on Heroes; The Killjoy as a Moses; Schmitz Francisco; Philosophy Up a Stump; Mr. Fairbanks Unmasks; Mr. Taft's Peril; "Strugglarian" Philosophy; The Fate of Finland; An Adirondack Amateur; Great Doings in Georgia; Mysteries of Eating; One Flag; One Bill of Fare!; The Opera; Stay at Home, Ladies!; Homiletics and the Spirit of Progress; Justice in France; What Women Admire; Ice and Immortality; An Elegy upon Fame; A Yacht Race in 1911; Manuel Goes a-Wooing; Charles N. Crittenton; Boston Faces a Horror; Brazil Is 20 Years Old; The Fraudulent Turkey; A Man Who Hated Babies; The Admirable Biddle; Why Homely Women Marry So Well; The Millennium Is at Hand; Crime and the Automobile; The Perfect Wife; The Colonel Backs His Magic with His Money; Spare the Rat!; The Aeroplane as a Business Proposition; Meditations on the Weather; Exit the Rabbit Foot; The Hookworm and Divorce; The New Morality; A Hymeneal Carnival; A Subtle Foe to Bachelors; The Reform of the Pulpit; Eusapia Palladino; The Godfather's Peril; The Income of a Poet; Automobile Horrors; Could Manila Be Easily Captured by the Japanese?; Dark Clouds in Cuba; Decay of Ancient Virtues.

Notes. Volume 15 of the Collected Essays and Journalism of H. L. Mencken.

166.   W. H. Pugmire, *An Ecstasy of Fear*
   a.   Lakewood, CO: Centipede Press, [July] 2019.

Contents: Introduction; The Black Winged Ones; Gathered Dust; An Ecstasy of Fear; Let Us Wash This Thing; Artifice; Letters from an Old Gent; The Imps of Innsmouth; Smooth Artifact of Bone; Some Unknown Gulf of Night; An Identity in Dream; Hempen Rope; Chamber of Dreams; Unhallowed Places; House of Legend; A Shadow of Your Own Design; Cesare; To See Beyond; A Quest of Dream; Pickman's Lazarus; To Dance among Your Puppets; Ye Horror on Tempest Hill; Underneath an Arkham Moon (with Jessica Amanda Salmonson); Sources and Credits.

Notes. A volume that had long been in the works—a follow-up to *The Tangled Muse* (item 87 above). Unfortunately, the author did not live to see it, having died on March 26, 2019.

167.   H. L. Mencken, *Writings in the* Baltimore Sun, *1909–1922*
   a.   Seattle: Sarnath Press, [July] 2019.

Contents: Faversham in New Role; Dr. Oscar Levy Completes His Remarkable Edition of Friedrich Nietzsche in English; Week of World-Bettering and High Endeavor; Mencken Throws Lifeline to Hon. Anderson; The Week in Review; London So Like Baltimore; How Germans Smashed Namur; Is This Why Germans Face a Hostile World?; Married Men Braver Than Bachelors? No!; Do You Speak English or American?; Where "American" Differs from the Old English Language; National Characteristics Are Shown in the Use of Words; They Differ Widely in the Spelling of Words; Schools Don't Attempt to Teach the Language Americans Speak; Germany

United: Mencken; Hapgood Analyzes Situation among the Entente Allies; Mencken and Hapgood Describe the Situation in Germany and in England; Berlin Calm, But Earnest, in Face of Action of U. S.; Mencken, at Kirkwall, Sees Searching of Ships; War Booms Norway—Mencken; Hapgood on Europe's Future; Henry Mencken Cables Story of "Ticklish Moments" in Berlin; "The Diary of a Retreat": Berlin at Time of Break; "The Diary of a Retreat": Berlin on Its Doubtful Day; Intervention Issue in Cuba; "The Diary of a Retreat": Americans Near Panic; Blow Dealt Cuban Rebels; "The Diary of a Retreat": Berlin Calm at Crisis; Cuban Liberals Hope to Force U. S. to Act; "The Diary of a Retreat": Dark Days for Americans; Cuban Revolt Blows Up; "The Diary of a Retreat": German Public Stirred Up; "The Diary of a Retreat": Americans Leave Berlin; "The Diary of a Retreat": Out of Germany at Last; "The Diary of a Retreat": Across French Border; "The Diary of a Retreat": Headed for Sunny Spain; "The Diary of a Retreat": In Sunny Spain at Last; "The Diary of a Retreat": Steaming Toward Home; "The Diary of a Retreat": Brought to Conclusion; G. O. P. Ticket Triumph for Old Bosses; Eyes Turning to Davis with Dark Horse Talk; Brief Battle Was Hopeless for Carpentier from First; Exile at Wieringen Says He Longs for Day When He Can Assist Germany; Who's Looney Now?; UNSIGNED EDITORIALS: The Baltimore Monument to Schiller; The Debutantes; The Twin Arts; The Coming of the Comet; The Folk Song; The Enrichment of the English Language; The Battle of the Poets; The Abominable Fly; Revoke the Reckless Automobilist's License; Good Luck to the Duke!; The Antique Lover; Mr. Bryan, the Constitution and the Public Utilities Commission; What They Eat in Pittsburg; Leave the Dead in Peace!; A Typical Melting Pot; The Pure Food Law; Pansies by the River Brim; A Chance for the Poets; Words Are Feminine—and Deeds?; Great Corkscrew Mystery; A Rebellion in Panama; Hats Off to Slatter; A Footnote on Education; A Linguistic Problem; A City Magnificent; Another Record Broken; Thoughts upon Jail Life; The Fried Smelt; Sir W. S. Gilbert Wages a Holy War; Diamonds in Maryland; First Blood for the Suffragettes; What Will Become of Mr. Morgan's Art Collection?; Thoughts on Mince Pie; The Woman Politician on Trial; The Deluded Dr. Wu; Who Owns the Presents?; A Truce for One Day; The Death of Romance; An Old-Time Christmas; Hash Week; A Council of 13 Plus 1; Gross Neglect of Duty; A Ridiculous Enterprise; Germany Is Ready for War; Weimar at the Bat Again; A Benevolent Monopoly; The Centennials of 1910; A Plea for 1909; More Work for the University of Copenhagen; Mr. Harriman Planned for a Great Hudson Park; Uncle Sam's Lost Citizens; A Blow to Literature; The Spirit of Brotherhood Invades St. Louis; A Hustling Youngster; By Train to Panama; Connubial Anarchy; A Noble Pair of Boots; Horrible Homogeneity; Mrs. Belmont Again; Plans for New States; Proposing a New Gender; After the Rabbit Foot—What?; A German Experiment; Astral Playmates; Vulgarity and Success; Common Sense Reforms; Walking as a Vice; The Charm of Kissing; The Modern Garden of Eden; On Etiquette at the Domestic Hearth; St. Louis' Ineffective Beau Brummel; The Roller Towel; The Dancing Grenadiers; Campaigning for Morse; The Deacon Moves; A Critic Confuted; An Indian Woman's Plea; Where the English Beat Us; The Poe Aftermath; Ireland Faces Opportunity; The Waltz Is Still King; Another Myth Exploded; The Evolution of Hazing; The Fat Man; Eating Still Goes On; A New Theory of Kissing; Ten More Colonels; The Rabbit Foot Again; Life in Arizona; A Bogus Garden of Eden; The School Boy; The Paris Flood; Land Values Increase; Pumpernickel as a Political Issue; The Goat; The Treason of McMillan; Russian Revolutionists and American Laws; Mr. Balfour's Peril; Riddles of the Day; How the French Faced Disaster; The Campaign for Business; As England Sees Us; Mendelssohn; The Congo Row Ends; Another Automobile Crime; The Failure of Terrorism; The Wireless Loses Its Romance; The Baffled Trusts; Human Progress and the Art of Love; The Span of Life Is Lengthening; The Czar's Troubles Increase; An Era of Railroad Building; The Gas of Halley's Comet Not So Bad as Some Other Things; Mayor Gaynor's Dilemma; Colonel Watterson at 70; The Medal Peril; In Defense of Poets; Spring Impends; The Gas Company's "Work"; Medicine and Newspapers; The Bottle in Battle; Gen. Latrobe at the Bat; Mr. Rockefeller's Stupendous Gift; The Corncob Pipe; The Dreams of St. Louis; The Censorship Problem; Children on the Stage; Exit the Cost of Living; More Trouble Ahead; The Scales of Fame; The Raid upon the Annex Paving Loan; A Double Anniversary; When Beethoven Wavered; Gambling in Works of Art; Raised from the Dead; Mr. Girdwood's Faux Pas; A Linguistic Outrage; The Dear Old Falls; The Pageant of Beauty; Bill and His Louisa; The Downfall of the Tyrannical Husband; The Planked Shad; A Fascinating Perennial; The Omaha Method of Census Enumeration.

Notes. Volume 16 of the Collected Essays and Journalism of H. L. Mencken.

168.   H. L. Mencken, *Writings in the* Baltimore Evening Sun, *April–June 1910*
  a.   Seattle: Sarnath Press, [August] 2019.

  Contents: Good Old Baltimore; Art and Red Hair; Socialism Today; "Huckleberry Finn"; Wars upon Alcohol; William Shakespeare;

Dr. Robert Koch; Joseph Conrad; The One Hundred Best Plays; A Great Norwegian; Psychotherapy; What Is Socialism?; On Whiskers; The Indian; The Charity Bill; The Literary Life; A Negro State?; Perils of the Ocean; "The Winter's Tale"; A Drama of Ideas; Thoughts on Eating; The Wedding Season; Notes in the Margin; The Pestiferous Fly; Victuals: A Reverie; More Psychotherapy; The Theatrical Year; A New Nation Arises; Notes in the Margin; The Slavic Invasion; A Plea for Comedy; In the Vestry Room; Sousa, et Cætera; First Editions; An Eternal Mystery; Mr. Taft at Work; Hidden Treasures; On Jurisprudence; The Play Record; Marginal Notes; Marginal Notes; Summer Novels; Marginal Notes; Theodore Roosevelt: A Study of the Man; China's New Senate; Marion Harland; Marginal Notes; The Pimlico Road; Marginal Notes; On Medical Fees; Lower California; Chiefly Musical; A Time of Change; "East Lynne" Wins; UNSIGNED EDITORIALS: The Ubiquitous Glucose; The Socialist Program; Tom Taggart; The King of Jokers; Roosevelt in Europe; Hunting the Leper; Samuel L. Clemens; Helping Mr. Johnson; The Peace Palace; Nuisances of the Sea; Another Blow to Taft; The New Justice; Bjoernstjerne Bjoernson; The Grand Opera Trust; Is Horsemanship Dead?; Dr. Pearce and the School Teachers; Tom Taggart; A National Health Department; A West Indian Zulu; The Clean-Food Ordinance; Colonel Roosevelt on Books; The Gorgeous Loden; Election Frauds in England; The Population Guess; The Saloons and the City Revenue; The Case of Tobacco; The Official Job Broker; The New King and His Problems; Why Not Some "Pops?"; The English Situation; The Imperilled Shad; The Son of Gladstone; The Circus; Mr. Seidel, of Milwaukee; Aldrich's Defeat; Customs-House Rows; A Lamentable Imposture; A Naval Battle Threatens; Mr. Taft's Explanation; Society by Moonlight; China Abolishes Slave Trading; Insurgents in Japan; Another Plague Conquered; Mr. Taft a Victim?; Boric Acid under Fire; The Eldest Son of the New King; The Prophetic Booby Prize; The Ballinger Trial Ends; A Beautiful Dream; The Rollins Case; Mr. Kronmiller; Music in the Parks; The Mad Dog Peril; A Matter of Etiquette; The Thieves Higher Up; A Bloodless Fourth; The Medical Expert; A Very High Private; Alaska in the Grip of an Octopus; A Noble Defiance of Newspaper Slanderers; A Carnival of Harmony; Is Piracy Legal?; The War of the Frohmans; The Woman's Medical College; Lorimer and His Friends; Another Victory for Peace; Socialists Fighting for a Square Deal in Prussia; A Cold-Storage June Day; Crusades Against Kissing; The Day of Reckoning; The Soft Crab; The New Role of the Kaiser; A Dubious Hybrid; Young Mr. Pittman; Havemeyer's Double Toll; The Pan-American Congress; Alas!; A Truce in the Rate War;

Goldwin Smith; The Limits of Warfare; What One Honest Man Has Accomplished; Love's Labor Lost; Romance in the Senate; A Wholesale Journalist; The Cruel Punishment of Mr. Harrison; The Critical Position of the Hon. John Dalzell; Porfirio Diaz; Enough!; The Case Against Ballinger; More Technicalities; The Statehood Fight Resumed; King George on the Turf; The Western Railroads and Their Strange Maneuvers; A Foul Blow; Breathless!; Mourners at the Feast; The Art of Lynching; Discords in the Harmony; Another Victory for the Square Deal in Congress; The Panama Exposition; Are There Any Insurgents in Maryland?; The Crew Takes a Holiday; The Triumph of Peanut Politics; Cuba Teaches Us a Lesson; A Study of Mr. Taft; The Watermelon; On Meteorology; The First Passenger Airship Line; The New Prince of Wales; Prosperity in Jamaica; The Charlton Case; The Collier Dinner; Will Mr. Hughes Run Again?; Senator Gore's Charges; Politics and Reforms in France; The German Turners; The Case of Charlton; A Shower of Gold; The Democratic Opportunity; The Father of the Automobile; Mr. Taft's Mistake; The Wedding Returns; Uncle Sam as a Banker; The White Slave Trade; The Band Begins to Play; Prosperity in the Dry States.

Notes. Volume 17 of the Collected Essays and Journalism of H. L. Mencken.

169.   W. H. Pugmire, *An Imp of Aether*
 a.   New York: Hippocampus Press, [August] 2019.

Contents: Introduction; The Hands That Reek and Smoke; The Zanies of Sorrow; Dust to Dust; The House of Idiot Children (with Maryanne K. Snyder); Beyond the Realm of Dream; An Implement of Ice; Garden of Shattered Faces; Pickman's Lazarus; Totem Pole; Visions of William Davis Manly; The Boy with the Bloodstained Mouth; Your Seventh Eikon (with Maryanne K. Snyder); Heritage of Hunger ; Born in Strange Shadow; An Imp of Aether; The Horror on Tempest Hill; Child of Dark Mania; Pale, Trembling Youth (with Jessica Amanda Salmonson); Your Kiss of Filth; Old Time Entombed; The Barrier Between; These Harpies of Carcosa; In Blackness Etched, My Name; This Weave of Witchery (with Maryanne K. Snyder); To Move Beneath Autumnal Oaks; The Ghoul's Dilemma; Acknowledgments.

Notes. A volume that was somewhat hastily assembled to capitalise on interest in Pugmire's work following his death.

170/171/172. Arthur Machen, *Collected Fiction*
 a.   New York: Hippocampus Press, [August] 2019. 3 vols.
  Contents:

Volume 1 (1888–1895): Introduction; A Chapter from the Book Called The Ingenious Geltmean Don Quijote de la Mancha Which by Some Mischance Has Not Till Now Been Printed; The Chronicle of Clemendy; The Spagyric Quest of Beroaldus Cosmopolita; The Great God Pan; A Remarkable Coincidence; The Autophone; A Double Return; A Wonderful Woman; The Lost Club; An Underground Adventure; Jocelyn's Escape; The Inmost Light; *The Three Impostors; or, The Transmutations*; The Red Hand; The Shining Pyramid; APPENDIX: Folklore and Legends of the North; Preface to "The Great God Pan" (1916); Introduction to *The Three Impostors* (1923); On Rereading *The Three Impostors* and the Wonder Story; Bibliography.

Volume 2 (1896–1910): Introduction; *The Hill of Dreams*; *Ornaments in Jade* (The Rose Garden; The Holy Things; The Turanians; The Idealist; Witchcraft; The Ceremony; Psychology; Torture; Midsummer; Nature); The White People; A Fragment of Life; *The Secret Glory*; APPENDIX: Introduction to *The Hill of Dreams* (1923); Preface to *The Secret Glory* (1922); Epilogue to *The Secret Glory* (1922); Bibliography.

Volume 3 (1911–1937): The Thousand and One Nights; The Bowmen; The Soldiers' Rest; The Monstrance; The Dazzling Light; The Great Return; The Little Nations; Out of the Earth; The Men from Troy; Munitions of War; The Light That Can Never Be Put Out; The Ghost of Whit-Monday; A New Christmas Carol; Scrooge and the Spirit—of Psycho-analysis; *The Terror*; The Happy Children; The Islington Mystery; The Gift of Tongues; The Cosy Room; Johnny Double; Awaking; Opening the Door; *The Green Round*; The Compliments of the Season; N; The Exalted Omega; The Children of the Pool; The Bright Boy; The Tree of Life; Out of the Picture; Change; The Dover Road; Ritual; APPENDIX: Introduction to *The Angels of Mons*; The Coming of the Terror; Bibliography.

Notes. This volume came together fairly quickly—it was given added urgency by the fact that Machen's work had gone into the public domain on January 1, 2018, and the market was flooded with all manner of trashy print-on-demand editions of his work. I carefully scrutinised the texts of his various tales, using the final two chapters of *The Secret Glory* (just about the only extant mss. of his fiction available) to establish a "style sheet" for his work. It includes one short piece ("The Thousand and One Nights") that has never been reprinted.

173. H. L. Mencken, *Writings in the* Baltimore Evening Sun, *July–October 1910*
a.   Seattle: Sarnath Press, [September] 2019.

Contents: Marginal Notes; A Wild German; The Early Drama; Notes on Morals; On Heredity; Marginal Notes; At Back River; In the Rosin Dust; French Marriages; Europe Since 1815; A Tale of 1904; Who's Who in 1910; The New Thought; The Noble Smiths; An Old-Time Actor; Back to Torture!; On Cigarettes; Marginal Notes; The Actor; World Languages; A French Scandal; Hymen's Handicap; The Common Negro; Henry Lavedan; A Moslem Revival; The Profane Art; Curbing the Cops; Neurasthenia; Trouble Ahead; Exit the Maxims; In Germany; Exit G. B. Shaw; The American; Genius vs. Cash; The Happy Life; A Russian Critic; The Census Returns; On Tobacco; About Best-Sellers; Cholera Again; The Two Englishes; Jim the Penman; UNSIGNED EDITORIALS: An Awe-Inspiring Armada; Round One; A Warning to the Duke; France Goes Back to Capital Punishment; Frank C. Wachter; The Treason of the Chautauqua Stars; China Adopts Our Decimal Coinage; What It Cost the Country; Hope Lingers; The Dawn in Turkey; A New Suffrage Bill in Parliament; England Begins to Understand the Race Problem; A Wise Decision; The Salvation Army under Fire; The War on the Bucketshop; An Extraordinary Woman; The Airships to the Fore; A Master of the Tone Art; Mr. Horwitz's Will; The New School of Lobbyists; Our Ridiculous Clothing; Mr. Roosevelt's Title to Leadership; Governor Harmon and the Newark Lynching; The Kaiser's Note; The Coroners under Fire; A Colonial Experiment; Safeguarding Passengers at Sea; King George's Wages; Robbing the Consumer; An Evil Custom; Dr. Wilson's Candidacy; The Charlton Case; The Weakness of the Aeroplane; On Chorus Girls; The Fruits of a Truce; Mr. Gaynor's Duty; Wedding Victuals; A Pennsylvania Horror; The Good Work Is Begun; Personal Journalism; The End of a Bitter Conflict; Art Languishes; The Modern Adam Smith; The Centre of Population; Launching the Ship; Canada Gives Notice; Mr. Taft's Advice; A Spanish Metternich; An Object Lesson; The Arts and Crafts Movement in Texas; A Man Worthy of Honor; Encouraging the Heroes; Politics in Georgia; A National Health Department; The Defeat of Bryan; In North Carolina; The British Immortals; Summer in Kansas; Nothing Doing!; A Defense of the King; The Decay of Swooning; The Jousting Begins; No Rest for the Explorers; A Missouri Methuselah; A British Dogberry; John G. Carlisle; The Accession Oath; The Quacks Are Prosperous; Insurance against Rain; The Carlists; The New Member; The Bank Thieves; The "Good" Lawyer; A Statesman's Fatal Mistake; A Monte Carlo in Cuba; The Returns from Cincinnati; The Treason of John D.; A Victory for Decency; Two Statesmen; The National Archives; The Peach Crop Liar; Progress against Leprosy; Mr. Betz and His

Holy War; Testing the Aeroplane; The Commission Curse; A Time of Change in England; On Spooning; The National Health Department and Its Critics; The Assassination Problem; The Right Kind of Despot; On the Golf Links; The Cost of Big Ships; The Decay of a Violin; In Defense of Kansas; The Gore Hearings; An Ignorant Judiciary; When Doctors Disagree; The Sorrows of the Goat; The Decay of Rowdyism; Demoralizing the Jackies; Florence Nightingale; The New Boss; Danger in Soothing Syrups; The Marrying Parson as a Social Menace; The Death of Applejack; The Incomparable Victual; The War in Illinois; The Awakening of Pittsburg; An "Independent" Republican; Improving an Ancient Art; In Colorado; Troubles of a New-Born Nation; Bryan Bolts the Ticket; Justice to the Boll Weevil; The Battle in New York; Another Hero Slain; Helping Mr. Harmon; Security against Typhoid; The Bad Actor Problem; Does Beauty Make Votes?; Explaining the Returns; We Come to the Scherzo; The Battle Begins; On Cancer Cures; The Learned Comedians; The Issue in November; The Best-Selling of All Best-Sellers; Bosses; A Meteorological Anodyne; The German Volcano; The Rooseveltian Japs; A First-Class Man; Dr. White's Advice; Baltimore vs. Panama; Political Slang; In Defense of the Gallus; The Maneuvers of Hearst; In the Glare of Greatness; The New Chinese Senate; The Red Flag in Portugal; The Passing of Queenstown; The Decay of Hearstism; What Mr. Hughes Has Done; The Portuguese Republic; The Kings Depart; The Man of Mystery; A Forgotten Delicacy; The Voter's Last Chance; Why Baltimore Shows a High Death Rate; The Operatic Ideal in America; The Cleveland Monument; Baltimore and Boston; The New Month of Weddings.

Notes. Volume 18 of the Collected Essays and Journalism of H. L. Mencken.

174. H. L. Mencken, *Writings in the* Baltimore Evening Sun, *October–December 1910*

   a. Seattle: Sarnath Press, [September] 2019.

     Contents: The Expurgators; England's English; American Cooking; Spoken American; More American; The Book; William V. Moody; American Pronouns; Empty Pessimism; William Gillette; A Call for Help; An Examination; Sunday Theatres; Nietzscheana; French Melodrama; Poor Old Ibsen!; A New Court?; Is a Capital Burlesque; Percy Mackaye; The Pension Grab; Good for the Reds!; The Printed Play; Henri Bataille; A Hall of Fame; The Moral Mind; Modjeska's Book; Jerome K. Jerome; On Hanging; The Tzs-Cheng Yuan; A Notable Novel; The Mikado; The Dramatic Critic; At the Pole; Mental Vibrations; Avery Hopwood; Eating, an Elegy; England's Crisis; An

English Issue; Tolstoiana; The Death Rate; A Maker of Tunes; August Strindberg; On "Life-Waste"; Various Matters; The Lords Spiritual; Christmas Books; Direct Elections; Various Matters; Christmas Sermon; The Fitch Plays; Wm. Clyde Fitch; In Liberia; Various Matters; UNSIGNED EDITORIALS: The Bird-Man of Politics; The Immortal Genoese; A Brace Race; The New Alpine Tunnel; Healing without Drugs; The French Strike; Figures Made Charming; Why Uncle Sam Is Robbed; Socialism under Fire; New Annexation Plans; Manuel Plays Politics; The Reform of a Socialist; Heroes of Other Days; The Census Padders; The Author of a Noble Hymn; The Land of Superstitions; Wellman's Failure; The Court of King's Bench; On Lawlessness; General Latrobe Wavers; Russia Battles with Trusts; Curbing the Police; Boston Prepares to Expand; A Man-Killing Machine; English Justice; Getting Rid of Ballinger; Socialism in Peril; The Opera Fund; Zion Church; The Department Store; The Portuguese Republic; A Hospital "for the Middle Classes"; Lady Warwick's Apostasy; Biplane vs. Monoplane; The Useless Balloon; The Battle in New York; Pumpkin Pie: A Fraud; Persecuting a Martyr; Another Burglary; Dr. Steiner's Reply to His Critics; Dr. Wilson's Campaign; John D. in Germany; Latham's Flight; Church Union; On Colds; Open-Air Weddings; Curbing the Tricksters; The Cholera Situation; The Colonel's Visit; A Vain Effort to Damage a Noble Character; The Aerotaxi Next; The End of the Battle; The Prophets Perform; A Prophet at Work; The Opportunity Ahead; The New York Senatorship; The Air-Men Surpass Themselves; Mr. Taft Still Pursues the Magazines; The Riots in Mexico; A Psychical Researcher Pays the Penalty; The Loans and the Tax Rate; A Waste of Talent; The Cost of Living Falls; England Faces a Crisis; A Constitution for Portugal; An Exquisite Victual; More Sugar Trust Thefts; Exit the Lords; Mr. Gaynor's Doctors' Bills; Lodge Follows Aldritch Hale and Burrows; China in the Throes of a Reformation; A Footnote on Tolstoi; The Mexican "Revolution"; The Shrieking Sisters; A Day of Judgment for the Stock Swindlers; The House Grows Unwieldy; On Pie; Col. Supplee and the Ancient Greeks; A Severe Blow to the Mexican Revolutionists; The Brazilian Navy; Peace in Mexico; The Price of Husbands; The Sugar Trust; Tammany's Choice; The Census Returns and Baltimore City; Dr. Cook's Confession; The Shady Lawyer; A Liar and His Lies; Gloom in Congress; Mr. Hitchcock's Work; Thirty Thousand Words; Germany Breaks Records; Ballinger Draws the Veil; The Garden of Eden; The Charlton Case; A Negro Invasion Causes Trouble in New York; Another Row in Honduras; A Plea for Originality; The Lorimer Case; A Notable Invention; The Carnegie Gift; The Civil Service Reformers; The Bald-Headed Man;

Extending the Merit System; Suspend the Rules!; The Mayor Before the Civil Service Reformers; The Fried Smelt; "Revision with Reservations"; The Spirit of Chicanery; The Direct Elections Amendment; The Fruits of Free Trade; John D.'s Latest Gift; The Seattle Spirit; The Belvedere; Loden Grows Obscure; The Season of Great Fires; An Obfuscated Carte; A Pleasing Blunder; The Flood of Bills; The Pistol-Toter; The Muckrake in the Country; Mr. Lucas under Fire; Sheehan for the Senate; The Pie of Pies; A New Pension Grab; American Music; Christmas Statistics; Uncle Joe a Capella; The Proposed Tariff Board.

Notes. Volume 19 of the Collected Essays and Journalism of H. L. Mencken.

175. H. L. Mencken, *Writings in the* Baltimore Evening Sun, *January–March 1911*

a.   Seattle: Sarnath Press, [September] 2019.

Contents: Lizette Reese; On Old Books; Concerning 'The Lily'; The Balalaika; Jones at the Bat; Do We Go Ahead?; Cowboy Songs; Various Matters; The 16th Amendment; Rupert Hughes; Various Matters; What Is Truth?; James Forbes; Literary Vandals; The Baconians; An Idol Smashed; On "Macbeth"; "Der Rosenkavalier"; England's Paupers; On Autographs; "La Samaritaine"; Health Laws; The Lowden Bill; Pinero's Latest; On Being Fat; A Notable Novel; Everywoman; The Trial of Joan; Home Rule!; On Bald Heads; Russian Fiction; Mrs. Fiske's Roles; Good and Bad at the Playhouses; The New Peers; Eugene Walter; On Quotations; An Irish Genius; Round One!; The Oregon Plan; About "The Faun"; Legalized Murder; Round Two!; Ambitious Bards; In Jackson's Day; Food Chemistry; The Child-Actor; Uncle Sam's Money; The Varieties; Mental Healing; The Novel Today; More Poetry!; The Literary Life; On Free Speech; Mr. Shakespeare; Stage Censors; The Bard Again; The Open Road; Round Three!; Slaying the Bard; UNSIGNED EDITORIALS: The Tricks of Sheehan; An Over-Gentle Law; A Tabloid Newspaper; The Errors of Reporters; The Battle of London; Exotic Weather; Tears: An Elegy; Pursuing the Trusts; The Centennials of 1911; A Campaign of Slander; Affairs in Portugal; The Rescue of Honduras; Lorimer Faces the Penalty; Mr. Underwood's Confession; The New House; Larceny in the Home; The Cost of Ocean Travel; The Fight in New York; The Tariff on Rats; Inaugurating a Governor; The Direct Elections Campaign; A Bachelor on the Bench; The Modern Detective; The Birthday of Germany; Electing Senators; "Of No Mean City"; A Chance to Save Money; The Carnegie Institution; Uncle Sam in Honduras; The Burial of the Colonel; David Graham

Phillips; Tearing Down Tariff Walls; The Schenk Trial; Oysters and Pseudo-Oysters; The Shakespeare Belt; The Florestan Club; Censoring Sarah; Sport for Dare-Devils; The Season of Colds; The Ambassador's House; On Marrying Titles; The Duty of a Jury; The Canadian Treaty; A Claque in Our Midst?; Jail for Smugglers; Why the Courts Have Lost the Confidence of the American People; A Peace Movement; Murdering the Muckrakers; Meningitis Is Conquered; A Political Puzzle; A Chance for Mr. Taft; The Cost of the Performance at Albany; The Maryland Delegation; The Delays of Justice; The Appeal from China; Mr. Clark's Indiscretion; The War in Mexico; A Herring Across the Trail; The Planked Shad; The Plague in China; On Train Speeds; The Mann Filibuster; The Georgia Seer; The Chances of Home Rule; Home Rule in Peril; The New Treaty with Japan; A Master of Figures; The Argentine Battleships; Mr. Lorimer's Defense; In Praise of Spring; Canada Bars the Negro; The Snarl in the Senate; In Defense of Lorimer; The Amendment's Chances; The Vote on the Amendment; The Case of Abe Ruef; The Direct Primary in Chicago; Ruef Goes to Prison; A Defect in Our Hospital System; Mr. Dix Changes Front; Miss Bates on Widows; Senator Rayner; A Rocky Road Ahead; The Vacant Leadership; Mr. Taft on Ballinger; The Colonel Redivivus; A Militant Governor; The Mexican Demonstration; The Rockefeller Pastor Quits; The Army at Work; The New Theatre; Alexandre Charles Lecocq; How and Why the Money of the People Is Squandered; Epidemics and the Public Mind; A Harmless Jest; Practical Tests of the Value of Vaccination; A Conqueror of Nature; Disrespect to St. Patrick; Sheehan Quits; Church Attendance; Patrolman Uncle Sam; Mayor Gaynor under Fire; The New York Fire.

Notes. Volume 20 of the Collected Essays and Journalism of H. L. Mencken.

176. H. L. Mencken, *Writings in the* Baltimore Evening Sun, *April–July 1911*
  a. Seattle: Sarnath Press, [October] 2019.

Contents: Up the Valley; In Re Shakespeare; At the Theatres; Bob the Eloquent; The Last Round; A Farewell; "The White Ship"; Some New Plays; The Indian Drama; Italian Bands; The Vernal Bards; Daniel Frohman; On Dreams; The Pied Piper; The New Theatre; Fortunata; The Party System; Flying by Night; A Woman's Plays; A Symphony; "The Honorable"; The Ueberbrettl'; On Bartenders; The Minstrel Men; Vaudeville Songs; "The Arrow Maker"; After Appomattox; On Alcohol; UNSIGNED EDITORIALS: Mr. Berger's Program; The Los Angeles Plan; The Perils of Bathing; The Lorimer Case Again; One of Spring's Delights; A Reformer's Opportunity; Memphis at the Bat Again; Progress in the Theatre; A New Health Resort; The Way Is Clear; Three-Cent Tom; The Coronation Oath; Reform at the Bar; Mr. Raynor's Speech; The Battle of Douglas; An Illinois Bill; The Passing of Joshua Whitcomb; Beware of the Flood!; A Grave Situation; A Good Idea; The Man in Chains; An Epoch-Making Decision; L'Art Nouveau in Kentucky; The Country Editor; Other Worlds Than Ours; A Great Debate; The Gutenberg Bible; A New National Anthem; The Hoe Sale; The Mexican Situation Clarifies; A Medical Exhibition; Enter the Strawberry; The Passing of a Great Ship; The Baconian Excavators; Up, Boomers, and at Him!; Summer Opera; On Pastry; The Problem of Problems; The Grand Master of the Simplified Spellers; The Minor Parties; On Wedding Presents; Bilingual Bards; The Criminal Lawyer; Diaz's Offer; Dr. Parker's Opera; The Empire Builders; The Broadway Carnival; The Country Is Saved!; Another Step Forward in China; To Europe by Way of Labrador; The New Slavery; Mexico and the United States; A Great Success; Madero's Rough Road; The Wireless Again; What the Decision in the Standard Oil Case Means; The Key Monument; Good Old Towson!; The Lords Take Heart; The Fly Meets Its Master; The Toils Close upon Lorimer; State Insurance against Disability; A Man of Sense; The Latest Type of Ocean Ship; The Mexican Peace Pact; The Canal Nears Completion; Making the House of Lords a Representative Senate; Governor Dix Fails; Lloyd-George Faces Difficulties; Mr. Taft's Wise Firmness; The Passing of Diaz; Unions of Government Employes; A Baltimore Boomer; The Second Phase in Portugal; The Second Visiting Day; The Passing of Gilbert; The Patent Medicine Case; "If I Owned Baltimore"; The Day Dawns in Pittsburg; A Wise Decision; A Blow to American Art; The New Chinese Dollar; An Old-Time Photographer; Wisdom Boiled Down; Harmon vs. Wilson; In Honor of the Cardinal; The Irish Census; An Idol Overturned; Learned Bodies; Postal Savings Banks; A Lamentable Attack upon (Prolonged Applause); Crimes and Punishments; The Chesapeake Crab; The Secrets of Happiness; Summer Amusements; The Senate Votes "Aye"; Mr. West's Resolution; A Warm Debate Impends; The Better Side of the Moving Picture; Havemeyer Again; A Pittsburg Gentleman; In Praise of Plumbers; The Mormon Peril; The Coronation; Sir William Osler, Bart.; The United States of Greater Britain; The Polytechnic's Future; The War on "Sure Cures"; The Powder Trust Case; A Golden Opportunity; The House Says No; Bad Politics; A Chance to Get a Big League Baseball Club; Jersey's Politicians Alarmed; The Parent's Part; The der Grosse; The English Census; An Economic Riddle; A Day of Old-Time Sport; The Johns Hopkins; The Recovery of June;

The Spring Opera Season; Half a Million Automobiles; One of the New Knights; A Right or a Duty?; Our Absurd Summer Clothes; The Gobbling of Morocco; Baltimore Is Lucky; The Whiskers Mystery; Jamaica Looks to Canada; Diplomatic Social Climbers; The Society of Christian Endeavor; The Silver Lining; One of the Wounded; The Servant Problem; The Morning After; Senators Afloat and Ashore; A Georgia Campaign; The "Dear Dick" Letter; The House-Fly; A Scholastic Reformer; A Georgia Magnifico; Germany and the Canal; The Income Tax; Dr. Wiley's "Crime"; New Navies; The Country's Verdict; A Blow to a Bugaboo; Mr. Wickersham; The Charms of Jail Life; The Cholera Situation; The Politicians Win Again; To Regulate Prices; A Dead-Letter Ordinance; The Identity of a Poet; Haiti Is at It Again; Simon on the Run; Mr. Taft's Victory; The Lords Admit Defeat; More Money for Postoffice Employes; Paris Cries "Enough!"; The Lords Take the Count; The Practical Effects of a State Guaranty of Bank Deposits; The Motive of Germany; The Downfall of Simon; Canada Balks at the Treaty; Germany in Morocco; Texas Is Still Wet; England Muddles Through; The Decay of the No. 2; Alaska Threatens Revolt; Marking Time; What Is Beer?; The Price of Novels.

Notes. Volume 21 of the Collected Essays and Journalism of H. L. Mencken.

177.   *Best of Black Wings: Tales of Lovecraftian Horror*
   a.   Hornsea, UK: PS Publishing, [October] 2019.

   Contents: Introduction; Acknowledgements; Norman Partridge, "Lesser Demons"; Darrell Schweitzer, "Howling in the Dark"; Sam Gafford, "Passing Spirits"; John Shirley, "When Death Wakes Me to Myself"; Richard Gavin, "The Abject"; Melanie Tem, "Dahlias"; John Langan, "Bloom"; Simon Strantzas, "Thistle's Find"; Jonathan Thomas, "Houdini Fish; Fred Chappell, "Artifact"; Lois H. Gresh, "Cult of the Dead"; Jason V Brock, "The Dark Sea Within"; Ann K. Schwader, "Night of the Piper"; Robert H. Waugh, "The Woman in the Attic"; Jason C. Eckhardt, "The Walker in the Night"; Donald Tyson, "The Organ of Chaos"; Stephen Woodworth, "Voodoo"; Don Webb, "The Shard"; W. H. Pugmire, "To Move Beneath Autumnal Oaks"; Wade German, "Lore."

   Notes. A book commissioned by the publisher. Selection of the "best" stories in the six-volume series was very difficult, as there were many fine stories I would have liked to include.

178. H. L. Mencken, *Writings in the* Baltimore Evening Sun, *August 1911– June 1912*

    a. Seattle: Sarnath Press, [November] 2019.

        Contents: Maude Adams Is Unable to Meet the Demands of the Role of Chantecler; True Comedy in "Green Stockings"; Agreeable Little Play Is "Pomander Walk"; 11 Fearful Hours of Democracy's Candidate-Making; UNSIGNED EDITORIALS: The Canadian Referendum; The English "Revolution" Ends; A Humane Device; The Water Supply; Mr. Soper's Task; A New Russian Navy; The Humane Mr. Wilson; The Downfall of Simon; On Christmas Gifts; Dr. Remsen on Newspapers; A House of 433 Members; The Arbitration Treaties; Grim Figures; The Liner and the Berg; The Third Degree; On American Stage Plays; Senator Borah's Speech; The New Battleships; A Hot Fight in Canada; The Hon. James K. Vardaman; Scotching the Joy Rider; Exit Pittsburg, Enter Pittsburgh; The Boy Scouts; The Madness of Bill; The Benzoate Campaign; An Invasion of Greeks; Home Rule Takes the Centre of the Stage; Unnecessary Noises; The Politicians' Ideal; Revising "God Save the King"; A Way out for Haiti; The Parcels Post; Curing Cancer by Mail; Dr. How's Figures; The Alsop Claim; The Practical Effect of the Arbitration Treaties; A Certain Bondholder; The Julep and Its Judges; Mr. Bryan's Position; How the Folly of Arizona May Work Good; China's Millions Shrink; Copyright in Architecture; Mr. Taft and the Tariff; Togo Takes the Count; The Visiting Irish Actors; A Case of Figures Lying; Lingering Barbarism; The Campaign in Canada; Pay for British Lawmakers; Lawmaking by Wholesale; To Europe by Way of Nova Scotia and Ireland; The Campaign in Mexico; The "Mona Lisa"; The Truth at Last; The Banana Trade; New Hope for the Schools; Santo Domingo; Are We Living Too Fast?; Handicapping the School Board; Muddling Through; The Queen of Grasses; Dr. Wilson's Star Rises; A New Flag on the Seas; Maine to Reconsider Prohibition; Americanizing the Porto Ricans; The Crop of Novels; The Safe and Sane Fourth: A Summary of Results; Abolishing "Honest" Graft; A Connubial Winkelreid; Sound-Proof Apartments; The Lafferty Mystery; Neglected Centennials; Troubles of the Weather Man; The Typhoid Situation; The War upon Lorimer; Elevating Two Professions; The Coroners; A Filipino Republic Protected by the Powers; Mr. M'Nulty's Charges; Party Platforms in Mexico; What the Parcels Post Will Do; A Red-Hot Campaign; "Pinafore" at 33; Mr. Baker's Enterprise; The M'Nulty Case Must Be Pushed to Trial; The Triumph of Reaction; The Ham Celestial; Improving the Primary Law; The Postal Savings Banks; The Increasing Safety of Aviation; Exit the Free Newspaper; A Hideous Gaud; The Greatest of Best-Sellers; The Battle for Prohibition; More Trouble in Portugal; How Canada Views the United States; A Decaying Profession; Will Mr. Bryan Give His Support to Mr. Wilson?; The Maryland Delegation; A Royal Match; Postal Bank Growth; The Wiley Verdict; The Convention Is Ours; Stolypin; On Eating the Oyster; Why the Chinese Rebel; The Stars Grow Dim; The Typhoid Situation; The Austrian Volcano; The New School Board; Arizona Clings to the Recall of Judges; A Monster Submarine; Pittsburgh's Dreams; Fixing the Blame; The Canadian Electors; Baltimore in the News; Our Natural Monopoly; The Canadian Landslide; A Proof of Progress; John L. in Congress? Why Not?; Step Up and Save the Opera Season!; Dreadnoughts and Superdreadnoughts; The Heavenly Twins; Enter the Mortician; Mr. Hughes' False Friends Once More Advise Him; Mr. J. Albert Hughes; A Moralist in Office; Gentlemen Horrified; A Time to Tell the Truth; The Role of the Police; Mr. Wickersham Considers; One Who Blundered; A Question of Etiquette; On Clerical Errors; The Horns of a Dilemma; A Patriotic Balm; Expert Advice; A Neutral; The Oyster in New Orleans; Good Government; An Auctioneer's Relaxations; The "Advisory" Committee; The Shame of Baltimore; What the Country Thinks; Where Badness Is a Fine Art; More Advertising; Leaders of the Opposition; A Brotherly Business; Oysters and "Oysters"; Once More That Curse!; Who Is Getting It?; The End Is in Sight; The Germans Indorse Wiley; Coatesville Will Not Tell; An "Old-Fashioned" Fire Department; Germany Faces a National Campaign; Equal Suffrage Advances; No Cause for Alarm; On Professors; The Dead Justice; The Chinese Rebellion; The Perils of Air-Sickness; Cholera in Italy; A Needed Trolley Line; The Chase of Spooks; Another War Scare; A Maryland Victual; The Opera Season; Islam in Africa; Baltimore in Kansas City; Lynching and Liquor; Fake Patent Medicines Next; Advertising Baltimore; Vaccination and Lockjaw; Mrs. Boswell's Theory; The Legislative Arm; Another Brave Foe of Newspaper Domination; The Chinese Parliament; Maine Is Still at It; A Victory for France; The Rise of Beer; Socialism as a Phase of Insurgency; A Statesman's Laborious Explanation; Free Advice to Kansas City; The Negro and the Census; Diplomacy and the Dollar; Arthur James Balfour; On Feminine Architecture; Home Rule: The Last Battle; The Humane Machine; The Opera Situation; The Chinese Elections; The Owen Bill; More Advertising; A Rising Political Power; The Queen of the Gramineae; What's Wrong with the Navy?; Ramon Caceres; Concerning a Name; Introducing the Yak; The Hand of Blood; The Avaricious Allopaths; The Airship in Actual War; The Meleagris Gallopavo; A Carnival, by All Means!; A Generation's Progress; The M'Namara Confession; Exit the Small

Manufacturer; Congress Again; Italy Faces Disaster; Salisbury's Decision; Where Baltimore Leads; A Friend to the Downtrodden; The Census and the Sexes; New York Justice; The Economists; The Typhoid Problem; Our National Library; Is It Constitutional?; The German Elections; Tempo: Adagio; Lorimer Again; The "Increase" of Cancer; The Carnival; Compulsory Insurance in England; England's Paupers; A Baltimorean by Free Choice; The Game of Grab; Oysters and Oysterians; A Chance for the Boomers; Modern Jail Life; The Smiths; The Next Step in China; A Lucky Year; In Ecuador; One Walking in Darkness; The Dean of Congress; Bernardo Reyes; An Abhorrent Trust; Two Professions; A Dangerous Practice; The Captain of the Old Guard Surrenders; Tuberculosis Is Decreasing; The Backward Germans; Americans of Tomorrow; "Fighting Bob"; A New Year's Gift to Man; The Throne; In China; The New Theatre's End; The Economists; Esperanto; A Dangerous Plan; Feeding the Visitors; The City Council as It Is; The Germans Vote Tomorrow; The Kentucky Mammoth; For Three Vice-Admirals; The German Socialists; A Censor of Stage Morals; Labouchere; Changing Inauguration Day; False Irishmen; The Decay of Maryland Victualry; Dr. Wiley Wins; The Flood of Bills; An Amazing Error; Another Typhoid Epidemic; The New Reichstag; Mexico at It Again.

Notes. Volume 22 of the Collected Essays and Journalism of H. L. Mencken.

179.   H. L. Mencken, *The Free Lance, May–August 1911*
    a.   Seattle: Sarnath Press, [December] 2019.

      Contents: 8 May 1911; 9 May 1911; 10 May 1911; 11 May 1911; 12 May 1911; 13 May 1911; 15 May 1911; 16 May 1911; 17 May 1911; 18 May 1911; 19 May 1911; 20 May 1911; 22 May 1911; 23 May 1911; 24 May 1911; 25 May 1911; 26 May 1911; 27 May 1911; 29 May 1911; 30 May 1911; 31 May 1911; 1 June 1911; 2 June 1911; 3 June 1911; 5 June 1911; 6 June 1911; 7 June 1911; 8 June 1911; 9 June 1911; 10 June 1911; 12 June 1911; 13 June 1911; 14 June 1911; 15 June 1911; 16 June 1911; 17 June 1911; 19 June 1911; 20 June 1911; 21 June 1911; 22 June 1911; 23 June 1911; 24 June 1911; 26 June 1911; 27 June 1911; 28 June 1911; 29 June 1911; 30 June 1911; 1 July 1911; 3 July 1911; 5 July 1911; 6 July 1911; 7 July 1911; 8 July 1911; 10 July 1911; 11 July 1911; 12 July 1911; 13 July 1911; 14 July 1911; 15 July 1911; 17 July 1911; 18 July 1911; 19 July 1911; 20 July 1911; 21 July 1911; 22 July 1911; 24 July 1911; 25 July 1911; 26 July 1911; 27 July 1911; 28 July 1911; 29 July 1911; 1 August 1911; 3 August 1911; 4 August 1911; 8 August 1911; 11 August 1911; 12 August 1911; 15 August 1911; 17 August 1911; 18 August

1911; 21 August 1911; 23 August 1911; 24 August 1911; 25 August 1911; 26 August 1911; 28 August 1911; 30 August 1911.

Notes. Volume 23 of the Collected Essays and Journalism of H. L. Mencken, and the first of as many as 12 volumes reprinting the totality of Mencken's "Free Lance" columns in the *Baltimore Evening Sun* (1911–15).

III. Editions of Works by H. P. Lovecraft

1. *Uncollected Prose and Poetry* (with Marc A. Michaud)
    a. West Warwick, RI: Necronomicon Press, 1978.

        Contents: Introduction; Letters to the Editor of the *Providence Sunday Journal* (No Transit of Mars, The Earth Not Hollow); Providence in 2000 A.D.; Two Letters to the Editor of the *Argosy* (Ad Criticos: Liber Primus, Correction for Lovecraft); New England; "Prologue" to "Fragments from an Hour of Inspiration" by Jonathan E. Hoag; The Simple Spelling Mania; The Case for Classicism; Helene Hoffman Cole [poem]; Trimmings; Editorial Notes in the *United Amateur* (issues of November 1920, September 1921, November 1921); Lucubrations Lovecraftian; East and West Harvard Conservatism; Letter to the Editor of *Weird Tales* (September 1923); Review of *Ebony and Crystal* by Clark Ashton Smith; The Omnipresent Philistine; The Very Old Folk; Biographical Notice; Sleepy Hollow To-day; Letter to the Editor of *Driftwind* (July 1932); The Sorcery of Aphlar (with Duane W. Rimel); The Odes of Horace: III, ix; The Night Ocean (with R. H. Barlow); Commentary [by Joshi]; Bibliography; Errata.

        Notes. My first book—an early product of my bibliographical work, during which I discovered many works by Lovecraft not previously known. The book was marred by many typographical errors, necessitating a hastily inserted errata sheet.

2. *Science vs. Charlatanry: Essays on Astrology* (with Scott Connors)
    a. Madison, WI: The Strange Co., 1979.

        Contents: Preface, by Joshi and Connors; Introduction, by Connors and Joshi; Hartmann, "Astrology and the European War"; Lovecraft, "Science versus Charlatanry"; Hartmann, [Letter to the Editor]; Lovecraft, "The Falsity of Astrology"; Lovecraft (as "Isaac Bickerstaffe, Jr."), "Astrology and the Future"; Hartmann, "The Science of Astrology"; Lovecraft (as "Isaac Bickerstaffe, Jr."), "Delavan's Comet and Astrology"; Hartmann, "A Defense of Astrology"; Lovecraft, "The Fall of Astrology"; Lovecraft (as "Isaac Bickerstaffe, Jr."), "[Isaac Bickerstaffe's Reply]"; Notes [by Joshi]; Bibliography.

Notes. A slim volume resulting from Scott Connors's discovery of the controversy between Lovecraft and Hartmann in the pages of the Providence *Evening News* of 1914.

3. *Uncollected Prose and Poetry II* (with Marc A. Michaud)
    a. West Warwick, RI: Necronomicon Press, 1980.
        Contents: Introduction; Ibid; The Trap (with Henry S. Whitehead); Collapsing Cosmoses (with R. H. Barlow); Ad Criticos: Liber Secundus; Brotherhood; Medusa: A Portrait; The Feast; Ave atque Vale; Poesy; Life for Humanity's Sake; Vermont—A First Impression; "Preface" to *Old World Footprints*; The Old Brick Row; In Memoriam: Henry St. Clair Whitehead; Robert Ervin Howard: 1906–1936; Notes.
        Notes. More reprints of rare Lovecraftiana.

4. *Uncollected Prose and Poetry 3* (with Marc A. Michaud)
    a. West Warwick, RI: Necronomicon Press, 1982.
        Contents: Introduction; Discarded Draft of "The Shadow over Innsmouth"; The Battle That Ended the Century (with R. H. Barlow); Earth and Sky; Hellas; On Religion; To an Infant; Festival; The Brief Autobiography of an Inconsequential Scribbler; What Amateurdom and I Have Done for Each Other; Cats and Dogs; Notes on Writing Weird Fiction; Notes.
        Notes. Still more reprints of rare Lovecraftiana.

5. *Saturnalia and Other Poems*
    a. Bloomfield, NJ: Cryptic Publications, 1984.
        Contents: Introduction; On the Creation of Niggers; To Mr. Munroe, on His Instructive and Entertaining Account of Switzerland; To an Accomplished Young Gentlewoman; The Decline and Fall of a Man of the World; The Road to Ruin; Verses Designed to Be Sent by a Friend of the Author to His Brother-in-Law on New-Year's Day; On an Accomplished Young Linguist; To "The Scribblers"; The Isaacsonio-Mortoniad; Providence Amateur Press Club (Deceased) to the Athenaeum Club of Journalism; Gryphus in Asinum Mutatus; To the Arcadian; To the Nurses of the Red Cross; To the A.H.S.P.C. on Receipt of the May *Pippin*; To the A.H.S.P.C. on Receipt of the Christmas *Pippin*; Sors Poetae; "The Poetical Punch" Pushed from His Pedestal; To Mr. Kleiner, on Receiving from Him the Poetical Works of Addison, Gay, and Somerville; To Col. Linkaby Didd; Epigrams; On Collaboration; With a Copy of Wilde's Fairy Tales; On Receiving a Portraiture of Mrs. Berkeley, yᵉ Poetess; To S. S. L.: Christmas 1920; To Samˡ Loveman Esq.; To Saml: Loveman, Gent.; To Two Epgephi; Damon and Lycë; To Mr. Baldwin, upon Re-

ceiving a Picture of Him in a Rural Bower; Saturnalia; To Xanthippe, on Her Birthday—March 16, 1925; Hedone; Veteropinguis Redivivus; My Lost Love; To a Young Poet in Dunedin; On an Unspoil'd Rural Prospect; Christmas Greetings; Notes.

Notes. A volume—commissioned by the editor of *Crypt of Cthulhu*, Robert M. Price—assembling Lovecraft's previously unpublished poetry. Special issue (No. 21) of *Crypt of Cthulhu.*

6.　*The Dunwich Horror and Others*
　　a.1. Sauk City, WI: Arkham House, 1984.
　　a.2. Sauk City, WI: Arkham House, 1985.
　　a.3. Sauk City, WI: Arkham House, 1988.
　　a.4. Sauk City, WI: Arkham House, 1992.
　　a.5. Sauk City, WI: Arkham House, 1997.
　　a.6. Sauk City, WI: Arkham House, 2000.

Contents: S. T. Joshi, "A Note on the Texts"; Robert Bloch, "Heritage of Horror"; In the Vault; Pickman's Model; The Rats in the Walls; The Outsider; The Colour out of Space; The Music of Erich Zann; The Haunter of the Dark; The Picture in the House; The Call of Cthulhu; The Dunwich Horror; Cool Air; The Whisperer in Darkness; The Terrible Old Man; The Thing on the Doorstep; The Shadow over Innsmouth; The Shadow out of Time.

Notes. The first volume of my corrected edition of Lovecraft's fiction.

7.　*Juvenilia: 1895–1905*
　　a.　West Warwick, RI: Necronomicon Press, 1984.

Contents: Introduction; The Little Glass Bottle; The Poem of Ulysses; Ovid's Metamorphoses; The Secret Cave; The Mystery of the Grave-Yard; An Account in Verse of the Marvellous Adventures of H. Lovecraft . . .; The Mysterious Ship; *Poemata Minora, Volume II* (Ode to Selene or Diana; To the Old Pagan Religion; On the Ruin of Rome; To Pan; On the Vanity of Human Ambition); De Triumpho Naturae; Notes.

Notes. A slim pamphlet assembling the entirety of Lovecraft's fictional and poetic juvenilia. The title should have been *Juvenilia: 1897–1905.*

8.　*In Defence of Dagon*
　　a.　West Warwick, RI: Necronomicon Press, 1985.

Contents: Introduction; The Defence Reopens!; The Defence Remains Open!; Final Words.

Notes. First complete publication of three essays sent by Lovecraft through the Transatlantic Circulator. A revised edition was prepared but never published; but the revised introduction appeared as "*In Defence of Dagon* and Lovecraft's Philosophy" in I.23.

9. *At the Mountains of Madness and Other Novels*
    a.1. Sauk City, WI: Arkham House, 1985.
    a.2. Sauk City, WI: Arkham House, 1987.
    a.3. Sauk City, WI: Arkham House, 1991.
    a.4. Sauk City, WI: Arkham House, 1997.

    Contents: S. T. Joshi, "A Note on the Texts"; James Turner, "A Mythos in His Own Image"; *At the Mountains of Madness; The Case of Charles Dexter Ward;* The Shunned House; The Dreams in the Witch House; The Statement of Randolph Carter; *The Dream-Quest of Unknown Kadath;* The Silver Key; Through the Gates of the Silver Key (with E. Hoffmann Price).

    Notes. The second volume of my corrected edition of Lovecraft's fiction.

10. *Medusa and Other Poems*
    a. Mount Olive, NJ: Cryptic Publications, 1986.

    Contents: Introduction; The Members of the Men's Club of the First Universalist Church . . .; Providence in 2000 A.D.; Ad Criticos; Frustra Praemunitus; To General Villa; To the Rev. James Pyke; New England; The Power of Wine; 1914; The Crime of Crimes; The Bookstall; An American to Mother England; The Teuton's Battle-Song; Ye Ballade of Patrick von Flynn; Content; The Beauties of Peace; Brotherhood; Britannia Victura; Iterum Conjunctae; To Greece, 1917; Prologue to "Fragments from an Hour of Inspiration" by Jonathan E. Hoag; Earth and Sky; To the Death of a Rhyming Critic; Autumn; Ver Rusticum; The Link; The Spirit of Summer; Hellas; Ambition; Spring; Damon—a Monody; Amissa Minerva; Hylas and Myrrha: A Tale; Helene Hoffman Cole; A Cycle of Verse; Monody on the Late King Alcohol; The Pensive Swain; Wisdom; Bells; Cindy: Scrub Lady in a State Street Skyscraper; Ex-Poet's Reply; October; To Alfred Galpin, Esq.; Theobaldian Aestivation; Medusa: A Portrait; To Zara; To Damon; To Rheinhart Kleiner, upon His Town Fables and Elegies; The Feast; Lines for Poets' Night at the Scribblers' Club; To an Infant; To Miss Beryl Hoyt; Ave atque Vale; Bouts Rimés; The Odes of Horace; Bibliography.

    Notes. Another special issue (No. 44) of *Crypt of Cthulhu,* containing all Lovecraft's unreprinted verse (i.e., those poems not included in *Collected Poems* [1963] or *A Winter Wish* [1977]).

11.   *Dagon and Other Macabre Tales*
        a.1. Sauk City, WI: Arkham House, 1986.
        a.2. Sauk City, WI: Arkham House, 1987.
        a.3. Sauk City, WI: Arkham House, 1991.
        a.4. Sauk City, WI: Arkham House, 1997.

   Contents: S. T. Joshi, "A Note on the Texts"; T. E. D. Klein, "A Dreamer's Tales"; The Tomb; Dagon; Polaris; Beyond the Wall of Sleep; The White Ship; The Doom That Came to Sarnath; The Tree; The Cats of Ulthar; The Temple; Facts concerning the Late Arthur Jermyn and His Family; Celephaïs; From Beyond; The Nameless City; The Quest of Iranon; The Moon-Bog; The Other Gods; Herbert West—Reanimator; Hypnos; The Hound; The Lurking Fear; The Unnamable; The Festival; Under the Pyramids (with Harry Houdini); The Horror at Red Hook; He; The Strange High House in the Mist; The Evil Clergyman; In the Walls of Eryx (with Kenneth Sterling); *Early Tales:* The Beast in the Cave; The Alchemist; The Transition of Juan Romero; The Street; Poetry and the Gods (with Anna Helen Crofts); *Fragments:* Azathoth; The Descendant; The Book; Supernatural Horror in Literature; [James Turner], Index to "Supernatural Horror in Literature"; [S. T. Joshi], "Chronology of the Fiction of H. P. Lovecraft.

   Notes. The third volume of my corrected edition of Lovecraft's fiction.

12.   *Uncollected Letters*
        a.   West Warwick, RI: Necronomicon Press, 1986.

   Contents: Introduction; Letters: To the Editor of the *Scientific American*, 16 July 1906; to the Editor of *The All-Story Weekly*, [c. January 1913]; to the Editor of the *All-Story Weekly*, [c. February 1914]; to Edwin Baird of *Weird Tales*, [c. May 1923]; to Edwin Baird of *Weird Tales*, [c. June 1923]; to Edwin Baird of *Weird Tales*, [c. October 1923]; to Edwin Baird of *Weird Tales*, [c. August 1923]; to Farnsworth Wright of *Weird Tales*, [c. January 1926]; to Farnsworth Wright of *Weird Tales*, 5 July 1927; to Farnsworth Wright of *Weird Tales*, [c. December 1927]; to Farnsworth Wright of *Weird Tales*, [c. January 1928]; to Bertrand K. Hart, [c. March 1930]; to Edwin Hadley Smith, 10 March 1933; to Farnsworth Wright of *Weird Tales*, [c. December 1933]; to Charles D. Hornig of the *Fantasy Fan*, 1933–34 (9 letters); to F. Lee Baldwin, [c. 1934]; to Vincent B. Haggerty, [c. June 1935]; to Donald A. Wollheim, [c. October 1935]; to Farnsworth Wright of *Weird Tales*, [c. June 1936]; to the Convention of the National Amateur Press Association, 22 June 1936; to Willis

Conover, 24 August 1936; to Willis Conover, 23 September 1936; to Ben Abramson, [c. January 1937]; to Rheinhart Kleiner, 1915–23 ("By Post from Providence"); to Duane W. Rimel, 19 November 1934; 10 March 1935; 16 April 1935 ("Excerpts from the Letters of H. P. Lovecraft"); to Jim Blish and William Miller, Jr., 13 May 1936; 19 May 1936; 3 June 1936; to Nils H. Frome, 19 December 1936; 20 January 1937; 8 February 1937; Notes; Bibliography.

Notes. A volume collecting many of Lovecraft's letters published during or shortly after his lifetime.

13. *The Horror in the Museum and Other Revisions*
     a.1. Sauk City, WI: Arkham House, 1989.
     a.2. Sauk City, WI: Arkham House, 1997.
     a.3. Sauk City, WI: Arkham House, 2000.
     b. New York: Del Rey, 2007.

Contents: S. T. Joshi, "A Note on the Texts"; August Derleth, "Lovecraft's 'Revisions'"; *Primary Revisions:* The Green Meadow (with Winifred V. Jackson); The Crawling Chaos (with Winifred V. Jackson); The Last Test (with Adolphe de Castro); The Electric Executioner (with Adolphe de Castro); The Curse of Yig (with Zealia Bishop); The Mound (with Zealia Bishop); Medusa's Coil (with Zealia Bishop); The Man of Stone (with Hazel Heald); The Horror in the Museum (with Hazel Heald); Winged Death (with Hazel Heald); Out of the Aeons (with Hazel Heald); The Horror in the Burying-Ground (with Hazel Heald); The Diary of Alonzo Typer (with William Lumley); *Secondary Revisions:* The Horror at Martin's Beach (with Sonia H. Greene); Ashes (with C. M. Eddy, Jr.); The Ghost-Eater (with C. M. Eddy, Jr.); The Loved Dead (with C. M. Eddy, Jr.); Deaf, Dumb, and Blind (with C. M. Eddy, Jr.); Two Black Bottles (with Wilfred B. Talman); The Trap (with Henry S. Whitehead); The Tree on the Hil (with Duane W. Rimel); The Disinterment (with Duane W. Rimel); "Till A' the Seas" (with R. H. Barlow); The Night Ocean (with R. H. Barlow).

Notes. A volume of my corrected texts of Lovecraft's revisions and collaborations. Several new revisions have been added, and the volume has been radically restructured from the original (1970) edition.

14. *The Conservative* (3rd ed.)
     a. West Warwick, RI: Necronomicon Press, 1990.

Contents: Introduction; Editorial (April 1915); The Crime of the Century; [Untitled notes on amateur journalism] (April 1915); Editorial (July 1915); Metrical Regularity; In a Major Key; The Allowable Rhyme; Editorial (October 1915); Gems from *In a Minor Key;*

The Renaissance of Manhood; Liquor and Its Friends; Symphony and Stress; Old England and the "Hyphen"; Revolutionary Mythology; The Symphonic Ideal; The Vers Libre Epidemic; A Remarkable Document; The Despised Pastoral; Time and Space; Merlinus Redivivus; Anglo-Saxondom; *Les Mouches Fantastiques*; The League; Bolshevism; Rursus Adsumus; Rudis Indigestaque Moles; In the Editor's Study (July 1923); [Untitled notes on amateur journalism] (July 1923).

Notes. A selection of Lovecraft's writings in his amateur journal, the *Conservative*. The first (1976) and second (1977) editions appeared without my involvement.

15.   *The Fantastic Poetry*
    a.   West Warwick, RI: Necronomicon Press, 1990.
    b.   West Warwick, RI: Necronomicon Press, 1993.

      Contents: Introduction; Unda; or, The Bride of the Sea; To the Late John H. Fowler, Esq.; The Poe-et's Nightmare; The Rutted Road; Nemesis; Astrophobos; Psychopompos: A Tale in Rhyme; The Eidolon; Despair; Revelation; A Cycle of Verse (Oceanus, Clouds, Mother Earth); The House; The City; To Edward John Moreton Drax Plunkett, Eighteenth Baron Dunsany; Bells; The Nightmare Lake; On Reading Lord Dunsany's *Book of Wonder*; To a Dreamer; To Zara; Nathicana; The Cats; Primavera; Hallowe'en in a Suburb; Festival; The Wood; The Outpost; The Messenger; The Ancient Track; Bouts Rimés (Beyond Zimbabwe, The White Elephant) (with R. H. Barlow); In a Sequester'd Providence Churchyard Where Once Poe Walk'd; To Mr. Finlay, upon His Drawing for Mr. Bloch's Tale, "The Faceless God"; To Clark Ashton Smith, Esq., upon His Phantastick Tales, Verses, Pictures, and Sculptures.

      Notes. A modest collection of Lovecraft's weird verse. The second edition includes "The Unknown."

16.   *Letters to Henry Kuttner* (with David E. Schultz)
    a.   West Warwick, RI: Necronomicon Press, 1990.

      Contents: Introduction, by Joshi and Schultz; Letters to Henry Kuttner: 16 February 1936; 12 March 1936; 16 April 1936; 18 May 1936; [c. 18 June 1936]; 29 July 1926; 29 August 1936; 15 October 1936; 30 November 1936; 8 February 1937.

      Notes. A slim volume, the first of the Joshi–Schultz unabridged editions of Lovecraft's letters to given correspondents.

17.   *Letters to Richard F. Searight* (with David E. Schultz and Franklyn Searight)
    a.   West Warwick, RI: Necronomicon Press, 1992.
       Contents: Franklyn Searight, "Introduction: Richard F. Searight"; Letters to Richard F. Searight.
       Notes. First complete publication of the letters to Searight.

18.   *Autobiographical Writings*
    a.   West Warwick, RI: Necronomicon Press, 1992.
       Contents: Introduction; The Brief Autobiography of an Inconsequential Scribbler; Within the Gates; A Confession of Unfaith; Selections from "News Notes"; Commercial Blurbs; [Biographical Notice]; Autobiography of Howard Phillips Lovecraft; Some Notes on a Nonentity; Bibliography.
       Notes. A slim volume of Lovecraft's writings about himself.

19.   *Letters to Robert Bloch* (with David E. Schultz)
    a.   West Warwick, RI: Necronomicon Press, 1993.
       Contents: Robert Bloch, "A Man of Letters"; Letters to Robert Bloch; Index.
       Notes. A volume containing nearly all of Bloch's letters to Lovecraft. Shortly after publication, additional letters were found, necessitating a slim "addendum."

20.   *The H. P. Lovecraft Dream Book* (with David E. Schultz and Will Murray)
    a.   West Warwick, RI: Necronomicon Press, 1994.
       Contents: Introduction; Letters to Rheinhart Kleiner, 16 November 1916; to Maurice W. Moe, 15 May 1918; to the Gallomo, 11 December 1919; to the Gallomo, [January <i.e. April>] 1920; to Rheinhart Kleiner, 21 May 1920; to Rheinhart Kleiner, 14 December 1920; to Frank Belknap Long, [November 1927?]; to Donald Wandrei, [3 November 1927]; to Bernard Austin Dwyer, [4 November 1927]; to Donald Wandrei, [24 November 1927]; to Robert Bloch, [c. 19–20 August 1933]; to Clark Ashton Smith, 3 October 1933; to Bernard Austin Dwyer, [August 1933?]; to Clark Ashton Smith, [22 October 1933]; to Clark Ashton Smith, 13 November 1933; to Clark Ashton Smith, 29 November 1933; to J. Vernon Shea, 4 February 1934; to Duane W. Rimel, 22 December 1934; to R. H. Barlow, [20 April 1935]; to R. H. Barlow, [11 May 1935]; to William Lumley, 20 June 1936; to Virgil Finlay, 24 October 1936; to Harry O. Fischer, [late February 1937].
       Notes. A volume containing accounts of weird dreams found in Lovecraft's letters. The volume was criticised as being a retread of

Dreams and Fancies (1962), but the selection is much more extensive and textually accurate.

21.   *The Shadow over Innsmouth* (with David E. Schultz)
    a.   West Warwick, RI: Necronomicon Press, 1994.
    b.   West Warwick, RI: Necronomicon Press, 1997.
        Contents: Introduction, by Joshi and Schultz; The Shadow over Innsmouth; Notes to "The Shadow over Innsmouth"; Discarded Draft of "The Shadow over Innsmouth"; Textual Notes; Publication History of "The Shadow over Innsmouth."
        Notes. Exhaustively annotated edition of the novella.

22.   *Letters to Samuel Loveman and Vincent Starrett* (with David E. Schultz)
    a.   West Warwick, RI: Necronomicon Press, 1994.
        Contents: Introduction, by Joshi and Schultz; Letters to Samuel Loveman; Letters to Vincent Starrett; Appendix (letters to the *Haldeman-Julius Weekly*, 20 January 1923; 17 March 1923); Appendix ("To Satan" and "Bacchanale" by Samuel Loveman).
        Notes. Small pamphlet of the few letters to Starrett and Loveman.

23.   *Miscellaneous Writings*
    a.   Sauk City, WI: Arkham House, 1995.
        Contents: Introduction; DREAMS AND FANCIES: [introductory note by Joshi]; The Little Glass Bottle; The Secret Cave; The Mystery of the Grave-Yard; The Mysterious Ship; A Reminiscence of Dr. Samuel Johnson; Old Bugs; Memory; Nyarlathotep (prose-poem); Ex Oblivione; What the Moon Brings; Sweet Ermengarde; The Very Old Folk; History of the *Necronomicon*; Ibid; Discarded Draft of "The Shadow over Innsmouth"; The Battle That Ended the Century (with R. H. Barlow); Collapsing Cosmoses (with R. H. Barlow); The Challenge from Beyond (Lovecraft portion only); THE WEIRD FANTASIST: [introductory note by Joshi]; Commonplace Book; Lord Dunsany and His Work; Notes on Writing Weird Fiction; Some Notes on Interplanetary Fiction; In Memoriam: Robert Ervin Howard; MECHANISTIC MATERIALIST: [introductory note by Joshi]; Idealism and Materialism—A Reflection; Life for Humanity's Sake; *In Defence of Dagon*; Nietzcheism and Realism; The Materialist Today; Some Causes of Self-Immolation; Heritage or Modernism: Common Sense in Art Forms; THE LITERARY CRITIC: [introductory note by Joshi]; Metrical Regularity; The Vers Libre Epidemic; The Case for Classicism; Literary Composition; Ars Gratia Artis; The Poetry of Lilian Middleton; Rudis Indigestaque Moles; In the Editor's Study; The Professional Incubus; The Omnipresent Philistine; What Belongs in

Verse; POLITICAL THEORIST: [introductory note by Joshi]; The Crime of the Century; More *Chain Lightning*; Old England and the "Hyphen"; Revolutionary Mythology; Americanism; The League; Bolshevism; Some Repetitions on the Times; ANTIQUARIAN TRAV-ELS: [introductory note by Joshi]; Vermont—A First Impression; Observations on Several Parts of America; Travels in the Provinces of America; An Account of Charleston; Some Dutch Footprints in New England; Homes and Shrines of Poe; AMATEUR JOURNALIST: [introductory note by Joshi]; In a Major Key; The Dignity of Journalism; Symphony and Stress; *United Amateur Press Association: Exponent of Amateur Journalism*; A Reply to *The Lingerer*; *Les Mouches Fantastiques*; For What Does the United Stand?; Amateur Journalism: Its Possible Needs and Betterment; What Amateurdom and I Have Done for Each Other; Lucubrations Lovecraftian; A Matter of Uniteds; Mrs. Miniter—Estimates and Recollections; *Some Current Motives and Practices*; EPISTOLARIAN: [introductory note by Joshi]; Trans-Neptunian Planets; The Earth Not Hollow; Letter to the *All-Story Weekly* (1914); Science versus Charlatanry; The Fall of Astrology; Letter to Edwin Baird (1923); Letter to Edwin Baird (1923); The Old Brick Row; Letter to Nils H. Frome (1937); PERSONAL: [introductory note by Joshi]; The Brief Autobiography of an Inconsequential Scribbler; Within the Gates; A Confession of Unfaith; Commercial Blurbs; Cats and Dogs; Some Notes on a Nonentity; Bibliography.

Notes. A major selection of Lovecraft's nonfictional writings (also including stray bits of fiction that did not appear in earlier Arkham House volumes of my corrected texts), with introduction and substantial section introductions.

24. *The Annotated H. P. Lovecraft*
  a. New York: Dell, August 1997.
     Contents: Introduction; The Rats in the Walls; The Colour out of Space; The Dunwich Horror; *At the Mountains of Madness*; Lovecraft on Weird Fiction (excerpts of letters to *Weird Tales* [March 1924], to *Weird Tales* [5 July 1927], to Frank Belknap Long [22 February 1931], to Harold S. Farnese [22 September 1932]); Appendix: Lovecraft in the Media; Select Bibliography.
     Notes. A volume commissioned by a book packager and containing numerous illustrations and extensive annotations. The book went through a number of reprintings, but I have no details on these.

25. *More Annotated H. P. Lovecraft* (with Peter Cannon)
  a. New York: Dell, August 1999.

Contents: Introduction, by Peter Cannon; The Picture in the House; Herbert West—Reanimator; The Hound; The Shunned House; The Horror at Red Hook; Cool Air; The Call of Cthulhu; Pickman's Model; The Thing on the Doorstep; The Haunter of the Dark.

Notes. A volume I tried to get out of editing, because I was already working on my first Penguin edition (see item 26 below); but the book packager demanded that my name remain on the book. I annotated only "Herbert West—Reanimator"; Cannon did the rest.

26.   *The Call of Cthulhu and Other Weird Stories*
   a.   New York: Penguin, [October] 1999.
   b.   New York: Penguin, [October] 2011 (deluxe ed.).
   c.   London: Folio Society, 2017.

      Contents: Introduction; Suggestions for Further Reading; Dagon; The Statement of Randolph Carter; Facts concerning the Late Arthur Jermyn and His Family; Celephaïs; Nyarlathotep; The Picture in the House; The Outsider; Herbert West—Reanimator; The Hound; The Rats in the Walls; The Festival; He; Cool Air; The Call of Cthulhu; The Colour out of Space; The Whisperer in Darkness; The Shadow over Innsmouth; The Haunter of the Dark; Explanatory Notes.

      Notes. The first of my annotated editions for Penguin; it has gone through at least 25 printings. The Folio Society edition was licenced by Penguin without my knowledge or permission.

27.   *Lord of a Visible World: An Autobiography in Letters* (with David E. Schultz)
   a.   Athens: Ohio University Press, [August] 2000.
   b.   New York: Hippocampus Press, [August] 2019.

      Contents: Introduction, by Joshi and Schultz; Childhood and Ancestry (1890–1914); Amateur Journalism (1914–1921); Expanding Horizons (1921–1924); Marriage and Exile (1924–1926); Homecoming (1926–1930); The Old Gentleman (1931–1937); Appendix: Some Notes on a Nonentity; Glossary of Names; Notes; Sources; Further Reading; Index.

      Notes. A volume I had long wished to assemble—a kind of autobiography covering the entirety of Lovecraft's life (also many of his philosophical beliefs), culled from his extensive correspondence.

28.   *The Annotated Supernatural Horror in Literature*
   a.1. New York: Hippocampus Press, [August] 2000.
   a.2. New York: Hippocampus Press, [July 2005].
   b.   New York: Hippocampus Press, [March] 2012 (rev. ed.).

Contents: Preface; Introduction; Supernatural Horror in Literature; Appendix: The Favourite Weird Stories of H. P. Lovecraft; Notes; Bibliography of Authors and Works; Index.

Notes. The first publication by Hippocampus Press. The book had largely been compiled as far back as 1981, when Greenwood Press had expressed tentative interest in it; but later Greenwood backed out of the project, leading me to shelve it for many years.

29. *The Shadow out of Time* (with David E. Schultz)
    a.1. New York: Hippocampus Press, [August] 2001.
    a.2. New York: Hippocampus Press, [October] 2003.
    Contents: Introduction, by Joshi and Schultz (includes "Discovery of the Manuscript," by John H. Stanley); The Shadow out of Time; Notes to "The Shadow out of Time"; Early Draft; Notes; Textual Notes.

    Notes. First publication of the corrected text of the novella, based on my consultation (in February 1994) of the recently discovered autograph manuscript, received by the John Hay Library in early 1994.

30. *The Ancient Track: Complete Poetical Works*
    a. San Francisco: Night Shade Books, [August] 2001.
    b. New York: Hippocampus Press, 2013. [Rev. ed.]
    Contents: Introduction; Juvenilia: The Poem of Ulysses, or The Odyssey; Ovid's Metamorphoses; H. Lovecraft's Attempted Journey betwixt Providence & Fall River on the N.Y.N.H. & H.R.R.; *Poemata Minora, Volume II* (Ode to Selene or Diana; To the Old Pagan Religion; On the Ruin of Rome; To Pan; On the Vanity of Human Ambition); C.S.A. 1861–1865: To the Starry Cross of the SOUTH; De Triumpho Naturae; Fantasy and Horror: To the Late John H. Fowler, Esq.; The Unknown; The Poe-et's Nightmare; The Rutted Road; Nemesis; Astrophobos; Psychopompos: A Tale in Rhyme; The Eidolon; A Cycle of Verse (Oceanus, Clouds, Mother Earth); Despair; Revelation; The House; The City; To Edward John Moreton Drax Plunkett, Eighteenth Baron Dunsany; The Nightmare Lake; Bells; On Reading Lord Dunsany's *Book of Wonder*; To a Dreamer; With a Copy of Wilde's Fairy Tales; [On *The Thing in the Woods* by Harper Williams]; The Cats; Primavera; Festival; Hallowe'en in a Suburb; [On Ambrose Bierce]; The Wood; The Outpost; The Ancient Track; The Messenger; *Fungi from Yuggoth*; Bouts Rimés (Beyond Zimbabwe; The White Elephant); In a Sequester'd Providence Churchyard Where Once Poe Walk'd; To Mr. Finlay, upon His Drawing for Mr. Bloch's Tale, "The Faceless God"; To Clark Ashton Smith, Esq., upon His Phantastick Tales, Verses, Pictures, and Sculptures; Nathicana; Occasional Verse: The Members of the Men's

Club of the First Universalist Church of Providence, R.I., to Its President, About to Leave for Florida on Account of His Health; To Mr. Terhune, on His Historical Fiction; To Mr. Munroe, on His Instructive and Entertaining Account of Switzerland; Regner Lodbrog's Epicedium; To an Accomplished Young Gentlewoman on Her Birthday, Decy. 2, 1914; On Receiving a Picture of Swans; To Charlie of the Comics; On the Cowboys of the West; To Samuel Loveman, Esquire, on His Poetry and Drama, Writ in the Elizabethan Style; The Bookstall; Content; The Smile; Inspiration; Respite; Brotherhood; Lines on Graduation from the R.I. Hospital's School of Nurses; Fact and Fancy; Percival Lowell; Prologue to "Fragments from an Hour of Inspiration' by Jonathan E. Hoag; Earth and Sky; To M. W. M.; Lines on the 25th. Anniversary of the *Providence Evening News*, 1892–1917; To the Nurses of the Red Cross; To the Arcadian; Laeta; a Lament; To Mr. Kleiner, on Receiving from Him the Poetical Works of Addison, Gay, and Somerville; A Pastoral Tragedy of Appleton, Wisconsin; Damon and Delia, a Pastoral; To Delia, Avoiding Damon; Hellas; Ambition; Damon: A Monody; Hylas and Myrrha: A Tale; John Oldham: A Defence; Myrrha and Strephon; Wisdom; Tryout's Lament for the Vanished Spider; Cindy: Scrub-Lady in a State Street Skyscraper; The Voice; On a Grecian Colonnade in a Park; The Dream; To Alfred Galpin, Esq.; On Receiving a Portraiture of Mrs. Berkeley, yᵉ Poetess; To a Youth; On the Return of Maurice Winter Moe, Esq., to the Pedagogical Profession; To Mr. Galpin; Sir Thomas Tryout; To Damon; To Rheinhart Kleiner, Esq.; Chloris and Damon; To Endymion; To Mr. Baldwin, on Receiving a Picture of Him in a Rural Bower; Damon and Lycë; [On the Pyramids]; [Stanzas on Samarkand]; To Samuel Loveman, Esq.; To George Kirk, Esq.; My Favourite Character; [On the Double-R Coffee House]; [On Rheinhart Kleiner Being Hit by an Automobile]; [To Frank Belknap Long on His Birthday]; A Year Off; To an Infant; To George Willard Kirk, Gent., of Chelsea-Village, in New-York, upon His Birthday, Novr. 25, 1925; [On *Old Grimes* by Albert Gorton Greene]; In Memoriam: Oscar Incoul Verelst of Manhattan: 1920–1926; The Return; Hedone; To Miss Beryl Hoyt; To a Sophisticated Young Gentleman; Veteropinguis Redivivus; To a Young Poet in Dunedin; [Metrical Example]; The Odes of Horace: Book III, ix; Gaudeamus; The Greatest Law; [Sonnet Study]; To Samuel Loveman Esq.; Verses Designed to Be Sent by a Friend of the Author to His Brother-in-Law on New Year's Day; [Last of an elder race . . .]; ['Tis a sprig of green shamrock . . .]; Satire: Providence in 2000 A.D.; Fragment on Whitman; [On Robert Browning]; Ad Criticos; Frustra Praemunitus; De Scriptore Mulieroso; On a Modern Lothario; The End of the Jackson War; The Power of Wine. A Satire; Gryphus in Asinurn Mutatus; The Simple Speller's Tale; [On Slang]; Ye Ballade of Patrick von Flynn; The Isaacsonio-Mortoniad; Undia; or, The Bride of the Sea; [On "Unda; or, The Bride of the Sea"]; Gems from *In a Minor Key*; The State of Poetry; The Magazine Poet; My Lost Love; The Beauties of Peace; Epitaph on ye Letterr Rrr ....; The Dead Bookworm; Ad Balneum; [On Kelso the Poet]; Futurist Art; The Nymph's Reply to the Modern Business Man; The Poet of Passion; On the Death of a Rhyming Critic; To the Incomparable Clorinda; To Saccharissa, Fairest of Her Sex; To Rhodoclia—Peerless among Maidens; To Belinda, Favourite of the Graces; To Heliodora—Sister of Cytheraea; To Mistress Sophia Simple, Queen of the Cinema; The Introduction; Grace; To Col. Linkaby Didd; Amissa Minerva; [On Prohibition]; Monody on the Late King Alcohol; The Pensive Swain; The Poet's Rash Excuse; On Religion; The Pathetic History of Sir Wilful Wildrake; Medusa: A Portrait; Simplicity: A Poem; Plaster-All; To Zara; Waste Paper; [On a Politician]; [On a Room for Rent]; [On J. F. Roy Erford]; Lines upon the Magnates of the Pulp; Dead Passion's Flame; Arcadia; Lullaby for the Dionne Quintuplets; The Decline and Fall of a Man of the World; [Epigrams]; Life's Mystery; On Mr. L. Phillips Howard's Profound Poem Entitled "Life's Mystery"; On an Accomplished Young Linguist; "The Poetical Punch" Pushed from His Pedestal; The Road to Ruin; Sors Poetae; Seasonal and Topographical: Quinsnicket Park; New England; March; A Mississippi Autumn; A Rural Summer Eve; Brumalia; On Receiving a Picture of the Marshes at Ipswich; Spring; A Garden; April; On Receiving a Picture of ye Towne of Templeton, in the Colonie of Massachusetts-Bay, with Mount Monadnock, in New-Hampshire, Shewn in the Distance; Autumn; Sunset; Old Christmas; A Summer Sunset and Evening; A Winter Wish; Ver Rusticum; A June Afternoon; The Spirit of Summer; August; April Dawn; January; October [1]; Christmas; [On Marblehead]; [On a Scene in Rural Rhode Island]; Providence; Solstice; October [2]; [On Newport, Rhode Island]; The East India Brick Row; On an Unspoil'd Rural Prospect; Saturnalia; [Christmas Greetings]; Amateur Affairs: To the Members of the Pin-Feathers on the Merits of Their Organisation, and of Their New Publication, *The Pinfeather*; To the Rev. James Pyke; To the Members of the United Amateur Press Association from the Providence Amateur Press Club; The Bay-Stater's Policy; R. Kleiner, Laureatus, in Heliconem; Providence Amateur Press Club (Deceased) to the Athenaeum Club of Journalism; To Mr. Lockhart, on His Poetry; To Jonathan E. Hoag, Esq.; To Arthur Goodenough, Esq.; To the Eighth of November; To the A.H.S.P.C., on Receipt of the Christmas *Pippin*; Greetings; To Jonathan Hoag, Esq.; In Memoriam: J. E. T. D.; To the A.H.S.P.C., on Receipt of the May *Pippin*; Helene Hoffman Cole: 1893–1919; On Collaboration; Birthday Lines to Margfred Galbraham; Ad Scribam; Ex-Poet's Reply; To Two Epgephi; Theobaldian Aestivation; The Prophecy of Capys Secundus; To Mr. Hoag; On a Poet's Ninety-first Birthday; To Saml: Loveman, Gent.; To Mr. Hoag; The Feast; Lines for Poets' Night at the Scribblers' Club; To Mr. Hoag; To Mr. Hoag; To Jonathan Hoag; To Jonathan E. Hoag, Esq.; The Absent Leader; Ave atque Vale; To "The Scribblers"; Politics and Society: New-England Fallen; On the Creation of Niggers; On a New-England Village Seen by Moonlight; To General Villa; The Teuton's Battle-Song; 1914; The Crime of Crimes; An American to Mother England; Temperance Song; The Rose of England; Lines on Gen. Robert Edward Lee; Britannia Victura; Iterum Conjunctae; The Peace Advocate; To Greece, 1917; Ode for July Fourth, 1917; An American to the British Flag [text not included]; Ad Britannos—1918; On a Battlefield in Picardy; The Volunteer; To Alan Seeger; Germania—1918; The Conscript; To Maj.-Gen. Omar Bundy, U.S.A.; Theodore Roosevelt; North and South Britons; Personal: [To His Mother on Thanksgiving]; An Elegy on Franklin Chase Ciark, M.D.; [The Solace of Georgian Poetry]; [On Phillips Gamwell]; An Elegy on Phillips Gamwell, Esq.; Sonnet on Myself; Phaeton; Monos: An Ode; Oct. 17, 1919; To S. S. L.—Oct. 17, 1920; S. S. L.—Christmas 1920; To Xanthippe, on Her Birthday—March 16, 1925; Εἰς Σφίγγην; [On Cheating the Post Office]; An Epistle to the Rt. Honble Maurice Winter Moe, Esq.; [Anthem of the Kappa Alpha Tau]; Edith Miniter; [Little Sam Perkins]; *Alfredo; a Tragedy*; Fragments; Notes; A Chronology of Lovecraft's Poems; Index of Titles; Index of First Lines.

Notes. First complete publication of Lovecraft's poetry, with extensive notes. The first edition was to have been published by Necronomicon Press, and Marc A. Michaud in fact formatted the interior pages; his formatting was used by Night Shade. The second edition gathers a few poems and poem fragments that had not been found at the time, and also includes poems revised by Lovecraft (with, where possible, the original texts of these poems) and poems to which Lovecraft responded with poems of his own. The notes have also been overhauled.

31. *The Thing on the Doorstep and Other Weird Stories*
   a. New York: Penguin, [August] 2001.
   b. New York: Penguin, [September] 2013 (as part of Penguin Horror, ed. Guillermo del Toro).

Contents: Introduction; Suggestions for Further Reading; The Tomb; Beyond the Wall of Sleep; The White Ship; The Temple; The Quest of Iranon; The Music of Erich Zann; Under the Pyramids (with Harry Houdini); Pickman's Model; *The Case of Charles Dexter Ward*; The Dunwich Horror; *At the Mountains of Madness*; The Thing on the Doorstep; Explanatory Notes.

Notes. The second of my annotated Penguin editions of Lovecraft.

32. *Mysteries of Time and Spirit: The Letters of H. P. Lovecraft and Donald Wandrei* (with David E. Schultz)
   a. San Francisco: Night Shade Books, [October] 2002.

   Contents: Introduction, by Joshi and Schultz; A Note on This Edition; Letters by H. P. Lovecraft and Donald Wandrei; Glossary of Frequently Mentioned Names; Bibliography; Index.

   Notes. First publication of the joint correspondence between Lovecraft and Wandrei, based on manuscripts in the John Hay Library.

33. *From the Pest Zone: The New York Stories* (with David E. Schultz)
   a. New York: Hippocampus Press, [January] 2003.

   Contents: Introduction, by Schultz and Joshi; The Shunned House; The Horror at Red Hook; He; In the Vault; Cool Air; Frank Belknap Long, "Preface to *The Shunned House*"; Little Sketches about Town (*New York Evening Post*, 29 August 1924); Notes; Textual Notes.

   Notes. Annotated edition of the tales Lovecraft wrote during his stay in New York (1924–26).

34. *Letters to Alfred Galpin* (with David E. Schultz)
   a. New York: Hippocampus Press, [June] 2003.

   Contents: Introduction, by Joshi and Schultz; Letters to Alfred Galpin; Works of Alfred Galpin: Mystery; Two Loves; Selenaio-Phantasma; Remarks to My Handwriting; Marsh-Mad; The Critic; Stars; Some Tendencies of Modern Poetry; The Spoken Tongue; The World Situation; The United's Policy 1920–1921 (with H. P. Lovecraft); Form in Modern Poetry; Picture of a Modern Mood; Nietzsche as a Practical Prophet; To Sam Loveman; The Vivisector (November 1921); Four Translations from *Les Fleurs du mal* by Charles Pierre Baudelaire (Au Lecteur, L'Ennemi, Remords Posthume, L'Ange Gardien); Scattered Remarks upon the Green Cheese Theory; Department of Public Criticism (May 1922); Intuition in the Philosophy of Bergson; A Critic of Poetry; From the French of Pierre de Ronsard ("Amours"–Livre II); Aubade; Echoes from Beyond Space; En Route (An American to Paris, 1931): I. New York Harbor; II. On Deck; November; A Partial Bibliography of Alfred Galpin.

Notes. First complete publication of the letters to Galpin, along with many writings by Galpin.

35.   *Collected Essays: Volume 1 (Amateur Journalism)*
    a.   New York: Hippocampus Press, [April] 2004.

    Contents: Introduction; A Task for Amateur Journalists; Department of Public Criticism (November 1914); Department of Public Criticism (January 1915); Department of Public Criticism (March 1915); What Is Amateur Journalism?; Consolidation's Autopsy; The Amateur Press; Editorial (April 1915); The Question of the Day; The Morris Faction; For President—Leo Fritter; Introducing Mr. Chester Pierce Munroe; [Untitled Notes on Amateur Journalism]; Department of Public Criticism (May 1915); Finale; New Department Proposed: Instruction for the Recruit; Our Candidate; Exchanges; For Historian—Ira A. Cole; Editorial (July 1915); The Conservative and His Critics (July 1915); Some Pohtical Phases; Introducing Mr. John Russell; In a Major Key; Amateur Notes; The Dignity of Journalism; Department of Public Criticism (September 1915); Editorial (October 1915); The Conservative and His Critics (October 1915); The Youth of Today; An Impartial Spectator; [Untitled Notes on Amateur Journalism]; Little Journeys to the Homes of Prominent Amateurs: II. Andrew Francis Lockhart; Report of First Vice-President (November 1915); Department of Public Criticism (December 1915); Systematic Instruction in the United; *United Amateur Press Association: Exponent of Amateur Journalism*; Introducing Mr. James Pyke; Report of First Vice-President (January 1916); Editorial (February 1916); Department of Public Criticism (April 1916); Among the New-Comers; Department of Public Criticism (June 1916); Department of Public Criticism (August 1916); Department of Public Criticism (September 1916); Among the Amateurs; Concerning "Persia—in Europe"; Amateur Standards; A Request; Department of Public Criticism (March 1917); Department of Public Criticism (May 1917); A Reply to *The Lingerer*; The United's Problem; Editorially; The "Other United"; Department of Public Criticism (July 1917); Little Journeys to the Homes of Prominent Amateurs: V. Eleanor J. Barnhart; News Notes (July 1917); President's Message (September 1917); President's Message (November 1917); President's Message (January 1918); Department of Public Criticism (January 1918); President's Message (March 1918); Department of Public Criticism (March 1918); President's Message (May 1918); Department of Public Criticism (May 1918); Comment; President's Message (July 1918); Amateur Criticism; The United 1917–1918; The Amateur Press Club; *Les Mouches Fantastiques*; Department of Public Criticism (September 1918); Department of Public Criticism (November 1918); News Notes (November 1918); [Letter to the Bureau of Critics]; Department of Public Criticism (January 1919); Department of Public Criticism (March 1919); Winifred Virginia Jordan: Associate Editor; Helene Hoffman Cole—Litterateur; Department of Public Criticism (May 1919); Trimmings; For Official Editor—Anne Tillery Renshaw; Amateurdom; Looking Backward; For What Does the United Stand?; The Pseudo-United; The Conquest of the Hub Club; News Notes (September 1920); Amateur Journalism: Its Possible Needs and Betterment; Editorial (November 1920); News Notes (November 1920); News Notes (January 1921); The United's Policy 1920-1921 (with Alfred Galpin); What Amateurdom and I Have Done for Each Other; News Notes (March 1921); The Vivisector (March 1921); [Letter to John Milton Heins]; Lucubrations Lovecraftian; News Notes (May 1921); The Vivisector (June 1921); The Haverhill Convention; News Notes (July 1921); Within the Gates; The Convention Banquet; Editorial (September 1921); News Notes (September 1921); A Singer of Ethereal Moods and Fancies; News Notes (November 1921); [Letter to John Milton Heins]; Editorial (January 1922); News Notes (January 1922); *Rainbow* Called Best First Issue; News Notes (March 1922); The Vivisector (March 1922); News Notes (May 1922); [Letter to the N.A.P.A.]; President's Message (November 1922-January 1923); President's Message (March 1923); Bureau of Critics (March 1923); Rursus Adsumus; The Vivisector (Spring 1923); President's Message (May 1923); Lovecraft's Greeting; President's Message (July 1923); [Untitled Notes on Amateur Journalism]; The President's Annual Report; Trends and Objects; Editorial (May 1924); News Notes (May 1924); Editorial (July 1925); News Notes (July 1925); A Matter of Uniteds; The Convention; Bureau of Critics (December 1931); Critics Submit First Report; Verse Criticism; Report of Bureau of Critics; Bureau of Critics Comment on Verse, Typography, Prose; Bureau of Critics (June 1934); Chairman of the Bureau of Critics Reports on Poetry; Mrs. Miniter—Estimates and Recollections; Report of the Bureau of Critics (December 1934); Report of the Bureau of Critics (March 1935); Lovecraft Offers Verse Criticism; Dr. Eugene B. Kuntz; Some Current Amateur Verse; Report of the Executive Judges (with Vincent B. Haggerty and Jennie K. Plaisier); *Some Current Motives and Practices*; [Letter to the N.A.P.A.]; [Literary Review]; Defining the 'Ideal' Paper; Appendix: [Miscellaneous Notes in the *United Amateur*]; Official Organ Fund; [Untitled Note on Amateur Poetry]; [On *Notes High and Low* by Carrie Adams Berry]; A Voice from the Grave; Index.

Notes. Another project long in the making, and the final component of my early idea to assemble the "Collected Works of H. P. Lovecraft."

36. *Collected Essays: Volume 2 (Literary Criticism)*
     a.   New York: Hippocampus Press, [April] 2004.

     Contents: Introduction; Metrical Regularity; The Allowable Rhyme; The Proposed Authors' Union; The Vers Libre Epidemic; Poesy; The Despised Pastoral; The Literature of Rome; The Simple Spelling Mania; The Case for Classicism; Literary Composition; Editor's Note to "A Scene for *Macbeth*" by Samuel Loveman; Winifred Virginia Jackson: A "Different" Poetess; The Poetry of Lilian Middleton; Lord Dunsany and His Work; Rudis Indigestaque Moles; Introduction [to *The Poetical Works of Jonathan E. Hoag*]; Ars Gratia Artis; In the Editor's Study; [Random Notes]; [Review of *Ebony and Crystal* by Clark Ashton Smith]; The Professional Incubus; The Omnipresent Philistine; The Work of Frank Belknap Long, Jr.; Supernatural Horror in Literature; Preface [to *White Fire* by John Ravenor Bullen]; Notes on "Alias Peter Marchall", by A. F. Lorenz; Foreword [to *Thoughts and Pictures* by Eugene B. Kuntz]; Notes on Verse Technique; Weird Story Plots; [Notes on Weird Fiction]; Notes on Writing Weird Fiction; Some Notes on Interplanetary Fiction; What Belongs in Verse; [Suggestions for a Reading Guide]; Appendix: The Poetry of John Ravenor Bullen; The Favourite Weird Stories of H. P. Lovecraft; Supernatural Horror in Literature [abridgment of 1936]; Index.

     Notes. The second volume of my complete edition of Lovecraft's essays.

37. *The Dreams in the Witch House and Other Weird Stories*
     a.   New York: Penguin, [August] 2004.

     Contents: Introduction; Suggestions for Further Reading; Polaris; The Doom That Came to Sarnath; The Terrible Old Man; The Tree; The Cats of Ulthar; From Beyond; The Nameless City; The Moon-Bog; The Other Gods; Hypnos; The Lurking Fear; The Unnamable; The Shunned House; The Horror at Red Hook; In the Vault; The Strange High House in the Mist; *The Dream-Quest of Unknown Kadath*; The Silver Key; Through the Gates of the Silver Key (with E. Hoffmann Price); The Dreams in the Witch House; The Shadow out of Time; Explanatory Notes.

     Notes. The third of my annotated Penguin editions of Lovecraft's fiction.

38. *Letters from New York* (with David E. Schultz)
     a.   San Francisco: Night Shade Books, [April] 2005.

     Contents: Introduction, by Joshi and Schultz; A Note on This Edition; Letters by H. P. Lovecraft; Glossary of Names; Index.

Notes. A selection of letters (mostly to Lillian D. Clark) recounting Lovecraft's visits to and life in New York (1922–26).

39. *Letters to Rheinhart Kleiner* (with David E. Schultz)
  a. New York: Hippocampus Press, [July] 2005.
      Contents: Introduction, by Joshi and Schultz; Letters to Rheinhart Kleiner; *Works* [by Rheinhart Kleiner]: A. Poems by Rheinhart Kleiner: Alas!; Dream Days; or, Metrical Musings; Another Endless Day; Motes; At Providence in 1918; Brooklyn, My Brooklyn; Epistle to Mr. and Mrs. Lovecraft; The Four of Us!; After a Decade; B. Essays by Rheinhart Kleiner: A Note on Howard P. Lovecraft's Verse; The Kleicomolo; After a Decade and the Kalem Club; Howard Phillips Lovecraft; Lovecraft in Brooklyn; Some Lovecraft Memories; C. Rheinhart Kleiner vs. H. P. Lovecraft: To Mary of the Movies [by Kleiner]; To Charlie of the Comics [by Lovecraft]; To a Movie Star [by Kleiner]; To Mistress Sophia Simple, Queen of the Cinema [by Lovecraft]; Ruth [by Kleiner]; Grace [by Lovecraft]; John Oldham: 1653–1683 [by Kleiner]; John Oldham: A Defence [by Lovecraft]; Ethel: Cashier in a Broad Street Buffet [by Kleiner]; Cindy: Scrub-Lady in a State Street Skyscraper [by Lovecraft]; On Collaboration [by Lovecraft and Kleiner]; D. Poems by H. P. Lovecraft Addressed to Rheinhart Kleiner: The Bookstall; Content; To Mr. Kleiner, on Receiving from Him the Poetical Works of Addison, Gay, and Somerville; R. Kleiner, Laureatus, in Heliconem; To Rheinhart Kleiner, Esq., Upon His Town Fables and Elegies; [On Rheinhart Kleiner Being Hit by an Automobile]; A Partial Bibliography of Rheinhart Kleiner; Index.
      Notes. First complete edition of Lovecraft's letters to Kleiner, with many writings by Kleiner.

40. *Collected Essays: Volume 3 (Science)*
  a. New York: Hippocampus Press, 2005 [February 2006].
      Contents: Introduction; My Opinion as to the Lunar Canals; No Transit of Mars; Trans-Neptunian Planets; The Moon; The Earth Not Hollow; [Astronomy Articles for the *Pawtuxet Valley Gleaner:*] The Heavens for August; The Skies of September; Is Mars an Inhabited World?; Is There Life on the Moon?; An Interesting Phenomenon; October Heavens; Are There Undiscovered Planets?; Can the Moon Be Reached by Man?; The Moon; [Untitled]; The Sun; The Leonids; Comets; December Skies; The Fixed Stars; Clusters—Nebulae; January Heavens; [Astronomy Articles for the Providence *Tribune:*] In the August Sky; The September Heavens; Astronomy in October; The Skies of November; The Heavens for December; The Heavens in January; The Heavens in February; The Heavens in

March; April Skies; The Heavens in May; The Heavens in June; Astronomy in August; The Heavens for September; The Skies of October; The Heavens in November; Heavens for December; The Heavens in January; February Skies; The Heavens in Month of March; Solar Eclipse Feature of June Heavens; Third Annual Report of the Prov. Meteorological Station; Celestial Objects for All; Venus and the Public Eye; [Astronomy Articles for the Providence *Evening News:*] The January Sky; The February Sky; The March Sky; The April Sky; May Sky; The June Sky; The July Sky; The August Sky; The September Sky; The October Sky; The November Sky; The December Sky; The January Sky; The February Sky; The March Sky; April Skies; The May Sky; The June Skies; The July Skies; The August Skies; September Skies; October Skies; November Skies; December Skies; January Skies; February Skies; March Skies; April Skies; May Skies; June Skies; July Skies; August Skies; September Skies; October Skies; November Skies; December Skies; January Skies; February Skies; March Skies; April Skies; May Skies; June Skies; July Skies; August Skies; September Skies; October Skies; November Skies; December Skies; January Skies; February Skies; March Skies; April Skies; May Skies; [Science versus Charlatanry:] Science versus Charlatanry; The Falsity of Astrology; Astrology and the Future; Delavan's Comet and Astrology; The Fall of Astrology; [Isaac Bickerstaffe's Reply]; *Mysteries of the Heavens Revealed by Astronomy:* I. The Sky and Its Contents; [II.] The Solar System; III. The Sun; IV. The Inferior Planets; V. Eclipses; VI. The Earth and Its Moon; VII. Mars and the Asteroids; VIII. The Outer Planets; [The Outer Planets, Part II]; IX. Cornets and Meteors; Comets and Meteors [Part II]; X. The Stars; [The Stars, Part II]; XI. Clusters and Nebulae; [Clusters and Nebulae, Part II]; XII. The Constellations; [The Constellations, Part II]; XIII. Telescopes and Observatories; [Telescopes and Observatories, Part II]; Editor's Note to "The Irish and the Fairies" by Peter J. MacManus; Brumalia; The Truth about Mars; The Cancer of Superstition; [Some Backgrounds of Fairyland]; *Appendix:* Does "Vulcan" Exist?; Astronomical Notebook; [Astrology Articles by J. F. Hartmann:] Astrology and the European War; [Letter to the Editor]; The Science of Astrology; A Defense of Astrology; Lovecraft's Juvenile Scientific Manuscripts; Index.

Notes. The third volume of my complete edition of Lovecraft's essays. His unpublished juvenile writings could not be printed because of the difficulty of reproducing them in facsimile, the only feasible way of printing them.

41. *Collected Essays: Volume 4 (Travel)*
    a. New York: Hippocampus Press, 2005 [February 2006].
        Contents: Introduction; The Trip of Theobald; Vermont—A First Impression; Observations on Several Parts of America; Travels in the Provinces of America; An Account of a Trip to the Antient Fairbanks House, in Dedham, and to the Red Horse Tavern in Sudbury, in the Province of the Massachusetts-Bay; Account of a Visit to Charleston, S.C.; An Account of *Charleston*, in His Maj$^{ty's}$ Province of South-Carolina; A Description of the Town of Quebeck in New-France, Lately Added to His Britannick Majesty's Dominions; European Glimpses; Some Dutch Footprints in New England; Homes and Shrines of Poe; The Unknown City in the Ocean; Charleston; Appendix: A Descent to Avernus; Sleepy Hollow To-day; Index.
        Notes. The fourth volume of my complete edition of Lovecraft's essays.

42. *Collected Essays: Volume 5 (Philosophy; Autobiography and Miscellany)*
    a. New York: Hippocampus Press, 2006 [January 2007].
        Contents: Introduction; Philosophy: The Crime of the Century; The Renaissance of Manhood; Liquor and Its Friends; More *Chain Lightning*; Symphony and Stress; Old England and the 'Hyphen'; Revolutionary Mythology; The Symphonic Ideal; Editor's Note to "The Genesis of the Revolutionary War" by Henry Clapham McGavack; A Remarkable Document; At the Root; Time and Space; Merlinus Redivivus; Anglo-Saxondom; Americanism; The League; Bolshevism; Idealism and Materialism—A Reflection; Life for Humanity's Sake; [*In Defence of Dagon*] (The Defence Reopens!, The Defence Remains Open!, Final Words); Nietzscheism and Realism; East and West Harvard Conservatism; The Materialist Today; Some Causes of Self-Immolation; Some Repetitions on the Times; A Layman Looks at the Government; The *Journal* and the New Deal; A Living Heritage: Roman Architecture in Today's America; Objections to Orthodox Communism; Autobiography and Miscellany: The Brief Autobiography of an Inconsequential Scribbler; A Confession of Unfaith; [Diary: 1925]; [Commercial Blurbs]; Cats and Dogs; Notes on Hudson Valley History; Autobiography of Howard Phillips Lovecraft; In Memoriam: Henry St. Clair Whitehead; Some Notes on a Nonentity; Correspondence between R. H. Barlow arid Wilson Shepherd of Oakman, Alabama—Sept.-Nov. 1932; In Memoriam: Robert Ervin Howard; Commonplace Book; Instructions in Case of Decease; [Diary—1937]; [Notes for Stories]: [Notes to "Medusa's Coil"]; [Notes to *At the Mountains of Madness*]; [Notes to "The Shadow over Innsmouth"]; [The Round Tower]; [The Rose Window]; Of Evil Sorceries Done in New-England, of Daemons in No Humane

Shape; [Notes to "The Shadow out of Time"]; [Notes to "The Challenge from Beyond"]; [Miscellaneous Lists and Notes]: [1] Catalogue of Prov. Press Co.; [2] [Catalogue of Works (1902)]; [3] [Postal Expenses]; [4] Old Farmer's Almanacks Wanted by H. P. Lovecraft; [5] [Notes on Clothing Stores]; [6] [Works Desired by H. Warner Munn]; [7] [Works of Weird Fiction]; [8] Tales by H. P. Lovecraft; [9] Basic Books for a Weird Library; [10] [Remembrancer]; [11] [List of Amateur Papers]; [12] [Possible Collections of Tales]; [13] [Magazine Addresses]; [14] [List of Individuals to Be Sent "The Battle That Ended the Century"]; [15] [List of Correspondents to Whom Postcards Have Been Sent]; [16] Suggested Recipients for Dragon Fly Outside Memb. List of NAPA; [17] Fungi from Yuggoth and Other Verses; [18] [Notable Stories in Recent Issues of *Weird Tales*]; [19] "Little Magazines"; [20] [Worthy Stories in Recent Issues of *Weird Tales*]; [21] [Pronunciation Guide]; [22] Tales of H. P. Lovecraft; Weird &c. Items in Library of H. P. Lovecraft; Appendix: [Advertisement of Revisory Services]; [Advertisement in the *New York Times*]; The Recognition of Temperance; [Advertisement in *Weird Tales*]; [Biographical Notice]; [E'ch-Pi-El Speaks]; Robert Ervin Howard: 1906–1936; Chronology of the Works of H. P. Lovecraft; Index of Titles (Volumes 1–5); Index (Volumes 1–5).

Notes. The fifth and final volume of my complete edition of Lovecraft's essays.

43.   *O Fortunate Floridian: H. P. Lovecraft's Letters to R. H. Barlow* (with David E. Schultz)
   a.   Tampa, FL: University of Tampa Press, 2007.
        Contents: Introduction, by Joshi and Schultz; A Note on This Edition [by Joshi and Schultz]; The R. H. Barlow, "The Wind That Is in the Grass: A Memoir of H. P. Lovecraft in Florida"; "Lovecraft's Coined Names for Friends and Associates" [by Joshi and Schultz]; Letters to R. H. Barlow (1931–37); Appendices: I. Autobiographical Writings of R. H. Barlow ([Memories of Lovecraft (1934)]; Autobiography); II. H. P. Lovecraft's Letters to Charles Blackburn Johnston; Glossary of Names; Bibliography; Index.

        Notes. First complete edition of Lovecraft's letters to Barlow. There was also a limited slipcased edition, signed by the editors.

44/45. *Essential Solitude: The Letters of H. P. Lovecraft and August Derleth* (with David E. Schultz)
   a.   New York: Hippocampus Press, 2008. 2 vols. [hardcover].
   b.   New York: Hippocampus Press, 2013. 2 vols. [paperback].

Contents: Volume 1: Introduction, by Schultz and Joshi; A Note on This Edition; Abbreviations; Letters: *Volume 2:* Letters; Appendix: One for the Black Bag, by H. P. Lovecraft; The Weird Tale in English Since 1890 [excerpt], by August Derleth; A Master of the Macabre, by August Derleth; H. P. Lovecraft, Outsider, by August Derleth; H. P. L.—Two Decades After, by August Derleth. Glossary of Frequently Mentioned Names; Bibliography; Index.

Notes. The first two volumes of our planned complete edition of Lovecraft's letters, projected to fill 25 or more volumes.

46. *The Complete Fiction* (uncredited)
   a. New York: Barnes & Noble, 2008.
   b. New York: Barnes & Noble, 2011.

Contents: Introduction; The Beast in the Cave; The Alchemist; The Tomb; Dagon; A Reminiscence of Dr. Samuel Johnson; Polaris; Beyond the Wall of Sleep; Memory; Old Bugs; The Transition of Juan Romero; The White Ship; The Street; The Doom That Came to Sarnath; The Statement of Randolph Carter; The Terrible Old Man; The Tree; The Cats of Ulthar; The Temple; Facts concerning the Late Arthur Jermyn and His Family; Celephaïs; From Beyond; Nyarlathotep; The Picture in the House; Ex Oblivione; Sweet Ermengarde; The Nameless City; The Quest of Iranon; The Moon-Bog; The Outsider; The Other Gods; The Music of Erich Zann; Herbert West—Reanimator; Hypnos; What the Moon Brings' Azathoth; The Hound; The Lurking Fear; The Rats in the Walls; The Unnamable; The Festival; Under the Pyramids (with Harry Houdini); The Shunned House; The Horror at Red Hook; He; In the Vault; Cool Air; The Call of Cthulhu; Pickman's Model; The Silver Key; The Strange High House in the Mist; *The Dream-Quest of Unknown Kadath; The Case of Charles Dexter Ward;* The Colour out of Space; The Descendant; History of the *Necronomicon;* The Very Old Folk; Ibid; The Dunwich Horror; The Whisperer in Darkness; *At the Mountains of Madness;* The Shadow over Innsmouth; The Dreams in the Witch House; Through the Gates of the Silver Key (with E. Hoffmann Price); The Thing on the Doorstep; The Evil Clergyman; The Book; The Shadow out of Time; The Haunter of the Dark; *Appendix: Juvenilia:* The Little Glass Bottle; The Secret Cave; The Mystery of the Grave-yard; The Mysterious Ship [short version]; The Mysterious Ship [long version]; Discarded draft of "The Shadow over Innsmouth"; Supernatural Horror in Literature.

Notes. A volume commissioned by the publisher, and containing—for the first time—all of Lovecraft's original tales, arranged in chronological order. Each story has a brief headnote supplying basic information on its writing and publication.

47/48. *A Means to Freedom: The Letters of H. P. Lovecraft and Robert E. Howard* (with David E. Schultz and Rusty Burke)
   a. New York: Hippocampus Press, [September] 2009. 2 vols. (hardcover).
   b. New York: Hippocampus Press, 2011. 2 vols. (paperback).
       Contents: Volume 1: Introduction; A Note on This Edition; Abbreviations; Letters; *Volume 2:* Letters; APPENDIX: With a Set of Rattlesnake Rattles; The Beast from the Abyss; Dr. I. M. Howard: Letters to H. P. Lovecraft; Glossary of Frequently Mentioned Names; Bibliography; Index.
       Notes. A volume long in the making, and containing the complete joint correspondence of Lovecraft and Howard.

49. *Against Religion*
   a. [New York]: Sporting Gentlemen, [May] 2010.
       Contents: Foreword, by Christopher Hitchens; Introduction; I. Some Personal Reflections: A Confession of Unfaith; The Insignificance of Man [Letter to the Kleicomolo, 8 August 1916]; What I Have against Religion [Letter to Maurice W. Moe, 15 May 1918]; II. General Thoughts on God and Religion: The Nature of God [Letters to the Kleicomolo, October 1916 and April 1917]; What Is Religion? [Letter to Emil Petaja, 6 March 1935]; Atheism and Probability [Letter to Robert E. Howard, 16 August 1932]; Religious Indoctrination [Letter to Maurice W. Moe, 3 August 1931]; III. Religion and Science: Idealism and Materialism—A Reflection; Remarks on Materialism [*In Defence of Dagon,* 1921]; The Materialist Today; Religion and Relativity [Letter to Frank Belknap Long, 20 February 1929]; Religion and Indeterminacy [Letter to Frank Belknap Long, 22 November 1930]; IV. Religion and Society: Religion, Art, and Emotion [Letter to Woodburn Harris, 25 February–1 March 1929]; Religion and Ethics [Letter to Natalie H. Wooley, 2 May 1936]; Religion and Social Progress [Letter to Helen Sully, 17 October 1933]; Protestants and Catholics [Letter to Frank Belknap Long, April 1931]; The Psychology of Puritanism [Letter to Robert E. Howard, 4 October 1930]; On Spiritualism [Letter to August Derleth, 12 November 1932]; Notes.
       Notes. A volume commissioned by the publisher, and featuring Lovecraft's provocative writings on religion, culled from essays and letters. It was something of a coup to have gotten Hitchens to write the foreword. He had reprinted a letter by Lovecraft in his *Portable Atheist* (2007)—a volume that plainly drew upon my *Atheism: A Reader* (II.26).

50. *The Case of Charles Dexter Ward*
     a.   Tampa, FL: University of Tampa Press, [September] 2010.
          Contents: The Case of Charles Dexter Ward; Notes; Afterword; Bibliography; Lovecraft's Providence: Photographs by Donovan K. Loucks.
          Notes. An extensively annotated edition of Lovecraft's Providence novel.

51. *The Crawling Chaos and Others* (The Annotated Revisions and Collaborations of H. P. Lovecraft, Volume 1)
     a.   Welches, OR: Arcane Wisdom, [August] 2011.
          Contents: Introduction; The Green Meadow (with Winifred V. Jackson); Poetry and the Gods (with Anna Helen Crofts); The Crawling Chaos (with Winifred V. Jackson); The Horror at Martin's Beach (with Sonia H. Greene); Under the Pyramids (with Harry Houdini); Two Black Bottles (with Wilfred Blanch Talman); The Last Test (with Adolphe de Castro); The Curse of Yig (with Zealia Bishop); The Electric Executioner (with Adolphe de Castro); The Mound (with Zealia Bishop); Appendix: Sonia H. Greene, "Four O'Clock"; Gustav Adolphe Danziger, "A Sacrifice to Science"; Gustav Adolphe Danziger, "The Automatic Executioner"; Notes; Bibliography.
          Notes. A volume that presents annotated versions of Lovecraft's revisions and collaborations.

52. *Letters to James F. Morton* (with David E. Schultz)
     a.   New York: Hippocampus Press, [December] 2011.
          Contents: Introduction; Letters to James F. Morton; *Appendix:* Lovecraft and Morton; Correspondence with William L. Bryant; Writings by James F. Morton; Writings about James F. Morton; Glossary of Frequently Mentioned Names; Bibliography; Index.
          Notes. First complete publication of Lovecraft's letters to Morton, with an appendix containing much material by and about Morton.

53. *Medusa's Coil and Others* (The Annotated Revisions and Collaborations of H. P. Lovecraft, Volume 2)
     a.   Welches, OR: Arcane Wisdom, [April] 2012.
          Contents: Introduction; Medusa's Coil (with Zealia Bishop); The Trap (with Henry S. Whitehead); The Man of Stone (with Hazel Heald); Winged Death (with Hazel Heald); The Horror in the Museum (with Hazel Heald); Out of the Aeons (with Hazel Heald); The Horror in the Burying-Ground (with Hazel Heald); The Slaying of the Monster (with R. H. Barlow); The Hoard of the Wizard-Beast

(with R. H. Barlow); The Tree on the Hill (with Duane W. Rimel); The Battle That Ended the Century (with R. H. Barlow); "Till A' the Seas" (with R. H. Barlow); Collapsing Cosmoses (with R. H. Barlow); The Challenge from Beyond (with C. L. Moore, A. Merritt, Robert E. Howard, and Frank Belknap Long); The Disinterment (with Duane W. Rimel); The Diary of Alonzo Typer (with William Lumley); In the Walls of Eryx (with Kenneth Sterling); The Night Ocean (with R. H. Barlow); Appendix: Notes to "Medusa's Coil"; Notes to "The Challenge from Beyond"; The Sorcery of Aphlar (with Duane W. Rimel); William Lumley, "The Diary of Alonzo Typer"; Notes; Bibliography.

Notes. The second volume of my annotated versions of Lovecraft's revisions and collaborations.

54. *Letters to Elizabeth Toldridge and Anne Tillery Renshaw* (with David E. Schultz)
a. New York: Hippocampus Press, [January] 2014.

Contents: Introduction; Letters to Elizabeth Toldridge; Letters to Anne Tillery Renshaw; *Appendix:* Poems by Elizabeth Toldridge; Toldridge's Poetry Manuscripts at JHL; Contents of *Winnings*; Letters by Elizabeth Toldridge; Unpublished Parts of *Well-Bred Speech* as Written by H. P. Lovecraft; Glossary of Frequently Mentioned Names; Bibliography; Index.

Notes. First complete publication of the letters to Toldridge and Renshaw.

55. *H. P. Lovecraft* (Library of Weird Fiction)
a. Lakewood, CO: Centipede Press, [April] 2014.

Contents: Introduction; Dagon; The Statement of Randolph Carter; Facts concerning the Late Arthur Jermyn and His Family; Nyarlathotep; The Picture in the House; The Outsider; The Music of Erich Zann; Herbert West—Reanimator; The Lurking Fear; The Rats in the Walls; The Festival; The Shunned House; Cool Air; The Call of Cthulhu; Pickman's Model; The Case of Charles Dexter Ward; The Colour out of Space; The Dunwich Horror; The Whisperer in Darkness; At the Mountains of Madness; The Shadow over Innsmouth; The Thing on the Doorstep; The Shadow out of Time; The Haunter of the Dark; Bibliography.

56/57/58. *Collected Fiction: A Variorum Edition*
a. New York: Hippocampus Press, [August] 2015. 3 vols.

Contents: Volume 1: Introduction; The Beast in the Cave; The Alchemist; The Tomb; Dagon; A Reminiscence of Dr. Samuel Johnson; Polaris; Beyond the Wall of Sleep; Memory; Old Bugs; The

Transition of Juan Romero; The White Ship; The Street; The Doom That Came to Sarnath; The Statement of Randolph Carter; The Terrible Old Man; The Tree; The Cats of Ulthar; The Temple; Facts concerning the Late Arthur Jermyn and His Family; Celephaïs; From Beyond; Nyarlathotep; The Picture in the House; Ex Oblivione; Sweet Ermengarde; or, The Heart of a Country Girl; The Nameless City; The Quest of Iranon; The Moon-Bog; The Outsider; The Other Gods; The Music of Erich Zann; Herbert West—Reanimator; Hypnos; What the Moon Brings; Azathoth; The Hound; The Lurking Fear; The Rats in the Walls; The Unnamable; The Festival; Under the Pyramids; The Shunned House; The Horror at Red Hook; He; In the Vault.

Volume 2: Introduction; Cool Air; The Call of Cthulhu; Pickman's Model; The Silver Key; The Strange High House in the Mist; The Dream-Quest of Unknown Kadath; The Case of Charles Dexter Ward; The Colour out of Space; The Descendant; History of the "Necronomicon"; Ibid; The Dunwich Horror; The Whisperer in Darkness.

Volume 3: Introduction; At the Mountains of Madness; The Shadow over Innsmouth; The Dreams in the Witch House; Through the Gates of the Silver Key (with E. Hoffmann Price); The Thing on the Doorstep; The Book; The Shadow out of Time; The Haunter of the Dark; APPENDIX: [Juvenilia] (The Little Glass Bottle, The Secret Cave, The Mystery of the Grave-Yard, The Mysterious Ship [short version], The Mysterious Ship [long version]); The Very Old Folk; Discarded Draft of "The Shadow over Innsmouth"; The Evil Clergyman; [Cigarette Characterizations]; Of Evil Sorceries done in New England, of Daemons in No Humane Shape; Bibliography.

Notes. An entirely revised edition of my corrected texts of Lovecraft's fiction, based on a renewed examination of the textual status of the tales. Textual variants in all significant appearances of each story are printed. Volumes 1–3 (to appear later in 2014) will contain the original fiction; Volume 4 will include the revisions and collaborations along with an index of names and titles to all four volumes. This, I hope, will be my last edition of Lovecraft's stories, pending any new discoveries.

59.   *Letters to Robert Bloch and Others* (with David E. Schultz)
   a.   New York: Hippocampus Press, [August] 2015.

     Contents: Introduction; Letters to Robert Bloch; Letters to Natalie H. Wooley; Letters to Robert and Mrs. Elmer Nelson; Letters to William F. Anger; Letters to Kenneth Sterling; Letters to Donald A. Wollheim; Letters to Wilson Shepherd; Letters to Willis Conover, Jr.; APPENDIX: Robert Bloch, "A Visit with H. P. Lovecraft," "Lilies,"

"The Black Lotus," "How I Get My Inspiration," "Milwaukee Youth Writes Horror Tales, Sells 'Em"; Natalie H. Wooley, "Admonition," "Dream Fantasy," "Antares," "Avatar," "The Alien," Flight," "A Heavenly Tragedy," "Lines to Cleopatra," "Coward," "Sailor's Child," "Western Night," "Mountain Trail," "Sanctuary," "Dream Tryst," "The Adventure Story," "Is Criticism Necessary?," "Have You a Hobby?," "The Dance," "Reminiscence," "Spurs of Death"; Robert Nelson, "Night of Unrest," "Fragment," "The Unremembered Realm," "Below the Phosphor," "Dream-Stair," "Jorgas," "Sable Revelry," "Under the Tomb," "Lost Excerpts," "The Weird Tale (A Dialogue)"; William F. Anger, "Fantastic Bread & Butter; or, the Mystery of the Missing Authors"; "An Interview with E. Hoffmann Price"; Donald A. Wollheim, "Review of THE NECRONOMICON," "Allalieor," "Umbriel," "Pure Fantasy," "Howard Phillips Lovecraft," "Editor's Preface [to "The Shadow out of Time"]," "The Future of Publishing"; Kenneth Sterling, "The Horror Element in Poe"; Wilson Shepherd, "Death"; "Willis Conover, Jr., "Observations and Otherwise," "The Lost Chord," "The Spirits Mourn"; Chronology; Glossary of Frequently Mentioned Names; Bibliography; Index.

Notes. A substantial volume that is of note for its publication of the complete extant letters to Wollheim, which were obtained after lengthy negotiations with Wollheim's heirs.

60.   *Early Stories* (with Steven Philip Jones)

    a.   Livonia, MI: Caliber Comics, [May] 2016.

       Contents: A Few Words on the Stories in This Anthology (by Steven Philip Jones); Foreword (by S. T. Joshi); The Alchemist; The Tomb; Dagon; Beyond the Wall of Sleep; The Statement of Randolph Carter; Arthur Jermyn; The Picture in the House; The Music of Erich Zann; The Lurking Fear.

       Notes. A slim volume of early Lovecraft stories to accompany graphic adaptations of them by Jones.

61.   *Letters to J. Vernon Shea, Carl F. Strauch, and Lee McBride White* (with David E. Schultz)

    a.   New York: Hippocampus Press, [May] 2016.

       Contents: Introduction; Letters to J. Vernon Shea; Letters to Carl Ferdinand Strauch; Letters to Lee McBride White; APPENDIX: J. Vernon Shea, Jr., "On Writing in Bed," "Four Playwrights"; Carl F. Strauch, "The Beauty of Decay," "The White Fiend Death," "A Library Goes Regionalist"; Lee McBride White, "For Aldous Huxley," "Out of Sorrow," "Look at Your Thumb"; Gossary of Frequently Mentioned Names; Bibliography; Index.

Notes. First publication of the complete letters to Shea.

62. *Letters to F. Lee Baldwin, Duane W. Rimel, and Nils Frome* (with David E. Schultz)
 a. New York: Hippocampus Press, [October] 2016.
      Contents: Introduction; Letters to F. Lee Baldwin; Letters to Duane W. Rimel; Letters to Nils Frome; APPENDIX: F. Lee Baldwin, "Writings in *The Fantasy Fan*," "H. P. Lovecraft: A Biographical Sketch," "Preface to the *Fantasy Fan Index*"; Duane W. Rimel, "H. P. Lovecraft as I Knew Him," "A Fan Looks Back," "Lee Baldwin—A Fan's Fan," "Weird Music," "The Forbidden Room," "The Sorcery of Aphlar," "Dreams of Yid," "Dreams of Yith," "The Ship," "Late Revenge," "The Snake," "Its Prayer"; Chronology; Glossary of Frequently Mentioned Names; Bibliography; Index.
      Notes. Letters to three young fans of Lovecraft's.

63. *Letters to C. L. Moore and Others* (with David E. Schultz)
 a. New York: Hippocampus Press, [August] 2017.
      Contents: Introduction; H. P. LOVECRAFT: Letters to and from C. L. Moore; to Henry Kuttner; to Fritz and Jonquil Leiber; to Harry O. Fischer; to Frederic Jay Pabody; APPENDIX: Verse by C. L. Moore; Henry Kuttner, "For H. P. Lovecraft"; Fritz Leiber, "My Correspondence with Lovecraft"; Glossary of Frequently Mentioned Names; Bibliography; Index.
      Notes. The volume is noteworthy for containing Moore's lengthy and substantial letters to Lovecraft.

64. *Dawnward Spire, Lonely Hill: the Letters of H. P. Lovecraft and Clark Ashton Smith* (with David E. Schultz)
 a. New York: Hippocampus Press, [August] 2017.
      Contents: Introduction; Letters; APPENDIX: Annie E. P. Gamwell, Postcard to Clark Ashton Smith; H. P. Lovecraft, "[Review of *Ebony and Crystal*]"; "From 'Supernatural Horror in Literature'"; Clark Ashton Smith, "[Fantasy and Human Experience]"; "[On 'Garbage-Mongering']"; "[Realism and Fantasy]"; "[On the Forbidden Books]"; "The Tale of Macrocosmic Horror"; "[Crossword Puzzles]"; Clifford Gessler, "Treader of Obscure Stars"; Various, "In re exhibitions of Smith's artwork"; "The Boiling Point"; Chronology; Glossary of Frequently Mentioned Names; Bibliography; Index.
      Notes. A volume many years in the making, as it required the piecing together of hundreds of letters by Lovecraft to Smith, which had been sold piecemeal after Smith's death. The overwhelming bulk of the work on the volume was done by Schultz.

65.   *Collected Fiction: A Variorum Edition* (Volume 4)
       a.   New York: Hippocampus Press, [August] 2017.
             Contents: Introduction; The Green Meadow (with Winifred V. Jackson); Poetry and the Gods (with Anna Helen Crofts); The Crawling Chaos (with Winifred V. Jackson); The Horror at Martin's Beach (with Sonia H. Greene); Two Black Bottles (with Wilfred Blanch Talman); The Last Test (with Adolphe de Castro); The Curse of Yig (with Zealia Bishop); The Electric Executioner (with Adolphe de Castro); The Mound (with Zealia Bishop); Medusa's Coil (with Zealia Bishop); The Trap (with Henry S. Whitehead); The Man of Stone (with Hazel Heald); Winged Death (with Hazel Heald); The Horror in the Museum (with Hazel Heald); Out of the Aeons (with Hazel Heald); The Horror in the Burying-Ground (with Hazel Heald); The Slaying of the Monster (with R. H. Barlow); The Hoard of the Wizard-Beast (with R. H. Barlow); The Tree on the Hill (with Duane W. Rimel); The Battle That Ended the Century (with R. H. Barlow); The Battle That Ended the Century (with R. H. Barlow); The Disinterment (with Duane W. Rimel); "Till A' the Seas" (with R. H. Barlow); Collapsing Cosmoses (with R. H. Barlow); The Challenge from Beyond (with C. L. Moore, A. Merritt, Robert E. Howard, and Frank Belknap Long); The Diary of Alonzo Typer (with William Lumley); In the Walls of Eryx (with Kenneth Sterling); The Night Ocean (with R. H. Barlow); APPENDIX: Sonia H. Greene, "Four O'Clock"; Gustav Adolphe Danziger, "A Sacrifice to Science"; Gustav Adolphe Danziger, "The Automatic Executioner"; Duane W. Rimel, "The Sorcery of Aphlar"; William Lumley, "The Diary of Alonzo Typer"; Bibliography; Index.

             Notes. A collection of all the tales Lovecraft ghostwrote or revised for clients, along with his avowed collaborations. (Two such stories, "Under the Pyramids" and "Through the Gates of the Silver Key," were placed in volumes 1 and 3 of the variorum edition.)

66.   *Letters to Maurice W. Moe and Others* (with David E. Schultz)
       a.   New York: Hippocampus Press, [September] 2018.
             Contents: Introduction; Letters to Maurice W. Moe; Letters to Robert E. Moe; Letters to Bernard Austin Dwyer; Letters to Samuel Loveman; Letters to Vincent Starrett; APPENDIX: Maurice W. Moe, "Why I Am Not a Freethinker," "The Church and the World," "Life for God's Sake," "Looking Backward," "'Once an Amateur, Always an Amateur,'" "First Steps in the Appreciation of Poetry," "Maurice W. Moe on Amateur Criticism," "Through the Eyes of the Poet," "Imagism," "Literary Appreciation," "From *Poem Comments*," "From *Imagery Aids*," "Introduction to Poetry," "In a Sequestered Church-

yard Where Once Poe Walked," "Seven O'Clock"; Bernard Austin Dwyer, "Ol' Black Sarah," "Beautiful Night," "Fairies," "The Snake-God," "Letters to *Weird Tales*," "Letter to *Strange Tales*"; Samuel Loveman, "Collecting Curious Books," "A Conversation with Ambrose Bierce," "A Holiday Post-Card," "The Coast of Bohemia," "A Whittier Discovery," "[Untitled]"; Vincent Starrett, [Letter to Samuel Loveman, 24 May 1928]; Glossary of Frequently Mentioned Names; Bibliography; Index.

Notes. First complete publication of the letters to Moe and Dwyer.

67.   *The H. P. Lovecraft Cat Book*
   a.   West Warwick, RI: Necronomicon Press, [June] 2019.

   Contents: Introduction; The Cats of Ulthar; Sir Thomas Tryout; The Rats in the Walls; The Cats; In Memoriam: Oscar Incoul Verelst of Manhattan; Cats and Dogs; *From* The Dream-Quest of Unknown Kadath; Veteropinguis Redivivus; [To a Cat]; [Little Sam Perkins]; [Christmas Greetings]; The Cats of New York; Old Man; The Kappa Alpha Tau; Musings of an Ailurophile; Extracts from Letters; APPENDIX: Felis: A Prose Poem, by Frank Belknap Long.

   Notes. Another book designed to help in the revival of Necronomicon Press. I culled not only HPL's stories, essays, and poems, but his letters for discussions of felines. The best feature of the volume was Jason C. Eckhardt's artwork, scattered throughout the book.

68.   *Selected Essays*
   a.   West Warwick, RI: Necronomicon Press, [July] 2019.

   Contents: Introduction; I. ON WEIRD FICTION: Lord Dunsany and His Work; [Review of *Ebony and Crystal* by Clark Ashton Smith]; Notes on Writing Weird Fiction; Some Notes on Interplanetary Fiction; In Memoriam: Robert Ervin Howard; II. ON PHILOSOPHY AND POLITICS: Idealism and Materialism—A Reflection; Life for Humanity's Sake; [In Defence of Dagon]; Nietzscheism and Realism; Some Repetitions on the Times; III. ON LITERARY CRITICISM: The Case for Classicism; Rudis Indigestaque Moles; The Professional Incubus; The Omnipresent Philistine; Notes on Verse Technique; IV. ON SCIENCE: Can the Moon Be Reached by Man?; [Science versus Charlatanry]; The Truth about Mars; [Some Backgrounds of Fairyland]; V. ON TRAVEL: Vermont—A First Impression; Travels in the Provinces of America; Homes and Shrines of Poe; VI. ON AMATEUR JOURNALISM: The Dignity of Journalism; *Les Mouches Fantastiques*; Amateur Journalism: Its Possible Needs and Betterment; What Amateurdom and I Have Done for Each Other; Lucubrations Lovecraftian; Within the Gates; A Matter of Uniteds; Mrs. Miniter—Estimates and Recollections; Some Current Motives and Practices; VII. ON H. P. LOVECRAFT: A Confession of Unfaith; Cats and Dogs; Some Notes on a Nonentity.

Notes. A volume initially designed for Hippocampus Press (for those readers who might not want to wade through the five volumes of *Collected Essays*), then scheduled for publication with Sarnath Press, then handed to Necronomicon Press.

69.   *To a Dreamer: Best Poems of H. P. Lovecraft*
  a.   West Warwick, RI: Necronomicon Press, [July] 2019.

    Contents: Introduction; I. FANTASY AND HORROR: The Poe-et's Nightmare; The Rutted Road; Nemesis; Astrophobos; Psychopompos: A Tale in Rhyme; The Eidolon; A Cycle of Verse; Despair; Revelation; The House; The City; Bells; The Nightmare Lake; On Reading Lord Dunsany's *Book of Wonder*; To a Dreamer; The Cats; Primavera; Festival; Hallowe'en in a Suburb; The Wood; The Outpost; The Ancient Track; The Messenger; *Fungi from Yuggoth*; In a Sequester'd Providence Churchyard Where Once Poe Walk'd; To Mr. Finlay, upon His Drawing for Mr. Bloch's Tale, "The Faceless God"; To Clark Ashton Smith, Esq., upon His Phantastick Tales, Verses, Pictures, and Sculptures; II. OCCASIONAL VERSE: Regner Lodbrog's Epicedium; To Charlie of the Comics; The Bookstall; Inspiration; Respite; Brotherhood; Fact and Fancy; Laeta; a Lament; To Mr. Kleiner, on Receiving from Him the Poetical Works of Addison, Gay, and Somerville; A Pastoral Tragedy of Appleton, Wis.; Hellas; Tryout's Lament for the Vanished Spider; Cindy: Scrub Lady in a State Street Skyscraper; On a Grecian Colonnade in a Park; Sir Thomas Tryout; To Endymion; Damon and Lycë; My Favourite Character; A Year Off; To an Infant; In Memoriam: Oscar Incoul Verelst of Manhattan; Hedone; To a Sophisticated Young Gentleman; To a Young Poet in Dunedin; Gaudeamus; III. SATIRE: Providence in 2000 A.D.; Ad Criticos; Gryphus in Asinum Mutatus; The Power of Wine: A Satire; The Simple Speller's Tale; The Isaacsonio-Mortoniad; The Magazine Poet; My Lost Love; The Dead Bookworm; On the Death of a Rhyming Critic; To the Incomparable Clorinda; Amissa Minerva; On Religion; The Pathetick History of Sir Wilful Wildrake; Medusa: A Portrait; Plaster-All; Waste Paper; Lines upon the Magnates of the Pulp; IV. SEASONAL AND TOPOGRAPHICAL: New England;   Brumalia; A Garden; Sunset; Old Christmas; A Winter Wish; Providence; October [II]; The East India Brick Row; Saturnalia; [Christmas Greetings]; V. AMATEUR AFFAIRS: To the Members of the United Amateur Press Association from the Providence Amateur Press Club; Providence Amateur Press Club

(Deceased) to the Athenaeum Club of Journalism; Greetings; In Memoriam: J. E. T. D.; Helene Hoffman Cole: 1893–1919; Theobaldian Aestivation; The Feast; VI. POLITICS AND SOCIETY: The Crime of Crimes; The Rose of England; To Greece, 1917; The Volunteer; On a Battlefield in Picardy; The Conscript; Theodore Roosevelt; VII. PERSONAL: [The Solace of Georgian Poetry]; Sonnet on Myself; Phaeton; Monos: An Ode; Edith Miniter; [Little Sam Perkins]; Notes; Index of Titles; Index of First Lines.

Notes. This volume was also initially compiled for Hippocampus (as a compact version of *The Ancient Track*), then for Sarnath Press, then for Necronomicon Press.

70.   *Letters to Wilfred B. Talman and Helen V. and Genevieve Sully* (with David E. Schultz)

a.   New York: Hippocampus Press, [August] 2019.

Contents: Introduction; LETTERS: To Wilfred B. Talman; To Helen V. Sully; To Genevieve Sully; APPENDIX: H. P. Lovecraft, "[Some Backgrounds of Fairyland]," "The Pool"; Wilfred Blanch Talman, *Chinoiserie and Other Verses,* "Dream Ships," "Death," "Haunted Island," "Ballade of Creatures Abroad by Night," "Adventure Land," "Fragment," "Izrim," "The Curse of Alabad and Ghinu and Aratza," "A Horror in Profile," "Texaco at Home: V.–Providence," "The Story Teller," "Bookplates," "Lovecraft Revisited," "Letterst to *Weird Tales*"; Rheinhart Kleiner, "To Mistress Katherine Ann Talman"; Genevieve Sully, "Letters to *Weird Tales*"; Glossary of Frequently Mentioned Names; Bibliography; Index.

Notes. A volume difficult to prepare, since the letters to Talman had been scattered and were not easy to reassemble; many of the letters were also undated.

71.   *Letters with Donald and Howard Wandrei and to Emil Petaja* (with David E. Schultz)

a.   New York: Hippocampus Press, [December] 2019.

Contents: Introduction; Letters of H. P. Lovecraft and Donald Wandrei; Letters of H. P. Lovecraft and Howard Wandrei; Letters to Emil Petaja; APPENDIX: Donald Wandrei Interviewed; Other Known Letters to Howard Wandrei; Emil Petaja: Elemental; Dream within a Dream Within; Lost Dream; Partings . . . ; The Warrior; Asphodel; Marmok; The Witch's Berceuse; Famous Fantasy Fiction; The Mist; [Fragmentary story]; Glossary of Frequently Mentioned Names; Bibliography; Index.

Notes. A revision of *Mysteries of Time and Spirit* (item 32 above), along with other letters.

IV. Books Translated

1.   Maurice Lévy, *Lovecraft: A Study in the Fantastic*
      a.   Detroit: Wayne State University Press, 1988.
           Contents: Translator's Preface; Author's Preface; Introduction; 1. The Outsider; 2. Dwellings and Landscapes; 3. The Metamorphoses of Space; 4. The Horrific Bestiary; 5. The Depths of Horror; 6. The Horrors of Heredity; 7. Cthulhu; 8. Unholy Cults; 9. In the Chasms of Dream; 10. From Fable to Myth; Conclusion; Abbreviations; Notes; Bibliography; Index.
           Notes. A volume I had begun translating in 1976, and still one of the best critical analyses of Lovecraft.

V. Joshi as Series Editor

A. New Millennium Mythos

1.   Michael Shea. *Copping Squid and Other Mythos Tales*
      a.   [Lynnwood, WA:] Perilous Press, [October] 2009.
           Contents: Foreword; Tsathoggua; Dagoniad; Copping Squid; Nemo Me Impune Lacessit; The Pool; The Battery; The Presentation; Fat Face.

2.   Brian Stableford. *The Womb of Time*
      a.   Lynnwood, WA: Perilous Press, 2010.
           Contents: Foreword; The Womb of Time; The Legacy of Erich Zann.

B. The Modern Mythos Library

1.   Rick Dakan. *The Cthulhu Cult*
      a.   Welches, OR: Arcane Wisdom, 2011.

2.   Jonathan Thomas. *The Color over Occam*
      a.   Welches, OR: Arcane Wisdom, 2012.

C. Studies in Supernatural Literature

1.   Robert H. Waugh, ed. *Lovecraft and Influence: His Predecessos and His Contemporaries*
      a.   Lanham, MD: Scarecrow Press, 2013.
           Contents: Abbreviations; Robert H. Waugh, "Intro-duction"; I. LOVECRAFT'S PREDECESSORS: Robert M. Price, "Biblical Bits in

Lovecraft"; J. D. Worthington, "Queen Anne Is [Not] Dead: Lovecraft and the Augustans"; James Goho, "The Shape of Darkness: Origins for H. P. Lovecraft within the American Gothic Tradition"; Donald R. Burleson, "Hawthorne's Influence on Lovecraft"; Alex Houstoun, "'Hearken . . . I Can Tell You the Whole Story': Monologues and Confessions in the Early Works of H. P. Lovecraft and Edgar Allan Poe"; Darrell Schweitzer, "Lovecraft's Debt to Lord Dunsany"; Gavin Callaghan, "A Reprehensible Habit: H. P. Lovecraft and the Munsey Magazines"; T. R. Livesey, "Green Storm Rising: Lovecraft's Roots in Invasion Literature"; II. LOVECRAFT'S SUCCESSORS: Norm Gayford, "What Stays in Lovecraft's Sieve Once Frank Belknap Long Is Strained Through It"; S. T. Joshi, "From the Cosmic to the Human: H. P. Lovecraft's Influence on Ramsey Campbell"; Robert H. Waugh, "Lovecraft's Influence in Science Fiction: The Tides of His Dark Star in the Works of Arthur C. Clarke, Fritz Leiber, and Philip K. Dick"; Michael Cisco, "Reanimator and Exterminator: H. P. Lovecraft and William S. Burroughs"; John Langan, "Nature's Other, Ghastly Face: H. P. Lovecraft and the Animal Sublime in Stephen King"; Steven J. Mariconda, "Easy as Falling Off Logic: A Consideration of Lovecraft and Ligotti as 'Weird Realists'"; Selected Bibliography; Index; About the Contributors; About the Editor.

Notes. A volume that I recommended to Waugh, although I am still tempted to write a book on the subject myself.

2.   S. T. Joshi, ed. *Critical Essays on Lord Dunsany*
a.   Lanham, MD: Scarecrow Press, [August] 2013.
       See II.102.

3.   William F. Touponce. *Lord Dunsany, H. P. Lovecraft, Ray Bradbury: Spectral Journeys*
a.   Lanham, MD: Scarecrow Press, [October] 2013.
       Contents: Introduction; Lord Dunsany, or Beauty; H. P. Lovecraft, or Shock; Ray Bradbury, or Nostalgia; Index; About the Author.

       Notes. A fine monograph, containing some of the best discussions of the three authors in recent years.

4.   Gary William Crawford, ed. *Ramsey Campbell: Critical Essays on the Master of Modern Horror*
a.   Lanham, MD: Scarecrow Press, [December] 2013.
       Contents: Gary William Crawford, "Introduction"; Andy Sawyer, "'That Ill-Rumoured and Evilly-Shadowed Seaport': Ramsey Campbell's Lovecraftian Secret Hitories of Liverpool"; Leigh Blackmore, "'A Puppet's Parody of Joy': Dolls, Puppets, and Mannikins as Diabolical

Other in Ramsey Campbell"; Richard Bleiler, "Ramsey Campbell and the Twenty-First-Century Weird Tale"; James Goho, "An Archaeology of Urban Dread: The Short Fiction of Ramsey Campbell"; Simon MacCulloch, "Glimpses of Absolute Power: Ramsey Campbell's Concept of Evil"; S. T. Joshi, "Master and Pupil: August Derleth and Ramsey Campbell's First Book"; Stefan Dziemianowicz, "Mastering Darkness: An Interview with Ramsey Campbell"; John Llewellyn Probert, "Grinning in the Dark: The Humor of Ramsey Campbell"; Joel Lane, "A Local Afterlife"; Anthony J. Fonseca, "What Develops in the Darkest Rooms of the Mind: The Photographic Technique in *Nazareth Hill* and *The Seven Days of Cain*"; Gary William Crawford, "A Religion of His Own Making: Peter in *Obsession*"; Selected Bibliography; Index; About the Editor; About the Contributors.

Notes. A much overdue volume of criticism on the leading writer of weird fiction after HPL.

5.   S. T. Joshi and Darrell Schweitzer. *Lord Dunsany: A Comprehensive Bibliography.*
       a.   Lanham, MD: Scarecrow Press, [December] 2013.
            See I.11.b.

6.   James Goho. *Journeys into Darkness: Critical Essays on Gothic Horror.*
       a.   Lanham, MD: Scarecrow Press, [March] 2014.
            Contents: Dark Beginnings: Fear and Trembling in the Novels of Charles Brockden Brown; Poe's "The Fall of the House of Usher": A Predecessor to Lovecraft's "The Outsider"?; The Realm of Suffering: Ambrose Bierce and the Phantoms of the American Civil War; Suffering and Evil in the Short Fiction of Arthur Machen; The Haunted Wood: Algernon Blackwood's Canadian Stories; The Sickness unto Death in H. P. Lovecraft's "The Hound"; What Is "the Unnamable?: H. P. Lovecraft and the Problem of Evil; The Aboriginal in the Works of H. P. Lovecraft; From Salem to Eastwick: Witchcraft in the American Gothic; The City of Darkness: Fritz Leiber and the Beginnings of Modern Urban Horror; Selected Bibliography; Filmography; Index; About the Author.
            Notes. A splendid and wide-ranging collection of essays.

7.   Jason V Brock. *Disorders of Magnitude: A Survey of Dark Fantasy.*
       a.   Lanham, MD: Rowman & Littlefield, [July] 2014.
            Contents: Preface; Acknowledgments; PART ONE: THE DARKEST AGE: 1. The Smoldering Past: The Creation of the Modern from *Frankenstein* and *Dracula* to the Great War and Beyond; 2. "Cosmic Introspection": Lovecraft's Attainment of Personal Value by Way of

Infinite Insignificance; 3. Forrest J Ackerman: Fan Zero; 4. Gathering Darkness: In Appreciation of the Artists of *Weird Tales*; 5. Frank M. Robinson: First Fandom and Beyond; PART TWO: THINGS BECOME: 6. The Burden of Now: Welles's "Panic Broadcast," World War II, and Creeping Anomie; 7. Ray Bradbury: The Boy Who Never Grew Up' 8. Cinematic Dream Logic: How Movies Permanently Altered the Fabric of Reality; 9. Individual Sexual Liberation Becomes Social Emancipation: *Playboy* Changes the World; 10. Harlan Ellison: *L'enfant terrible* (Sort Of); PART THREE: THE RISE OF THE SPECULATIVE MIND: 11. Rod Serling: Articulating the American Nightmare; 12. A Howling at Owl Creek Bridge: Observations on Two Important *Twilight Zone* Episodes; 13. George Clayton Johnson: A Touch of Strange; 14. *L'Age d'Or* to *Götterdämmerung*: How Bradbury, Serling, Beaumont, and "The Group" Shaped a Pop Future; 15. Roger Corman: Socially Conscious Auteur; 16. Finding Sanctuary: Running from the *Zone* to *Logan*; 17. The Long Nuclear Shadow: Atomic Horror, *Godzilla*, and the Cold War; 18. The Horror of It All!: EC and the Beginnings of Modern Media HOOHAH!; 19. Madly Yours, Al Feldstein; 20. An End, a Middle, a Beginning: Richard Matheson and His Impact; PART FOUR: SLASHERS, BLOCKBUSTERS, AND BEST SELLERS: 21. Riding the Dark Wave: The Role of Dystopian Science Fiction in Popular Culture; 22. Celluloid Asylum: O'Bannon, Romero, Carpenter, and the Liberals Lose (and Find) Their Collective Minds; 23. Terrible Beauty: Slasher Film Connections to Conservatism, Pornography, and Misogyny; 24. King of the Dead: Filmmaker George A. Romero on Politics, Film, and the Future; 25. Dan O'Bannon: Not Gone, Not Forgotten; 26. H. R. Giger: A Darkness Faster Than light; 27. The Emperor's New Book: How Stephen King Saved Horror, Created Clive Barker (and Sam Raimi) . . . and Killed Publishing; 28. The Doctor Is In: F. Paul Wilson; 29. Sounds Horrific: Art Rock, Soundtracks, and the Zeitgeist; PART FIVE: A CENTURY OF SPECULATION: 30. Carnivora: The Dark Art of Automobiles; 31. David J. Skal: Monster Kid Ambassador of Horror; 32. Seasons in Hell; 33. Kris Kuksi: Dark Horizons in the Realm of the Senses; 34. Bluewater Comics' Darren G. Davis: On the Run in the Digital Age of Comics; 35. The H. P. Lovecraft Film Festival: Cosmic Chaos on the Silver Screen; 36. S. T. Joshi: Champion of the Weird Tale; 37. Marc Scott Zicree: As Timeless as Infinity; PART SIX: FROM (AND INTO) THE BEYOND: 38. *Fangoria*'s Chris Alexander: Cinephilia, Music, and All the Rest of It; 39. Bruce Campbell: From *The Evil Dead* to *Burn Notice* and Beyond; 40. The Inner World of William F. Nolan; 41. *The Mammoth Book of Body*

Horror; 42. Two of a Kind: Lee-Anne Raymond and Demetrios Vakras; 43. "Cthulhu, a Vampire, and a Zombie Walk into a Bar . . .": Why These Things, Why Now, and What's the Matter with Hollyweird?; 44. John Shirley: The Tao of Identity; 45. Ray Harryhausen: A Note on the Passage of Giants; 46. Kneeling at the Dandelion Shrine: An Appreciation; 47. William F. Nolan and Ray Bradbury: Reflections; 48. Introduction: The Pope of Speculative Fiction; 49. Future Shock? (De)Parting Thoughts; Appendix A: Select Books and Other Publications; Appendix B: Select Radio, Film, and Television Productions; Appendix C: Select Authors, Artists, Filmmakers, and Musicians; Index.

Notes. A provocative assemblage of essays, interviews, reivews, and other matter.

8.   Justin Everett and Jeffrey H. Shanks, ed. *The Unique Legacy of* Weird Tales: *The Evolution of Modern Fantasy and Horror.*
   a.   Lanham, MD: Rowman & Littlefield, 2015.
      Contents: Acknowledgments; Justin Everett and Jeffrey H. Shanks, "Introduction: *Weird Tales*—Discourse Community and Genre Nexus"; PART I: THE UNIQUE MAGAZINE: *WEIRD TALES,* MODERNISM, AND GENRE FORMATION: Jason Ray Carney, "'Something That Swayed as if in Unison': The Artistic Authenticity of *Weird Tales* in the Interwar Periodical Culture of Modernism"; Jonas Prida, "Weird Modernism: Literary Modernism in the First Decade of *Weird Tales*"; Dániel Nyikos, "The Lovecraft Circle and the 'Weird Class': 'Against the Complacency of an Orthodox Sun-Dweller'"; Nicole Emmelhainz, "Strnage Collaborations: *Weird Tales*'s Discourse Community as a Site of Collaborative Writing"; Morgan T. Holmes, "Gothic to Cosmic: Sword-and-Sorcery Fiction in *Weird Tales*"; PART II: EICH-PI-EL AND TWO-GUN BOB: LOVECRAFT AND HOWARD IN *WEIRD TALES:* Clancy Smith, "A Nameless Horror: Madness and Metamorphosis in H. P. Lovecraft and Postmodernism"; Bobby Derie, "Great Phallic Monoliths: Lovecraft and Sexuality"; Jeffrey H. Shanks, "Evolutionary Otherness: Anthropological Axiety in Robert E. Howard's 'Worms of the Earth'"; Justin Everett, "Eugenic Thought in the Works of Robert E. Howard"; PART III: MASTERS OF THE WEIRD: OTHER AUTHORS OF *WEIRD TALES:* Scott Connors, "Pegasus Unbridled: Clark Ashton Smith and the Ghettoization of the Fantastic"; Geoffrey Reiter, "'A Round Cipher': Word-Building and World-Building in the Weird Works of Clark Ashton Smith"; Jonathan Holland, "C. L. Moore, M. Brundage, and Jirel of Joiry: Women and Gender in the October 1934 *Weird Tales*"; Paul W.

Shovlin, "*Psycho*-ology 101: Incipient Madness in the Weird Tales of Robert Bloch"; Sidney Sondergard, "'To Hell and Gone': Harold Lawlor's Self-Effacing Pulp Metafiction"; Index; About the Editors and Contributors.

9.   June Pulliam and Anthony J. Fonseca. *Richard Matheson's Monsters: Gender in the Stories, Scripts, Novels, and* Twilight Zone *Episodes.*
    a.   Lanham, MD: Rowman & Littlefield, 2016.
        Contents: Introduction: The Most Famous Horror Author You've Never Heard Of; 1. The Life of the Legend: A Bio-bibliography; 2. EarlyStories and Novels: The Pre-*Legend* Years; 3. *I Am Legend* and *The Shrinking Man:* The Benchmark Novels; 4. The *Twilight Zone* Years; 5. From Legendary Scripts to Film; 6. Novels and Tales to Film, Part I: Multiple Masculinities; 7. Novels and Tales to Film, Part II: "The Most Monstrous of Monsters"; 8. Minor Novels and Teleplays; Bibliography; Index; About the Authors.

VI. Contributions to Books and Periodicals

A. Essays and Introductions

1.   "Adam Nevill: The Sense of Dread."
        a. *Dead Reckonings* No. 24 (Fall 2018): 62–67.
        Condensed version of the chapter on Nevill in I.51.

2.   "Adnotationes Criticae."
    a.   *Life Is a Hideous Thing* 1, No. 2 (January 1981): 8-10; 1, No. 4 (July 1981): 7-10; 2, No. 2 (July 1982): 5-7; 2, No. 3 (January 1983): 5-6; 2, No. 4 (April 1983): 2-4; 3, No. 1 (September 1983): 3-6.

3.   "Afterword."
    a.   In H. P. Lovecraft. *A History of the Necronomicon.* West Warwick, RI: Necronomicon Press, 1980. [5-7].
    b.   In I.43 (as "'History of the *Necronomicon*'").

4.   "Afterword."
    a.   In [R. H. Barlow and] H. P. Lovecraft. *The Night Ocean.* West Warwick, RI: Necronomicon Press, 1982. [24].

5.   "Afterword."
    a.   In Brian McNaughton. *The Throne of Bones.* Black River, NY: Terminal Fright, 1997. 338-41.

6. "Afterword."
   a. In Michael Aronovitz. *Alice Walks.* Lakewood, CO: Centipede Press, 2013. 201–3.

7. "Afterword."
   a. In Salomé Jones, ed. *Cthulhu Lives!* London: Ghostwood Books, 2014. 230–32.

8. "Afterword."
   a. H. P. Lovecraft. *The Annual Report on the Science of Astronomy, 1904.* West Warwick, RI: Necronomicon Press, 2018. 17–19.

9. "Afterword."
   a. In Kyla Lee Ward. *The Macabre Modern and Other Morbidities.* Sydney, Australia: P'rea Press, 2019. 147–48.

10. "Afterword: Gorman and Lovecraft."
    a. In Herbert Gorman. *The Place Called Dagon.* New York: Hippocampus Press, 2003. 185–87.

11. "Agnosticism and Atheism."
    a. In Tom Quirk and Gary Scharnhorst, ed. *American History through Literature 1870–1920.* Detroit: Thomson Gale, 2006, 1.31–35.

12. "Algernon Blackwood."
    a. In Scott Brewster and Luke Thurston, ed. *The Routledge Handbook to the Ghost Story.* New York: Routledge, 2017. 116–23.
    b. In I.52.

13. "An Annotated List of Lovecraft's Juvenile Manuscripts in the John Hay Library."
    a. *Les Bibliothèques* 2, No. 2 (April 1985): 1–7.

14. "Arthur Machen: Philosophy and Fiction."
    a. *Studies in Weird Fiction* No. 2 (Summer 1987): 3–26.
    b. In I.7 (as "Arthur Machen: The Mystery of the Universe").
    c. In Darrell Schweitzer, ed. *Discovering Classic Horror Fiction I.* Mercer Island, WA: Starmont House, 1992. 1–33.
    d. In *Short Story Criticism,* Volume 20. Detroit: Thomson Gale, 2005. 193–201 (as "Arthur Machen: The Mystery of the Universe").

15. "Arthur Machen: The Evils of Materialism."
    a.   In Stephen Jones, ed. *Flotsam Fantastique: The Souvenir Book of World
         Fantasy Convention 2013*. Wembley, UK: World Fantasy Conven-
         tion, 2013. 96–105.
              Extract from I.40/41.

Articles in *Muncie Evening Press*, 1975–76.

16. "Burris Intensive Courses Popular." 22 November 1975, "Next Week"
    section. T-10.

17. "Burris Singers in BSU Concert." 13 December 1975, "Next Week"
    section. T-11.

18. "Burris Has New Lounge." 10 January 1976, "Next Week" section. T-8.

19. "Burris to Do 'The Apple Tree.'" 31 January 1976, "Next Week" sec-
    tion. T-10.

20. "Many Enjoy Burris Open House." 21 February 1976, "Next Week"
    section. T-10.

21. "Burris Group Wins Gold Medal." 13 March 1976, "Next Week" sec-
    tion. T-10.

22. "Eleven Burris String Groups Plan Concert." 24 April 1976, "Next
    Week" section. T-10.

23. "Burris Players into Baroque Tuesday Night." 15 May 1976, "Next
    Week" section. T-10.

24. "Autobiography in Lovecraft."
    a.   *Lovecraft Studies* No. 1 (Fall 1979): 7–19.
    b.   In The Necon Committee, ed. *Necon Stories*. Providence: Three
         Bobs Press, 1990. 142–59 (revised).
    c.   In I.23.
    d.   In I.43.

25. "Barbarism vs. Civilization: Robert E. Howard and H. P. Lovecraft in
    Their Correspondence."
    a.   *Studies in the Fantastic* No. 1 (Summer 2008): 95–124.
    b.   In Darrell Schweitzer, ed. *The Robert E. Howard Reader*. [Holicong,
         PA:] Borgo Press, 2010. 51–81.
    c.   In I.43.

26. "The Beatification of St. Kim."
    a. *American Rationalist* 61, No. 6 (November/December 2015): 6–7.
    b. In I.46.

27. "The Beauties of Cosmicism: The Poetry and Prose of Clark Ashton Smith" (with Marc A. Michaud).
    a. *Books at Brown* 27 (1979): 81–87 (as "The Prose and Poetry of Clark Ashton Smith").

28. "Books by Lovecraft's Colleagues: A Preliminary Listing."
    a. *New Lovecraft Collector* No. 11 (Summer 1995): 3–4; No. 13 (Winter 1996): 2–4.

29. "Bran Mak Morn and History."
    a. In Benjamin Szumskyj, ed. *Two-Gun Bob: A Centennial Study of Robert E. Howard.* New York: Hippocampus Press, 2006. 120–31.
    b. In I.47.

30. "Briefly Noted."
    a. *Lovecraft Studies* No. 2 (Spring 1980): 20, 29; No. 3 (Fall 1980): 39; No. 4 (Spring 1981): 9, 19, 38, 43, 44; No. 5 (Fall 1981): 40; No. 6 (Spring 1982): 13, 17, 32; No. 7 (Fall 1982): 29, 39; No. 9 (Fall 1984): 71, 73, 79–80; No. 10 (Spring 1985): 12, 17, 28, 35; No. 11 (Fall 1985): 80; No. 12 (Spring 1986): 33, 37; No. 14 (Spring 1987): 38, 44; No. 15 (Fall 1987): 64, 68; No. 16 (Spring 1988): 18, 24, 40; No. 17 (Fall 1988): 13, 23, 29; No. 18 (Spring 1989): 17; Nos. 19/20 (Fall 1989): 27, 62, 69, 71; No. 21 (Spring 1990): [separate insert]; Nos. 22/23 (Fall 1990): 9, 32, 65 (without title); No. 24 (Spring 1991): 5, 17, 29; No. 25 (Fall 1991): 22; No. 26 (Spring 1992): 25, 34; No. 27 (Fall 1992): 9, 25, 31; No. 32 (Spring 1995): 11 (without title).

31. "Briefly Noted."
    a. *Lovecraft Annual* No. 1 (2007): 26, 83, 90, 93, 160; No. 2 (2008): 103, 138, 191, 215; No. 3 (2009): 9, 53, 95, 146, 183, 199; No. 4 (2010): 30, 123, 135, 165, 170, 215; No. 5 (2011): 111, 120, 154, 180; No. 6 (2012): 35, 75, 152, 178; No. 7 (2013): 35, 74, 135.

32. "Briefly Noted."
    a. *Studies in Weird Fiction* No. 2 (Summer 1987): 35, 44; No. 4 (Fall 1988): 12, 22, 33, 40; No. 5 (Spring 1989): 19, 26, 36; No. 6 (Fall 1989): 9, 14, 24, 27; No. 7 (Spring 1990): [separate insert]; No. 12 (Spring 1993): 6 (without title); No. 14 (Winter 1994): 28, 36 (without title).

33. "The 'Cake Artist' and His Bigotry."
    a. *Free Inquiry* 38, No. 2 (February/March 2018): 11.
    b. In I.46.b.

34. "The Canon of Weird Fiction."
    a. *Necrofile* No. 19 (Winter 1996): 23–25.

35. "Christianity and Paganism in Two Dunsany Novels."
    a. In S. T. Joshi, ed. *Critical Essays on Lord Dunsany.* Lanham, MD: Scarecrow Press, 2013. 203–11.
    b. In I.47.

36. "A Chronology of Selected Works by H. P. Lovecraft."
    a. In Kenneth W. Faig, Jr. *H. P. Lovecraft: His Life, His Work.* West Warwick, RI: Necronomicon Press, 1979. 29–36.
    b. In II.2. 27–41.

37. "Clive Barker: Sex, Death, and Fantasy."
    a. *Studies in Weird Fiction* No. 9 (Spring 1991): 2–12.
    b. In I.18.
    c. In *Contemporary Literary Criticism*, Volume 205. Detroit: Thomson Gale, 2005. 57–66.

38. "Commentary" [on Lovecraft to Charles W. Hornig, 7 August 1933].
    a. *Crypt of Cthulhu* No. 49 (Lammas 1987): 29–30.

39. "Concluding Address."
    a. *Books at Brown* 38–39 (1991–92): 149–55.
    b. In II.5.

40. "A Confession of Unfaith."
    a. *American Rationalist* 60, No. 4 (July/August 2014): 6–7.
    b. In I.46.

41. "The Cthulhu Mythos."
    a. In S. T. Joshi, ed. *Icons of Horror and the Supernatural.* Westport, CT: Greenwood Press, 2006. 97–128 (Vol. 1).
    b. In I.43.

42. "The Cthulhu Mythos: Lovecraft vs. Derleth."
    a. In David Wynn, ed. *Mythos Tales & Others: Number One.* Poplar Bluff, MO: Mythos Books, 1996. 76–87.

43. "Cthulhu's Empire: H. P. Lovecraft's Influence on His Contemporaries and Successors."
    a.   In Gary Hoppenstand, ed. *Pulp Fiction in the 1920s and 1930s.* Salem, OR: Salem Press, 2013. 19–35.

44. "David J. Schow and Splatterpunk."
    a.   *Studies in Weird Fiction* No. 13 (Summer 1993): 21–27.
    b.   In I.24.

45. "The Demise of the White Inferiorists."
    a.   *Free Inquiry* 39, No. 3 (April/May 2019): 14–15.

46. "Dennis Etchison: Spanning the Genres."
    a.   *Studies in Weird Fiction* No. 15 (Summer 1994): 30–36.
    b.   *Studies in Weird Fiction* No. 19 (Summer 1996): 29–36 (revised).
    c.   In I.24.

47. "The Development of Lovecraftian Studies, 1971–1982."
    a.   *Lovecraft Studies* No. 8 (Spring 1984): 32–36 (Part IB; as "Lovecraft in the Foreign Press, 1971–1982"); No. 9 (Fall 1984): 62–71 (Part IA); No. 10 (Spring 1985): 18–28 (Part IIA); No. 11 (Fall 1985): 54–65 (Part IIB).
    b.   In I.43.

48. "Difficile Est Saturam Non Scribere."
    a.   *Lovecraftian Ramblings* No. 11 (5 February 1979): 14.

49. "Dorothy L. Sayers: The Highbrow Detective Story."
    a.   *Million* No. 14 (March–June 1993): 13–17.

50. "The Dream World and the Real World in Lovecraft."
    a.   *Crypt of Cthulhu* No. 15 (Lammas 1983): 4–15.
    b.   In I.23.
    c.   In I.43.

51. "Dunsany, Lord."
    a.   In David Pringle, ed. *St. James Guide to Fantasy Writers.* Detroit: St. James Press, 1996. 170–71.

52. "Eckhardt's Art."
    a.   *Damned Thing* No. 3 (August 1992): 34–36.

53. "Editorial."
    a. *Vanguard* 5, No. 9 (16 January 1975): 2 (with subtitle: "Buycenten-nial?").

54. "Editorial."
    a. *Lovecraft Studies* No. 1 (Fall 1979): 1–2.

55. "Editorial."
    a. *Lovecraft Studies* Nos. 19/20 (Fall 1989): 3–4.

56. "Editorial."
    a. *Dead Reckonings* No. 1 (Spring 2007): 3–4 (as by "The Editors").

57. "Editorial."
    a. *American Rationalist* 57, No. 4 (July/August 2011): 3.

58. "Editorial."
    a. *Spectral Realms* No. 1 (Summer 2014): 4–5.

59. "Editorial Postscript" to "Xenophobia in the Life and Work of H. P. Lovecraft" by Barry L. Bender.
    a. *Lovecraft Studies* No. 5 (Fall 1981): 27–28.

60. "Editorial Postscript" to "The Lovecraft–Derleth Connection" by Robert M. Price.
    a. *Lovecraft Studies* No. 7 (Fall 1982): 23–24, 7.

61. "Editor's Note" to "The Doom That Came to Sarnath" by H. P. Lovecraft.
    a. *Lovecraftian Ramblings* No. 10 (31 October 1978): 6–7.

62. "Editor's Note" to "The Other Gods" by H. P. Lovecraft.
    a. *Lovecraftian Ramblings* No. 12 (1 August 1979): 3–4.

63. "Editor's Note" to "'Till A' the Seas'" by H. P. Lovecraft and R. H. Barlow.
    a. *Lovecraftian Ramblings* No. 9 (20 August 1978): 6.
    b. *Crypt of Cthulhu* No. 17 (Hallowmass 1983): 33 (abridged; as "Lovecraft's Contribution to '"Till A' the Seas"'").

64. "Edgar Allan Poe and the Revolution in Horror Fiction."
    a. In [Jerad Walters, ed.] *The Man That Was Used Up: A Celebration of Edgar Allan Poe*. Lakewood, CO: Centipede Press, 2009. 437–81.
    b. In I.40/41 (as "Edgar Allan Poe").

65. [Entries.]
    a.   In David Pringle, ed. *St. James Guide to Horror, Ghost & Gothic Writ-
         ers.* Detroit: St. James Press, 1998.
             Entries on Robert Aickman, Ambrose Bierce, William Peter
         Blatty, Ramsey Campbell, F. Marion Crawford, Les Daniels, Thomas
         Harris, L. P. Hartley, William Hjortsberg, Shirley Jackson, T. E. D.
         Klein, H. P. Lovecraft, Peter Straub, Thomas Tryon.

66. [Entries.]
    a.   In Tom W. Flynn, ed. *The New Encyclopedia of Unbelief.* Amherst,
         NY: Prometheus Books, 2007.
             Entries on Euripides, H. L. Mencken, Voltaire, and Witchcraft
         and Unbelief.

67. "Establishing the Canon of Weird Fiction."
    a.   *Studies in Weird Fiction* No. 27 (Spring 2005): 10–15.
    b.   In I.47.
             Revised version of my keynote address to the International Con-
         ference on the Fantastic in the Arts, Fort Lauderdale, FL (March
         2003).

68. "'The Events at Poroth Farm' and the Literature of Horror."
    a.   *Dagon* Nos. 18/19 (July-October 1987): 10–12.

69. "Excised Passages in 'The Thing on the Doorstep.'"
    a.   *Lovecraft Annual* No. 7 (2013): 171–77.
    b.   In I.43.

70. "A Failed Experiment: Family and Humanity in *The Sundial.*"
    a.   In Melanie R. Anderson and Lisa Kröger, ed. *Shirley Jackson, Influences
         and Confluences.* London & New York: Routledge, 2016. 25–34.
    b.   In I.52.

71. "The Fiction of Ambrose Bierce: A Bibliographical Survey."
    a.   *Studies in Weird Fiction* No. 23 (Summer 1998): 31–37.

72. "Finney, Charles G."
    a.   In Jack Sullivan, ed. *The Penguin Encyclopedia of Horror and the Super-
         natural.* New York: Viking, 1986. 152–53.

73. "Foreword."
    a.   In H. P. Lovecraft. *Writings in* The Tryout. West Warwick, RI:
         Necronomicon Press, 1977. 3–4.

74. "Foreword."
    a. In Joseph S. Pulver, Sr. *Blood Will Have Its Season.* New York: Hippocampus Press, 2009. 11–12.

75. "Foreword."
    a. In Michael Aronovitz. *Seven Deadly Pleasures.* New York: Hippocampus Press, 2009. 7–8.

76. "Foreword."
    a. In William F. Nolan and Jason V Brock, ed. *The Bleeding Edge: Dark Barriers, Dark Frontiers.* Vancouver, WA: Cycatrix Press, 2009. [9–12]. New York: Hippocampus Press, 2015. 7–11.
    b. In I.45 (as "The Anthologies of Jason V Brock and William F. Nolan").

77. "Foreword."
    a. In Jason V Brock and William F. Nolan, ed. *The Devil's Coattails: More Dispatches from the Dark Frontier.* Vancouver, WA: Cycatrix Press, 2011. 13–15.
    b. In I.45 (as "The Anthologies of Jason V Brock and William F. Nolan").

78. "Foreword."
    a. In Danel Olson, ed. *21st Century Gothic: Great Gothic Novels Since 2000.* Lanham, MD: Scarecrow Press, 2011. xi–xvii.
    b. In I.45 (as "From Gothic to Weird").

79. "Foreword."
    a. In Charles Lovecraft, ed. *Avatars of Wizardry.* Sydney, Australia: P'rea Press, 2012. 9–12.

80. "Foreword."
    a. In David Simmons, ed. *New Critical Essays on H. P. Lovecraft.* New York: Palgrave Macmillan, 2013. xi–xvi.
    b. In I.45 (as "The Emergence of H. P. Lovecraft").

81. "Foreword."
    a. In Mark Howard Jones, ed. *Cthulhu Cymraeg: Lovecraftian Tales from Wales.* Cardiff: Screaming Dreams, 2013. 1–4.

82. "Foreword."
    a. In Kenneth W. Faig, Jr. *Lovecraftian Voyages.* n.p.: Ultratelluric Press, 2013. vii–viii.
    b. In Kenneth W. Faig, Jr. *Lovecraftian Voyages.* New York: Hippocampus Press, 2017. vii–viii.

83. "Foreword."
   a. In Sammy Maine. *Necronomicon: Dark Fantasy, Digital Art and H. P. Lovecraft.* London: Flame Tree Publishing, 2015. 6.

84. "Foreword."
   a. In David Hambling. *The Dulwich Horror and Others.* Hornsea, UK: PS Publishing, 2015. ix–x.

85. "Foreword."
   a. In Nicole Cushing. *The Mirrors.* Vancouver, WA: Cycatrix Press, 2015. 11–13.

86. "Foreword."
   a. In H. P. Lovecraft. *Short Stories: An Anthology of Classic Tales.* London: Flame Tree Publishing, 2017. 8–9.

87. "Foreword."
   a. In Curtis M. Lawson. *Black Heart Boy's Choir.* n.p.: Wyrd Horror, 2019. vii–ix.

88. "Foreword: Poe and Lovecraft."
   a. In Sean Moreland, ed. *The Lovecraftian Poe: Essays on Influence, Reception, Interpreation and Transformation.* Bethlehem: Lehigh University Press, 2017. ix–xiii.

89. "From the Cosmic to the Human: H. P. Lovecraft's Influence on Ramsey Campbell."
   a. In Robert H. Waugh, ed. *Lovecraft and Influence: His Predecessors and Successors.* Lanham, MD: Scarecrow Press, 2013. 109–23.

90. "Further Notes on Lovecraft and Music."
   a. *Romantist* 4–5 (1980/81): 47–49.
   b. In I.43.

91. "Gems from *Unquiet* 21."
   a. *Lovecraftian Ramblings* No. 10 (31 October 1978): 19.

92. "The Genesis of 'The Shadow out of Time.'"
   a. *Lovecraft Studies* No. 33 (Fall 1995): 24–29.
       Extract from I.14.

93. "Ghost Stories."
   a. In Tom Quirk and Gary Scharnhorst, ed. *American History through Literature 1870–1920.* Detroit: Thomson Gale, 2006. 1.417–24.

94. "Gore Vidal (1925–2012)."
    a.   *Free Inquiry* 32, No. 6 (October/November 2012): 8.

95. "The Great Meadow Country Clubhouse."
    a.   *Crypt of Cthulhu* No. 110 (Roodmas 2018): 13.

96. "The Group: Bradbury, Matheson, Beaumont, Nolan."
    a.   *Nameless* 1, No. 2 (Fall/Winter 2012): 129–43.
        Extract from I.40/41.

97. "A Guide to the Lovecraft Fiction Manuscripts at the John Hay Library."
    a.   *Cynick* 2, No. 4 (September 1981): 2–19.
    b.   *Lovecraft Studies* No. 16 (Spring 1988): 24–33; No. 17 (Fall 1988): 14–20.
    c.   In I.43.

98. "Gun Nuts on the Run."
    a.   *Free Inquiry* 38, No. 5 (August/September 2018): 12–13.

99. "H. P. Lovecraft (1890–1937)."
    a.   *Life Is a Hideous Thing* 1, No. 3 (April 1981): 6–7.

100. "H. P. Lovecraft: Letters to August Derleth, 1926–1937."
    a.   *Cynick* 1, No. 1 (April 1977): 1–10.

101. "H. P. Lovecraft: Letters to John T. Dunn" (editor; with David E. Schultz and John H. Stanley).
    a.   *Books at Brown* 38–39 (1991–92): 157–223.

102. "H. P. Lovecraft: The Books" (by Lin Carter; annotated by Robert M. Price and S. T. Joshi)
    a.   In Darrell Schweitzer, ed. *Discovering H. P. Lovecraft.* Rev. ed. Holicong, PA: Wildside Press, 2001. 107–47.

103. "H. P. Lovecraft: The Fiction of Materialism."
    a.   In Douglas Robillard, ed. *American Supernatural Fiction: From Edith Wharton to the* Weird Tales *Writers.* New York: Garland, 1996. 141–66.
    b.   In I.24.
    c.   In I.43.

104. "H. P. Lovecraft and Lovecraft Criticism: An Annotated Bibliography: Supplement."
    a.   *Cynick* 1, No. 1 (April 1977): 23–33; 1, No. 2 (June 1977): 5–28; 1, No. 3 (September 1977): 9–36; 1, No. 4 (December 1977): 11–23.

105. "How Bad Are Lovecraft's Revisions?"
    a. *Scream Factory* No. 10 (Autumn 1992): 18–22.
    b. In Peter Enfantino, Robert Morrish, and John Scoleri, ed. *The Best of the Scream Factory.* Baltimore: Cemetery Dance Publications, 2018. 106–9.

106. "H[oward] P[hillips] Lovecraft."
    a. In Douglass H. Thomson, Jack G. Voller, and Frederick S. Frank, ed. *Gothic Writers: A Critical and Bibliographical Guide.* Westport, CT: Greenwood Press, 2001. 270–82.

107. "Humour and Satire in Lovecraft."
    a. *Crypt of Cthulhu* No. 61 (Yuletide 1988): 3–13.
    b. In Scott Connors, ed. *A Century Less a Dream: Selected Criticism on H. P. Lovecraft.* Holicong, PA: Wildside Press, 2002. 124–36.
    c. In I.43.

108. "In Memoriam: Paul Kurtz (1925–2012)."
    a. *American Rationalist* 58, No. 6 (November/December 2012): 11.

109. "An Index of Titles to the *Selected Poems* of Clark Ashton Smith."
    a. *Cynick* 2, No. 2 (February 1981): 2–12.

110. "Interview with S. T. Joshi."
    a. *Carnage Hall* No. 4 (n.d.): 36–45.

111. "Introduction."
    a. *Forum* 2, No. 1 (September 1975): 3.

112. "Introduction."
    a. *Cynick* 3, No. 1 (February 1982): 1–12.
        Introduction to III.8.

113. "Introduction."
    a. In Walter de la Mare. *The Return.* Mineola, NY: Dover, 1997. iii–vi.
    b. In I.52.

114. "Introduction."
    a. In Algernon Blackwood. *Incredible Adventures.* New York: Hippocampus Press, 2004. 9–13.
    b. In I.52.

115. "Introduction."
    a. In Clark Ashton Smith. *The Sword of Zagan and Other Writings*. New York: Hippocampus Press, 2004. 7–9.

116. "Introduction."
    a. In Bram Stoker. *Five Novels*. New York: Barnes & Noble, 2006. vii–x.
    b. In I.47 (as "Bram Stoker: *Dracula* and Others").

117. "Introduction."
    a. In Barry Pain. *An Exchange of Souls* [with Henri Béraud's *Lazarus*]. New York: Hippocampus Press, 2007. 5–8.
    b. In I.52 (as "Barry Pain: The Occasional Weirdist").

118. "Introduction."
    a. In Henri Béraud. *Lazarus* [with Barry Pain's *An Exchange of Souls*]. New York: Hippocampus Press, 2007. 5–6.
    b. In I.52.

119. "Introduction."
    a. In Ambrose Bierce. *An Occurrence at Owl Creek Bridge and Other Stories*. Leyburn, UK: Tartarus Press, 2008. v–xviii.

120. "Introduction."
    a. In Leland Hall. *Sinister House* [with Francis Brett Young's *Cold Harbour*]. New York: Hippocampus Press, [June] 2008. 5–8.
    b. In I.52.

121. "Introduction."
    a. In Francis Brett Young. *Cold Harbour* [with Leland Hall's *Sinister House*]. New York: Hippocampus Press, [June] 2008. 9–13.
    b. In I.52.

122. "Introduction."
    a. In Washington Irving. *The Legend of Sleepy Hollow and Other Stories*. Leyburn, UK: Tartarus Press, 2009. v–xi.

123. "Introduction."
    a. In Arthur Ransome. *The Elixir of Life* [with R. E. Spencer's *The Lady Who Came to Stay*]. New York: Hippocampus Press, 2009. 7–11.
    b. In I.52.

124. "Introduction."
  a. In R. E. Spencer. *The Lady Who Came to Stay* [with Arthur Ransome's *The Elixir of Life*]. New York: Hippocampus Press, 2009. 9–13.
  b. In I.52.

125. "Introduction."
  a. In H. B. Drake. *The Shadowy Thing.* New York: Hippocampus Press, 2010. 5–7.

126. "Introduction."
  a. In Voltaire. *God and Human Beings.* Translated by Michael Shreve. Amherst, NY: Prometheus Books, 2010. 11–16.

127. "Introduction."
  a. In H. P. Lovecraft. *The Complete Cthulhu Mythos Tales.* New York: Fall River Press, 2013; New York: Barnes & Noble, 2016. vii–xiii.

128. "Introduction."
  a. In H. P. Lovecraft. *The Dream-Quest of Unknown Kadath.* (Lovecraft Illustrated, Volume 1.) Hornsea, UK: PS Publishing, 2014. ix–xii.

129. "Introduction."
  a. In H. P. Lovecraft. *The Dreams in the Witch House.* (Lovecraft Illustrated, Volume 2.) Hornsea, UK: PS Publishing, 2014. ix–xii.

130. "Introduction."
  a. In H. P. Lovecraft. *The Dunwich Horror.* (Lovecraft Illustrated, Volume 3.) Hornsea, UK: PS Publishing, 2014. ix–xii.

131. "Introduction."
  a. In Clint Smith. *Ghouljaw and Other Stories.* New York: Hippocampus Press, 2014. 11–12.

132. "Introduction."
  a. In Nate Pederson, ed. *The Starry Wisdom Library.* Hornsea, UK: PS Publishing, 2014, n.p.

133. "Introduction."
  a. In H. P. Lovecraft. *The Shadow out of Time.* (Lovecraft Illustrated, Volume 4.) Hornsea, UK: PS Publishing, 2015. ix–xii.

134. "Introduction."
  a. In H. P. Lovecraft. *The Shadow over Innsmouth.* (Lovecraft Illustrated, Volume 5.) Hornsea, UK: PS Publishing, 2015. ix–xii.

135. "Introduction."
    a.   In H. P. Lovecraft. *At the Mountains of Madness.* (Lovecraft Illustrated, Volume 6.) Hornsea, UK: PS Publishing, 2015. ix–xii.

136. "Introduction."
    a.   In Lois H. Gresh. *Cult of the Dead and Other Weird and Lovecraftian Tales.* New York: Hippocampus Press, 2015. 9–10.

137. "Introduction."
    a.   In H. P. Lovecraft. *The Spirit of Revision: Lovecraft's Letters to Zealia Brown Reed Bishop.* Ed. Sean Branney and Andrew Leman. Glendale, CA: H. P. Lovecraft Historical Society, 2015. 7–14.

138. "Introduction."
    a.   In Darrell Schweitzer. *Awaiting Strange Gods: Weird and Lovecraftian Fictions.* Nampa, ID: Fedogan & Bremer, 2015. i–v.
    b.   In I.45 (as "Darrell Schweitzer and the Mythos").

139. "Introduction."
    a.   In Caitlín R. Kiernan. *Beneath an Oil-Dark Sea: The Best of Caitlín R. Kiernan, Volume Two.* Burton, MI: Subterranean Press, 2015. 11–16.
    b.   In I.47 (as "Caitlín R. Kiernan and Sensuous Prose").

140. "Introduction."
    a.   In H. P. Lovecraft. *The Call of Cthulhu.* (Lovecraft Illustrated, Volume 7.) Hornsea, UK: PS Publishing, 2015. ix–xii.

141. "Introduction."
    a.   In H. P. Lovecraft. *The Colour out of Space.* (Lovecraft Illustrated, Volume 8.) Hornsea, UK: PS Publishing, 2015. ix–xii.

142. "Introduction."
    a.   In H. P. Lovecraft. *The Whisperer in Darkness.* (Lovecraft Illustrated, Volume 9.) Hornsea, UK: PS Publishing, 2015. ix–xii.

143. "Introduction."
    a.   In H. P. Lovecraft. *The Colour out of Space.* Orange, MA: Amy Borezo, Publisher, 2016, n.p.

144. "Introduction."
    a.   In Don Swaim. *The Assassination of Ambrose Bierce: A Love Story.* New York: Hippocampus Press, 2016. 9–11.

145. "Introduction."
     a. In H. P. Lovecraft [and Zealia Bishop]. *The Mound.* (Lovecraft Illustrated, Volume 10.) Hornsea, UK: PS Publishing, 2016. ix–xii.

146. "Introduction."
     a. In H. P. Lovecraft. *The Haunter of the Dark (with The Thing on the Doorstep).* (Lovecraft Illustrated, Volume 11.) Hornsea, UK: PS Publishing, 2016. xi–xviii.

147. "Introduction."
     a. In H. P. Lovecraft. *The Case of Charles Dexter Ward.* (Lovecraft Illustrated, Volume 12.) Hornsea, UK: PS Publishing, 2016. ix–xvi.

148. "Introduction."
     a. In Eleanor M. Ingram. *The Thing from the Lake.* Seattle: Sarnath Press, 2017. 5–8.
     b. In I.52.

149. "Introduction."
     a. In Robert Hichens. *The Dweller on the Threshold.* Seattle: Sarnath Press, 2017. 5–8.
     b. In I.52.

150. "Introduction."
     a. In H. P. Lovecraft. *The Festival and Other Abnormalities.* (Lovecraft Illustrated, Volume 13.) Hornsea, UK: PS Publishing, 2017. ix–xiv.

151. "Introduction."
     a. In H. P. Lovecraft. *Herbert West–Reanimator and Kindred Night Spawn.* (Lovecraft Illustrated, Volume 14.) Hornsea, UK: PS Publishing, 2017. ix–xix.

152. "Introduction."
     a. In H. P. Lovecraft. *Dagon and Diverse Monstrosities.* (Lovecraft Illustrated, Volume 15.) Hornsea, UK: PS Publishing, 2017. ix–xx.

153. "Introduction."
     a. In H. P. Lovecraft. *The Other Gods and Various Ethereal Effusions.* (Lovecraft Illustrated, Volume 16.) Hornsea, UK: PS Publishing, 2017. ix–xxi.

154. "Introduction."
    a. In H. P. Lovecraft. *The Curse of Yig and Selected Ghastly Ghostwritings.* (Lovecraft Illustrated, Volume 17.) Hornsea, UK: PS Publishing, 2017. ix–xvi.

155. "Introduction."
    a. In Caitlín R. Kiernan. *Houses Under the Sea: Mythos Tales.* Lakewood, CO: Centipede Press, 2018. 11–16.

156. "Introduction."
    a. In [Alex and Bobbi Scully, ed.] *Birthing Monsters: Frankenstein's Cabinet of Curiosities and Cruelties.* n.p.: Firbolg Publishing, 2018. 1–7.

157. "Introduction."
    a. In Edgar Allan Poe. *The Masque of the Red Death and Others.* Illustrated by Jason Eckhardt. Warren, RI: Ulthar Press, 2018. 7–11.

158. "Introduction."
    a. In H. P. Lovecraft. *The Lurking Fear.* West Warwick, RI: Necronomicon Press, 2019. 1.

159. "Introduction" to "Cats and Dogs" by H. P. Lovecraft.
    a. *Twilight Zone* 3, No. 3 (July–August 1983): 30.

160. "Introduction" to *H. P. Lovecraft's Favourite Horror Stories* (ed. S. T. Joshi and Marc A. Michaud).
    a. *Twilit Grotto* 1, No. 4 (May 1984): [2–5].

161. "Introduction to the Cooper Square Edition."
    a. In H. P. Lovecraft and Willis Conover. *Lovecraft at Last.* New York: Cooper Square Press, 2002. xi–xvi.
    b. In I.43 (as "*Lovecraft at Last*").

162. "Introduction" to *The Hoard of the Wizard-Beast and One Other* by R. H. Barlow.
    a. West Warwick, RI: Necronomicon Press, 1994. 5–8.

163. "Introduction" to *The Night Ocean and Other Tales.*
    a. *Cynick* 2, No. 3 (June 1981): 8–14.

164. "Irvin S. Cobb and Gouverneur Morris: A Taste for the Weird."
    a. *Weird Fiction Review* No. 6 (2015): 171–85.
    b. In I.47.

Originally written as the introduction to a volume of Cobb's and Morris's weird tales for the Classics of Gothic Horror series (scheduled to come out in 2020).

165. "J. Vernon Shea (1912–1981)."
  a. In J. Vernon Shea. *H. P. Lovecraft: The House and the Shadows*. West Warwick, RI: Necronomicon Press, 1982. 19–20.

166. "Jacques Bergier and H. P. Lovecraft."
  a. *Cynick* 1, No. 4 (December 1977): 2–3.
  b. *Lovecraftian Ramblings* No. 11 (5 February 1979): 7–8.

167. "Killing Women with Robert Bloch, Thomas Harris, and Bret Easton Ellis."
  a. *Armchair Detective* 26, No. 1 (Winter 1993): 38–45, 98–102 (as "Weird Tales").
  b. In I.18.

168. "*The King of Elfland's Daughter* and *The Blessing of Pan*."
  a. *Damned Thing* No. 5 (Yuletide 1993): 40–49.
          Extract from I.12.

169. "The King's New Clothes."
  a. *Million* No. 13 (January–February 1993): 27–37.
  b. In I.18 (as "Stephen King: the King's New Clothes").

170. "Kipling, [Joseph] Rudyard."
  a. In Jack Sullivan, ed. *The Penguin Encyclopedia of Horror and the Supernatural*. New York: Viking, 1986. 246–47.

171. "L. P. Davies: The Workings of the Mind."
  a. *Armchair Detective* 24, No. 2 (Spring 1991): 174–85 (as "The Powers of the Mind").
  b. In I.24.

172. "Lands Forgotten or Unfound: The Prose Poetry of Clark Ashton Smith."
  a. In Scott Connors, ed. *The Freedom of Fantastic Things: Selected Criticism on Clark Ashton Smith*. New York: Hippocampus Press, 2006. 138–47.
  b. In I.52.

173. "Les Daniels."
  a. *Studies in Weird Fiction* No. 8 (Fall 1990): 16–24.
  b. In I.24 (as "Les Daniels: The Horror of History").

174. "Letters: Mencken-Sterling."
   a. *Menckeniana* No. 155 (Fall 2000): 3–7.
   Introduction to II.29.

175. "Letters to Carl Ferdinand Strauch" by H. P. Lovecraft (editor; with David E. Schultz).
   a. *Lovecraft Annual* No. 4 (2010): 46–119.

176. "Letters to Farnsworth Wright" by H. P. Lovecraft (editor; with David E. Schultz).
   a. *Lovecraft Annual* No. 8 (2014): 5–59.

177. "Letters to Lee McBride White" by H. P. Lovecraft (editor; with David E. Schultz).
   a. *Lovecraft Annual* No. 1 (2007): 31–64.

178. "The Life and Work of Rod Serling."
   a. *Studies in Weird Fiction* No. 7 (Spring 1990): 22–28.
   b. In I.24 (as "Rod Serling: The Moral Supernatural").

179. "Life Is *Not* a Hideous Thing."
   a. *Crypt of Cthulhu* No. 7 (Lammas 1982): 36–38.
   b. In [Sam Gafford, ed.] *The Providence Pals: Memories and Miscellany.* Warren, RI: Ulthar Press, 2015. 14–17.

180. [Liner Notes.]
   a. In H. P. Lovecraft. *The Hound; The Music of Erich Zann.* Read by Andrew Leman. Syracuse, NY: Cadabra Records, 2016. [LP]

181. [Liner notes.]
   a. In H. P. Lovecraft. *Fungi from Yuggoth and Other Poems.* Read by William E. Hart. Nampa, ID: Fedogan & Bremer, 2016. [CD. Notes printed in separate booklet.]

182. [Liner notes.]
   a. In Robert W. Chambers. *The Yellow Sign.* Read by Anthony D. P. Mann. Syracuse, NY: Cacabra Records, 2017. [LP]

183. [Liner notes.]
   a. In H. P. Lovecraft. *Dagon; The Cats of Ulthar; The Music of Erich Zann.* Read by Andrew Leman. Syracuse, NY: Cadabra Records, 2018. [LP]

184.   [Liner notes.]
    a.   In H. P. Lovecraft. *The Call of* Cthulhu. Read by Andrew Leman. Syracuse, NY: Cadabra Records, 2018. [LP]

185.   "A Literary Tutelage: Robert Bloch and H. P. Lovecraft."
    a.   *Studies in Weird Fiction* No. 16 (Winter 1995): 13–25.
    b.   In I.24.
    c.   In Benjamin Szumskyj, ed. *The Man Who Collected Psychos: Critical Essays on Robert Bloch.* Jefferson, NC: McFarland, 2009. 23–40.
    d.   In I.43.

186.   "Living in a Religious Society."
    a.   *American Rationalist* 62, No. 6 (November/December 2016): 6–7.
    b.   In I.46.

187.   "The Long View."
    a.   *Free Inquiry* 39, No. 2 (February/March 2019): 9–10.

188.   "A Look at Lovecraft's Fantastic Poetry."
    a.   *Aklo* (Summer 1991): 20–30.
    b.   In I.43 (as "Lovecraft's Fantastic Poetry").

189.   "A Look at Lovecraft's Letters."
    a.   *Crypt of Cthulhu* No. 46 (Eastertide 1987): 3–12.
    b.   In I.6.
    c.   In I.23.
    d.   In I.43.

190.   "Lord Dunsany: The Career of a Fantaisiste."
    a.   In I.7.
    b.   In *Twentieth-Century Literary Criticism,* Volume 59. Detroit: Gale, 1995. 16–29.
    c.   In Darrell Schweitzer, ed. *Discovering Classic Fantasy Fiction.* San Bernadino, CA: Borgo Press, 1996. 7–48.

191.   "Lost on a Desert Island Department."
    a.   *Lovecraftian Ramblings* No. 14 (1 May 1980): 5.

192.   "Lovecraft and a World in Transition."
    a.   *Mage* (Winter 1985): 23–32.
    b.   In I.43.

193.   "Lovecraft and Classical Antiquity."
    a.   *Cynick* 2, No. 2 (February 1981): 13–24.

194. "Lovecraft and Dunsany's *Chronicles of Rodriguez.*"
    a. *Crypt of Cthulhu* No. 82 (Hallowmass 1992): 3–6.
    b. In I.23.
    c. In I.43.

195. "Lovecraft and Providence."
    a. Radio talk, WBRU (Providence), 15 March 1977, 6.45–7.15 p.m.

196. "Lovecraft and the 'Big Issue.'"
    a. *Providence Sunday Journal Magazine* (5 August 1990): 14 (as "An Enormous Break with Literary Tradition. . . .").
    b. *Lovecraft Studies* Nos. 22/23 (Fall 1990): 49–50.
    c. In I.43.

197. "Lovecraft and *The Dream-Quest of Unknown Kadath.*"
    a. *Cynick* 2, No. 1 (December 1979): 2–13.
    b. *Crypt of Cthulhu* No. 37 (Candlemas 1986): 25–34, 59.

198. "Lovecraft and the Films of His Day."
    a. *Crypt of Cthulhu* No. 77 (Eastertide 1991): 8–10.
    b. In I.23.
    c. In I.43.

199. "Lovecraft and the *Regnum Congo.*"
    a. *Crypt of Cthulhu* No. 28 (Yuletide 1984): 13–17.
    b. In I.23.
    c. In I.43.

200. "Lovecraft and the Titans: A Critical Legacy."
    a. In Sean Moreland, ed. *New Directions in Supernatural Horror in Literature: The Critical Influence of H. P. Lovecraft.* New York: Palgrave Macmillan, 2018. 155–70.

201. "Lovecraft and *Weird Tales.*"
    a. In II.1 (as "Introduction").
    b. In I.23.
    c. In I.43.
    d. In Tom Roberts, ed. *Windy City Pulp Stories #15.* Normal, IL: Black Dog Books, 2015. 57–65.

202. "Lovecraft Criticism: A Study."
    a. *Miskatonic* 5, No. 1 (2 February 1977): [2–6].
    b. In III.8.

203.   "Lovecraft, H. P."
   a.   In John A. Garraty and Mark C. Carnes, ed. *American National Biography*. New York: Oxford University Press, 1999, Vol. 13. 953–54.

204.   "Lovecraft, H. P."
   a.   In Matt Cardin, ed. *Mummies around the World*. Santa Barbara, CA: ABC-CLIO, 2014. 207–10.

205.   "Lovecraft in School."
   a.   *Damned Thing* No. 5 (Yuletide 1993): 2–14.
         Extract from I.14.

206.   "Lovecraft in *Weird Tales*."
   a.   *New Lovecraft Collector* No. 10 (Spring 1995): 3–4.

207.   "Lovecraft on Human Knowledge: An Exchange" (with K. Setiya).
   a.   *Lovecraft Studies* No. 24 (Spring 1991): 22–23, 34.

208.   "Lovecraft, Regner Lodbrog, and Olaus Wormius."
   a.   *Crypt of Cthulhu* No. 89 (Eastertide 1995): 3–7.
   b.   In I.23.
   c.   In I.43.

209.   "Lovecraft's Aesthetic Development: From Classicism to Decadence."
   a.   *Lovecraft Studies* No. 31 (Fall 1994): 24–34.
         Extract from I.14.

210.   "Lovecraft's Alien Civilisations: A Political Interpretation."
   a.   *Crypt of Cthulhu* No. 32 (St John's Eve 1985): 8–24, 31 (abridged).
   b.   In I.6.
   c.   In I.23.
   d.   In I.43.

211.   "Lovecraft's 'Dunsanian Studies.'"
   a.   In S. T. Joshi, ed. *Critical Essays on Lord Dunsany*. Lanham, MD: Scarecrow Press, 2013. 241–64.
         Extract from I.34/35.

212.   "Lovecraft's Earliest Writings."
   a.   *New Lovecraft Collector* No. 3 (Summer 1993): 3–4.

213.   "Lovecraft's Early Pamphlets."
   a.   *New Lovecraft Collector* No. 4 (Fall 1993): 3–4.

214. "Lovecraft's Ethical Philosophy."
    a. *Lovecraft Studies* No. 21 (Spring 1990): 24–37, 39.
        Extract from I.9.

215. "Lovecraft's Juvenile Fiction."
    a. *Crypt of Cthulhu* No. 84 (Lammas 1993): 3–16.
        Extract from I.14.

216. "Lovecraft's Other Planets."
    a. *Crypt of Cthulhu* No. 4 (Eastertide 1982): 3–11 (abridged).
    b. In I.6.
    c. In I.43.

217. "Lovecraft's Revisions: How Much of Them Did He Write?"
    a. *Crypt of Cthulhu* No. 11 (Candlemas 1983): 3–14.
    b. In I.6.
    c. In I.43.

218. "M. R. James and the Limitations of the Ghost Story."
    a. *Spectral Tales* No. 1 (June 1988): 27–33.
    b. In I.7 (as "M. R. James: The Limitations of the Ghost Story").
    c. In *Short Story Criticism*, Volume 16. Detroit: Gale, 1991. 254–58 (as
        "M. R. James: The Limitations of the Ghost Story").

219. "The Magical Spirituality of a Lapsed Catholic: Atheism and Anticler-
    icalism."
    a. In John W. Morehead, ed. *The Supernatural Cinema of Guillermo del
        Toro.* Jefferson, NC: McFarland, 2015. 11–21.
    b. In I.52.

220. "Man's Mistreatment of Woman."
    a. *Free Inquiry* 39, No. 5 (August/September 2019): 11–12.

221. "Master and Pupil: August Derleth and Ramsey Campbell's First
    Book."
    a. In Gary William Crawford, ed. *Ramsey Campbell: Critical Essays on
        the Master of Modern Horror.* Lanham, MD: Scarecrow Press, 2013.
        101–12.
    b. In I.47.

222. "Mencken and Terrorism."
    a. *Menckeniana* No. 173 (Spring 2005): 13–15.
    b. In I.50.

223.   "Mencken Bibliography Addenda."
   a.   *Menckeniana* No. 165 (Spring 2003): 12–16.

224.   "Mosig at Last: My Years with the Greatest of Lovecraft Scholars."
   a.   *Crypt of Cthulhu* No. 33 (Lammas 1985): 29–35, 23.

225.   "My Summer Readings."
   a.   *Life Is a Hideous Thing* 1, No. 1 (September 1980): 5–8.

226.   "My Work in Lovecraft Studies."
   a.   *Twilit Grotto* 2, No. 1 (February 1985): [2–3].

227.   "The Nastiness of Conservatives."
   a.   *Free Inquiry* 38, No. 6 (October/November 2018): 27–28.

228.   "News from Providence."
   a.   *Lovecraftian Ramblings* No. 12 (1 August 1979): 10.

229.   "News of Interest."
   a.   *Lovecraftian Ramblings* No. 11 (5 February 1979): 4 (unsigned).
        Ghostwritten for Ken Neily.

230.   "News of Interest."
   a.   *Lovecraftian Ramblings* No. 12 (1 August 1979): 2 (unsigned).
        Ghostwritten for Ken Neily.

231.   "*The Nightmare Factory* by Thomas Ligotti."
   a.   In Stephen Jones and Kim Newman, ed. *Horror: Another 100 Best Books.* New York: Carroll & Graf, 2005. 385–89.
   b.   In I.47.

232.   "A Note on Post-Lovecraftian Fantasy."
   a.   *Lovecraftian Ramblings* No. 20 (2 February 1985): 13–21; No. 21 (1 August 1985): 8–22; No. 22 (2 February 1986): 12–23.

233.   "The Old Gods Waken."
   a.   In Stephen Jones, ed. *The Art of Horror: An Illustrated History.* London: Elephant Books; Montclair, NJ: Applause Theatre & Cinema Books, 2015. 178–203.

234.   "On 'A Wine of Wizardry.'"
   a.   *Spectral Realms* No. 7 (Summer 2017): 105–10.
   b.   In I.52.

235. "On 'In Amundsen's Tent' by John Martin Leahy."
    a. In H. P. Lovecraft. *At the Mountains of Madness*. (Lovecraft Illustrated, Volume 6.) Hornsea, UK: PS Publishing, 2015. 171–73.

236. "On James Wade and English Spellings."
    a. *Outré* 1, No. 5 (May 1977): 69–73.

237. "On Joshi's *Critical Analysis*."
    a. *Forum* 2, No. 7 (March 1976): 6.

238. "On 'Polaris.'"
    a. *Crypt of Cthulhu* No. 15 (Lammas 1983): 22–26.
    b. In I.23.
    c. In I.43.

239. "On Rod Serling's 'Clean Kills and Other Trophies.'"
    a. In [Angel McCoy, ed.] *Another Dimension Anthology*. n.p.: Wily Writers, 2016. 43–45.

240. "On 'Supernatural Horror in Literature.'"
    a. *Fantasy Commentator* 5, No. 3 (Fall 1985): 194–204.
    b. In III.28 (as "Introduction"; revised).
    c. In I.43.

241. "On 'The Book.'"
    a. *Cynick* 2, No. 3 (June 1981): 2–7.
    b. *Nyctalops* 3, No. 4 (April 1983): 9–13.
    c. *Crypt of Cthulhu* No. 53 (Candlemas 1988): 3–7.
    d. In I.23.
    e. In I.43.

242. "On 'The Descendant.'"
    a. *Crypt of Cthulhu* No. 53 (Candlemas 1988): 10–11.
    b. In I.23.
    c. In I.43.

243. "On 'The Tree on the Hill.'"
    a. *Crypt of Cthulhu* No. 17 (Hallowmass 1983): 6–9.
    b. In I.43.

244. "An Outline of Trends in Post-Lovecraftian Fantasy."
    a. *Life Is a Hideous Thing* 1, No. 3 (April 1981): 2–5.

245. "The Party of Traitors."
    a. *Free Inquiry* 38, No. 3 (April/May 2018): 14–15.

b.   In I.46.b.

246.   "Passing the Torch: H. P. Lovecraft's Influence on Fritz Leiber."
a.   *Studies in Weird Fiction* No. 24 (Winter 1999): 17–25.
b.   *Fantasy Commentator* 11, Nos. 1 & 2 (Summer 2004): 65–74.
c.   In I.24.
d.   In I.43.

247.   "Poems Not in *The Ancient Track*" (editor).
a.   *Lovecraft Annual* No. 3 (2009): 184–89.

248.   "The Poetry of Donald Wandrei."
a.   *Studies in Weird Fiction* No. 3 (Spring 1988): 9–18, 34.
b.   In II.71 (as "Introduction").
c.   In I.52.

249.   "The Political and Economic Thought of H. P. Lovecraft."
a.   *Miskatonic* 6, No. 4 (February 1979): [20–24].
b.   In I.43.

250.   "Preface."
a.   In Andrew Migliore and John Strysik. *The Lurker at the Lobby: A Guide to the Cinema of H. P. Lovecraft.* Seattle: Armitage House, 2000. viii, x–xi.

251.   "Preface."
a.   In James Arthur Anderson. *Out of the Shadows: A Structuralist Approach to Understanding the Fiction of H. P. Lovecraft.* [San Bernardino, CA:] Borgo Press, 2011. 9–12.

252.   "Preface."
a.   In Ann K. Schwader. *Dark Energies.* Sydney, Australia: P'rea Press, 2015. 15–17.

253.   "Preface to the Illustrated Edition."
a.   In H. P. Lovecraft. *Supernatural Horror in Literature.* Pawtucket, RI: Montilla Publications, 1992. 5–8.

254.   "The Problem of Islamic Extremism."
a.   *American Rationalist* 61, No. 2 (March/April 2015): 7–8.
b.   In I.46.

255.   "Prospectus to the Collected Works of H. P. Lovecraft."
a.   *Lovecraftian Ramblings* No. 13 (31 October 1979): 3–15.

256. "R. H. Barlow and the Recognition of Lovecraft."
  a. *Crypt of Cthulhu* No. 60 (Hallowmass 1988): 45–51, 32.
  b. In I.43.

257. "Ramsey Campbell."
  a. In [Darrell Schweitzer, ed.] *The World Horror Convention, 1997.* [Philadelphia: Owlswick Press, 1997.] 8–10.

258. "Ramsey Campbell: The Fiction of Paranoia."
  a. *Studies in Weird Fiction* No. 17 (Summer 1995): 22–33 (abridged).
  b. In I.18.

259. "Random Memories of Noreascon II."
  a. *Lovecraftian Ramblings* No. 15 (31 October 1980): 22–23.
  b. In [Sam Gafford, ed.] *The Providence Pals: Memories and Miscellany.* Warren, RI: Ulthar Press, 2015. 7–10.

260. "The Rationale of Lovecraft's Pseudonyms."
  a. *Crypt of Cthulhu* No. 80 (Eastertide 1992): 15–24, 29.
  b. In I.23.
  c. In I.43.

261. "The Readings of S. T. Joshi: September 1982ff."
  a. *Life Is a Hideous Thing* 2, No. 3 (January 1983): 2–4.

262. "'Reality' and Knowledge: Some Notes on the Aesthetic Thought of H. P. Lovecraft."
  a. *Lovecraft Studies* 1, No. 3 (Fall 1980): 17–27.
  b. In I.23.
  c. In I.43.

263. "The Recognition of H. P. Lovecraft" (with Marc A. Michaud).
  a. *Lovecraftian Ramblings* No. 8 (5 February 1978): 2–7.

264. "The Recognition of H. P. Lovecraft."
  a. In *NecronomiCon Providence 2013*. Cranston, RI: Lovecraft Arts & Sciences Council Press, 2013. 10–11.

265. "The Recognition of H. P. Lovecraft, 1937–2013."
  a. In I.43.
       Transcript of keynote address at the NecronomiCon convention, 22 August 2013.

266. [Response to "The Defense Reopens!" by Peter Cannon.]
  a. *Lovecraft Studies* No. 24 (Spring 1991): 36.

267.   [Response to Letter by Patrick Miller.]
    a.   *Lovecraft Studies* No. 18 (Spring 1989): 32.

268.   [Response to Letter by Patrick Miller.]
    a.   *Lovecraft Studies* Nos. 19/20 (Fall 1989): 73.

269.   [Response to Letter by Stefan Dziemianowicz.]
    a.   *New Lovecraft Collector* No. 9 (Winter 1995): 4.

270.   [Response to Review of *H. P. Lovecraft: The Decline of the West* by Donald R. Burleson.]
    a.   *Lovecraft Studies* Nos. 22/23 (Fall 1990): 59.

271.   "Richard Gavin: the Nature of Horror."
    a.   *Vastarien* 1, No. 3 (Autumn 2018): 23–42.
    b.   In I.51.

272.   "Robert Aickman: 'So Little Is Definite.'"
    a.   *Million* No. 12 (November–December 1992): 15–22 (as "'So Little Is Definite'").
    b.   *Studies in Weird Fiction* No. 18 (Winter 1996): 22–33.
    c.   In I.18.

273.   "Robert W. Chambers."
    a.   *Crypt of Cthulhu* No. 22 (Roodmas 1984): 26–33, 17.
    b.   In Harold Bloom, ed. *Twentieth-Century American Literature.* New York: Chelsea House, 1986, Vol. 2. 725–26 (excerpt).
    c.   In *Twentieth-Century Literary Criticism,* Volume 41. Detroit: Gale, 1991. 113–15.
    d.   In I.24.

274.   "S. T. Joshi: Forthcoming Volumes."
    a.   *Life Is a Hideous Thing* 1, No. 2 (January 1981): 3–4; 2, No. 2 (July 1982): 8 (update).

275.   "S. T. Joshi: Re-editor" (with Will Murray).
    a.   *Dagon* No. 24 (January–March 1989): 24–29.

276.   "S. T. Joshi and Joshi Criticism: An Annotated Bibliography."
    a.   *Life Is a Hideous Thing* 2, No. 1 (January 1982): 1–5; *What Is Anything?* 1, No. 3 (April 1986): 3–14 (as "Bibliography of S. T. Joshi").

277. "Science and Superstition: Fritz Leiber's Modernization of Gothic."
    a. In Benjamin Szumskyj, ed. *Fritz Leiber: Critical Essays*. Jefferson, NC: McFarland, 2007. 116–30.
    b. In I.47.

278. "Select Bibliography of S. T. Joshi."
    a. *Damned Thing* No. 5 (Yuletide 1993): 58–60 (unsigned).

279. "Shirley Jackson: Domestic Horror."
    a. *Studies in Weird Fiction* No. 14 (Winter 1994): 9–28.
    b. In I.18.

280. "Slumming with Stoker and Others."
    a. *Weird Fiction Review* No. 1 (Fall 2010): 190–201.
        Extract from I.40/41.

281. "Solar Pons Meets Cthulhu: Detective Elements in Derleth's Mythos Tales."
    a. *Crypt of Cthulhu* No. 6 (St John's Eve 1982): 9–12.

282. "Some Notes on Modern Mystery Fiction."
    a. *Lovecraftian Ramblings* No. 16 (31 October 1981): 9–19; No. 17 (2 May 1982): 7–15.

283. "Some Sources for 'The Mound' and *At the Mountains of Madness*."
    a. In I.23.
    b. In I.43.

284. "The Sources for 'From Beyond.'"
    a. *Crypt of Cthulhu* No. 38 (Eastertide 1986): 15–19.
    b. In I.23.
    c. In I.43.

285. "Sources for the Chronology of Lovecraft's Fiction."
    a. *Lovecraft Studies* No. 2 (Spring 1980): 21–29.

286. "Steven J. Mariconda: Scholar Extraordinaire."
    a. In *NecronomiCon Providence 2017 Memento Book*. Cranston, RI: Lovecraft Arts & Science Council Press, 2017. 47–51.

287. "The Structure of Lovecraft's Longer Narratives."
    a. *Cynick* 3, No. 3 (September 1982): 1–16.
    b. *Crypt of Cthulhu* No. 37 (Candlemas 1986): 3–17.
    c. In I.6.
    d. In I.43.

288. "The Stupidity Watch."
    a. *American Rationalist* 57, No. 4 (July/August 2011): 15; 57, No. 5 (September/October 2011): 13–14; 57, No. 6 (November/December 2011): 15; 58, No. 1 (January/February 2012): 15; 58, No. 2 (March/April 2012): 15; 58, No. 3 (May/June 2012): 15; 58, No. 4 (July/August 2012): 15; 58, No. 5 (September/October 2012): 15; 58, No. 6 (November/December 2012): 15; 59, No. 1 (January/February 2013): 15; 59, No. 2 (March/April 2013): 15; 59, No. 3 (May/June 2013): 15; 59, No. 4 (July/August 2013): 15; 59, No. 5 (September/October 2013): 15; 59, No. 6 (November/December 2013): 15; 60, No. 1 (January/February 2014): 15; 60, No. 2 (March/April 2014): 15; 60, No. 3 (May/June 2014): 15; 60, No. 4 (July/August 2014): 15; 60, No. 5 (September/October 2014): 15; 60, No. 6 (November/December 2014): 15; 61, No. 1 (January/February 2015): 15; 61, No. 2 (March/April 2015): 15; 61, No. 3 (May/June 2015): 15; 61, No. 4 (July/August 2015): 15; 61, No. 5 (September/October 2015): 15; 61, No. 6 (November/December 2015): 15; 62, No. 1 (January/February 2016): 15; 62, No. 2 (March/April 2016): 15; 62, No. 3 (May/June 2016): 15; 62, No. 4 (July/August 2016): 15; 62, No. 5 (September/October 2016): 15; 62, No. 6 (November/ December 2016): 15; 63, No. 1 (January/February 2017): 15; 63, No. 2 (March/April 2017): 15; 63, No. 3 (May/June 2017): 15; 63, No. 4 (July/August 2017): 15; 63, No. 5 (September/October 2017): 15.
    b. In I.46.

289. "Surprised by Horror: The Fantasy Short Stories of C. S. Lewis."
    a. *Crypt of Cthulhu* No. 13 (Roodmas 1983): 31–34.
    b. In I.52.

290. "Survey of Four Decades of Ramsey Campbell."
    a. *Extrapolation* 44, No. 4 (Winter 2003): 420–24.

291. "A Style Sheet for Lovecraftian Studies."
    a. *Lovecraft Studies* No. 1 (Fall 1979): 27–29.

292. "Suspense vs. Horror: The Case of Thomas Harris."
    a. In Benjamin Szumskyj, ed. *Dissecting Hannibal Lecter.* Jefferson, NC: McFarland, 2008. 118–32.
        Expansion of my essay on Harris in *The Modern Weird Tale* (I.18).

293. "T. E. D. Klein: Urban Horror."
    a. *Studies in Weird Fiction* No. 10 (Fall 1991): 6–18.
    b. In I.18.

294. "A Talk with S. T. Joshi."
    a.   *Damned Thing* No. 5 (Yuletide 1993): 24–39.

295. "A Textual Commentary on *A Winter Wish*."
    a.   Providence, RI: Privately printed, [1978].
    b.   *Miskatonic* 6, No. 2 (May 1978): [11–21].
    c.   *Crypt of Cthulhu* No. 20 (Eastertide 1984): 31–45 (revised; as "An Errata List to *A Winter Wish*").

296. "Textual Problems in *At the Mountains of Madness*."
    a.   *Crypt of Cthulhu* No. 75 (Michaelmas 1990): 16–21.

297. "Textual Problems in Lovecraft."
    a.   *Lovecraft Studies* No. 6 (Spring 1982): 18–32.
    b.   In Darrell Schweitzer, ed. *Discovering H. P. Lovecraft*. Mercer Island, WA: Starmont House, 1987. 118–38. Rev. ed. Holicong, PA: Wildside Press, 2001. 92–106.
    c.   In I.43.

298. "The Theory and Practice of Satirical Criticism."
    a.   *Dead Reckonings* No. 23 (Spring 2018): 98–102.

299. "Things from the Sea: The Early Weird Fiction of Frank Belknap Long."
    a.   *Studies in Weird Fiction* No. 25 (Summer 2001): 33–39.
    b.   In I.24 (as "Frank Belknap Long: Things from the Sea").

300. "Thomas Ligotti: The Escape from Life."
    a.   *Studies in Weird Fiction* No. 12 (Spring 1993): 30–36.
    b.   In *Short Story Criticism*, Volume 16. Detroit: Gale, 1994. 284–89.
    c.   In I.18.
    d.   In Darrell Schweitzer, ed. *The Thomas Ligotti Reader*. Holicong, PA: Wildside Press, 2003. 135–53.

301. "Thomas Tryon: Rural Horror."
    a.   *Studies in Weird Fiction* No. 11 (Spring 1993): 5–12.
    b.   In I.18.

302. "Time, Space, and Natural Law: Science and Pseudo-Science in Lovecraft."
    a.   *Lovecraft Annual* 4 (2010): 171–201.
    b.   In I.43.

303.   "Title Changes in Lovecraft: Some Bibliographic Oddities."
    a.   *Cynick* 1, No. 4 (December 1977): 24–30.

304.   "Topical References in Lovecraft."
    a.   *Extrapolation* 25, No. 3 (Fall 1984): 247–65.
    b.   In Harold Bloom, ed. *Twentieth-Century American Literature.* New York: Chelsea House, 1986, Vol. 4. 2311–14.
    c.   In I.23.
    d.   In I.43.

305.   "'The Tree' and Ancient History."
    a.   *Nyctalops* 4, No. 1 (April 1991): 68–71.
    b.   In I.23.
    c.   In I.43.

306.   "A Triumvirate of Fantastic Poets: Ambrose Bierce, George Sterling, and Clark Ashton Smith."
    a.   *Extrapolation* 54, No. 2 (Summer 2013): 147–61.
    b.   In I.47.

307.   "Trump and the Religious Right."
    a.   *American Rationalist* 63, No. 1 (January/February 2017): 8, 10.
    b.   In I.46.b.

308.   "Two Spurious Lovecraft Poems."
    a.   *Crypt of Cthulhu* No. 20 (Eastertide 1984): 25–26.
    b.   In I.43.

309.   "Weird Fiction and Ordinary People."
    a.   *Necrofile* No. 6 (Fall 1992): 20–22.

310.   "The Weird Work of F. Marion Crawford."
    a.   *Studies in Weird Fiction* No. 22 (Winter 1998): 20–29.
    b.   In I.24 (as "F. Marion Crawford: Blood-and-Thunder Horror").

311.   "The Weird Work of L. P. Hartley."
    a.   *Niekas* No. 45 (1998): 27–32.
    b.   In I.24 (as "L. P. Hartley: The Refined Ghost").

312.   "What Happens in 'Arthur Jermyn.'"
    a.   *Crypt of Cthulhu* No. 75 (Michaelmas 1990): 27–28.
    b.   In I.23.
    c.   In I.43.

313. "What Happens in Ambrose Bierce's 'The Dead of Halpin Frayser.'"
    a.   *Studies in the Fantastic* No. 2 (Winter 2008/Spring 2009): 94–101.
    b.   In I.47 (as "What Happens in 'The Death of Halpin Frayser'").

314. "What Happens in *The Hashish-Eater?*"
    a.   *Dark Eidolon* No. 3 (Winter 1993): 16–20.
    b.   In Scott Connors, ed. *The Freedom of Fantastic Things: Selected Criticism on Clark Ashton Smith.* New York: Hippocampus Press, 2006. 99–107.
    c.   In I.52.

315. "What Is Anything?"
    a.   *Lovecraftian Ramblings* No. 13 (31 October 1979): 27.

316. "What Is the Cthulhu Mythos?" (panel discussion; with Donald R. Burleson, Will Murray, Robert M. Price, and David E. Schultz).
    a.   *Lovecraft Studies* No. 14 (Spring 1987): 3–30.

317. "What the Anti-Abortionists Want."
    a.   *Free Inquiry* 39, No. 6 (October/November 2019): 9–10.

318. "Who Was the Real Charles Dexter Ward?" (with M. Eileen McNamara).
    a.   *Lovecraft Studies* Nos. 19/20 (Fall 1989): 40–41, 48.

319. "Who Wrote 'The Mound'?"
    a.   *Nyctalops* No. 14 (March 1978): 41–42.
    b.   *Crypt of Cthulhu* No. 11 (Candlemas 1983): 27–29, 38 (revised).
    c.   In I.43.
    d.   In H. P. Lovecraft [and Zealia Bishop]. *The Mound.* (Lovecraft Illustrated, Volume 10.) Hornsea, UK: PS Publishing, 2016. 103–7.

320. "Why Michel Houellebecq Is Wrong about Lovecraft's Racism."
    a.   *Lovecraft Annual* No. 12 (2018): 43–50.

321. "William Peter Blatty: The Catholic Weird Tale."
    a.   *Damned Thing* No. 4 (Winter 1992–93): 2–14.
    b.   In I.18.

322. "The Works of H. P. Lovecraft: A Listing by Magazine."
    a.   *New Lovecraft Collector* No. 14 (Spring 1996): 3–4; No. 15 (Summer 1996): 3–4; No. 16 (Fall 1996): 3–4; No. 17 (Winter 1997): 3–4; No. 18 (Spring 1997): 3–4; No. 19 (Summer 1997): 3–4; No. 20 (Fall 1997): 3–4; No. 21 (Winter 1998): 3–4; No. 22 (Spring 1998): 3–4;

No. 23 (Summer 1998): 3–4; No. 24 (Fall 1998): 3–4; No. 25 (Winter 1999): 3–4; No. 26 (Spring 1999): 3–4.

323.   "The Writing of *Mystery and Horror Writers of the Twentieth Century*."
    a.   In *200 Books by S. T. Joshi* (I.44).

324.   [Untitled.]
    a.   *Lovecraftian Ramblings* No. 10 (31 October 1978): 18; No. 12 (1 August 1979): 1 (unsigned); No. 17 (2 May 1982): 1 (unsigned), 22.

325.   [Untitled.]
    a.   *New Lovecraft Collector* No. 1 (Winter 1993): 1–3 (unsigned); No. 2 (Spring 1993): 1–4 (unsigned); No. 3 (Summer 1993): 1–3 (unsigned); No. 4 (Fall 1993): 1–3 (unsigned); No. 5 (Winter 1994): 1–2 (unsigned); No. 6 (Spring 1994): 1–3 (unsigned); No. 7 (Summer 1994): 1–4 (unsigned); No. 8 (Fall 1994): 1–3 (unsigned); No. 9 (Winter 1995): 1–3 (unsigned); No. 10 (Spring 1995): 1–3 (unsigned); No. 11 (Summer 1995): 1–2 (unsigned); No. 12 (Fall 1995): 1–2 (unsigned); No. 13 (Winter 1996): 1; No. 14 (Spring 1996): 1–2 (unsigned); No. 15 (Summer 1996): 1–2 (unsigned); No. 16 (Fall 1996): 1 (unsigned); No. 17 (Winter 1997): 1–2 (unsigned); No. 18 (Spring 1997): 1–2 (unsigned); No. 19 (Summer 1997): 1–2 (unsigned); No. 20 (Fall 1997): 1–2 (unsigned); No. 21 (Winter 1998): 1–2 (unsigned); No. 22 (Spring 1998): 1–2 (unsigned); No. 23 (Summer 1998): 1–2 (unsigned); No. 24 (Fall 1998): 1–2 (unsigned); No. 25 (Winter 1999): 1–2 (unsigned); No. 26 (Spring 1999): 1–2 (unsigned).

326.   [Untitled.]
    a.   *Extrapolation* 50, No. 1 (Spring 2009): 20–21.
          A brief piece on the recent scholarship on Lovecraft.

B. Reviews

i. Columns

1.   "The Den." *Worlds of Fantasy & Horror*
    a.   No. 2 (Spring 1995): 8–13. Rpt. in I.29 (extracts; as "The Small Press" and "Norman Partridge: Here to Stay").
          [Small-press publications.]
    b.   No. 4 (Winter 1996–97): 7–11. Rpt. in I.24 (as "Poppy Z. Brite: Sex, Horror, and Rock-&-Roll").
          [Poppy Z. Brite.]

2.   "The Den." *Weird Tales*

a.   No. 314 (Fall 1998): 10–13. Rpt. in I.29 (as "Arkham House and Its Legacy").

[Successors to Arkham House.]

b.   No. 316 (Summer 1999): 9–13. Rpt. in I.29 (as "Some Thoughts on Weird Poetry").

[Weird poetry.]

c.   No. 318 (Winter 1999/2000): 11–15. Rpt. in I.29 (extracts; as "Thomas Harris: Lecter as Albatross," "Stephen King and God," and "Ramsey Campbell: Alone with a Master").

[Thomas Harris, *Hannibal*; Stephen King, *The Girl Who Loved Tom Gordon*; Ramsey Campbell, *The Last Voice They Hear*.]

d.   No. 320 (Summer 2000): 11–15. Rpt. in I.29 (as "Arkham House and Its Legacy").

[Recent Arkham House publications.]

e.   No. 322 (Winter 2000/2001): 11–14. In I.29 (extracts; as "Dennis Etchison and His Masters," "Peter Straub and the Blue Pencil," and "Ramsey Campbell: Alone with a Master").

[Ramsey Campbell, *Ghosts and Grisly Things*; Dennis Etchison, *The Death Artist*; Peter Straub, *Magic Terror*; Stefan Dziemianowicz, *Bloody Mary and Other Tales for a Dark Night*.]

f.   No. 324 (Summer 2001): 12–16. Rpt. in I.29 (as "The Cthulhu Mythos").

[Recent Cthulhu Mythos work.]

g.   No. 326 (Winter 2001–02): 15–18. Rpt. In I.29 (extracts; as "Ramsey Campbell: Alone with a Master" and "Norman Partridge: Here to Stay").

[Ramsey Campbell, *Pact of the Fathers*; Norman Partridge, *The Man with the Barbed-Wire Fists*.]

h.   No. 328 (Summer 2002): 12–16. Rpt. in I.29 (extracts; as "Algernon Blackwood: The Starlight Man" and "The Cthulhu Mythos").

[Mike Ashley, *Algernon Blackwood: An Extraordinary Life*; John Pelan and Benjamin Adams (ed.), *The Children of Cthulhu*.]

3.   "The Weird Scholar." *Dead Reckonings*

a. No. 4 (Fall 2008): 86–92.

[The weird work of Washington Irving. Extract from I.40/41.]

b. No. 5 (Spring 2009): 84–89.

[Edgar Allan Poe. Extract from I.40/41.]

c. No. 6 (Fall 2009): 89–94. Rpt. in I.45 (as "The Canon of American Weird Fiction").

[*American Fantastic Tales*, ed. Peter Straub.]

d. No. 8 (Fall 2010): 107–11. Rpt. in I.45 (as "Shirley Jackson as a Classic").

   [Shirley Jackson, *Novels and Stories* (Library of America).]

e. No. 9 (Spring 2011): 78–83.

   [British horror writers in the mid-20th century. Extract from I.40/41.]

f. No. 10 (Fall 2011): 65–70.

   [On bestselling horror of the 1970s and 1980s. Extract from I.40/41.]

g. No. 11 (Spring 2012): 94–99.

   [On Laird Barron and Joe Hill. Extract from I.40/41.]

h. No. 12 (Fall 2012): 86–91.

   [On D. H. Lawrence.]

i. No. 13 (Spring 2013): 56–59.

   [On Lord Dunsany. Extract from introduction to II.102.]

j. No. 14 (Fall 2013): 89–95.

   [On Sax Rohmer. Extract from introduction to II.103.]

k. No. 18 (Fall 2015): 53–61.

   [On Thomas Burke. Introduction to II.143.]

ii. Separate Reviews

1. Achtemeier, Mark. *The Bible's Yes to Same-Sex Marriage: An Evangelical's Change of heart.* Vines, Matthew. *God and the Gay Christian.*
   a.   *American Rationalist* 61, No. 5 (September/October 2015): 11–12.
   b.   In I.46 (as part of "The Bible and Gays").

2. Ashley, Mike. *Algernon Blackwood: A Bio-Bibliography.*
   a.   *Studies in Weird Fiction* No. 4 (Fall 1988): 34.
   b.   In I.29 (as "Algernon Blackwood: The Starlight Man").

3. Austin, Sherry. *Mariah of the Spirits and Other Southern Ghost Stories.*
   a.   *Necropsy* No. 7 (Fall 2002).
   b.   *Studies in Weird Fiction* No. 26 (Summer 2003): 34–35.
   c.   In I.29 (as "Sherry Austin: The Southern Ghost Story").

4. Austin, Sherry. *When the Woodbine Twines.*
   a.   *Dead Reckonings* No. 1 (Spring 2007): 96–97.
   b.   In I.29 (as "Sherry Austin: The Southern Ghost Story").

5. Baker, Jacqueline. *The Broken Hours: A Novel of H. P. Lovecraft.*
   a.   *Dead Reckonings* Nos. 19/20 (Fall 2016): 5–9.
   b.   In I.45 (as "'Life Is More Horrible Than Death'").

6. Barker, David, and W. H. Pugmire. *In the Gulfs of Dream and Other Love-craftian Tales.*
   a. *Dead Reckonings* No. 18 (Fall 2015): 75–79.
   b. In I.45 (as "Working Together").

7. Barker, David, and W. H. Pugmire. *The Revenant of Rebecca Pascal.*
   a. *Dead Reckonings* No. 16 (Fall 2014): 77–80.
   b. In I.45 (as "Working Together").

8. Barrass, Glynn Owen, ed. *In the Court of the Yellow King.* Jesse Bullington, ed. *Letters to Lovecraft.*
   a. *Dead Reckonings* No. 16 (Fall 2014): 57–63.
   b. In I.45 (as "Chambers, Lovecraft, and Pastiche").

9. Barrett, Mike. *Doors to Elsewhere.*
   a. *Dead Reckonings* No. 15 (Spring 2014): 92–93.

10. Barron, Laird. *The Beautiful Thing That Awaits Us All.*
    a. *Former People* (formerpeople.wordpress.com/2013/10/30/a-northwesterly-chill/).
    b. In I.45 (as "Terror in the Northwest").

11. Barron, Neil, ed. *Horror Literature.*
    a. *Necrofile* No. 1 (Summer 1991): 5–6.
    b. In I.29 (as "The Charting of Horror Literature").

12. Bell, Ian, ed. *William Hope Hodgson: Voyages and Visions.*
    a. *Studies in Weird Fiction* No. 2 (Summer 1987): 40–41.
    b. In I.29 (as "William Hope Hodgson: Writer on the Borderland").

13. Benson, E. F. *The Collected Ghost Stories of E. F. Benson.*
    a. *Necrofile* No. 11 (Winter 1994): 17–19.
    b. In Max Duperray, ed. *La Littérature fantastique en Grand Bretagne au tournant du siècle.* Aix-en-Provence: Publications de l'Université de Provence, 1997. 71–77.
    c. In I.24 (as "E. F. Benson: Spooks and More Spooks").
    d. In I.29 (as "E. F. Benson: Spooks and More Spooks").

14. Bierce, Ambrose. *The Devil's Dictionary.*
    a. *Vanguard* 4, No. ? (1975).

15. Blackmore, Leigh. *Spores from Sharnoth and Other Madnesses.*
    a. *Dead Reckonings* No. 4 (Fall 2008): 93.

16. Blackwood, Algernon. *The Magic Mirror.*
    a.   *Studies in Weird Fiction* No. 6 (Fall 1989): 35.
    b.   In I.29 (as "Algernon Blackwood: The Starlight Man").

17. Boston, Robert. *Taking Liberties: Why Religious Freedom Doesn't Give You the Right to Tell Other People What to Do.*
    a.   *American Rationalist* 60, No. 2 (March/April 2014): 9–10.
    b.   In I.46 (as "Religious Freedom or Religious Coercion?").

18. Brock, Jason V. *Milton's Children.*
    a.   *Dead Reckonings* No. 13 (Spring 2013): 102.

19. Broocks, Rice. *God's Not Dead: Evidence for God in an Age of Uncertainty.*
    a.   *American Rationalist* 61, No. 6 (November/December 2015): 9–11.
    b.   In I.46 (as "Atheism, Christianity, and Insanity").

20. Burleson, Donald R. *Arroyo.*
    a.   *Necrofile* No. 31 (Winter 1999): 18–20.
    b.   In I.29 (as "Donald R. Burleson: Enmeshed in the Bizarre").

21. Burleson, Donald R. *Beyond the Lamplight.*
    a.   *Necrofile* No. 24 (Spring 1997): 15, 18.
    b.   In I.29 (as "Donald R. Burleson: Enmeshed in the Bizarre").

22. Burleson, Donald R. *Flute Song.*
    a.   *Necrofile* No. 19 (Winter 1996): 20–21.
    b.   In I.29 (as "Donald R. Burleson: Enmeshed in the Bizarre").

23. Burleson, Donald R. *H. P. Lovecraft: A Critical Study.*
    a.   *Lovecraft Studies* No. 9 (Fall 1984): 77–79.
    b.   In I.29 (as "Some Lovecraft Scholarship").

24. Burleson, Donald R. *Lovecraft: Disturbing the Universe.*
    a.   *Lovecraft Studies* Nos. 22/23 (Fall 1990): 53–56.
    b.   In I.29 (as "Some Lovecraft Scholarship").

25. Burpo, Todd, with Lynn Vincent. *Heaven Is for Real.*
    a.   *American Rationalist* 60, No. 3 (May/June 2014): 11–12.
    b.   In I.46 (as "Satan, Monsters, and Bad People").

26. Burrage, A. M. *Someone in the Room: Strange Tales Old and New.*
    a.   *Necrofile* No. 29 (Summer 1998): 8–9.
    b.   In I.29 (as "A. M. Burrage: The Ghost Man").

27. Cadieux, Keith, and Dustin Geeraert, ed. *The Shadow over Portage &* *Main: Weird Fictions.*
    a.   *Dead Reckonings* Nos. 19/20 (Fall 2016): 66–69.
    b.   In I.45.b (as "Horrors in Winnipeg").

28. Caldecott, Andrew. *Not Exactly Ghosts: Collected Weird Stories.*
    a.   *Necropsy* No. 7 (Fall 2002).
    b.   *Studies in Weird Fiction* No. 26 (Summer 2003): 35–36.
    c.   In I.29 (as "Andrew Caldecott: The Well-Crafted Ghost").

29. Campbell, Ramsey. *Alone with the Horrors.*
    a.   *Necrofile* No. 8 (Spring 1993): 68.
    b.   In I.29 (as "Ramsey Campbell: Alone with a Master").

30. Campbell, Ramsey. *Born to the Dark.*
    a.   *Dead Reckonings* No. 22 (Fall 2017): 7–12.
    b.   In I.45.b (in "Campbell and Lovecraft").

31. Campbell, Ramsey. *By the Light of My Skull* and *The Way of the Worm.*
    a.   *Dead Reckonings* No. 24 (Fall 2018): 6–13.
    b.   In I.45.b (in "Campbell and Lovecraft").

32. Campbell, Ramsey. *Creatures of the Pool* and *Just Behind You.*
    a.   *Dead Reckonings* No. 7 (Spring 2010): 29–34.
    b.   In I.45 (as "Rain, Rain, Everywhere").

33. Campbell, Ramsey. *The Darkest Part of the Woods.*
    a.   *Necropsy* No. 4 (Spring 2003).

34. Campbell, Ramsey. *The Face That Must Die.*
    a.   *Lovecraftian Ramblings* No. 16 (31 October 1981): 28–29.

35. Campbell, Ramsey. *Holes for Faces, The Kind Folk,* and *The Last Revelation of Gla'aki.*
    a.   *Dead Reckonings* No. 14 (Fall 2013): 47–52.
    b.   In I.45 (as "Fifty Years of Ramsey Campbell").

36. Campbell, Ramsey. *The Inhabitant of the Lake and Other Unwelcome Tenants* and *Ghosts Know.*
    a.   *Dead Reckonings* No. 11 (Spring 2012): 40–44.
    b.   In I.45 (extracts; as "Campbell and Lovecraft" and "Fifty Years of Ramsey Campbell").

37. Campbell, Ramsey. *The Long Way.*
    a.   *Dead Reckonings* No. 5 (Spring 2009): 89.

38. Campbell, Ramsey, ed. *New Tales of the Cthulhu Mythos.*
    a.   *Lovecraftian Ramblings* No. 15 (31 October 1980): 27–29.

39. Campbell, Ramsey. *The One Safe Place* and *The House on Nazareth Hill.*
    a.   *Necrofile* No. 23 (Winter 1997): 3–7.
    b.   In I.29 (as "Ramsey Campbell: Alone with a Master").

40. Campbell, Ramsey. *The Overnight.*
    a.   *Necropsy* No. 14 (Summer 2004).
    b.   *Studies in Weird Fiction* No. 27 (Spring 2005): 36, 9, 15, 22.
    c.   In I.29 (as "Ramsey Campbell: Alone with a Master").

41. Campbell, Ramsey. *The Pretence.*
    a.   *Dead Reckonings* No. 15 (Spring 2014): 93.

42. Campbell, Ramsey. *Secret Stories.*
    a.   *Dead Reckonings* No. 1 (Spring 2007): 17–21.
    b.   In I.29 (as "Ramsey Campbell: Alone with a Master").

43. Campbell, Ramsey. *Think Yourself Lucky.*
    a.   *Dead Reckonings* No. 17 (Spring 2015): 28–32.
    b.   In I.45 (as "Terror in a Sentence").

44. Campbell, Ramsey. *Told by the Dead.*
    a.   *Necropsy* No. 11 (Fall 2003).
    b.   In I.29 (in "Ramsey Campbell: Alone with a Master").

45. Campbell, Ramsey. *Visions from Brichester.* Tem, Steve Rasnic. *In the Lovecraft Museum.*
    a.   *Dead Reckonings* No. 18 (Fall 2015): 38–44.
    b.   In I.45.b (extract; in "Campbell and Lovecraft").

46. Cannon, Peter. *The Chronology out of Time.*
    a.   *Lovecraft Studies* No. 14 (Spring 1987): 42–44.
    b.   In I.29 (as "Some Lovecraft Scholarship").

47. Cannon, Peter. *The Early Cannon* (2 vols.).
    a.   *Crypt of Cthulhu* No. 95 (Eastertide 1997): 36, 34.

48. Cannon, Peter. *H. P. Lovecraft.*
    a.   *Lovecraft Studies* No. 18 (Spring 1989): 20–21.
    b.   In I.29 (as "Some Lovecraft Scholarship").

49. Cannon, Peter. *The Lovecraft Chronicles.*
    a. *Necropsy* No. 14 (Summer 2004).
    b. *Lovecraft Annual* No. 1 (2007): 151–55.
    c. In I.29 (as "Lovecraft as a Character in Fiction").

50. Cannon, Peter. *Pulptime.*
    a. *Crypt of Cthulhu* No. 25 (Michaelmas 1984): 48–49.
    b. In I.29 (as "Lovecraft as a Character in Fiction").

51. Cannon, Peter. *Scream for Jeeves: A Parody.* Jones, Stephen, and Dave Carson, ed. *H. P. Lovecraft's Book of Horror.* Price, Robert M., ed. *The Hastur Cycle.* Bloch, Robert. *The Mysteries of the Worm.*
    a. *Lovecraft Studies* No. 30 (Spring 1994): 32–35.
    b. In I.29 (extracts; as "The Cthulhu Mythos" and "Lovecraft as a Character in Fiction").

52. Cardin, Matt, ed. *Born to Fear: Interviews with Thomas Ligotti.* Thomas Ligotti. *The Spectral Link.*
    a. *Dead Reckonings* No. 16 (Fall 2014): 82–87.
    b. In I.45 (as "The Mystery Man of Weird Fiction").

53. Carr, John Dickson. *The Case of the Constant Suicides.*
    a. *Cosmic Meld* No. 1 (1973).

54. Castronovo, Russ. *Necro Citizenship: Death, Eroticism, and the Public Sphere in the Nineteenth-Century United States.*
    a. *American Literary Realism* 35, No. 2 (Winter 2003): 176–77.

55. Christie, Agatha. *Curtain.*
    a. *Vanguard* 5, No. 10 (30 January 1976): 2.

56. Christie, Agatha. *The Murder of Roger Ackroyd.*
    a. *Cosmic Meld* No. 1 (1973).

57. Cisco, Michael. *Secret Hours* and *The Traitor.*
    a. *Dead Reckonings* No. 2 (Fall 2007): 38–42.
    b. In I.29 (as "Michael Cisco: Ligotti Redivivus?").

58. Clark, Kenneth. *Civilisation.*
    a. *Vanguard* 5, No. 3 (3 October 1975): 2.

59. Crawford, Gary William. *Robert Aickman: An Introduction.*
    a. *Necropsy* No. 10 (Summer 2003).

60. Dahl, Roald. *Switch Bitch.*
    a.   *Vanguard* 4, No. ? (1975).

61. Daniels, Keith Allen. *What Rough Book.*
    a.   *Studies in Weird Fiction* No. 11 (Spring 1992): 31.

62. Daniels, Les. *No Blood Spilled.*
    a.   *Studies in Weird Fiction* No. 9 (Spring 1991): 40.
    b.   In I.29 (as "Les Daniels: The Sardonic Vampire").

63. Daniels, Les. *Yellow Fog.*
    a.   *Studies in Weird Fiction* No. 5 (Spring 1989): 33.
    b.   In I.29 (as "Les Daniels: The Sardonic Vampire").

64. Datlow, Ellen, ed. *Children of Lovecraft.*
    a.   *Dead Reckonings* Nos. 19/20 (Fall 2016): 86–90.
    b.   In I.45.b (in "What Makes a Lovecraftian Story?").

65. de Botton, Alain. *Religion for Atheists: A Non-Believers Guide to the Uses of Religion.*
    a.   *American Rationalist* 58, No. 5 (September/October 2012): 8–9.
    b.   In I.46 (as "Yearning for Paradise Lost").

66. Delderfield, R. F. *God Is an Englishman.*
    a.   *Vanguard* 4, No. ? (December? 1974).

67. Derleth, August, ed. *Tales of the Cthulhu Mythos* (rev. ed.).
    a.   *Lovecraft Studies* No. 21 (Spring 1990): 43–44, 42.
    b.   In I.29 (as "The Cthulhu Mythos").

68. Doyle, Sir Arthur Conan. *A Study in Scarlet.*
    a.   *Vanguard* 5, No. 1 (5 September 1975): 2.

69. Dreher, Rod. *The Benedict Option: A Strategy for Christians in a Post-Christian Nation.*
    a.   *American Rationalist* 63, No. 3 (May/June 2017): 11–13.
    b.   In I.46.b (as "Throwing In the Towel").

70. du Maurier, Daphne. "The Birds."
    a.   *Vanguard* 5, No. 7 (5 December 1975): 2.

71. du Maurier, Daphne. *Rebecca.*
    a.   *Vanguard* 4, No. ? (1975).

72. Eller, Jonathan R. *Becoming Ray Bradbury.*
    a.   *Dead Reckonings* No. 10 (Fall 2011): 16–20.
    b.   In I.45 (as "A Biography of the Mind").

73. Eller, Jonathan R. *Ray Bradbury Unbound.*
    a.   *Dead Reckonings* No. 17 (Spring 2015): 12–17.
    b.   In I.45 (as "A Biography of the Mind").

74. Etchison, Dennis, ed. *The Complete Masters of Darkness.*
    a.   *Necrofile* No. 1 (Summer 1991): 16–17.
    b.   In I.29 (as "Dennis Etchison and His Masters").

75. Etchison, Dennis. *Got to Kill Them All.* Garton, Ray. *Silvers of Bone.*
    a.   *Dead Reckonings* No. 3 (Spring 2008): 55–59.
    b.   In I.45 (as "The Sublime and the Ridiculous").

76. Faig, Kenneth W., Jr. *Some of the Descendants of Asaph Phillips and Esther Whipple of Foster, Rhode Island.* Beaman, Charles C., and Casey B. Tyler. *Early Historical Accounts of Foster, Rhode Island.* Rutherford, Brett. *Night Gaunts.* Stanley, Joan C. *Ex Libris Miskatonici.*
    a.   *Lovecraft Studies* No. 29 (Fall 1993): 33–35.
    b.   In I.29 (as "Some Lovecraft Scholarship").

77. Faig, Kenneth W., Jr. *Tales of the Lovecraft Collectors.*
    a.   *Lovecraft Studies* Nos. 19/20 (Fall 1989): 70–71.
    b.   In I.29 (as "Lovecraft as a Character in Fiction").

78. Gafford, Sam, ed. *Carnacki: The New Adventures.*
    a.   *Dead Reckonings* No. 15 (Spring 2014): 13–16.
    b.   In I.45.b (as "Carnacki Lives Again!").

79. Gafford, Sam, and Jason C. Eckhardt. *Some Notes on a Nonentity: The Life of H. P. Lovecraft.*
    a.   *Crypt of Cthulhu* No. 109 (Candlemas 2018): 39–40.
    b.   In I.45.b (as "Lovecraft Alive").

80. Garst, Karen L., ed. *Women Beyond Belief: Discovering Life without Religion.*
    a.   *American Rationalist* 63, No. 2 (March/April 2017): 12–13.
    b.   In I.46.b (as "Atheism and Women").

81. Gavin, Richard. *Sylvan Dread: Tales of Pastoral Darkness.*
    a.   *Dead Reckonings* No. 21 (Spring 2017): 44–47.
    b.   In I.45.b (as "Terrors of the Natural World").

82. Geisler, Norman L., and Daniel J. McCoy. *The Atheist's Fatal Flaw: Exposing Conflicting Beliefs.*
    a.   *American Rationalist* 60, No. 5 (September/October 2014): 11–12, 14.
    b.   In I.46 (as "The Pious Fight Back").

83. George, Robert P. *Conscience and Its Enemies: Confronting the Dogmas of Liberal Secularism.*
    a.   *American Rationalist* 59, No. 6 (November/December 2013): 10–12.
    b.   Unabridged version at: http://www.stjoshi.org/review_george.html.
    c.   In I.46 (as "A 'Christian Intellectual' Speaks").

84. Gorman, Herbert S. *The Place Called Dagon.*
    a.   *Necrofile* No. 14 (Fall 1994): 19–21.
    b.   In I.29 (as "Herbert S. Gorman: Where Is the Place Called Dagon?").

85. Grayling, A. C. *The God Argument.*
    a.   *American Rationalist* 59, No. 4 (July/August 2013): 9–10.
    b.   In I.46 (as "The Caspar Milquetoast Humanist").

86. Gresh, Lois H., ed. *Dark Fusions: Where Monsters Lurk!*
    a.   *Dead Reckonings* No. 14 (Fall 2013): 73–76.
    b.   In I.45 (as "A Smorgasbord of Weird").

87. Grey, Orrin. *Painted Monsters & Other Strange Beasts.*
    a.   *Dead Recknings* No. 19/20 (Spring 2016): 39–41.
    b.   In I.45 (as "Just Like the Movies").

88. Griffin, Michael. *The Lure of Devouring Light.*
    a.   *Dead Reckonings* Nos. 19/20 (Fall 2016): 106–10.
    b.   In I.45.b (as "A Promising Start").

89. Haefele, John D. *A Look Behind the Derleth Mythos.*
    a.   http://www.stjoshi.org/review_haefele.html.
    b.   In I.45 (as "The Derleth Mythos").

90. Haining, Peter, ed. *The Mammoth Book of Haunted House Stories.*
    a.   *Necropsy* No. 3 (Fall 2001).
    b.   In I.29 (as "The Haunted House").

91. Hall, Joan Wylie. *Shirley Jackson: A Study of the Short Fiction.*
    a.   *Necrofile* No. 9 (Summer 1993): 22–23.
    b.   In I.29 (as "Classics and Contemporaries").

92. Herron, Don, ed. *The Barbaric Triumph.*
    a.   *Dark Man* No. 8 (Winter 2004): 27–32.
    b.   In I.29 (as "Classics and Contemporaries").

93. Hite, Kenneth. *Tour de Lovecraft.* Robert M. Price. *Blasphemies & Revelations.*
    a.   *Dead Reckonings* No. 5 (Spring 2009): 55–60.
    b.   In I.45 (as "The Lovecraft Cult").

94. Jackson, Shirley. *Just an Ordinary Day.*
    a.   *Necrofile* No. 25 (Summer 1997): 13–15.
    b.   In I.29 (as "Rescuing Shirley Jackson").

95. Jackson, Shirley. *Novels and Tales.*
    a.   *Dead Reckonings* No. 7 (Spring 2010): 117–18.

96. Jacoby, Susan. *Strange Gods: A Secular History of Conversion.*
    a.   *American Rationalist* 62, No. 3 (May/June 2016): 9–10.
    b.   In I.46 (as "Why People Convert").

97. Jones, Robert P. *The End of White Christian America.*
    a.   *American Rationalist* 62, No. 6 (November/December 2016): 10–11.
    b.   In I.46 (as "A Fitting Burial").

98. Jones, Stephen, ed. *Clive Barker's Shadows in Eden.*
    a.   *Necrofile* No. 2 (Fall 1991): 1–3.
    b.   In I.29 (as "Clive Barker: Weird Fiction as Subversion").

99. Juvenal. *Satires.*
    a.   *Vanguard* 4, No. ? (1975).

100. Kelahan, Michael [i.e., Stefan Dziemianowicz], ed. *The Screaming Skull and Other Classic Horror Stories.* Kelahan, Michael, ed. *The End of the World: Classic Tales of Apocalyptic Science Fiction.* Doyle, Sir Arthur Conan, ed. *The Horror of the Heights and Other Strange Tales.* Irving, Washington. *The Legend of Sleepy Hollow and Other Macabre Tales.* Stoker, Bram. *Dracula's Guest and Other Tales of Horror.* Wilde, Oscar. *The Picture of Dorian Gray and Other Fantastic Tales.*
    a.   *Dead Reckonings* No. 8 (Fall 2010): 57–61.

101. Kendrick, Walter. *The Thrill of Fear.*
    a.   *Washington Post Book World* (27 October 1991): 8–9.
    b.   In I.29 (as "The Charting of Horror Literature").

102.   Kiernan, Caitlín R. *The Ammonite Violin and Others.*
   a.   *Dead Reckonings* No. 9 (Spring 2011): 3–5.
   b.   In I.45 (as "Sculptures in Prose").

103.   Kiernan, Caitlín R. *The Red Tree.*
   a.   *Dead Reckonings* No. 6 (Fall 2009): 55–58.
   b.   In I.45 (as "A Modern 'Heart of Darkness'").

104.   Kiernan, Caitlín R. *Tales of Pain and Wonder.* Rev. ed.
   a.   *Dead Reckonings* No. 4 (Fall 2008): 16–19.
   b.   In I.45 (as "A Slow-Moving Tsunami").

105.   King, Stephen. *Four Past Midnight.* Straub, Peter. *Houses without Doors* (with Sam Gafford).
   a.   *Studies in Weird Fiction* No. 9 (Spring 1991): 34–36.
      I wrote the review of the Straub book; Gafford wrote the review of the King book.

106.   Koblas, Jack. *The Lovecraft Circle and Others as I Remember Them.*
   a.   *Lovecraft Annual* No. 8 (2014): 205–8.
   b.   In I.45 (as "The World of Lovecraft Fandom").

107.   Korn, M. F. *Confessions of a Ghoul and Other Stories.*
   a.   *Necropsy* No. 4 (Winter 2002).

108.   Kruse, Kevin M. *One Nation under God: How Corporate America Invented Christian America.*
   a.   *American Rationalist* 61, No. 4 (July/August 2015): 9–10.
   b.   In I.46 (as "Christianity and Free Enterprise").

109.   Lane, Joel. *This Spectacular Darkness: Critical Essays.*
   a.   *Dead Reckonings* No. 21 (Spring 2017): 16–20.
   b.   In I.45.b (as "Existential and Ontological Horror").

110.   Lansdale, Karen and Joe R., ed. *Dark at Heart.* Chizmar, Richard, ed. *Cold Blood.* Bloch, Robert, ed. *Psycho-Paths.*
   a.   *Necrofile* No. 5 (Summer 1992): 16–18.
   b.   In I.29 (as "What the Hell Is Dark Suspense?").

111.   LaValle, Victor. *The Ballad of Black Tom.*
   a.   *Lovecraft Annual* No. 10 (2016): 224–27.
   b.   In I.45 (as "Conflicted about Lovecraft").

112.   Leithauser, Brad, ed. *The Norton Book of Ghost Stories.*
    a.   *Necrofile* No. 15 (Winter 1995): 8–11.
    b.   In I.29 (as "Professionals and Amateurs").

113.   Lewis, Matthew Gregory. *Tales of Wonder.* Brett Rutherford, ed. *Last Flowers: The Romance and Poetry of Edgar Allan Poe & Sarah Helen Whitman.* Brett Rutherford. *Whippoorwill Road: The Supernatural Poems of Brett Rutherford.*
    a.   *Dead Reckonings* No. 12 (Fall 2012): 16–21.
    b.   In I.45 (as "Weird Poetry, Then and Now").

114.   Ligotti, Thomas. *My Work Is Not Yet Done.*
    a.   *Necropsy* No. 6 (Summer 2002).
    b.   *Studies in Weird Fiction* No. 26 (Summer 2003): 32–34.
    c.   In I.29 (as "Thomas Ligotti: The Long and the Short of It").

115.   Ligotti, Thomas. *Noctuary.*
    a.   *Necrofile* No. 12 (Spring 1994): 11–14.
    b.   In *Short Story Criticism*, Volume 16. Detroit: Gale, 1994. 296–98.
    c.   In I.29 (as "Thomas Ligotti: The Long and the Short of It").

116.   Ligotti, Thomas. *Death Poems.*
    a.   *Dead Reckonings* No. 13 (Spring 2013): 102–3.

117.   Lockhart, Ross E., ed. *The Book of Cthulhu;* Guran, Paula, ed. *New Cthulhu.*
    a.   *Dead Reckonings* No. 11 (Spring 2012): 18–22.
    b.   In I.45 (as "Old and New Cthulhu").

118.   Lockhart, Ross E., ed. *Cthulhu Fhtagn! Weird Tales Inspired by H. P. Lovecraft.*
    a.   *Dead Reckonings* Nos. 19/20 (Fall 2016): 27–33.
    b.   In I.45 (as "Is the Well Running Dry?").

119.   Lovecraft, H. P. *At the Mountains of Madness.*
    a.   *Cosmic Meld* No. 2 (January 1974).

120.   Lovecraft, H. P. *At the Mountains of Madness.*
    a.   *Vanguard* 4, No. ? (1975).

121.   Lovecraft, H. P. Ballantine paperback editions.
    a.   *Lovecraft Studies* No. 6 (Spring 1982): 38–39.
    b.   In I.29 (as "Some Lovecraft Editions").

122. Lovecraft, H. P. *The Best of H. P. Lovecraft.*
    a. *Crypt of Cthulhu* No. 11 (Candlemas 1983): 48–49.
    b. In I.29 (as "Some Lovecraft Editions").

123. Lovecraft, H. P. *The Classic Horror Stories* (ed. Roger Luckhurst).
    a. *Lovecraft Annual* No. 7 (2013): 204–10.
    b. In I.45 (as "How Not to Edit Lovecraft").

124. Lovecraft, H. P. *Collected Poems.*
    a. *Cosmic Meld* No. 2 (January 1974).

125. Lovecraft, H. P. *Crawling Chaos: Selected Works 1920–1935*; Stratman, Thomas M. K., ed. *Cthulhu's Heirs.*
    a. *Lovecraft Studies* No. 31 (Fall 1994): 34–36.
    b. In I.29 (as "Some Lovecraft Editions").

126. Lovecraft, H. P. *The Dream Cycle of H. P. Lovecraft.*
    a. *Necrofile* No. 18 (Fall 1995): 28.
    b. In I.29 (as "Some Lovecraft Editions").

127. Lovecraft, H. P. *The New Annotated Lovecraft* (ed. Leslie S. Klinger).
    a. *Lovecraft Annual* No. 8 (2014): 208–15.
    b. In I.45 (as "How Not to Edit Lovecraft").

128. Lupoff, Richard A. *Lovecraft's Book.*
    a. *Lovecraft Studies* No. 11 (Fall 1985): 75–76.
    b. In I.29 (as "Lovecraft as a Character in Fiction").

129. McGrath, Aleister E. *Mere Apologetics: How to Help Seekers and Skeptics Find Faith.*
    a. *American Rationalist* 58, No. 2 (March/April 2012): 10–11.
    b. In I.46 (as "Circling the Wagons").

130. Machen, Arthur. *Chapters Five and Six of The Secret Glory*; Russell, R. B., ed. *Machenalia* (2 vols.).
    a. *Studies in Weird Fiction* No. 11 (Spring 1992): 34–35.
    b. In I.29 (as "Arthur Machen: A Minor Classic").

131. Machen, Arthur. *Ornaments in Jade; Ritual and Other Stories; Tales of Horror and the Supernatural.*
    a. *Necrofile* No. 27 (Winter 1998): 28.
    b. In I.29 (as "Arthur Machen: A Minor Classic").

132. Machen, Arthur. *Ritual and Other Stories.*
  a. *Necrofile* No. 7 (Winter 1993): 25.

133. Machin, James. *Weird Fiction in Britain 1880–1939*
  a. *Dead Reckonings* No. 25 (Spring 2019): 16–21.

134. Morris, Roy, Jr. *Ambrose Bierce: Alone in Bad Company.*
  a. *Necrofile* No. 20 (Spring 1996): 6–9.
  b. In I.45 (as "The Life and Work of Ambrose Bierce").

135. [Murray, Will.] *The Destroyer #77: Coin of the Realm.*
  a. *Crypt of Cthulhu* No. 70 (Candlemas 1990): 62–63.

136. [Murray, Will.] *The Destroyer #81: Hostile Takeover.*
  a. *Crypt of Cthulhu* No. 75 (Michaelmas 1990): 60–61.

137. Nolan, William F. *Like a Dead Man Walking.*
  a. *Dead Reckonings* No. 15 (Spring 2014): 41–45.
  b. In I.45 (as "Spanning the Genres with William F. Nolan").

138. Nolan, William F. *Soul Trips: Collected Poems.* Brett Rutherford. *Trilobite Love Song: Selected Poems & Revisions.*
  a. *Spectral Realms* No. 5 (Summer 2016): 131–34.

139. Nolan, William F., and Martin H. Greenberg, ed. *The Bradbury Chronicles.*
  a. *Necrofile* No. 4 (Spring 1992): 26.

140. O'Brien, Edward. *Insidious Garden.*
  a. *Lovecraft Studies* No. 17 (Fall 1988): 36.
  b. In I.29 (as "Some Lovecraft Scholarship").

141. Oliver, Reggie. *The Sea of Blood.*
  a. *Dead Reckonings* No. 18 (Fall 2015): 3–6.
  b. In I.45 (as "Of Revenants and Seedy Taverns").

142. Partridge, Norman. *Lesser Demons.*
  a. *Dead Reckonings* No. 7 (Spring 2010): 63–66.
  b. In I.45 (as "Road Dogs and Iron Dead").

143. Preiss, Byron, et al., ed. *The Ultimate Dracula; The Ultimate Frankenstein; The Ultimate Werewolf.*
  a. *Necrofile* No. 3 (Winter 1992): 12–13, 16.
  b. In I.29 (as "Bram and Mary and Bela and Boris").

144. Price, Robert M. *H. P. Lovecraft and the Cthulhu Mythos*; Cannon, Peter. *"Sunset Terrace Imagery in Lovecraft" and Other Essays*; Faig, Kenneth W., Jr. *The Parents of Howard Phillips Lovecraft*.
    a. *Lovecraft Studies* Nos. 22/23 (Fall 1990): 60–63.
    b. In I.29 (as "Some Lovecraft Scholarship").

145. Pugmire, W. H. *The Strange Dark One: Tales of Nyarlathotep; Bohemians of Sesqua Valley; Encounters with Enoch Coffin* (with Jeffrey Thomas).
    a. *Dead Reckonings* No. 13 (Spring 2013): 24–28.
    b. In I.45 (as "A Distinctive Talent").

146. Ringel, Faye. *New England's Gothic Literature*.
    a. *Studies in Weird Fiction* No. 17 (Summer 1995): 35–36.
    b. In I.29 (as "The Charting of Horror Literature").

147. Roberts, Bette B. *Anne Rice*.
    a. *Necrofile* No. 18 (Fall 1995): 21–22.
    b. In I.29 (as "Classics and Contemporaries").

148. Ross, Kevin, ed. *Dead But Dreaming 2*.
    a. *Dead Reckonings* No. 10 (Fall 2011): 43–47.
    b. In I.45 (as "The Return of Cosmic Horror").

149. St Armand, Barton L. *H. P. Lovecraft: New England Decadent*.
    a. *Lovecraft Studies* No. 3 (Fall 1980): 35–38.
    b. In I.29 (as "Some Lovecraft Scholarship").

150. Sammons, Brian M., and Glynn Owen Barrass, ed. *The Children of Gla'aki: A Tribute to Ramsey Campbell's Great Old One*.
    a. *Dead Reckonings* No. 21 (Spring 2017): 103–8.
    b. In I.45.b (as "Pastiches of Pastiches").

151. Samuels, Mark. *The Prozess Manifestations*.
    a. *Dead Reckonings* No. 23 (Spring 2018): 20–23.
    b. In I.45.b (as "Who Is Dr. Prozess?").

152. Scarborough, Joe. *The Right Path*.
    a. *American Rationalist* 60, No. 6 (November/December 2014): 12–13.
    b. In I.46 (as "Republicans: An Endangered Species").

153. Schow, David J. *Black Leather Required*.
    a. *Necrofile* No. 13 (Summer 1994): 10–13.
    b. In I.29 (as "David J. Schow: Zombies, Tapeworms, and Kamikaze Butterflies").

154. Schweitzer, Darrell. *Living with the Dead.*
   a.   *Dead Reckonings* No. 5 (Spring 2009): 91–92.

155. Schweitzer, Darrell. *Pathways to Elfland: The Writings of Lord Dunsany.*
   a.   *Studies in Weird Fiction* No. 6 (Fall 1989): 32–33.
   b.   In I.29 (as "Classics and Contemporaries").

156. Schweitzer, Darrell, and John Ashmead, ed. *Tales from the Miskatonic University Library.*
   a.   *Dead Reckonings* No. 21 (Spring 2017): 25–29.
   b.   In I.45.b (as "The Horror in the Card Catalog").

157. Shershow, Scott Cutler, and Scott Michaelsen. *The Love of Ruins: Letters on Lovecraft.*
   a.   *Lovecraft Annual* No. 12 (2018): 189–97.
   b.   In I.45.b (as "How Not to Read Lovecraft").

158. Sidney-Fryer, Donald. *Songs and Sonnets Atlantean: Third Series;* Alan Gullette, *Acts of Love.*
   a.   *Necropsy* No. 11 (Fall 2003).

159. Silverman, David. *Fighting God: An Atheist Manifesto for a Religious World.*
   a.   *American Rationalist* 62, No. 5 (September/October 2016): 11–12.
   b.   In I.46 (as "In-Your-Face Atheism").

160. Skeel, David. *True Paradox: How Christianity Makes Sense of Our Complex World.*
   a.   *American Rationalist* 61, No. 1 (January/February 2015): 11–12.
   b.   In I.46 (as "Christianity and Complexity").

161. Smith, Clark Ashton [attrib.]. *As It Is Written.*
   a.   *Lovecraft Studies* No. 7 (Fall 1982): 32–34.

162. Smith, Clark Ashton. *The Hashish-Eater and Other Poems* (read by Donald Sidney-Fryer).
   a.   *Lost Worlds* No. 3 (2006): 40–41.

163. Smith, Clark Ashton. *Letters to H. P. Lovecraft.*
   a.   *Lovecraft Studies* No. 15 (Fall 1987): 83–84, 64.

164. Smith, Clark Ashton. *Selected Letters* and *The Red World of Polaris.*
   a.   *Necropsy* No. 12 (Winter 2004).

165. Steele, Justin, and Sam Cowan, ed. *Looming Low, Volume 1.*
   a.   *Dead Reckonings* No. 22 (Fall 2017): 73–79.

   b.   In I.45.b (as "A Mixed Bag").

166.   Stoker, Bram. *Dracula.*
   a.   *Vanguard* 5, No. 2 (19 September 1975): 2.

167.   Strantzas, Simon, ed. *Shadows Edge.* Joseph S. Pulver, Sr., ed. *A Season in Carcosa.*
   a.   *Dead Reckonings* No. 13 (Spring 2013): 66–70.
   b.   In I.45 (as "Driven to Madness with Fright").

168.   Sullivan, Jack. *Elegant Nightmares.*
   a.   *Lovecraft Studies* No. 1 (Fall 1979): 37–40.

169.   Sunquist, Scott W. *The Unexpected Christian Century: The Reversal and Transformation of Global Christianity, 1900–2000.*
   a.   *American Rationalist* 62, No. 1 (January/February 2016): 12, 14.
   b.   In I.46 (as "The Rise and Fall of Christianity").

170.   Szumskyj, Benjamin, ed. *Studies in Australian Weird Fiction,* issues 1 and 2.
   a.   *Dead Reckonings* No. 4 (Fall 2008): 94–95.

171.   Talley, Sharon. *Ambrose Bierce and the Dance of Death.*
   a.   *Dead Reckonings* No. 7 (Spring 2010): 119–20.

172.   Thackeray, William Makepeace. *Vanity Fair.*
   a.   *Vanguard* 4, No. ? (1975).

173.   Tibbetts, John C. *The Gothic Worlds of Peter Straub.*
   a.   *Dead Reckonings* Nos. 19/20 (Fall 2016): 111.

174.   Tierney, Richard L. *Collected Poems.*
   a.   *Crypt of Cthulhu* No. 14 (St John's Eve 1983): 38–40.
   b.   In I.29 (as "Some Thoughts on Weird Poetry").

175.   Toffler, Alvin. *Future Shock.*
   a.   *Vanguard* 5, No. 4 (17 October 1975): 2.

176.   Tryon, Thomas. *Harvest Home.*
   a.   *Cosmic Meld* No. 2 (January 1974).

177.   Tryon, Thomas. *Night Magic.*
   a.   *Necrofile* No. 18 (Fall 1995): 14–15.
   b.   In I.29 (as "Thomas Tryon: The Return of the Posthumous Collaboration").

178.   Tryon, Thomas. *The Other.*
   a.   *Vanguard* 4, No. 3? (September? 1973): 3?

179.   Tymn, Marshall, ed. *Horror Literature.*
   a.   *Lovecraft Studies* No. 5 (Fall 1981): 35–38.
   b.   In I.29 (as "The Charting of Horror Literature").

180.   Ulmer, James. *The Fire Doll: Stories.*
   a.   *Dead Reckonings* No. 23 (Spring 2018): 72–75.
   b.   In I.45.b (as "An Exponent of Quiet Horror").

181.   Valentine, Mark, and Roger Dobson, ed. *Arthur Machen: Apostle of Wonder.*
   a.   *Studies in Weird Fiction* No. 1 (Summer 1986): 37–38.
   b.   In I.29 (as "Arthur Machen: A Minor Classic").

182.   Vidal, Gore. *Julian.*
   a.   *Vanguard* 5, No. 11 (13 February 1976): 6.

183.   Vidal, Gore. *Thieves Fall Out.*
   a.   *Publishers Weekly* 262, No. 6 (9 February 2015): 46.

184.   Voltaire. *Works.*
   a.   *Vanguard* 4, No. ? (1975).

185.   Waldman, Michael. *The Second Amendment: A Biography.*
   a.   *American Rationalist* 60, No. 4 (July/August 2014): 10–11.
   b.   In I.46 (as "Guns, Guns, and More Guns").

186.   Waugh, Evelyn. *The Loved One.*
   a.   *Vanguard* 4, No. ? (1975).

187.   Waugh, Robert H. *The Monster in the Mirror: Looking for H. P. Lovecraft.*
   a.   *Lovecraft Annual* No. 1 (2007): 155–60.
   b.   In I.29 (as "Some Lovecraft Scholarship").

188.   Weinberg, Robert; Dziemianowicz, Stefan R.; and Greenberg, Martin H., ed. *Rivals of Weird Tales.*
   a.   *Crypt of Cthulhu* No. 75 (Michaelmas 1990): 58–60.

189.   Weinberg, Robert, and Martin H. Greenberg, ed. *Lovecraft's Legacy.*
   a.   *Lovecraft Studies* No. 24 (Spring 1991): 31–33.
   b.   In I.29 (as "The Cthulhu Mythos").

190. West, Nathanael. *Works.*
      a. *Vanguard* 5, No. 5 (31 October 1975): 3.

191.   Whitmarsh, Tim. *Battling the Gods: Atheism in the Ancient World.*
      a. *American Rationalist* 62, No. 2 (March/April 2016): 11–12.
      b. In I.46 (as "Atheism in Classical Antiquity").

192. Wilde, Oscar. *The Picture of Dorian Gray.*
      a. *Vanguard* 4, No. ? (1975).

193. Willis, Connie. *Inside Job.*
      a. *Menckeniana* No. 176 (Winter 2005): 14–15.

194. Zuckerman, Phil. *Faith No More: Why People Reject Religion.*
      a. *American Rationalist* 58, No. 1 (January/February 2012): 10–11.
      b. In I.46 (as "What Apostats Have to Say").

C. Fiction

1. "Back from the Dead."
    a. *Forum* 1, No. 9 (March 1975): 12.
    b. *Best of Forum* 1 (1975): 11–12.

2. "Book-World."
    a. *Forum* 2, No. 5 (January 1976): 6–9.

3. "The Daemoniac Ride: A Fantasy."
    a. *Forum* 1, No. 8 (March 1975): 11–12.

4. "'Disposall, Inc.'"
    a. *Forum* 1, No. 2 (December 1974): 12–14.

5. "The Evil Captain James."
    a. *Forum* 1, No. 5 (January 1975): [3–9].

6. "Fact and Fiction."
    a. *Lovecraftian Ramblings* No. 14 (1 May 1980): 11.
    b. In [Sam Gafford, ed.] *The Providence Pals: Memories and Miscellany.* Warren, RI: Ulthar Press, 2015. 13–14.

7. "Incident at Ferney."
    a. In Darrell Schweitzer, ed. *That Is Not Dead.* Hornsea, UK: PS Publishing, 2015. 123–44.
    b. In I.53.

8. "Murder."
    a. *Literary Lapses* 19? (1972–73).
    b. In *200 Books by S. T. Joshi* (I.44).

9. "A Musical Theory."
    a. *Forum* 1, No. 11 (April 1975): 8.
    a. *Issues* [Brown University] 7, No. 5 (March 1977): 41 (revised).

10. "The Narrative of a Murderer."
    a. *Forum* 2, No. 1 (September 1975): 6–9.
    b. *Issues* [Brown University] 7, No. 3 (December 1976): 11–12 (revised; as "I Am a Murderer").

11. "Parables (After Schopenhauer and Bierce)."
    a. *Lovecraftian Ramblings* No. 14 (1 May 1980): 12.
    b. *Twilit Grotto* 1, No. 1 (n.d.): [2–3].

12. "Personals."
    a. In I.53.

13. "Philosophical Tale."
    a. *Forum* 1, No. 7 (February 1975): 14.

14. "The Picture."
    a. *Double Take* (1973).

15. "The Recurring Doom."
    a. *Lovecraftian Ramblings* No. 15 (31 October 1980): 5–18.
    b. *Crypt of Cthulhu* No. 34 (Michaelmas 1985): 3–18.
    c. In Robert M. Price, ed. *Acolytes of Cthulhu*. Minneapolis, MN: Fedogan & Bremer, 2001. 296–315.
    d. In I.53.

16. "Saucers from Yaddith" [with others].
    a. New York: Privately printed, 1983. Part III: pp. 16–21.

17. "Scherzo in D-flat."
    a. *Forum* 2, No. 4 (December 1975): 5–6.
    b. *From the Dark Spaces* 2, No. 2 (May 1976): 1–2.
    c. In [Sam Gafford, ed.] *The Providence Pals: Memories and Miscellany*. Warren, RI: Ulthar Press, 2015. 10–11.

18. "Smith and Jones."
    a. *Forum* 1, No. 6 (February 1975): 13.

19. "Some Kind of Mistake."
    a.   In Lois H. Gresh, ed. *Innsmouth Nightmares*. Hornsea, UK: PS Publishing, 2015. 291–313.
    b.   In I.53.

20. "Suicide in Brooklyn."
    a.   See I.41 above.
    b.   In I.53.

21. "The Touch of Death."
    a.   *Double Take* (1973).

22. "The Wells Manuscript."
    a.   *Forum* 1, No. 11 (April 1975): 11–13.

23. "'You'll Reach There in Time.'"
    a.   *Forum* 1, No. 12 (May 1975): 7–13.
    b.   *Lovecraftian Ramblings* No. 24 (2 February 1987): 6–14.
    c.   In Jason V Brock, ed. *A Darke Phantastique*. Vancouver, WA: Cycatrix Press, 2014. 543–53 (revised).
    d.   In I.53.

D. Poetry

1.   "Autobiography."
    a.   *Forum* 2, No. 2 (October 1975): 7.

2.   "Epilogue" to "Poem: Untitled" [by Emily R. Huston].
    a.   *Forum* 2, No 6 (February 1976): 4.

3.   "Finale: Adagio ma non tanto."
    a.   *Forum* 2, No. 6 (February 1976): 12.
    b.   *Best of Forum* 2 (1976): 13.
    c.   *Life Is a Hideous Thing* 2, No. 1 (January 1982): 6 (with commentary. 6–8).

4.   "Four Poetic Ironies."
    a.   *Forum* 2, No. 3 (November 1975): 11.

5.   "Fragments of Men."
    a.   *Forum* 2, No. 5 (January 1976): 3.

6.   "Julius Caesar; Poe."
    a.   *Forum* 2, No. 3 (November 1975): 5.

7. "Motives for Suicide."
    a. *Forum* 2, No. 7 (March 1976): 10.
    b. *Best of Forum* 2 (1976): 5.

8. "The Nothing Verses."
    a. *Forum* 1, No. 4 (January 1975): 10–11.
    b. *Best of Forum* 1 (1975): 7.

9. "Poem I."
    a. *Forum* 1, No. 3 (December 1974): 22 (without title).

10. "Poem VII."
    a. *Forum* 1, No. 6 (February 1975): 8.
    b. *Best of Forum* 1 (1975): 17.
            Untitled in both printings.

11. "Poem VIII."
    a. *Forum* 2, No. 2 (October 1975): [6]-7.

12. "Poem X."
    a. *Forum* 1, No. 10 (April 1975): 13 (without title).

13. "Poem XII."
    a. *Forum* 1, No. 7 (February 1975): 12 (without title).

14. "Poem XIV: Poetic Conversation III."
    a. *Forum* 2, No. 8 (April 1976): 16 (as "Poetic Conversation III").

15. "Poem XXII: Poetic Conversation VI."
    a. *Forum* 1, No. 9 (March 1975): 10 (without title).

16. "Poem XXIV."
    a. *Forum* 2, No. 5 (January 1976): 4 (without title).

17. "Poem XLIX: Poetic Conversation XVIII."
    a. *Forum* 2, No. 1 (September 1975): 5 (as "Poetic Conversation XVIII").

18. "Poem LVII."
    a. *Forum* 2, No. 2 (October 1975): 8.

19. "The Production of Decadence."
    a. *Forum* 2, No. 4 (December 1975): 10.

20. "Symphony in Seven Sharps."
    a.   *Forum* 2, No. 8 (April 1976): 7–8.

21. "Time and Men."
    a.   *Forum* 1, No. 10 (April 1975): 10-12.

22. "To H. P. Lovecraft."
    a.   *Outré* 2, No. 3 (November 1977): 20.
    b.   In [Sam Gafford, ed.] *The Providence Pals: Memories and Miscellany.* Warren, RI: Ulthar Press, 2015, p. 12.

23. "Two Poems."
    a.   *Forum* 2, No. 6 (February 1976): 8.
             Contains "A Dismal Paradox" and Poem LXV.

E. Published Letters

1.   [Letter of Response.]
     a.   *Cimmerian* 2, No. 2 (April 2005): 32.

2.   To the Editor of *Crypt of Cthulhu.*
     a.   *Crypt of Cthulhu* No. 5 (Roodmas 1982): 41–42

3.   To the Editor of *Crypt of Cthulhu.*
     a.   *Crypt of Cthulhu* No. 13 (Roodmas 1983): 41–42.

4.   To the Editor of *Crypt of Cthulhu.*
     a.   *Crypt of Cthulhu* No. 14 (St John's Eve 1983): 44–47.

5.   To the Editor of *Crypt of Cthulhu.*
     a.   *Crypt of Cthulhu* No. 22 (Roodmas 1984): 57.

6.   To the Editor of *Crypt of Cthulhu.*
     a.   *Crypt of Cthulhu* No. 25 (Michaelmas 1984): 54.

7.   To the Editor of *Crypt of Cthulhu.*
     a.   *Crypt of Cthulhu* No. 26 (Hallowmass 1984): 51–52, 23.

8.   To the Editor of *Crypt of Cthulhu.*
     a.   *Crypt of Cthulhu* No. 34 (Michaelmas 1985): 61.

9.   To the Editor of *Crypt of Cthulhu.*
     a.   *Crypt of Cthulhu* No. 40 (St John's Eve 1986): 60.

10. To the Editor of *Crypt of Cthulhu*.
    a. *Crypt of Cthulhu* No. 42 (Michaelmas 1986): 67.

11. To the Editor of *Crypt of Cthulhu*.
    a. *Crypt of Cthulhu* No. 48 (St John's Eve 1987): 48–49.

12. To the Editor of *Crypt of Cthulhu*.
    a. *Crypt of Cthulhu* No. 56 (Roodmas 1988): 46.

13. To the Editor of *Crypt of Cthulhu*.
    a. *Crypt of Cthulhu* No. 76 (Hallowmass 1990): 18, 35.

14. To the Editor of *Crypt of Cthulhu*.
    a. *Crypt of Cthulhu* No. 88 (Hallowmass 1994): 53.

15. To the Editor of *Interzone*.
    a. *Interzone* No. 77 (November 1993): 4.

16. To the Editor of *Lovecraftian Ramblings*.
    a. *Lovecraftian Ramblings* No. 11 (5 February 1977): 17–18 (as "A Letter from S. T. Joshi").

17. To the Editor of *Lovecraftian Ramblings*.
    a. *Lovecraftian Ramblings* No. 12 (1 August 1979): 17–18 (as "Still Another Letter from S. T. Joshi").

18. To the Editor of the *Musical Heritage Review*.
    a. *Musical Heritage Review* [date unknown].

19. To the Editors of *Necrofile*.
    a. *Necrofile* No. 23 (Winter 1997): 26–27.

20. To the Editor of the *New York Review of Books*.
    a. *New York Review of Books* 62, No. 3 (19 February 2015): 41–42.

21. To the Editor of the *New York Times* (sports section).
    a. *New York Times* (13 September 1987).

22. To the Editor of the *New York Times* (Op-Ed page).
    a. *New York Times* (6 November 1990).

23. To the Editor of the *New York Times* (Op-Ed page).
    a. *New York Times* (19 November 2015).

24. To the Editor of the *New York Times Book Review*.
    a.   *New York Times Book Review* (24 November 1985).

25. To the Editor of the *New York Times Book Review*.
    a.   *New York Times Book Review* (8 May 1994).

26. To the Editor of *Outré*.
    a.   *Outré* 1, No. 3 (October 1976): [38].

27. To the Editor of *Outré*.
    a.   *Outré* 1, No. 4 (February 1977): 43.

28. To the Editor of *Science-Fiction Studies*.
    a.   *Science-Fiction Studies* 7, No. 1 (March 1980): 111–12 (as "In Defense of Lovecraft").

29. To the Editor of *Science-Fiction Studies*.
    a.   *Science-Fiction Studies* 19, No. 3 (November 1992): 437–39.

30. To the Editor of *Spectral Tales*.
    a.   *Spectral Tales* No. 2 (December 1989): 62, 58.

31. To the Editor of *Weird Tales*.
    a.   *Weird Tales* No. 323 (Spring 2001): 10–11.

32. To the Editor of *Weird Tales*.
    a.   *Weird Tales* No. 326 (Winter 2001–02): 14.

F. Translations

1. Bergier, Jacques. "Lovecraft: Genius, Outsider."
   a.   *Cynick* 1, No. 4 (December 1977): 4–8.
   b.   *Lovecraftian Ramblings* No. 11 (5 February 1979): 9–13.

2. Catullus. Poem 63.
   a.   *Life Is a Hideous Thing* 2, No. 2 (July 1982): 2–4.
   b.   *Crypt of Cthulhu* No. 72 (Roodmas 1990): 6–8 (as "Attis and Cybele: A Translation of Catullus 63").

3. Euripides. *Medea* 1118f.
   a.   *Life Is a Hideous Thing* 1, No. 2 (January 1981): 5–8.

4. Juvenal. Satire XV.
   a.   *Life Is a Hideous Thing* 1, No. 4 (July 1981): 2–7.

5. Lévy, Maurice. *Lovecraft.*
   a. *Cynick* 1, No. 1 (April 1977): 20-23; 3, No. 3[i.e. 4] (December 1982): 2-?; [etc.].

6. Marigny, Jean. "Clark Ashton Smith and His World of Fantasy."
   a. *Crypt of Cthulhu* No. 26 (Hallowmass 1984): 3-8.

7. Menegaldo, Gilles. "The City in H. P. Lovecraft's Work."
   a. *Lovecraft Studies* No. 4 (Spring 1981): 10-19.

8. Meurger, Michel. "'Retrograde Anticipation': Primitivism and Occultism in the French Response to Lovecraft 1953-1957."
   a. *Lovecraft Studies* Nos. 19/20 (Fall 1989): 5-19.

9. Zachrau, Thekla. "The 'Cthulhu Mythos': Between Horror and Science Fiction" (with Leslie G. Boba).
   a. *Lovecraft Studies* Nos. 19/20 (Fall 1989): 56-62.

VII. Journals Edited

1. *Double Take* (with others). (Burris Laboratory School, Muncie, IN.) [No. 1] (1972).

2. *The Cosmic Meld* (with others). (Burris Laboratory School, Muncie, IN.) No. 1 (1973); No. 2 (January 1974).

3. *The Forum* (with Joe Lauck and Jeff Turner). (Burris Laboratory School, Muncie, IN.)
   1, No. 1 (November 1974); 1, No. 2 (December 1974); 1, No. 3 (December 1974); 1, No. 4 (January 1975); 1, No. 5 (January 1975); 1, No. 6 (February 1975); 1, No. 7 (February 1975); 1, No. 8 (March 1975); 1, No. 9 (March 1975); 1, No. 10 (April 1975); 1, No. 11 (April 1975); 1, No. 12 (May 1975); 2, No. 1 (September 1975); 2, No. 2 (October 1975); 2, No. 3 (November 1975); 2, No. 4 (December 1975); 2, No. 5 (January 1976); 2, No. 6 (February 1976); 2, No. 7 (March 1976); 2, No. 8 (April 1976).

4. *The Best of Forum* (with Joe Lauck and Jeff Turner). (Burris Laboratory School, Muncie, IN.)
   No. 1 (1975); No. 2 (1976).

5. *The Cynick* (Necronomicon apa).
   1, No. 1 (March 1977); 1, No. 2 (June 1977); 1, No. 3 (September 1977); 1, No. 4 (December 1977); 2, No. 1 (?); 2, No. 2 (February

1981); 2, No. 3 (June 1981); 2, No. 4 (September 1981); 3, No. 1 (February 1982); 3, No. 2 (April 1982); 3, No. 3 (September 1982); 3, No. 4 (December 1982); 4, No. 1 (n.d.); 4, No. 2 (n.d.).

6. *Lovecraft Studies* (Necronomicon Press).
    No. 1 (Fall 1979); No. 2 (Spring 1980); No. 3 (Fall 1980); No. 4 (Spring 1981); No. 5 (Fall 1981); No. 6 (Spring 1982); No. 7 (Fall 1982); No. 8 (Spring 1984); No. 9 (Fall 1984); No. 10 (Spring 1985); No. 11 (Fall 1985); No. 12 (Spring 1986); No. 13 (Fall 1986); No. 14 (Spring 1987); No. 15 (Fall 1987); No. 16 (Spring 1988); No. 17 (Fall 1988); No. 18 (Spring 1989); Nos. 19/20 (Fall 1989); No. 21 (Spring 1990); Nos. 22/23 (Fall 1990); No. 24 (Spring 1991); No. 25 (Fall 1991); No. 26 (Spring 1992); No. 27 (Fall 1992); No. 28 (Spring 1993); No. 29 (Fall 1993); No. 30 (Spring 1994); No. 31 (Fall 1994); No. 32 (Spring 1995); No. 33 (Fall 1995); No. 34 (Spring 1996); No. 35 (Fall 1996); No. 36 (Spring 1997); No. 37 (Fall 1997); No. 38 (Spring 1998); No. 39 (Summer 1998); No. 40 (Fall 1998); No. 41 (Spring 1999); Nos. 42–43 (Fall 2001 [issued by Hippocampus Press]); No. 44 (2004); No. 45 (Spring 2005).

7. *Life Is a Hideous Thing* (Esoteric Order of Dagon apa).
    1, No. 1 (September 1980); 1, No. 2 (January 1981); 1, No. 3 (April 1981); 1, No. 4 (July 1981); 2, No. 1 (January 1982); 2, No. 2 (July 1982); 2, No. 3 (January 1983); 2, No. 4 (April 1983); 3, No. 1 (September 1983).

8. *What Is Anything?* (Esoteric Order of Dagon apa).
    1, No. 1 (October 1985); 1, No. 2 (January 1986); 1, No. 3 (April 1986); [etc.]

9. *Studies in Weird Fiction* (Necronomicon Press).
    No. 1 (Summer 1986); No. 2 (Summer 1987); No. 3 (Spring 1988); No. 4 (Fall 1988); No. 5 (Spring 1989); No. 6 (Fall 1989); No. 7 (Spring 1990); No. 8 (Fall 1990); No. 9 (Spring 1991); No. 10 (Fall 1991); No. 11 (Spring 1992); No. 12 (Spring 1993); No. 13 (Summer 1993); No. 14 (Winter 1994); No. 15 (Summer 1994); No. 16 (Winter 1995); No. 17 (Summer 1995); No. 18 (Winter 1996); No. 19 (Summer 1996); No. 20 (Winter 1997); No. 21 (Summer 1997); No. 22 (Winter 1998); No. 23 (Summer 1998); No. 24 (Winter 1999); No. 25 (Summer 2001); No. 26 (Summer 2003); No. 27 (Spring 2005).

Notes: *Studies in Weird Fiction* 25 was issued by Hippocampus Press. Awkwardly, Necronomicon Press itself issued its own No. 25 (i.e., Summer 2003), followed by the final issue, No. 27 (Spring 2005). There never was an actual "No. 26."

10. *Necrofile: The Review of Horror Fiction* (with Stefan Dziemianowicz and Michael A. Morrison) (Necronomicon Press).
     No. 1 (Summer 1991); No. 2 (Fall 1991); No. 3 (Winter 1992); No. 4 (Spring 1992); No. 5 (Summer 1992); No. 6 (Fall 1992); No. 7 (Winter 1993); No. 8 (Spring 1993); No. 9 (Summer 1993); No. 10 (Fall 1993); No. 11 (Winter 1994); No. 12 (Spring 1994); No. 13 (Summer 1994); No. 14 (Fall 1994); No. 15 (Winter 1995); No. 16 (Spring 1995); No. 17 (Summer 1995); No. 18 (Fall 1995); No. 19 (Winter 1996); No. 20 (Spring 1996); No. 21 (Summer 1996); No. 22 (Fall 1996); No. 23 (Winter 1997); No. 24 (Spring 1997); No. 25 (Summer 1997); No. 26 (Fall 1997); No. 27 (Winter 1998); No. 28 (Spring 1998); No. 29 (Summer 1998); No. 30 (Fall 1998); No. 31 (Winter 1999); No. 32 (Spring 1999).

11. *The New Lovecraft Collector* (Necronomicon Press).
     No. 1 (Winter 1993); No. 2 (Spring 1993); No. 3 (Summer 1993); No. 4 (Fall 1993); No. 5 (Winter 1994); No. 6 (Spring 1994); No. 7 (Summer 1994); No. 8 (Fall 1994); No. 9 (Winter 1995); No. 10 (Spring 1995); No. 11 (Summer 1995); No. 12 (Fall 1995); No. 13 (Winter 1996); No. 14 (Spring 1996); No. 15 (Summer 1996); No. 16 (Fall 1996); No. 17 (Winter 1997); No. 18 (Spring 1997); No. 19 (Summer 1997); No. 20 (Fall 1997); No. 21 (Winter 1998); No. 22 (Spring 1998); No. 23 (Summer 1998); No. 24 (Fall 1998); No. 25 (Winter 1999); No. 26 (Spring 1999).

12. *Dead Reckonings* (Hippocampus Press).
     No. 1 (Spring 2007); No. 2 (Fall 2007); No. 3 (Spring 2008); No. 4 (Fall 2008); No. 5 (Spring 2009); No. 6 (Fall 2009); No. 7 (Spring 2010); No. 8 (Fall 2010); No. 9 (Spring 2011); No. 10 (Fall 2011).

13. *The Lovecraft Annual* (Hippocampus Press).
     No. 1 (2007); No. 2 (2008); No. 3 (2009); No. 4 (2010); No. 5 (2011); No. 6 (2012); No. 7 (2013); No. 8 (2014); No. 9 (2015); No. 10 (2016); No. 11 (2017); No. 12 (2018); No. 13 (2019).

14. *Studies in the Fantastic* (University of Tampa Press).
     No. 1 (Summer 2008); No. 2 (Winter 2008/Spring 2009).

15.	*Weird Fiction Review* (Centipede Press).
No. 1 (2010); No. 2 (2011); No. 3 (2012); No. 4 (2013); No. 5 (2014); No. 6 (2015); No. 7 (2016); No. 8 (2017); No. 9 (2018).

16.	*The American Rationalist* (Center for Inquiry).
57, No. 4 (July/August 2011); 57, No. 5 (September/October 2011); 57, No. 6 (November/December 2011); 58, No. 1 (January/February 2012); 58, No. 2 (March/April 2012); 58, No. 3 (May/June 2012); 58, No. 4 (July/August 2012); 58, No. 5 (September/October 2012); 58, No. 6 (November/December 2012); 59, No. 1 (January/February 2013); 59, No. 2 (March/April 2013); 59, No. 3 (May/June 2013); 59, No. 4 (July/August 2013); 59, No. 5 (September/October 2013); 59, No. 6 (November/December 2013); 60, No. 1 (January/February 2014); 60, No. 2 (March/April 2014); 60, No. 3 (May/June 2014); 60. No. 4 (July/August 2014); 60, No. 4 (July/August 2014); 60, No. 5 (September/October 2014); 60, No. 6 (November/December 2014); 61, No. 1 (January/February 2015); 61, No. 2 (March/April 2015); 61, No. 3 (May/June 2015); 61, No. 4 (July/August 2015); 61, No. 5 (September/October 2015); 61, No. 6 (November/December 2015); 62, No. 1 (January/February 2016); 62, No. 2 (March/April 2016): 15; 62, No. 3 (May/June 2016); 62, No. 4 (July/August 2016); 62, No. 5 (September/October 2016); 62, No. 6 (November/December 2016); 63, No. 1 (January/February 2017); 63, No. 2 (March/April 2017); 63, No. 3 (May/June 2017); 63, No. 4 (July/August 2017); 63, No. 5 (September/October 2017).

17.	*Nameless* (Cycatrix Press).
1, No. 1 (Spring/Summer 2012); 1, No. 2 (Fall/Winter 2012); 2, No. 1 (Spring/Summer 2013).
I was managing editor; Jason V Brock was editor-in-chief.

18.	*Sargasso: The Journal of William Hope Hodgson Studies* (Ulthar Press).
1, No. 1 (2013); 1, No. 2 (2014); 1, No. 3 (2016).
I was co-editor; Sam Gafford was editor-in-chief. My name does not appear in the third issue.

19.	*Spectral Realms* (Hippocampus Press).
No. 1 (Summer 2014); No. 2 (Winter 2015); No. 3 (Summer 2015); No. 4 (Winter 2016); No. 5 (Summer 2016); No. 6 (Winter 2017); No. 7 (Summer 2017); No. 8 (Winter 2018); No. 9 (Summer 2018); No. 10 (Winter 2019); No. 11 (Summer 2019).

VIII. Translations of Works by S. T. Joshi

A. Books

1.   H. P. Lovecraft. *Lettres d'Innsmouth.*
      a.   Amiens: Encrage, 1989. Tr. Joseph Altairac.
           Notes. Translation of *In Defence of Dagon* (III.8) and *Uncollected Letters* (III.12).

2.   *Clefs pour Lovecraft.*
      a.   Amiens: Encrage, 1990. Tr. Joseph Altairac.
           Notes. Translation of *H. P. Lovecraft* (I.4).

3.   *Moderne Horrorautoren.*
      a.   Almersbach: Festa Verlag, 2001. 2 vols. Tr. Andreas Diesel, Frank Festa, Erik Hauser, Michael Plogmann and Michael Siefener.
           Notes. Translation of *The Modern Weird Tale* (I.18) with the extra chapters that had been dropped in the McFarland edition.

4.   *H. P. Lovecraft: Biografia.*
      a.   Poznań, Poland: Zysk I S-ka, 2010. Tr. Mateusz Kopacz.
           Notes. Translation of *H. P. Lovecraft: A Life* (I.14).

5.   H. P. Lovecraft. *Das übernaturaliche Grauen in der Literatur.*
      a.   Berlin: Golkonda Verlag, 2014. Tr. Alexander Pechmann.
           Translation of *The Annotated Supernatural Horror in Literature* (III.28).

6.   *Černá křídla Cthulhu.*
      a.   Plzeň, Czech Republic: Laser, 2014. Tr. Milan Žáček.
           Translation of *Black Wings I* (II.82).

7.   *Alas tenebrosas.*
      a.   Madrid: Valdemar, 2014. Tr. Marta Lila Murillo.
           Translation of *Black Wings I* (II.82).

8.   *Černá křídla Cthulhu 2.*
      a.   Plzeň, Czech Republic: Laser, 2015. Tr. Milan Žáček.
           Translation of *Black Wings II* (II.96).

9.   H. P. Lovecraft. *Der Fall Charles Dexter Ward.*
      a.   Munich: Golkonda Verlag, 2016. Tr. Andreas Fliedner.
           Translation of *The Case of Charles Dexter Ward* (III.50).

10.   *Černá křídla Cthulhu 3.*
       a.   Plzeň, Czech Republic: Laser, 2017. Tr. Milan Žáček.
             Translation of *Black Wings III* (II.110).

11.   *Chroniques de Cthulhu.*
       a.   Paris: Bragelonne, 2017. Tr. Arnaud Demaegd.
             Translation of *Black Wings I* (II.82).

12.   *H. P. Lovecraft: Leben und Werk.*
       a.   Munich: Golkonda Verlag, 2017-__. Tr. Andreas Fliedner. 2
             vols.
             Translation of *I Am Providence* (I.34/35).

13.   H. P. Lovecraft. *Contro la religione.*
       a.   [Rome]: Nessun Dogma, [May] 2018. Tr. Guido Negretti.
             Translation of *Against Religion* (III.49).

14.   R. H. Barlow. *La noche del océano y otros cuentos.*
       a.   Madrid: Distinta Tinta Ediciones, 2018.
             Translation of *Eyes of the God* (II.41). Introduction and bibliog-
             raphy omitted.

15.   *Je suis Providence: Vie et oeuvre de H. P. Lovecraft.*
       a.   Chambéry, France: Éditions ActuSF, March 2019. Ed. Chris-
             tophe Thill. Tr. Thomas Bauduret et al. 2 vols.
             Translation of *I Am Providence* (I.34/35).

16.   *Io sono Providence: La vita e I tempi di H. P. Lovecraft.*
       a.   n.p.: Providence Press, October 2019. Ed. Giacomo Ortolani. Tr.
             Elena Cervi, Lara Baldini, and Gianfranco Calvitti. Bibliography
             ed. Pietro Guarriello.
             The first of a three-volume translation of *I Am Providence* (I.34/35).

B. Contributions to Books and Periodicals

1.   "Een studie: Lovecraft-kritiek."
      a. *Rigel Magazine* No. 59 (November 1977): 9–16.
             Translation of "Lovecraft Criticism: A Study."

2.   "H. P. Lovecraft."
      a.   In H. P. Lovecraft. *Il libro dei gatti.* Ed. Gianfranco de Turris and
            Claudio De Nardi, with Pietro Guarriello. n.p.: Il Cerchio, 1996,
            2012. 23–26.

3.   "Introdução."
      a.   In H. P. Lovecraft. *Contos reunidos*. Ed. Bruno Costa. Sao Paolo: Editora Ex Machina, 2017. 9–14.

4.   "Postface."
      a.   In Clark Ashton Smith. *Clark Ashton Smith Intégrale, Volume 1: Mondes derniers*. Paris: Mnémos, 2017. 448–57.

5.   "Postface."
      a.   In Clark Ashton Smith. *Clark Ashton Smith Intégrale, Volume 2: Mondes premiers*. Paris: Mnémos, 2017. 240–49.

6.   "Postface."
      a.   In Clark Ashton Smith. *Clark Ashton Smith Intégrale, Volume 3: Autres mondes*. Paris: Mnémos, 2017. 202–10.
            The above three afterwords were written specifically for these editions. They appear as part of "Clark Ashton Smith: Poet of the Stars" in I.52.

7.   "Jeff VanderMeer: Una catástrofe estética."
      a.   *Ulthar* 2, No. 4 (April 2018): 84–101 (tr. Ana Colchero).
            Translation of "Jeff VanderMeer: An Aesthetic Catastrophe," a chapter in *21st-Century Horror* (I.51).

IX. Work in Media

A. Recordings

1.   Clark Ashton Smith. *Inferno*.
      a.   Syracuse, NY: Cadabra Records, 2016. 45 rpm.
            Contents: "Inferno"; "The Eldritch Dark"; "Nyctalops"; "Nightmare"; "To Howard Phillips Lovecraft."
            Notes. Limited to 100 copies.

2.   Clark Ashton Smith. *The Muse of Hyperborea*.
      a.   Syracuse, NY: Cadabra Records, 2016. LP.
            Contents: "The Harlot of the World"; "Nyctalops"; "Ode to thre Abyss"; "A Dream of Lethe"; "The Tears of Lilith"; "Nero"; "From the Crypts of Memory"; "The Sorcerer Departs"; "The Touch-stone"; "The Litany of the Seven Kisses"; "To the Daemon"; "The Nightmare Tarn"; "Memnon at Midnight"; "The Muse of Hyperborea"; "The Memnons of the Night"; "The Mortuary"; "The Traveller"; "Love Malevolent."
            Notes. Sound by Theologian. Art by C. M. Koseman.

3. *Selections from H. P. Lovecraft: A Short Biography*
    a. Syracuse, NY: Cadabra Records, [July] 2019. LP.
        Notes. Read by S. T. Joshi. Score by Chris Bozzone. Art by Dave Felton.

B. Appearances in Documentaries

1. *The Eldritch Influence: The Life, Vision, and Phenomenon of H. P. Lovecraft.* Directed by Shawn Owens. Hermetic Productions, 2003.

2. *Lovecraft: Fear of the Unknown.* Directed by Frank H. Woodward. 2008.

3. *Charles Beaumont: The Short Life of Twilight Zone's Magic Man.* Directed by Jason V Brock. JaSunni Productions, 2010.

4. *The AckerMonster Chronicles!* Directed by Jason V Brock. JaSunni Productions, 2012.

5. *Shooting for the Butler.* Directed by Digby Rumsey. 2014.
        A documentary on Lord Dunsany.

6. *The Life and Various Deaths of Ambrose Bierce.* Directed by Kirk Whitham. 2016.

7. *Lovecraftia: Crafting Lovecraft.* Directed by Gordon Clatworthy. Weird Howard Films, 2017.

8. *Clark Ashton Smith: The Emperor of Dreams.* Directed by Darin Coelho Spring. 2018.

9. *Memory: The Origins of* Alien. Directed by Alexandre O. Philippe. Exhibit A Pictures, 2019.

C. Musical Compositions

1. "Sunset."
    a. *Lovecraft Annual* No. 13 (2019): 102–10 (with introductory note; as "H. P. Lovecraft's 'Sunset'").
    b. In *A Very Choral Springtime 2019.* CD. [Seattle: RealTime Pip, 2019.]
        World premiere: Northwest Chorale, 11 May 2019, at the First Free Methodist Church (Seattle, WA). Available on YouTube www.youtube.com/watch?v=Hy8sLLmj9RA; recorded by Greg Lowney).

Appendix

Murder

by S. T. Joshi

The following are my thoughts from this moment until my death.

She was dead. My wife had fallen down the stairs, which I had neatly broken off, and then she had broken her neck. That makes it murder, doesn't it? I guess so. Well, Elanor deserved it!

The police had come and gone faster than I expected. I, acting as the grieved husband, pretending to be in shock while inside I was laughing at my cleverness. The police asked relatively few questions. It seemed like they didn't care.

So I was alone. No one to bug me anymore. I could do anything I want when I want. No nagging, no pressure, no worries.

The only time I was ever worried was one question the police asked. They said, "Now, Mr. Feldman, how come that stair was broken?"

I replied, "Well, Inspector, I had meant to get that fixed, but I never got around to it." And those idiots believed me!

So here I am, reading my book. Now I hear something mumbling. I look outside, but nobody is there. I look in the house, but nobody is there. The mumblings are getting louder, I can make them out:

"Jonathon, why did you kill me?"

It was her! It was Elanor! The voice was coming from . . . no, it's impossible . . . the walls!

The voice died down. It was just a hallucination. Yeah, that's what it was, a hallucination.

The voice again:

"JONATHON, WHY DID YOU KILL ME?"

Louder and louder, over and over again! I couldn't stand it! I had to get out.

I am now in an apartment building. Here, there is no voice to bother me. Or is there? No, I was just imagining it. The funeral will be tomorrow, so she can't bother me anymore. She'll be six feet under, and can't get out. What am I saying? She's dead. How can she get out? I'll have to relax.

I think I'll go watch some TV. Oh, there's a good movie on now. I'll just sit back and relax while I watch this movie. So I turn it on, and sit in the easy chair.

"We interrupt this movie for a special bulletin."

Oh, no!! It can't be! It's Elanor again! She's on the TV: That mocking voice, the sound of a crow screeching:

"JONATHON, WHY DID YOU KILL ME?"

No! Go away! You're dead! Why are you doing this??

The funeral was short and went fast. Not many people attended. Only Elanor's parents and a few friends. It seemed like nobody missed her much. I know *I* didn't. I was still shaken by that ugly face on the TV screen. It must be another hallucination.

So now I'm walking back to the apartment. I think I'll get something to eat. I'll go to some restaurant. Ah, there's one now.

I say, "Waitress, I'd like a menu!"

The waitress turns around. It's HER AGAIN! Elanor's back! She couldn't have gotten out of that grave! It's impossible!! She's coming nearer, nearer. . . . . .

"Go away, you . . . you ghost! Get out of here!"

Nearer, nearer . . .

I'm frozen to the spot. Go away!!!!

I scream, "Leave me alone! Leave me alone!"

NEARER, NEARER . . .

She's putting her ice-cold hands around my neck!

Eleanor, go away!!! Elanor, Ela—

[Fall 1972?]

The Writing of *Mystery and Horror Writers of the Twentieth Century*

I've used that little phrase of L. Sprague de Camp's, "literary miscarriage", so many times—in my *H. P. Lovecraft: A Critical Analysis*, in letters, in my journals—simply because it so aptly describes my work on my inchoate volume of literary criticism, *Mystery and Horror Writers of the Twentieth Century*. Ever since I began writing, I've had dreams of grandeur, and have always undertaken huge projects with the idea that, upon their completion and publication (!), they would immediately thrust me into literary fame. So it was with *Mystery and Horror Writers*.

The germ of the idea was, I suppose, two-fold, and I can't tell which influence came first. I at once wanted to write a continuation of H. P. Lovecraft's *Supernatural Horror in Literature* and to pen a criticism of mystery/horror writers and works. My adoration of Lovecraft was such that I thought that, if I could somehow write this "meagre" continuation of his own analysis, my name would thereupon become inextricably joined with his, just as August Derleth's, Robert Bloch's, Frank Belknap Long's, and even Edgar Poe's are. Perhaps, I considered, someone else would write, in fifty or seventy-five years, another continuation, so that we could have a great critical trio. . . .

I had always liked mystery fiction, and I began devouring it after I read Agatha Christie's *Ten Little Indians*, in September of 1972. Weird fiction also suited me: I'd read the fairy-like businesses of C. S. Lewis when I was younger, and by late 1972 I was into the Alfred Hitchcock anthologies; in time, of course, I progressed to Lovecraft, Bloch, Tryon, Shirley Jackson, and other 20th-century writers. I'd never cared much for the Gothics: the windy outpourings of Radcliffe and Maturin were dashed wearisome. I enjoyed *The Monk* when I read it in 1975, but I never became addicted to the Gothics as did Lovecraft.

My initial exposure to Lovecraft came when I read *At the Mountains of Madness and Other Novels* in either late 1972 or early 1973. However, I didn't care for him greatly then: I distinctly remember giving up trying to wade through the title novel, and exactly at page 53. This reaction was similar to my original disliking of Evelyn Waugh: when, at the encouragement of my English teacher, Dr Anthony Tovatt, I read *The Loved One* (late 1972), I found it positively hideous. Obviously, I was too young, literarily, to understand either Waugh or Lovecraft at this point in time.

At any rate, I decided to try Lovecraft again in late 1973, and was mesmerised by his *The Dunwich Horror and Others*. My love affair with him began then and there, and at the time of this writing, I've still only scratched the surface of my Lovecraftian studies.

All through 1973 and 1974, I read voraciously in mystery and horror—and almost nothing else. Then, on 17 July 1974, I decided to begin *Mystery and Horror Writers.* By then I had read—though most only once—many of the authors and works that I would cover, though I was still reading and reviewing as late as the summer of 1975, when I actually destroyed the thing. That week in July, from the 17th to the 23rd, saw the writing of the first five essays, on "Dorothy L. Sayers", "John Creasey", "Agatha Christie", "John D. MacDonald and Ross MacDonald", and "Mickey Spillane, Alistair McLean, and Erle Stanley Gardner", plus the Introduction. Also, I began compiling the major appendix to the volume: the Recommended Reading List of Books of Mystery and Horror. In time, I added the following appendices and addenda: Top Twenty Mystery and Horror Novels of the Twentieth Century, Best Short Stories of Mystery and Detection, Best Novelettes of Mystery and Detection, Best Short Stories of Horror and the Macabre, Best Novelettes of Horror and the Macabre, the Acknowledgements, and the Chronology of the Mystery and Horror Story in the Twentieth Century.

At that time, I was still trying to compose music, and the time spent on that was still great. I was also still trying to finish a collection of short stories (in fact, three of them). In December of 1974 I began my first collection of poems, *The Nothing Verses and Other Poems* (finished October 1975), and I was also continuing the compilation of my Addenda. However, *Mystery and Horror Writers* soon overshadowed all these concerns (which were greatly simplified by the surcease of my composing in November 1975), and this was the primary reason for both the remarkable burgeoning of the "extended essay" (reaching 250 pages in January 1975), and the subsequent atrophying of all my other projects, save my poems. The time spent on reading and writing for the volume became so great that I could quite literally work on nothing else (though the death of my fiction did not actually occur until September 1975; however, the fact that in August of 1974, when I began the heavy work for *Mystery and Horror Writers,* I wrote no fiction at all when in the previous months I had averaged over 44 pages a month, and the fact that all but three pages of the 281 pages of non-fiction written in 1974 were penned during the months of July to December, is significant).

After my original spurt of five essays, I began working mainly on horror writers: the rest of 1975 saw the writing (or at least the beginning) of the essays on "The Anthologies of Alfred Hitchcock", "H. P. Lovecraft", "Rod Serling", "Roald Dahl", "H. P. Lovecraft's Circle", "Shirley Jackson", "The Anthologies of Peter Haining", "Thomas Tryon", "Ray Bradbury", "Other Notables

(Horror)", and "Robert Bloch". Around November I reversed the trend, and penned the mystery essays, "Margery Allingham", "Ngaio Marsh", "Other Notables (Mystery)", and "John Dickson Carr".

On 13 October I divided the "Horror Writers" section into two parts, "Horror Writers" and "Writers of the Macabre". Originally, the essay was in two distinct sections, "Mystery Writers" and "Horror Writers". However, due to the fact that such authors and editors as Bradbury, Bloch, Hitchcock, Dahl, and others wrote works which bordered on mystery and/or suspense, I felt it *à propos* to make this further division. The new "Horror Writers" section included now only those writers of pure horror: Lovecraft, his "Circle", Peter Haining, Shirley Jackson, Rod Serling, and Thomas Tryon. The "Mystery" section remained the same.

Many of the essays went through a great amount of revision, the most being the "H. P. Lovecraft" essay. I rewrote many portions of this at least three or four times; of course, none of even these reached any levels of decency, and in fact, when I began *H. P. Lovecraft: A Critical Analysis* in May of 1975 (at that time, *Mystery and Horror Writers* was not destroyed, and my intention was to make the "H. P. Lovecraft" essay a general account, and the *Critical Analysis* a more in-depth one), I was so dissatisfied with that when it was completed (June 1975), that, even before it was published and released by Shroud, Publishers, I began a total revision and extension of it (October 1975).

The other essays that I recall greatly revising were "Dorothy L. Sayers", "Agatha Christie" (these took place in the new version of *Mystery and Horror Writers*, June 1975), "The Anthologies of Alfred Hitchcock", "The Anthologies of Peter Haining", "Roald Dahl", "H. P. Lovecraft's Circle", and "L. P. Davies". Those essays that were practically untouched from the first draft were the joke essays, "John Creasey", "John D. MacDonald and Ross MacDonald", "Charlotte Armstrong", and "Mickey Spillane, Alistair MacLean, and Erle Stanley Gardner", plus others as "Rod Serling", "Thomas Tryon", "Georges Simenon", "Robert Bloch", "John Dickson Carr", and "Philip MacDonald".

I remember that the Introduction also went through a number of revisings and re-writings (as did the Introduction to the *Critical Analysis*).

It was rather sad that I realised the worthlessness of the whole thing at the very time I had deemed it complete: 21 January 1975. It was then that the book reached its largest size, 250 pages, two and a half times as much as I'd originally expected it to be. I began a ferocious revising and re-writing task in March, and kept at it all the way through early June. Then I came to the realisation that the whole thing was simply so superfluous that even infinite revision could not bring it up to par. This whole period, the summer of 1975, was the time of awakening for me literarily: I took stock of all my work and found it all ineffably revolting. My fiction was worse than dreadful; my criticism was putrid; and only my poems were of any vague decency. (What dastardly irony! I thought:—that those works which took the least time to write, those works which went through absolutely no revision, should be the best I had written, such as that may be!) At any rate, on 11 June, I totally revised the format of *Mystery and Horror Writers*, and made it resemble Lovecraft's *Supernatural Horror in Literature* much more than it did before. Originally, the only similarity between the two was to have been the fact that both were written by writers of fiction. My goal, when I started writing, was to be a short-story writer/novelist/poet, and this volume of criticism was to be, as with Lovecraft, the sole example of my nonfiction work (his letters and other autobiographical works, just as my Addenda, Accounts, Journal, ad infinitum, aside). This new revision changed matters. The thing was still divided into the two sections of "Mystery" and "Horror", but I now gathered up my authors into groups or "schools", as Lovecraft did with his Gothic writers, later Gothics, American writers, etc. As a final, quaint relation to the Lovecraft essay, I had separate sections on both Agatha Christie and Lovecraft himself, as he did with Edgar Poe. The sections of *Mystery and Horror Writers* now were, to the best of my recollection:

Mystery Writers.
  I. The Sayersian School: Dorothy L. Sayers, Margery Allingham, Ngaio Marsh, and Others.
  II. The Americans: John Dickson Carr, August Derleth, Ellery Queen, Margaret Millar, and Others.
  III. Agatha Christie.
  IV. The English: L. P. Davies, John Creasey, Philip MacDonald, and Others.

Horror Writers.
  I.   H. P. Lovecraft.
  II. H. P. Lovecraft's Circle.
  III. The Horror Novelists: Thomas Tryon, Robert Bloch, Shirley Jackson.
  IV. The Anthologists: Alfred Hitchcock, Peter Haining, August Derleth.
  V.   The Miniaturists: Roald Dahl, Shirley Jackson, and Others.

This rearrangement gave me new life for a time, and I reeled off in quick succession two essays, "The Sayersian School" and "The Americans". I was learning succinction to an extent, and my new prediction for the length of the volume, based on these essays, was about 150 pages. During this time, however (June 1975), I was putting the finishing touches—for the moment—on the *Critical Analysis,* and was also launching a huge destruction campaign of my more stomach-turning works. A great deal of fiction went away, and eventually *Mystery and Horror Writers* became swept into the maelstrom: it was shelved "indefinitely" on 26 June 1975, and this was tantamount to outright destruction. The only things I preserved were the essays in this volume and the six appendices. This latter I combined and used as an appendix to my other volume, *H. P. Lovecraft: A Critical Analysis; Other Essays on Literature.**

This volume, which is to contain the revised *Critical Analysis*, the essay "Some Notes on Modern Mystery Fiction", and other related essays, is the relative outcome of *Mystery and Horror Writers*, and it is this book which makes the eleven months' work on the "literary miscarriage" not a total waste of time. The *Critical Analysis*, in its original version, is merely the enormous revision of the "H. P. Lovecraft" essay, and the revised *Critical Analysis*, however much I revise it, will still bear some traces, however minute, to that original piece. The entire outcome of the "Mystery" section was "Some Notes on Modern Mystery Fiction" (August 4–29, 1975), an essay which I still consider decent, though flawed.

The essential problem of the whole *Mystery and Horror* business was that I began it too early in my literary career. When I began it, I had been writing for only a year, and then only fiction. Though I may have had the intrinsic qualities of a literary critic, I had not the refinement nor the experience to be a good one. It might be said that *Mystery and Horror Writers* was simply a huge practice effort for my subsequent criticisms, but however true that is, the actual fact of the matter is that if I had started on a smaller scale, I might have prevented the whole fiasco, which so devastated my writing and my ego. That hellish summer of 1975, with the purging of my fiction, was painful enough in itself, and the added horror of *Mystery and Horror Writers* was something almost too intolerable to bear. All authors, however, go through the same thing, and it would have been a sign only of amateurishness and characteristic weakness had I let the thing too greatly affect me. If the development of my writing has been slow and anguished, I am at least thankful that there has been a development.

Thanksgiving Day (27 November), 1975.

---

*I subsequently destroyed even these.—S.T.J. (May 1976).

Books Published by Year

1978: 1	1992: 3	2006: 9
1979: 2	1993: 3	2007: 9
1980: 4	1994: 4	2008: 9
1981: 1	1995: 3	2009: 9
1982: 2	1996: 3	2010: 12
1983: 0	1997: 4	2011: 10
1984: 3	1998: 2	2012: 9
1985: 4	1999: 6	2013: 11
1986: 3	2000: 11	2014: 15
1987: 0	2001: 10	2015: 8
1988: 3	2002: 9	2016: 8
1989: 3	2003: 9	2017: 13
1990: 6	2004: 9	2018: 19
1991: 3	2005: 11	2019: 33

Index

A. Names

Æ (George William Russell) II.101
Abbott, Lyman II.61
Abramson, Ben III.12
Achtemeier, Mark VI.B.ii.1
Ackerman, Forrest J IX.B.4
Adams, Benjamin VI.B.i.2.h
Adams, Hannah II.20
Aickman, Robert I.18, 145/146,
    162; VI.A.65n, 272
Aiken, Conrad II.101
Alcott, Louisa May II.24
Alcott, William A. II.61
Alder, Emily II.123
Aldrich, Thomas Bailey II.20, 24,
    101
Allen, Ethan II.109
Allen, William F. II.20
Allingham, William II.101
Altairac, Joseph VIII.A.1, 2
Anderson, Angelee Sailer II.106
Anderson, Douglas A. II.41
Anderson, James Arthur
    VI.A.251.a
Anderson, Kevin J. II.127
Anderson, Melanie R. VI.A.70.a
Andersson, Martin II.134
Anderson, Wilda II.77
Anger, William Frederick III.59
Archibald, W. J. II.12
Arney, Lance II.70
Aronovitz, Michael I.51; II.112,
    113; VI.A.6.a, 75.a
Ashley, Mike II.67/68, 123;
    VI.B.i.2.h, ii.2
Ashmead, John VI.B.ii.156
Asimov, Isaac II.71
Astor, William Waldorf II.35

Atherton, Gertrude I.47; II.35, 76,
    129
Austin, Sherry I.29; VI.B.ii.3, 4
Autolycus II.86
Ayer, A. J. II.28

B., A. F. II.12
B., H. F. II.12
Bailey, J. O. II.86
Baird, Edwin III.12, 23
Baird, Robert II.20
Baker, Jacqueline VI.B.ii.5
Balch, Emily Greene II.61
Baldini, Lara VIII.A.16
Baldwin, F. Lee II.13; III.12, 62
Bancroft, Hubert Howe II.20
Barker, Clive I.18, 29; VI.A.37
Barker, David II.133; VI.B.ii.6, 7
Barlow, R. H. I.43; II.10, 21, 35,
    41, 154; III.3, 4, 13, 20, 43, 53,
    65; VI.A.4.a, 63, 162.a, 256;
    VIII.A.14
Barnes, Harry Elmer II.71
Barnitz, Park II.101
Barr, Amelia E. II.61
Barrass, Glynn Owen VI.B.ii.8,
    150
Barrett, Mike VI.B.ii.9
Barron, Laird I.51; II.82, 120,
    127, 131; VI.B.i.3.g, ii.10
Barron, Neil VI.B.ii.11
Bassnett, Susan II.106
Baudelaire, Charles II.69, 101
Bauduret, Thomas VIII.A.15
Bazinet, Julien II.120
Beaman, Charles C. VI.B.ii.76
Bear, Erik II.127
Bear, Greg II.100, 127

Browning, Robert II.101
Brownson, Orestes Augustus II.61
Brunner, John II.86
Bryant, William L. III.52
Buchan, John II.94
Buckley, James Monroe II.61
Buckley, William F., Jr. I.22, 25
Buhle, Paul II.8
Bullington, Jesse VI.B.ii.8
Burgess, John W. II.20
Burke, Rusty II.6, 7
Burke, Thomas II.35, 143;
   VI.B.i.3.k
Burks, Arthur J. II.94
Burleson, Donald R. I.29; II.8, 9,
   67/68, 77, 82, 110, 130, 132;
   V.C.1; VI.A.270, 316, B.ii.20,
   21, 22, 23, 24
Burleson, Mollie L. II.82, 110,
   130, 132
Burns, Robert II.101
Burpo, Todd VI.B.ii.25
Burr, Clinton Stoddard II.20
Burr, John II.12
Burrage, A. M. I.29; VI.B.ii.26
Bushnell, Horace II.20, 61
Butts, Mary II.70
Byron, George Gordon, Lord
   II.101

C., E. F. W. II.12
Cadieux, Keith VI.B.ii.27
Calcaño, José A. II.69
Caldecott, Andrew I.29; VI.B.ii.28
Callaghan, Gavin V.C.1
Calvitti, Gianfranco VIII.A.16
Campbell, Ramsey I.13, 18, 20,
   29, 45, 47; II.11, 39, 57/58/59,
   82, 113, 120, 122, 126, 133,
   136; V.C.4; VI.A.65n, 89, 221,
   257, 258, 266, 290; B.i.2.c, e, g,
   ii.29–25
Cannon, Peter I.29; II.2, 8, 9, 13n,
   62, 110, 154n; III.25; VI.B.ii.49,
   50, 51, 144

Cardin, Matt II.67/68;
   VI.A.204.a, B.ii.52
Carnes, Mark C. VI.A.203.a
Carney, Jason Ray V.C.8
Carr, John Dickson I.8; VI.B.ii.53
Carroll, Charles II.20
Carrool, Raymond G. II.20
Carson, Dave VI.B.ii.51
Carter, Lin VI.A.102
Carter, Margaret L. II.67/68
Carter, Stephen L. I.22
Case, David II.126
Castronovo, Russ VI.B.ii.54
Catullus (C. Valerius Catullus)
   II.101; VI.F.2
Cervi, Elena VIII.A.16
Cawein, Madison II.101
Cervone, Skye II.106
Chamberlain, Houston Stewart
   II.20
Chambers, Robert II.20
Chambers, Robert W. I.24, 45;
   II.27, 72, 97, 115; VI.A.182.a,
   273
Chappell, Fred II.8, 121, 124,
   125, 177
Chesterton, G. K. I.22
Chevalier, Mrs. A. V. II.12
Child, Lydia Maria II.20
Chizmar, Richard VI.B.ii.110
Chocaño, José Santos II.68
Chopin, Kate II.24
Christie, Agatha VI.B.ii.55, 56
Cisco, Michael I.29; II.82; V.C.1;
   VI.B.ii.57
Clancy, Tom I.31
Clare, John II.101
Clark, Kenneth VI.B.ii.58
Clark, Lillian D. III.38n
Clark, Mary Higgins I.31
Clarke, Arthur C. II.49, 106, 121
Clarke, Edward H. II.61
Clatworthy, Gordon IX.B.7
Clifford, W. K. II.71
Clore, Dan II.91

B. Titles of Books

C. Periodicals